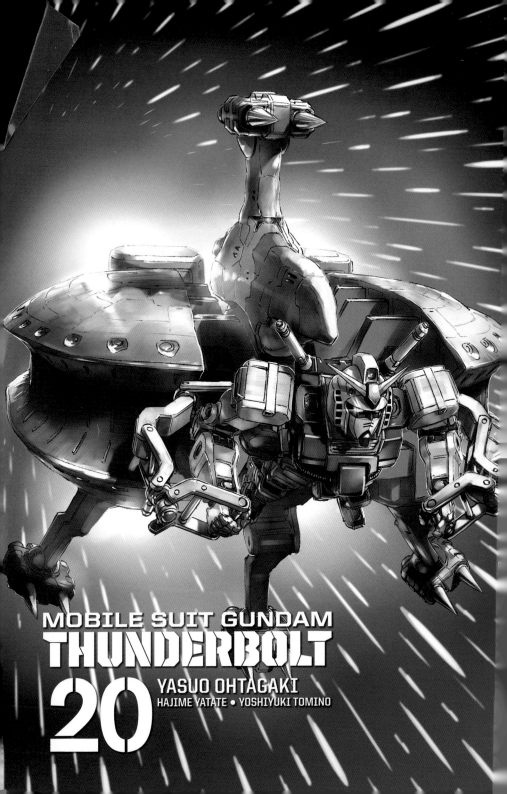

MOBILE SUIT GUNDAM
THUNDERBOLT
20

YASUO OHTAGAKI
HAJIME YATATE • YOSHIYUKI TOMINO

MOBILE SUIT GUNDAM
THUNDERBOLT

20
OPERATION MAITREYA

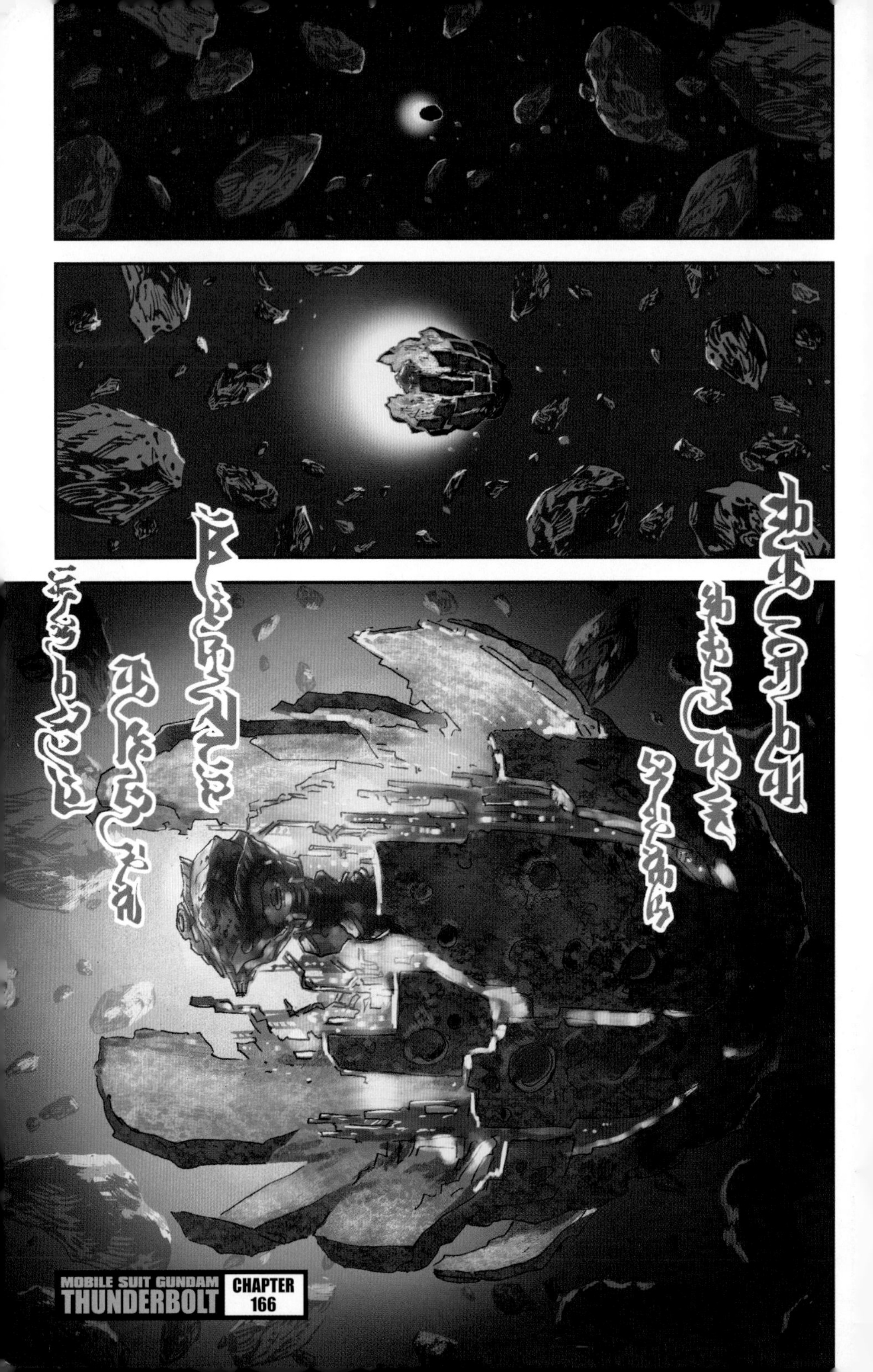
MOBILE SUIT GUNDAM
THUNDERBOLT
CHAPTER
166

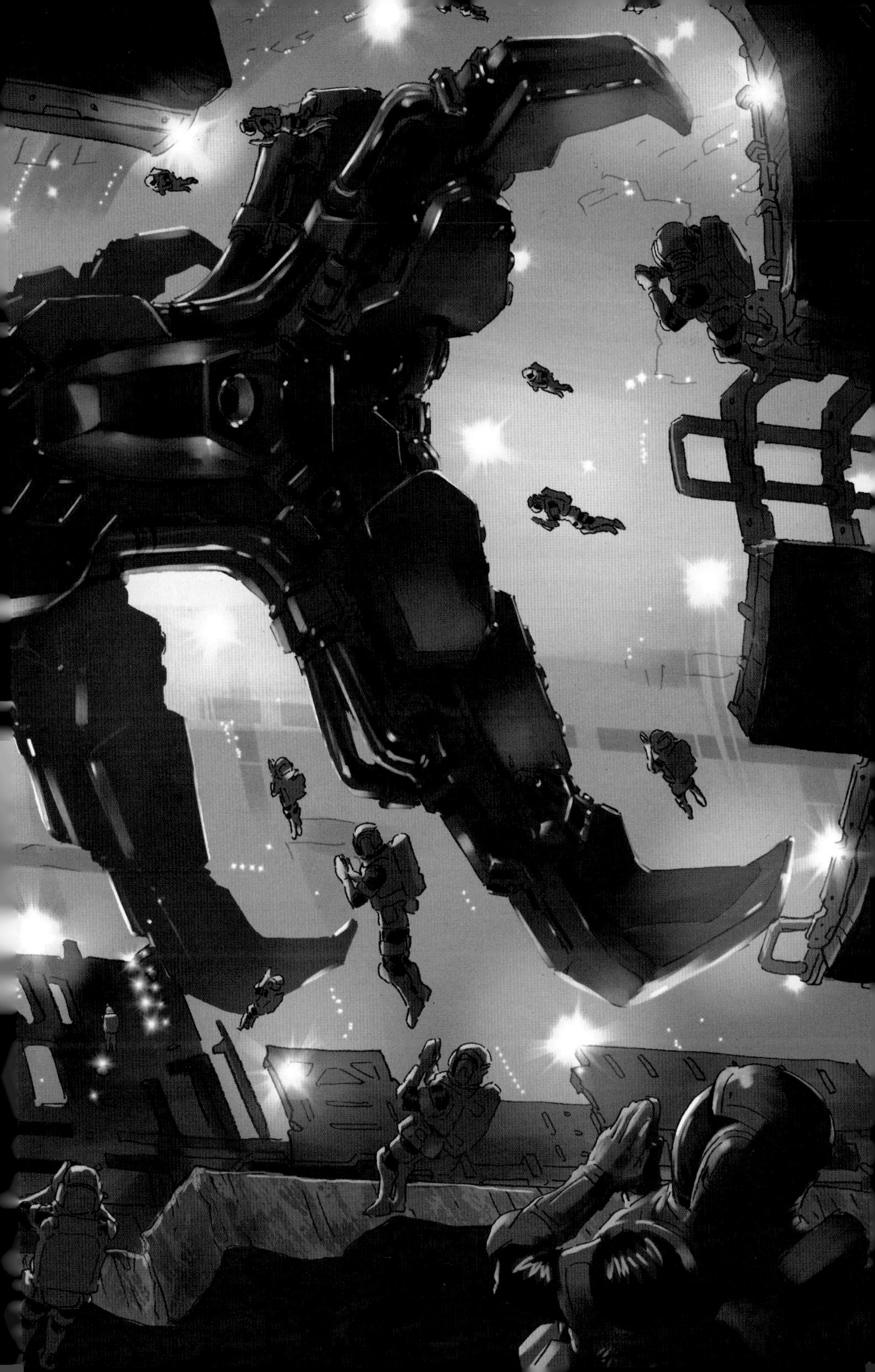

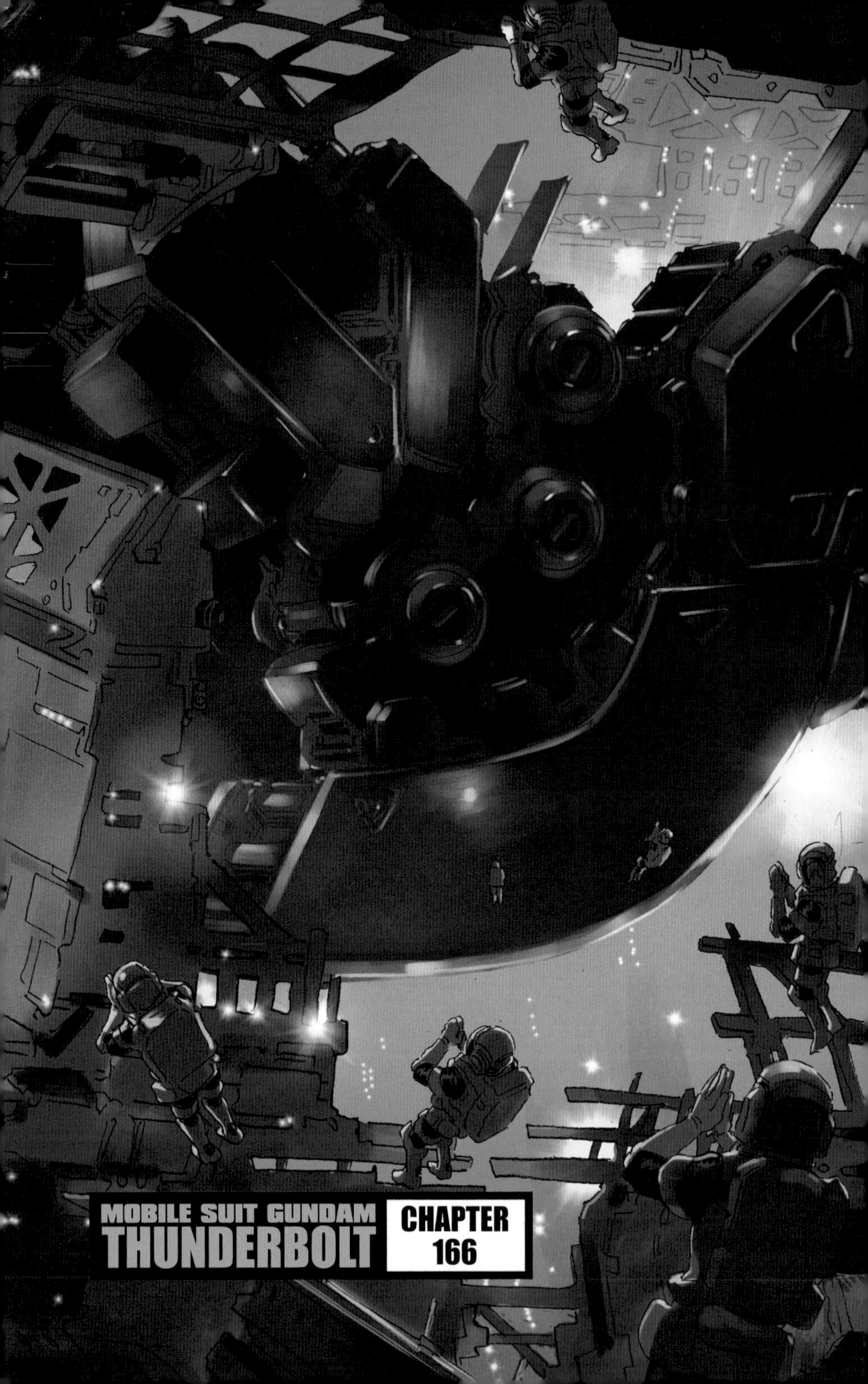
MOBILE SUIT GUNDAM
THUNDERBOLT
CHAPTER
166

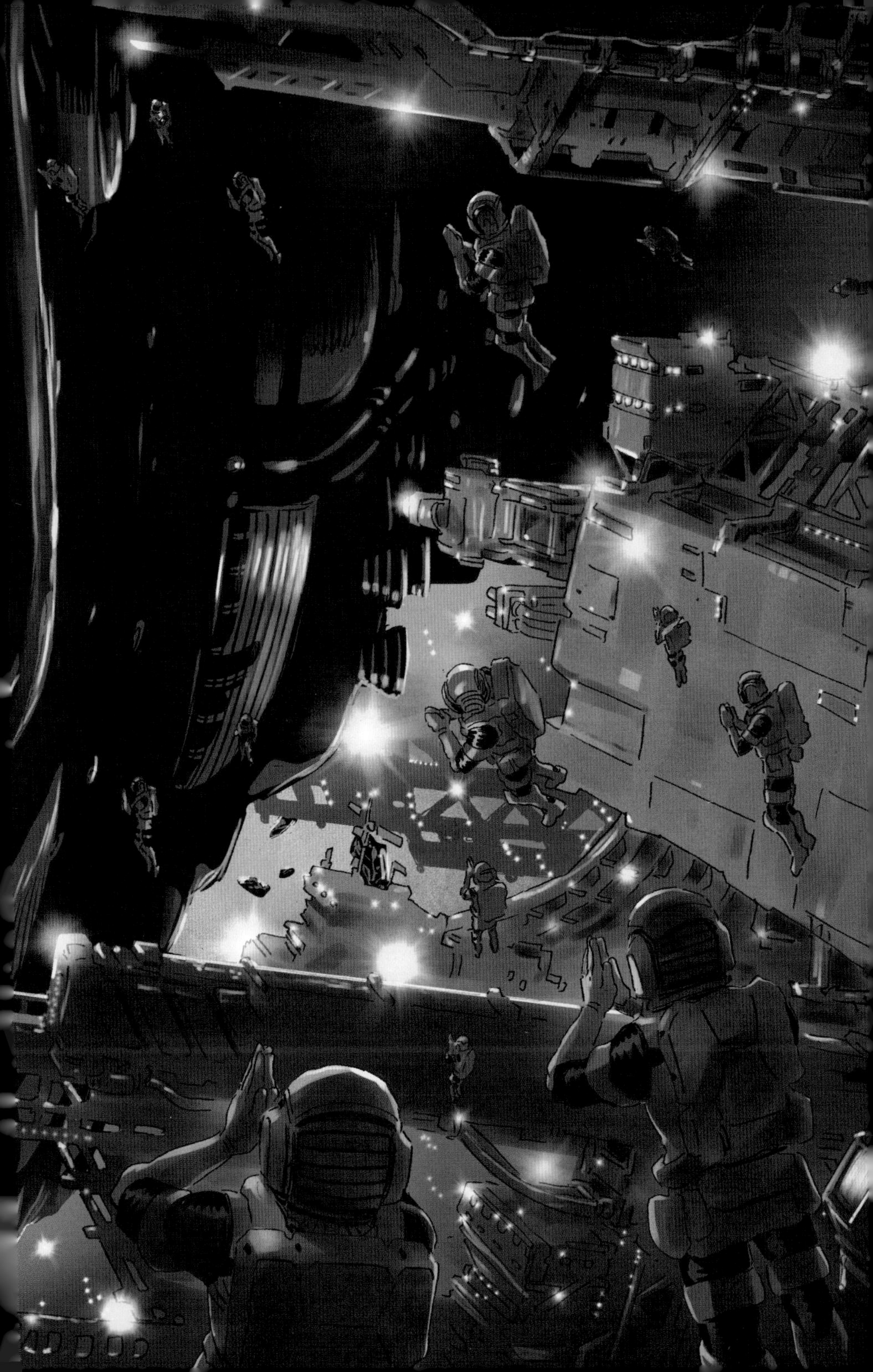

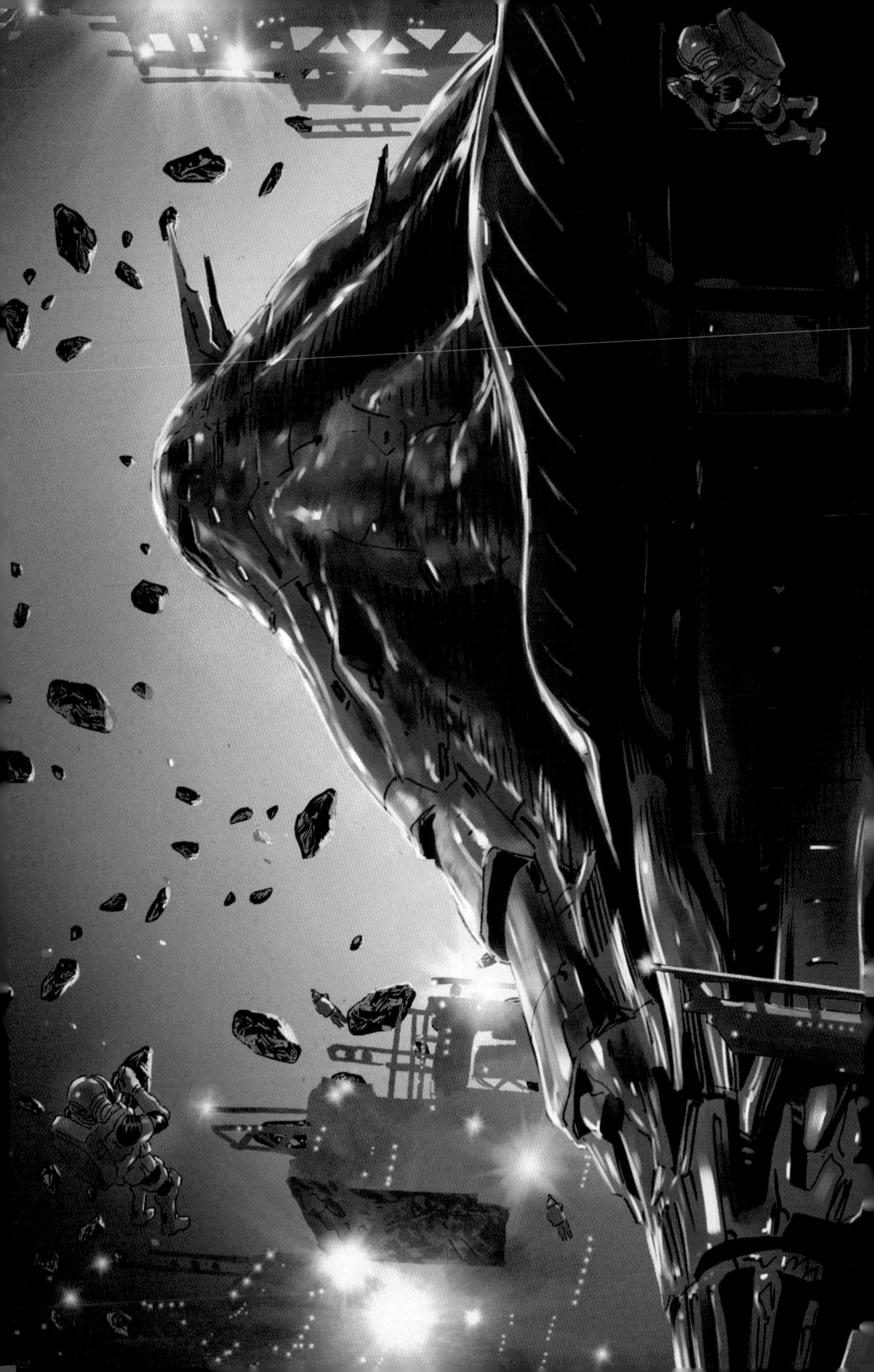

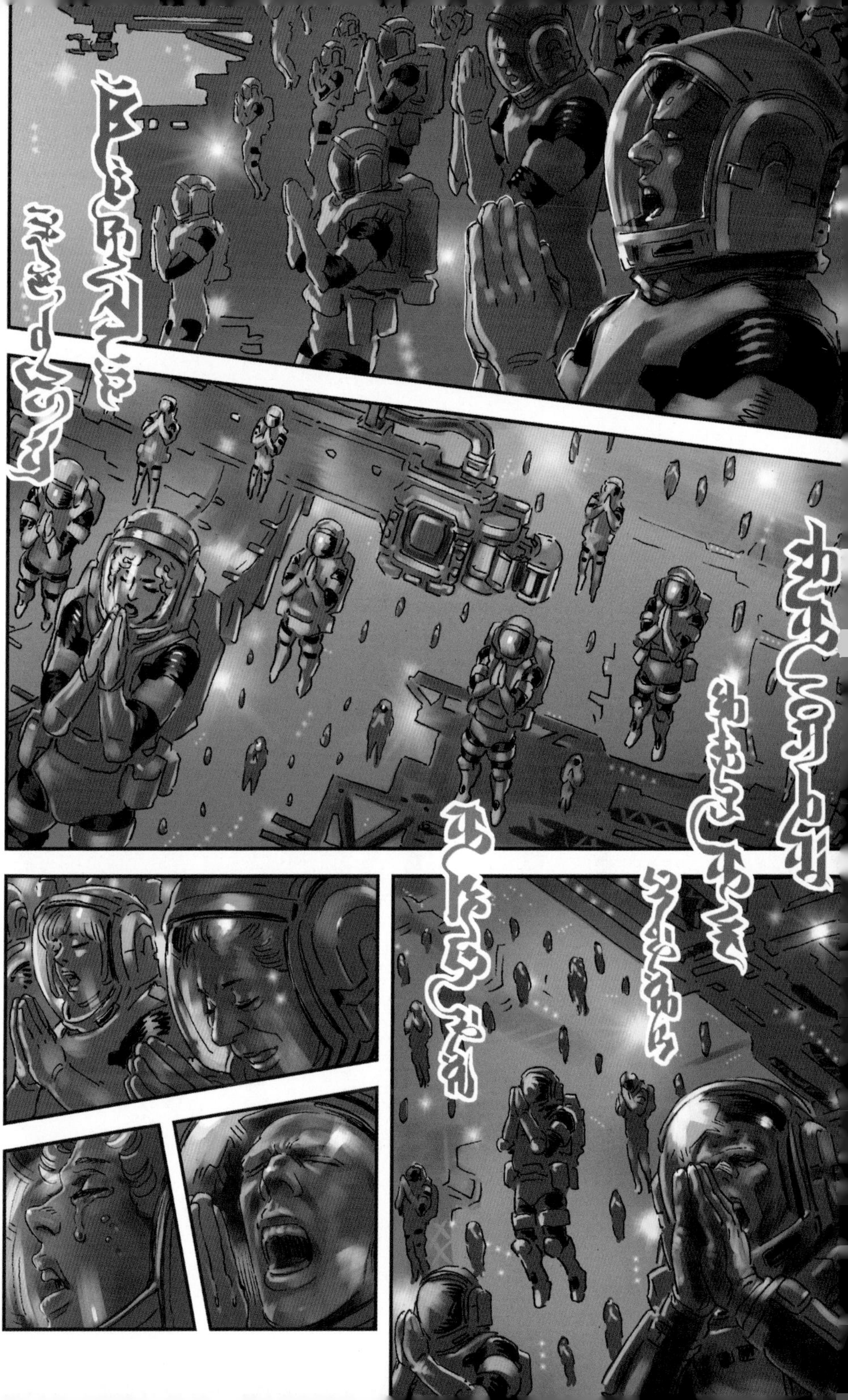

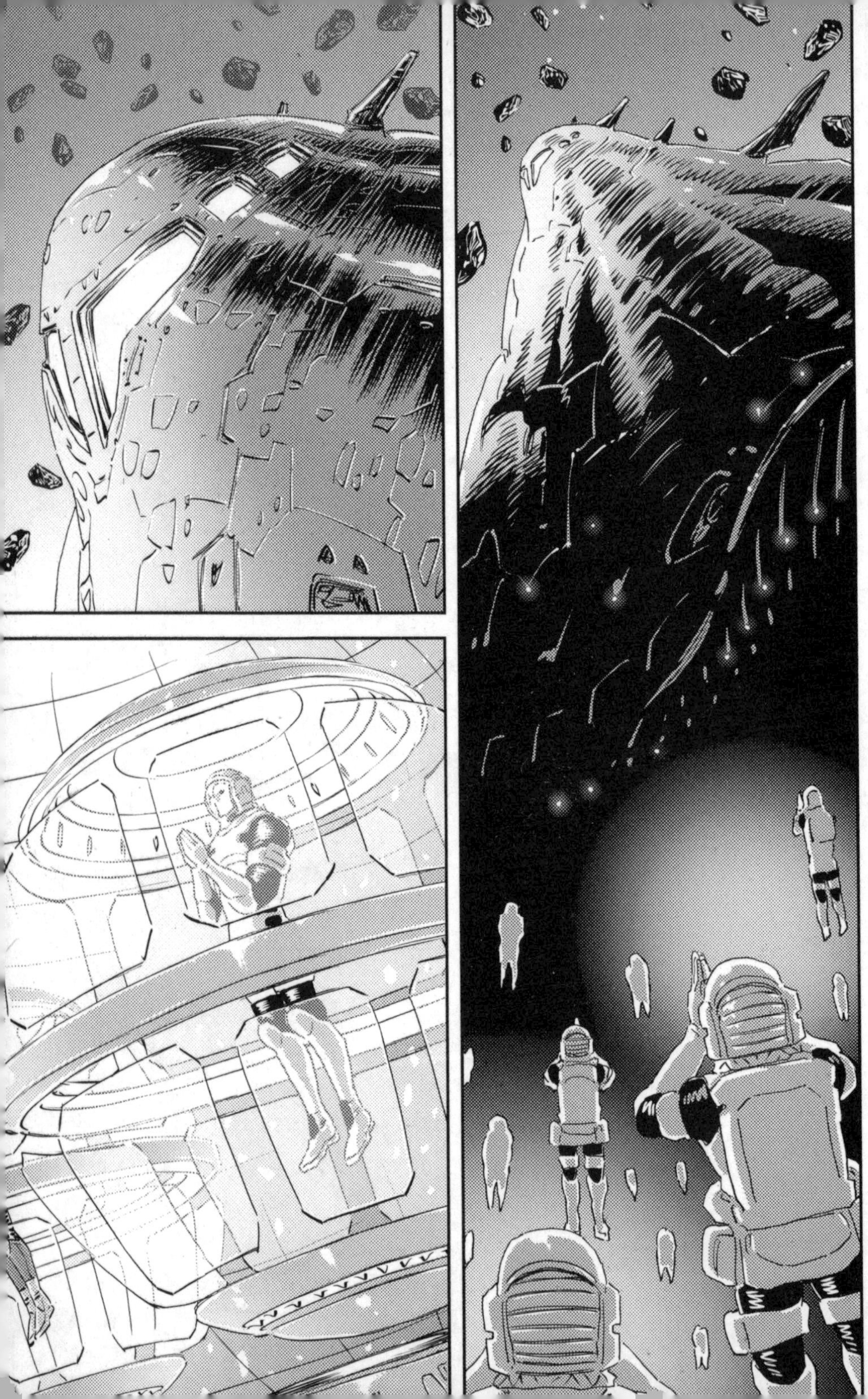

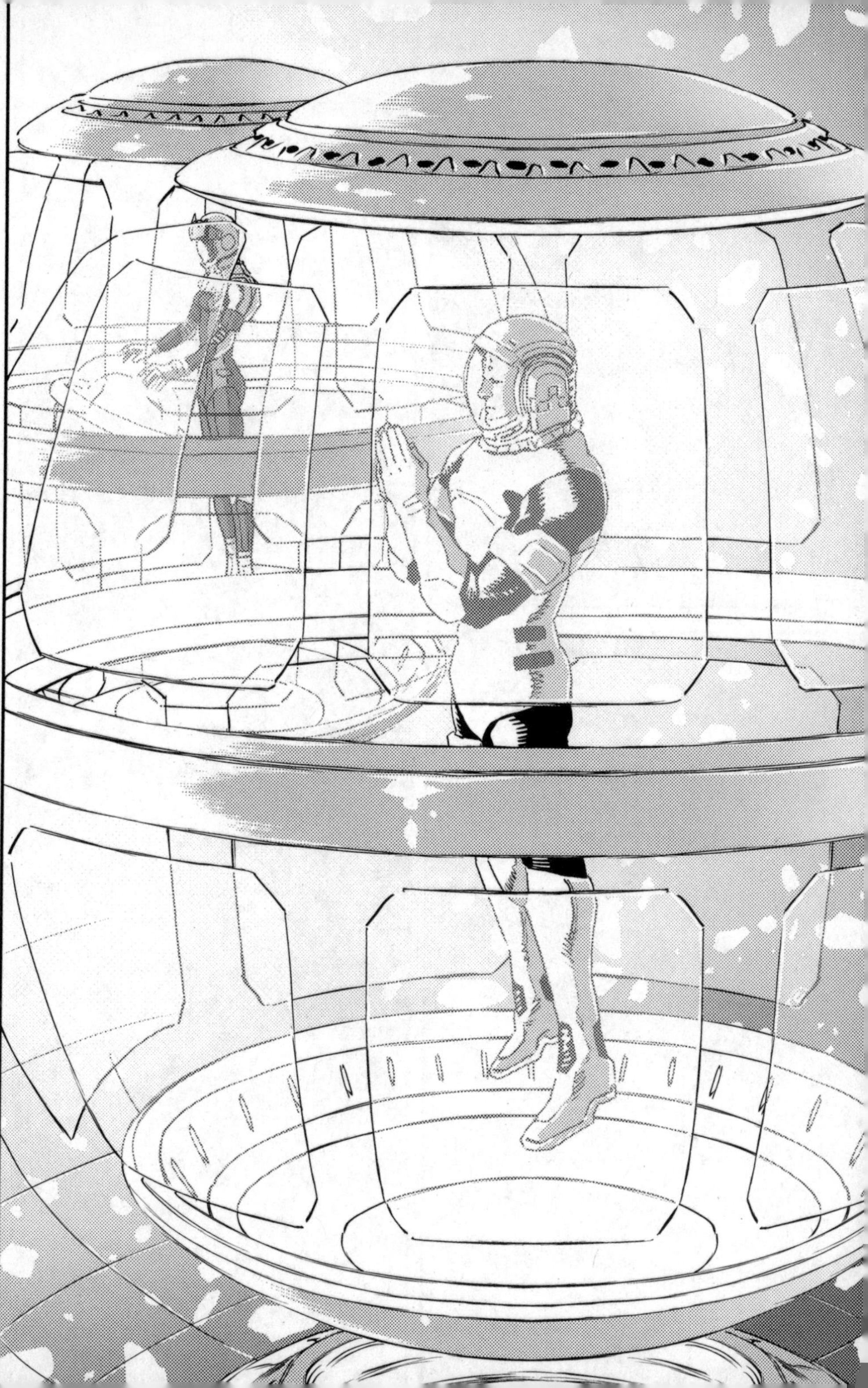

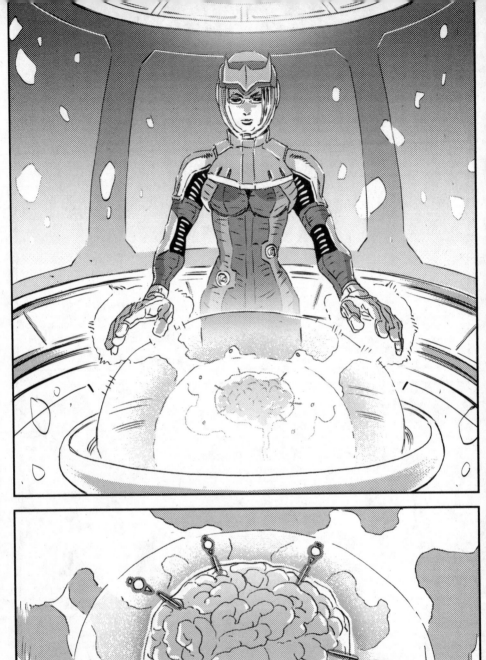
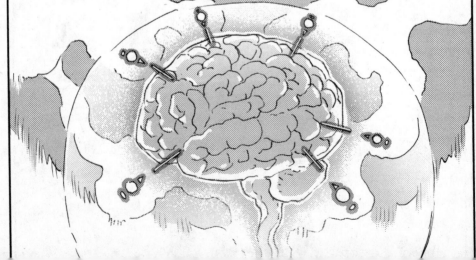

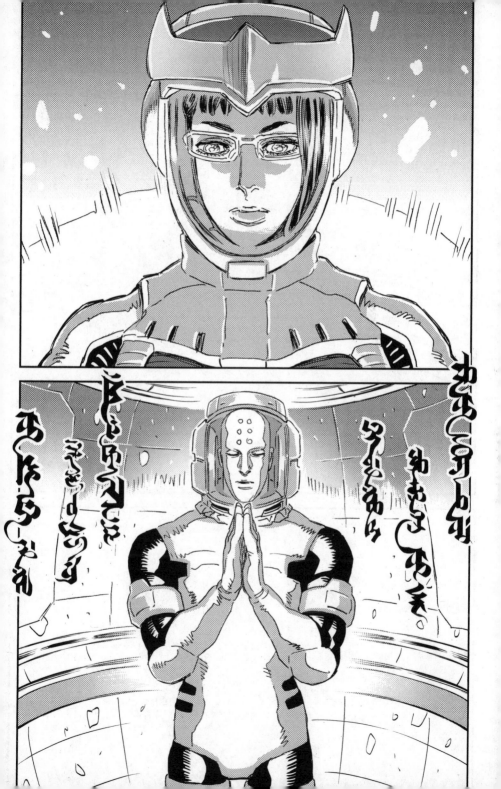

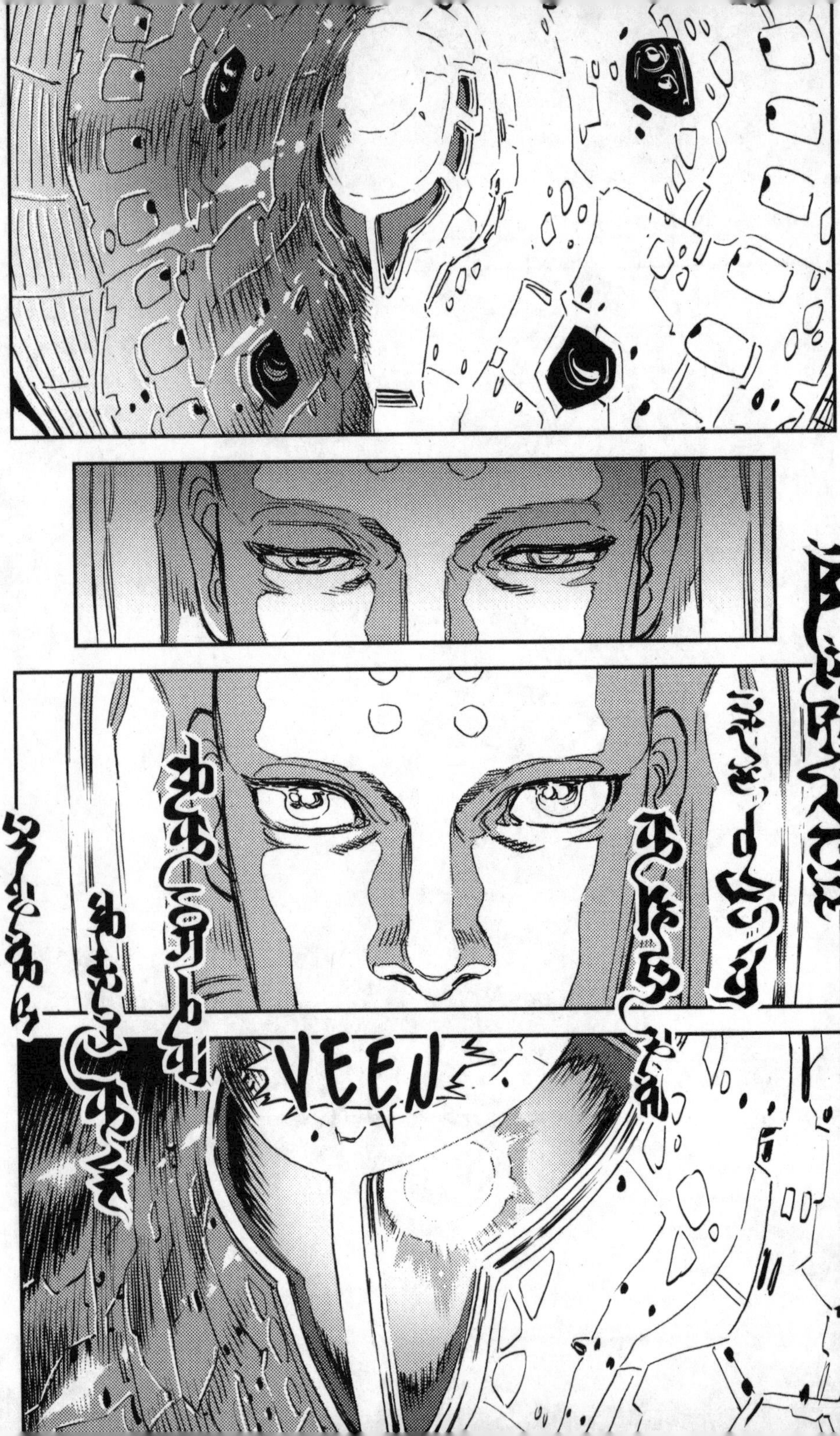
VEEN

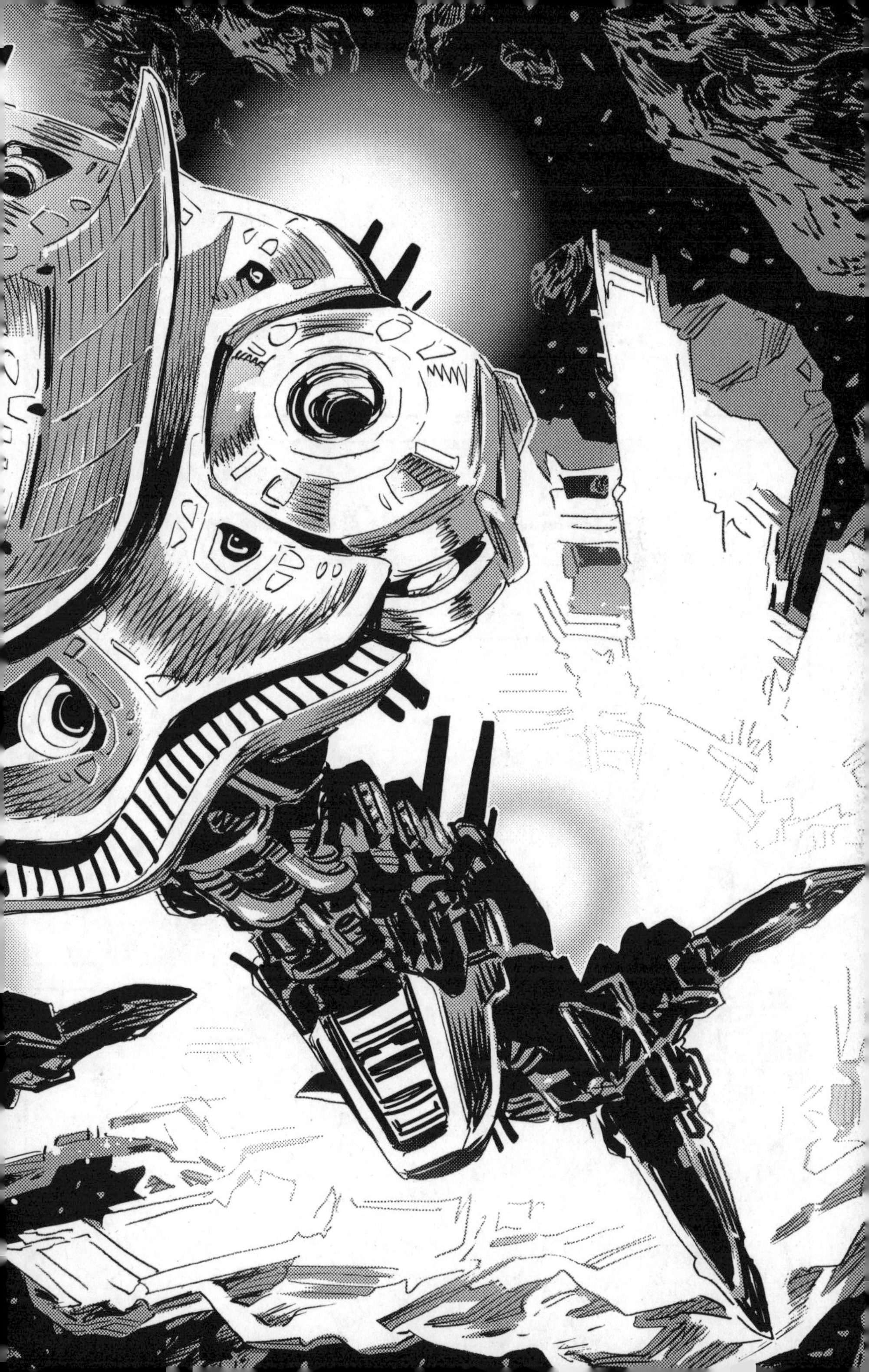

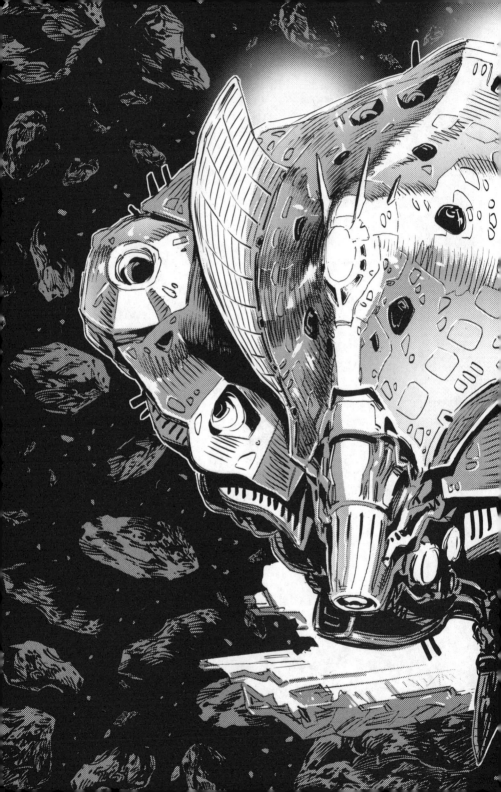

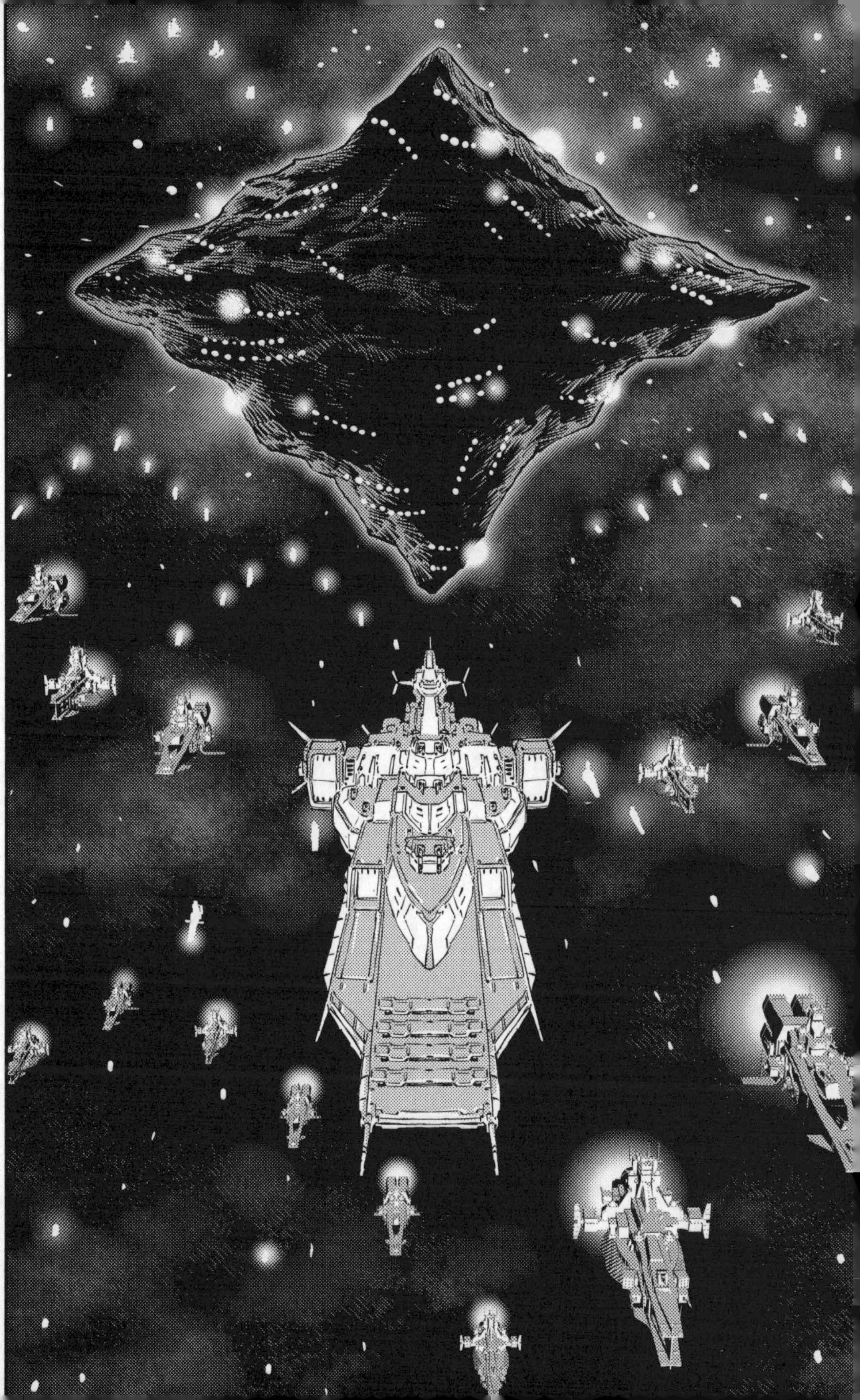

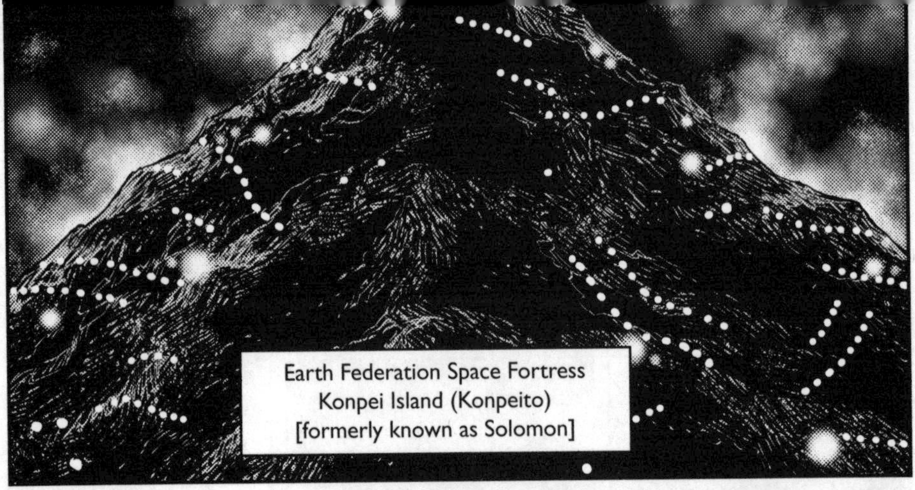
Earth Federation Space Fortress
Konpei Island (Konpeito)
[formerly known as Solomon]

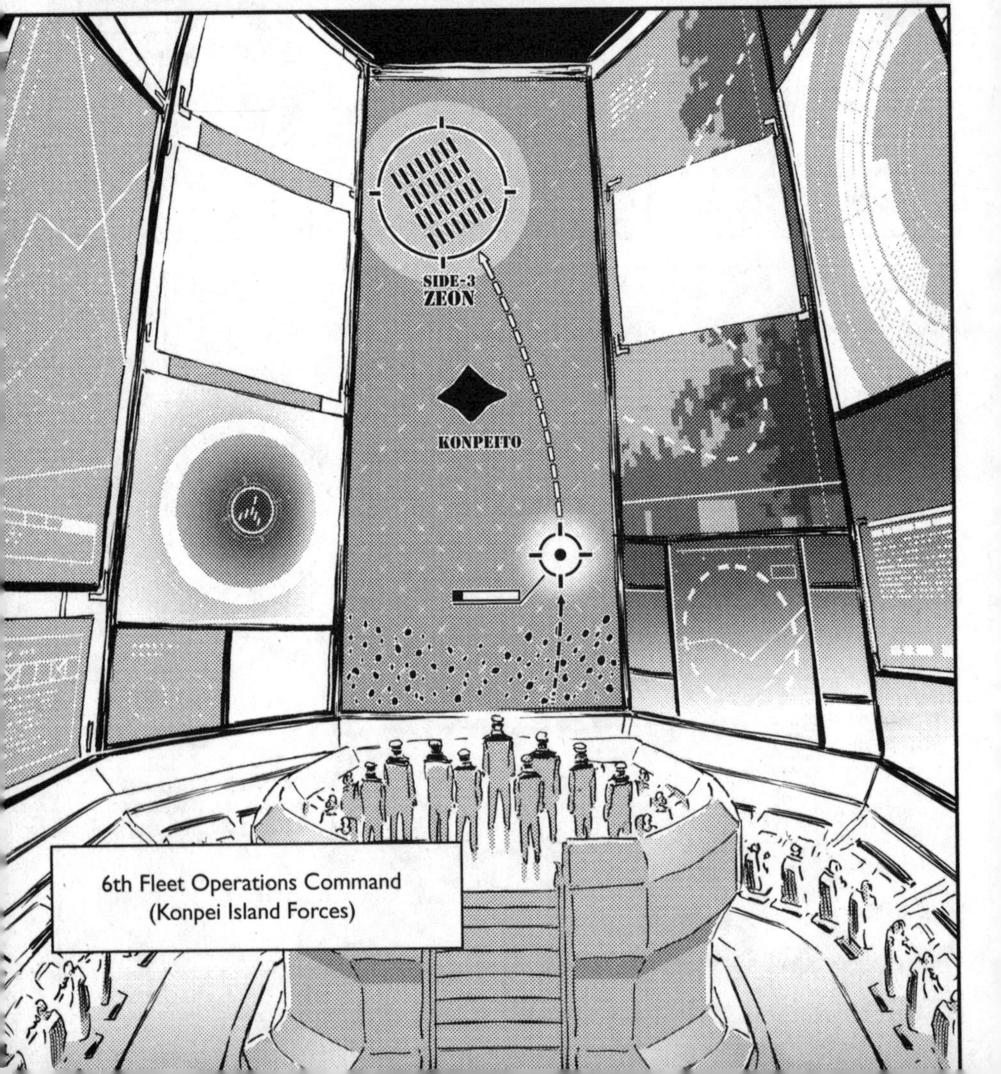
SIDE-3
ZEON
KONPEITO
6th Fleet Operations Command
(Konpei Island Forces)

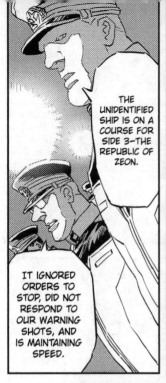

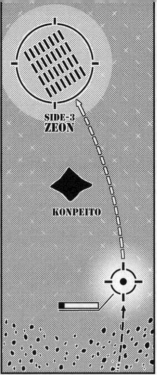

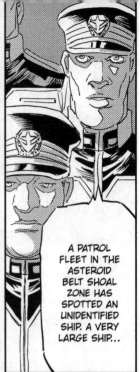

A PATROL FLEET IN THE ASTEROID BELT SHOAL ZONE HAS SPOTTED AN UNIDENTIFIED SHIP. A VERY LARGE SHIP...
SIDE-3
ZEON
KONPEITO
THE UNIDENTIFIED SHIP IS ON A COURSE FOR SIDE 3—THE REPUBLIC OF ZEON.
IT IGNORED ORDERS TO STOP, DID NOT RESPOND TO OUR WARNING SHOTS, AND IS MAINTAINING SPEED.
CONSIDERING THE SITUATION, IT COULD BE A TACTICAL OPERATION BY THAT TERRORIST ORGANIZATION JABURO ISSUED A WARNING ABOUT.
THE NANYANG ALLIANCE AND THEIR RELIGIOUS LEADER, LEVAN FU.
THE NEWTYPE THAT FLEW THE PSYCHO ZAKUS INTO SPACE.

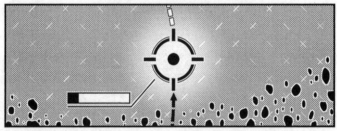

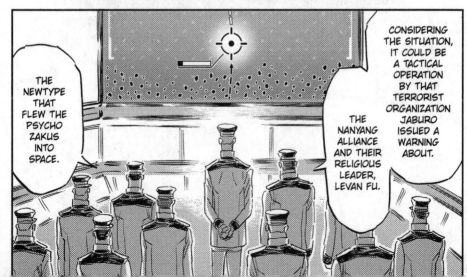

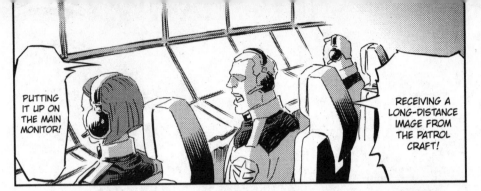

RECEIVING A LONG-DISTANCE IMAGE FROM THE PATROL CRAFT!
PUTTING IT UP ON THE MAIN MONITOR!
PIP
VEEM
WHAT...?!
HUH?!
IS...IS THAT THE BYG-ZAM ...?!

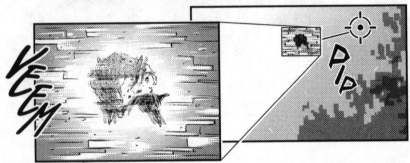

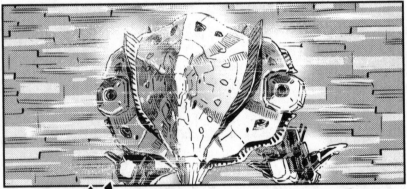

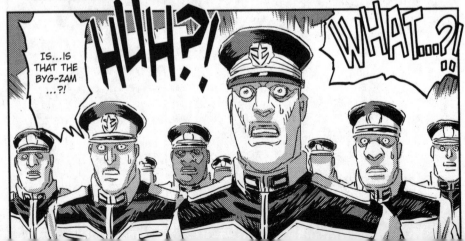

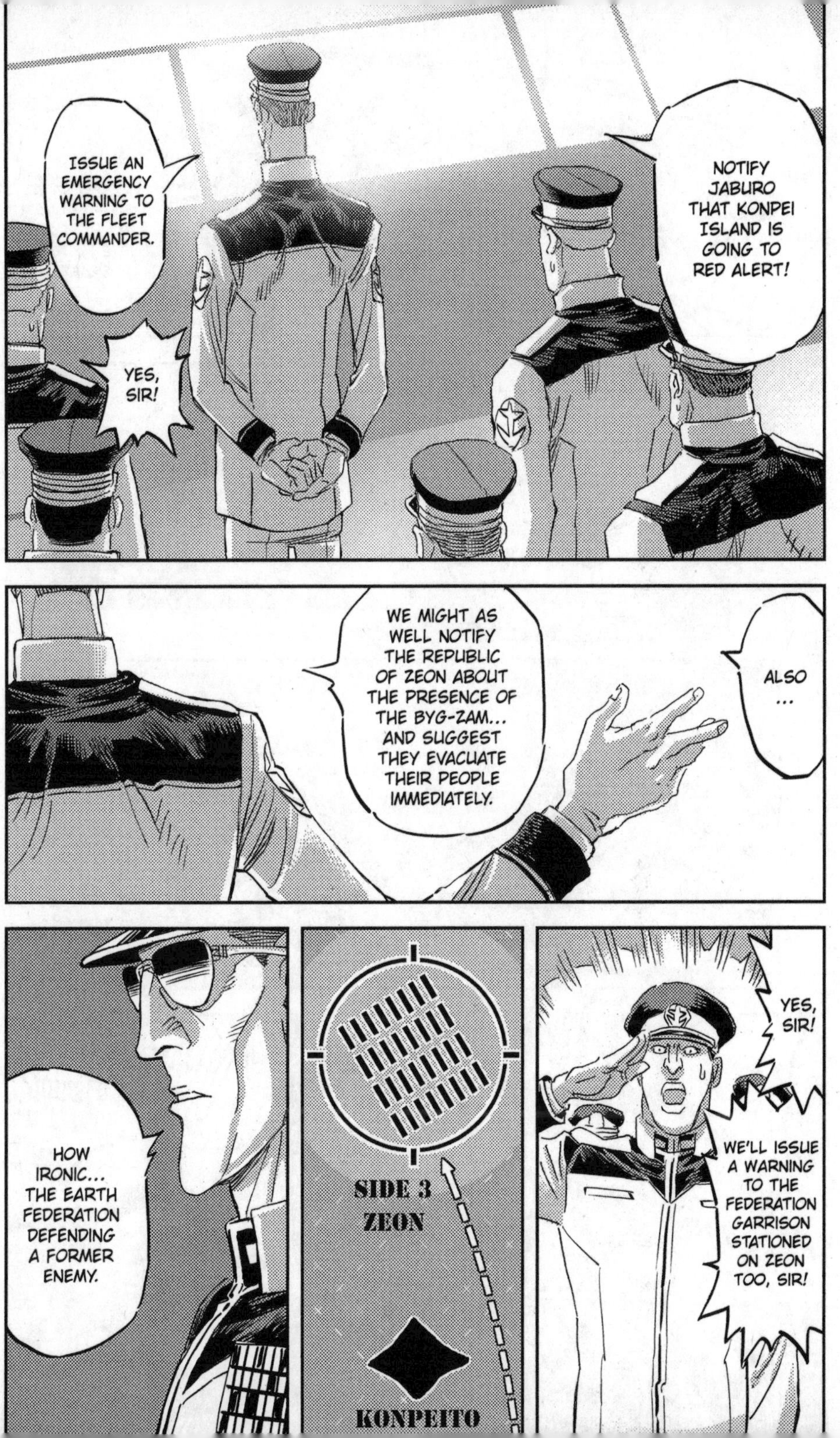
NOTIFY JABURO THAT KONPEI ISLAND IS GOING TO RED ALERT!
ISSUE AN EMERGENCY WARNING TO THE FLEET COMMANDER.
YES, SIR!
ALSO ...
WE MIGHT AS WELL NOTIFY THE REPUBLIC OF ZEON ABOUT THE PRESENCE OF THE BYG-ZAM... AND SUGGEST THEY EVACUATE THEIR PEOPLE IMMEDIATELY.
YES, SIR!
WE'LL ISSUE A WARNING TO THE FEDERATION GARRISON STATIONED ON ZEON TOO, SIR!
SIDE 3
ZEON
KONPEITO
HOW IRONIC... THE EARTH FEDERATION DEFENDING A FORMER ENEMY.

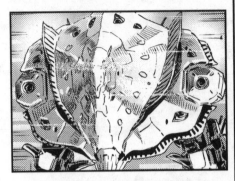

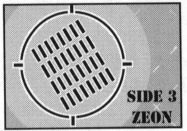

SIDE 3
ZEON

BECAUSE THE REPUBLIC OF ZEON AVOIDED COMBAT ON THEIR HOME SOIL, THEY ENTERED THE POSTWAR PERIOD UNSCATHED AND NOW HAVE ONE OF THE SYSTEM'S LARGEST ECONOMIES.

THE FEDERATION CANNOT AFFORD TO LOSE ITS CASH COW.

Admiral Fitz McGregor
Konpei Island Commander

HOW DARE THEY SEND OUT OUR MOST FORMIDABLE ADVERSARY FROM THE ONE-YEAR WAR!

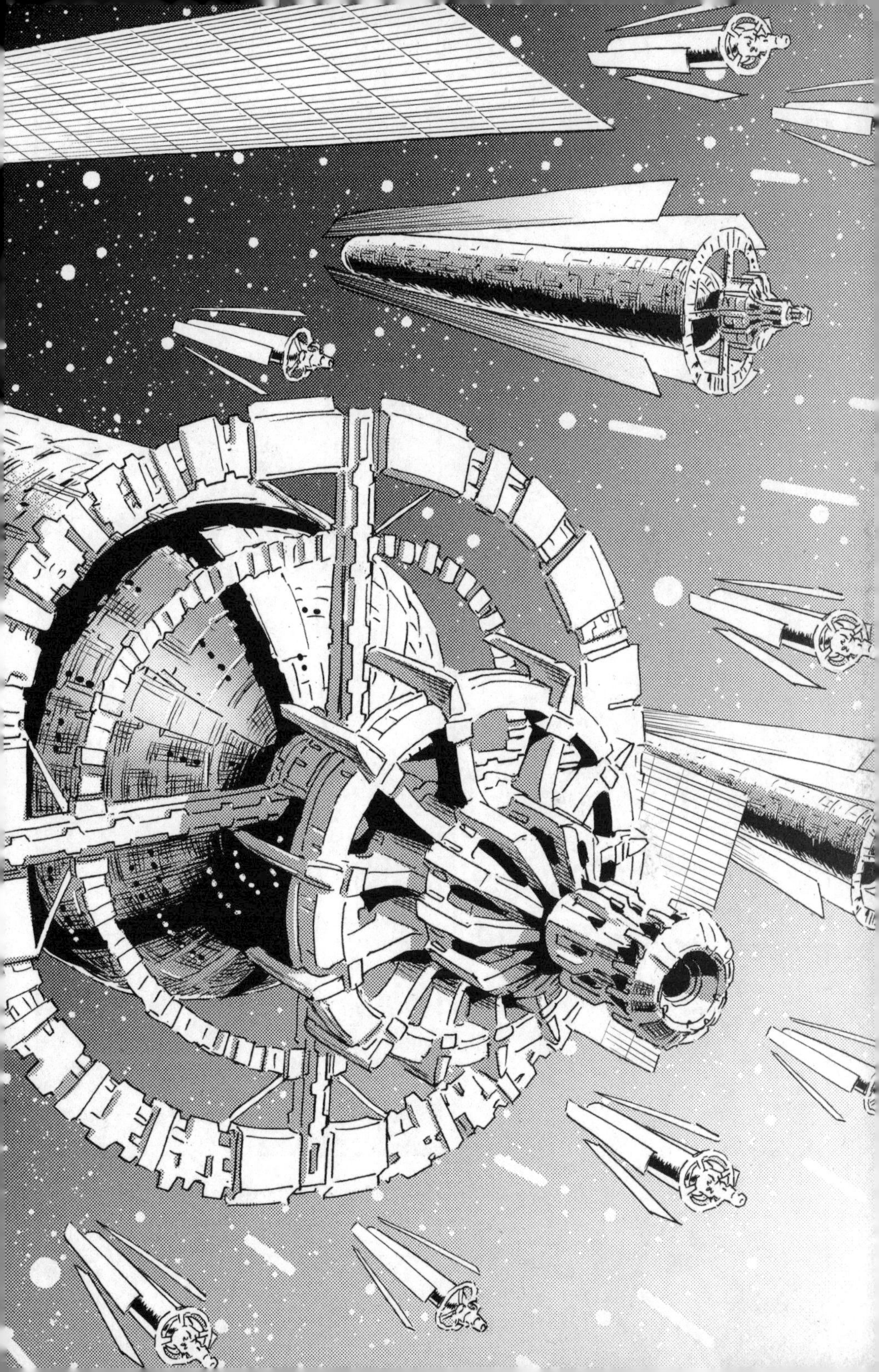

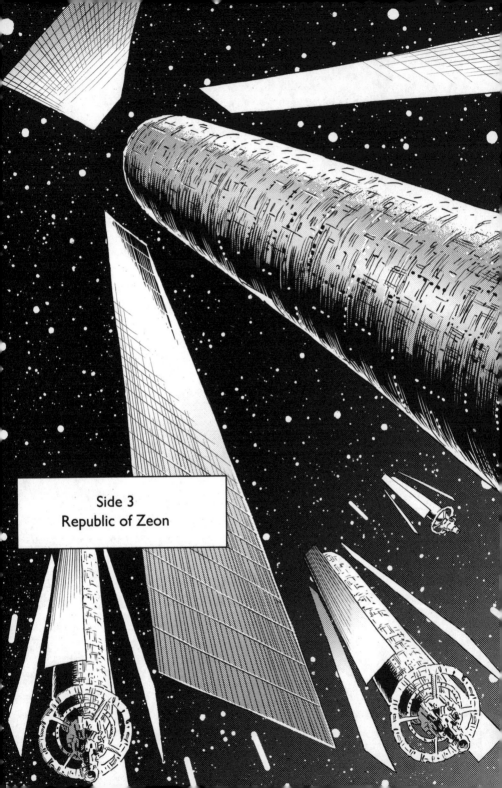

Side 3
Republic of Zeon

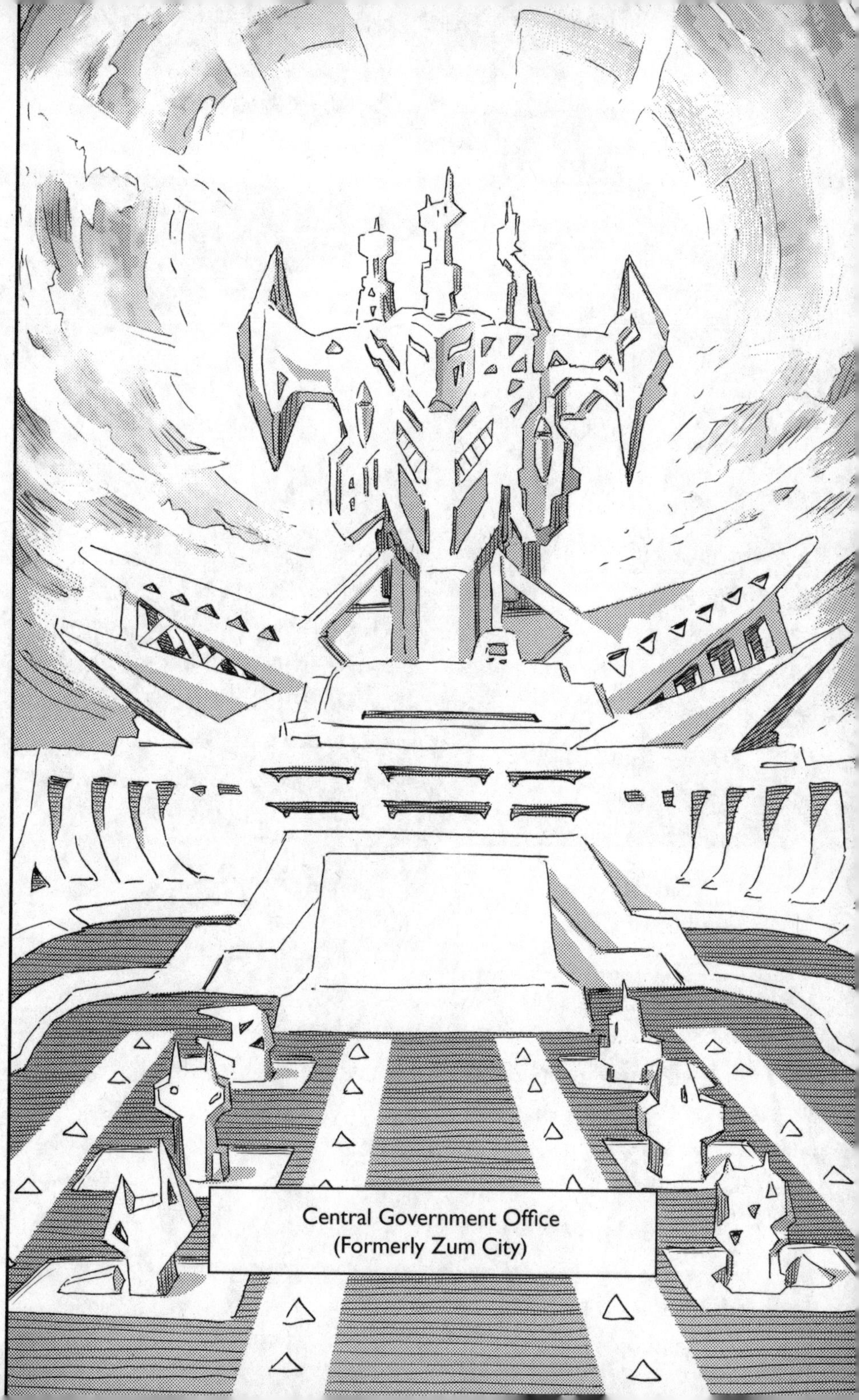
Central Government Office
(Formerly Zum City)

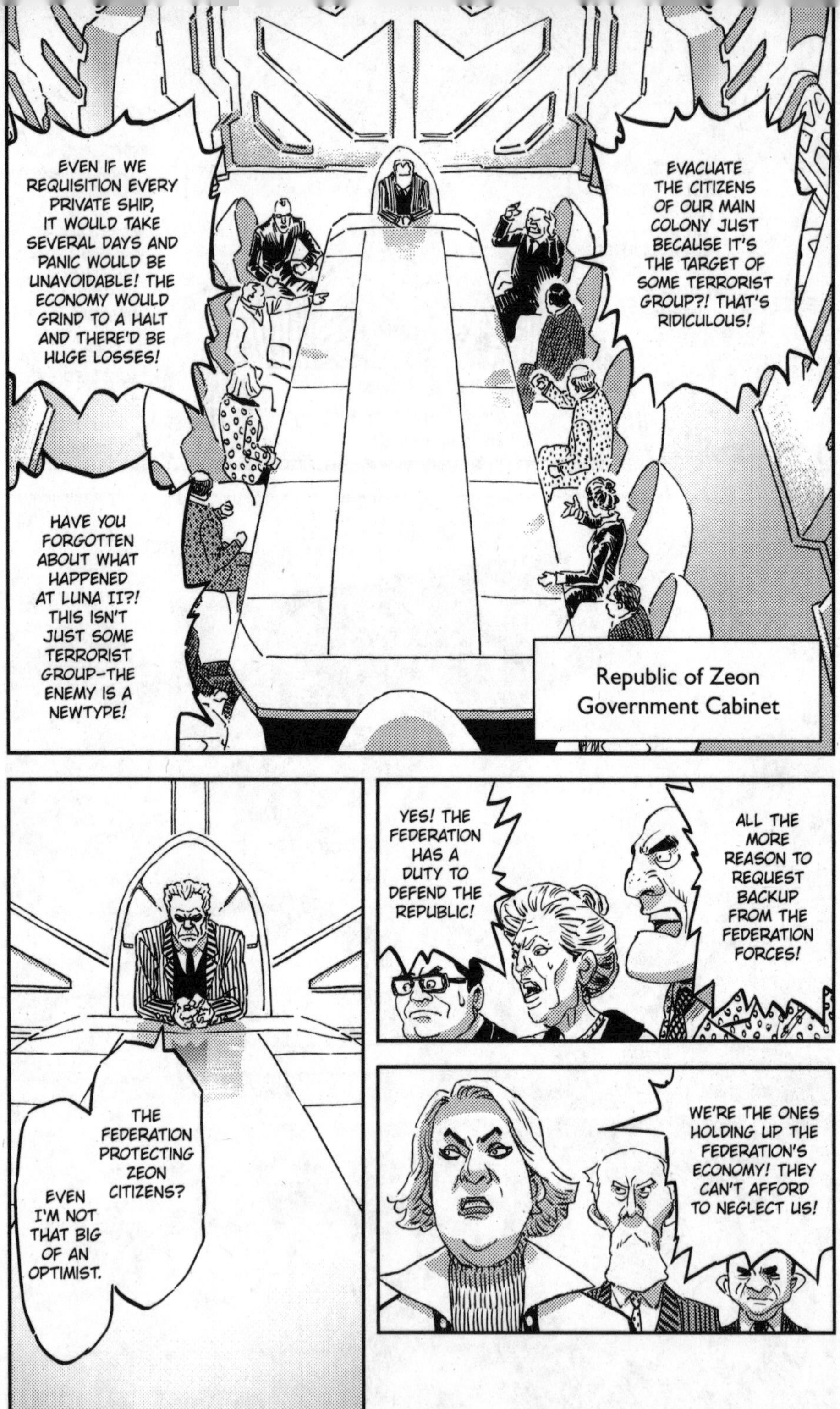
EVACUATE THE CITIZENS OF OUR MAIN COLONY JUST BECAUSE IT'S THE TARGET OF SOME TERRORIST GROUP?! THAT'S RIDICULOUS!
EVEN IF WE REQUISITION EVERY PRIVATE SHIP, IT WOULD TAKE SEVERAL DAYS AND PANIC WOULD BE UNAVOIDABLE! THE ECONOMY WOULD GRIND TO A HALT AND THERE'D BE HUGE LOSSES!
HAVE YOU FORGOTTEN ABOUT WHAT HAPPENED AT LUNA II?! THIS ISN'T JUST SOME TERRORIST GROUP—THE ENEMY IS A NEWTYPE!
Republic of Zeon Government Cabinet
ALL THE MORE REASON TO REQUEST BACKUP FROM THE FEDERATION FORCES!
YES! THE FEDERATION HAS A DUTY TO DEFEND THE REPUBLIC!
WE'RE THE ONES HOLDING UP THE FEDERATION'S ECONOMY! THEY CAN'T AFFORD TO NEGLECT US!
THE FEDERATION PROTECTING ZEON CITIZENS?
EVEN I'M NOT THAT BIG OF AN OPTIMIST.

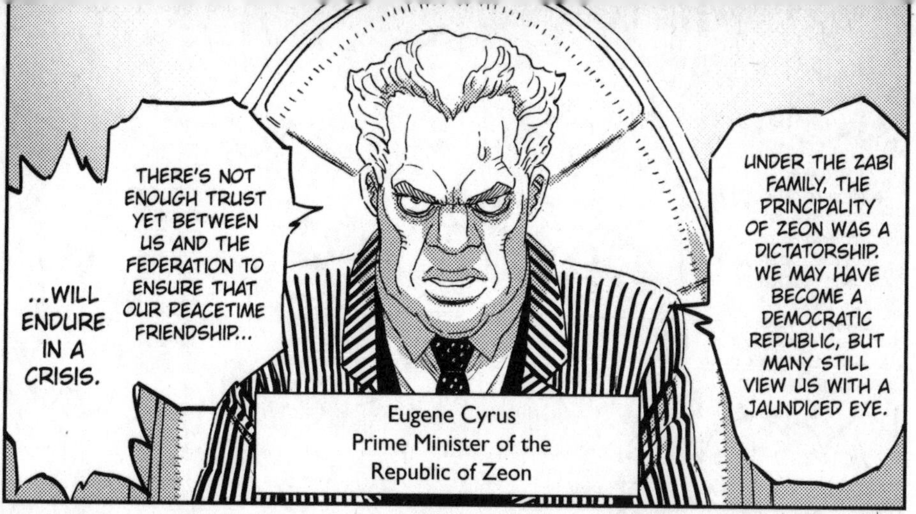
UNDER THE ZABI FAMILY, THE PRINCIPALITY OF ZEON WAS A DICTATORSHIP. WE MAY HAVE BECOME A DEMOCRATIC REPUBLIC, BUT MANY STILL VIEW US WITH A JAUNDICED EYE.
THERE'S NOT ENOUGH TRUST YET BETWEEN US AND THE FEDERATION TO ENSURE THAT OUR PEACETIME FRIENDSHIP...
...WILL ENDURE IN A CRISIS.
Eugene Cyrus
Prime Minister of the
Republic of Zeon

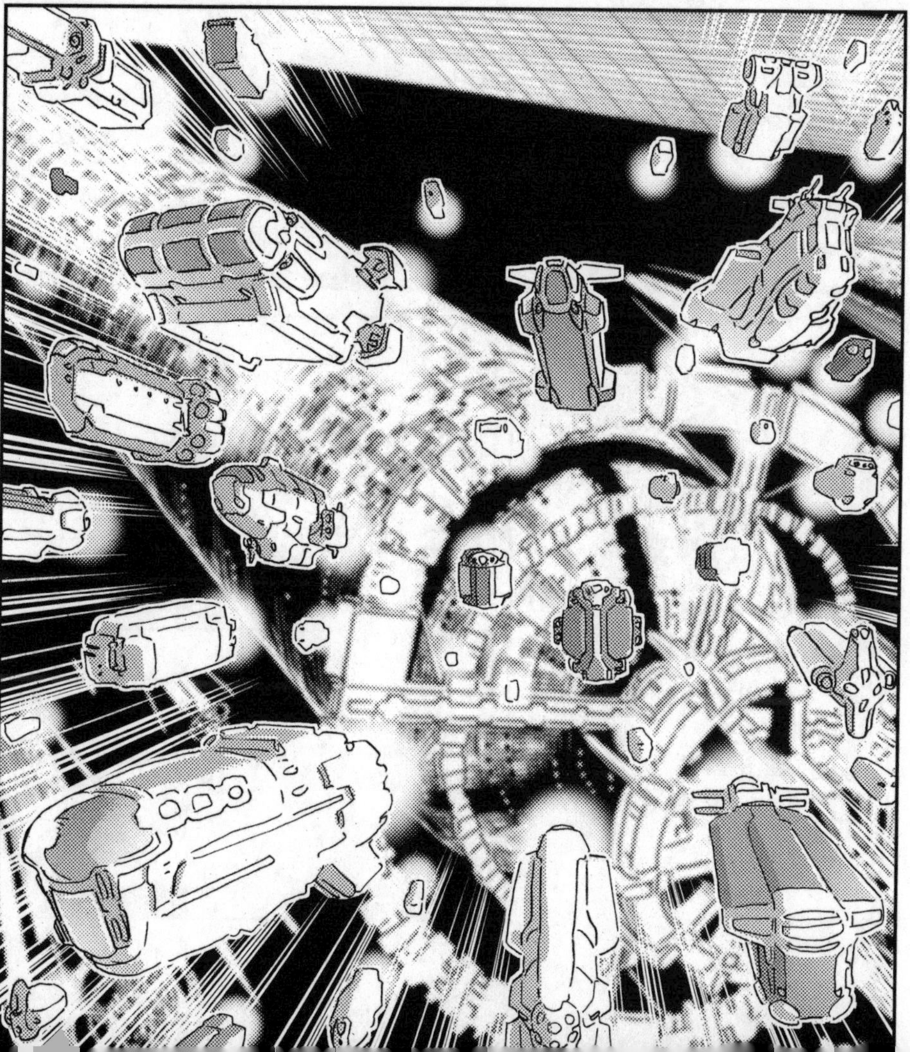

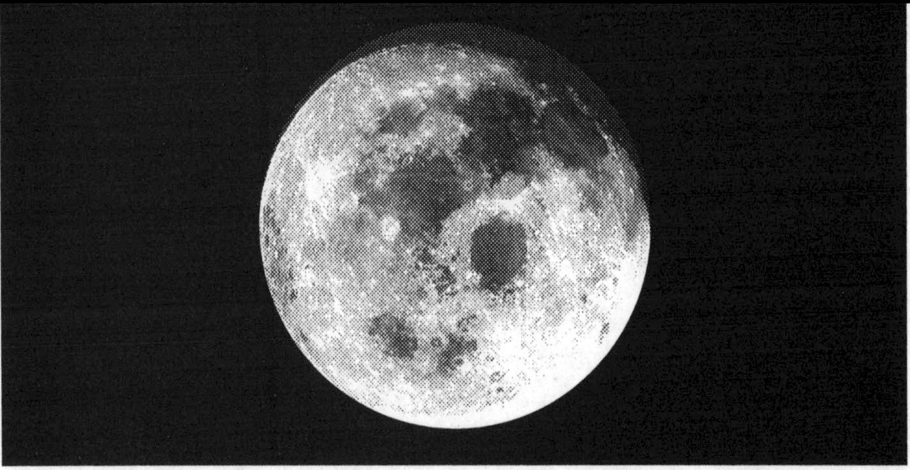

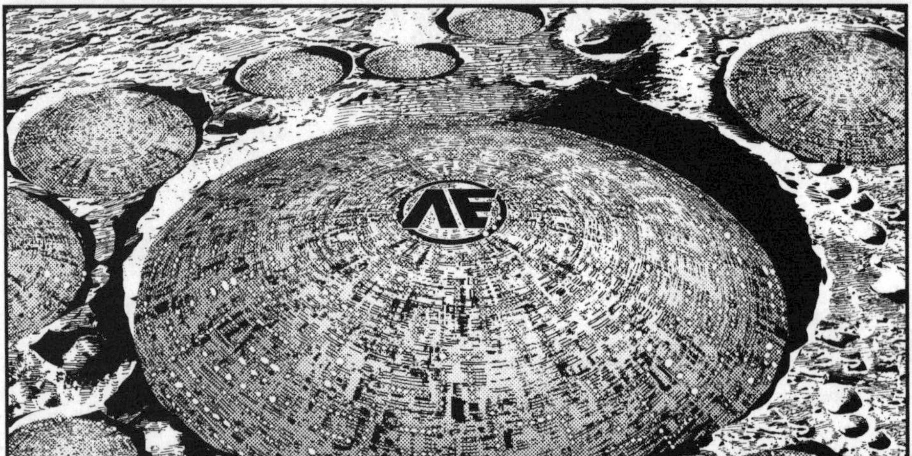
AE

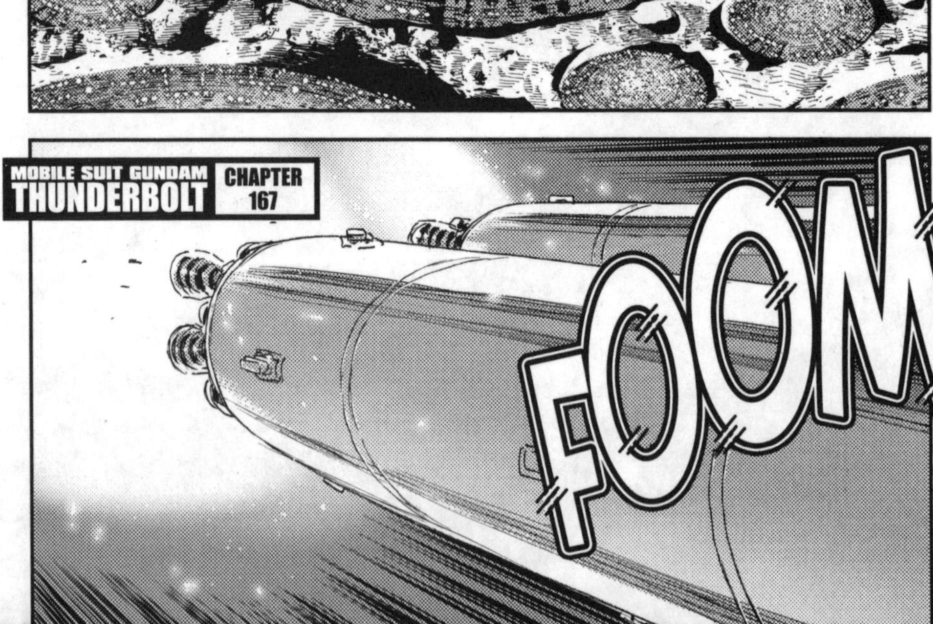
MOBILE SUIT GUNDAM
THUNDERBOLT
CHAPTER 167
FOOM

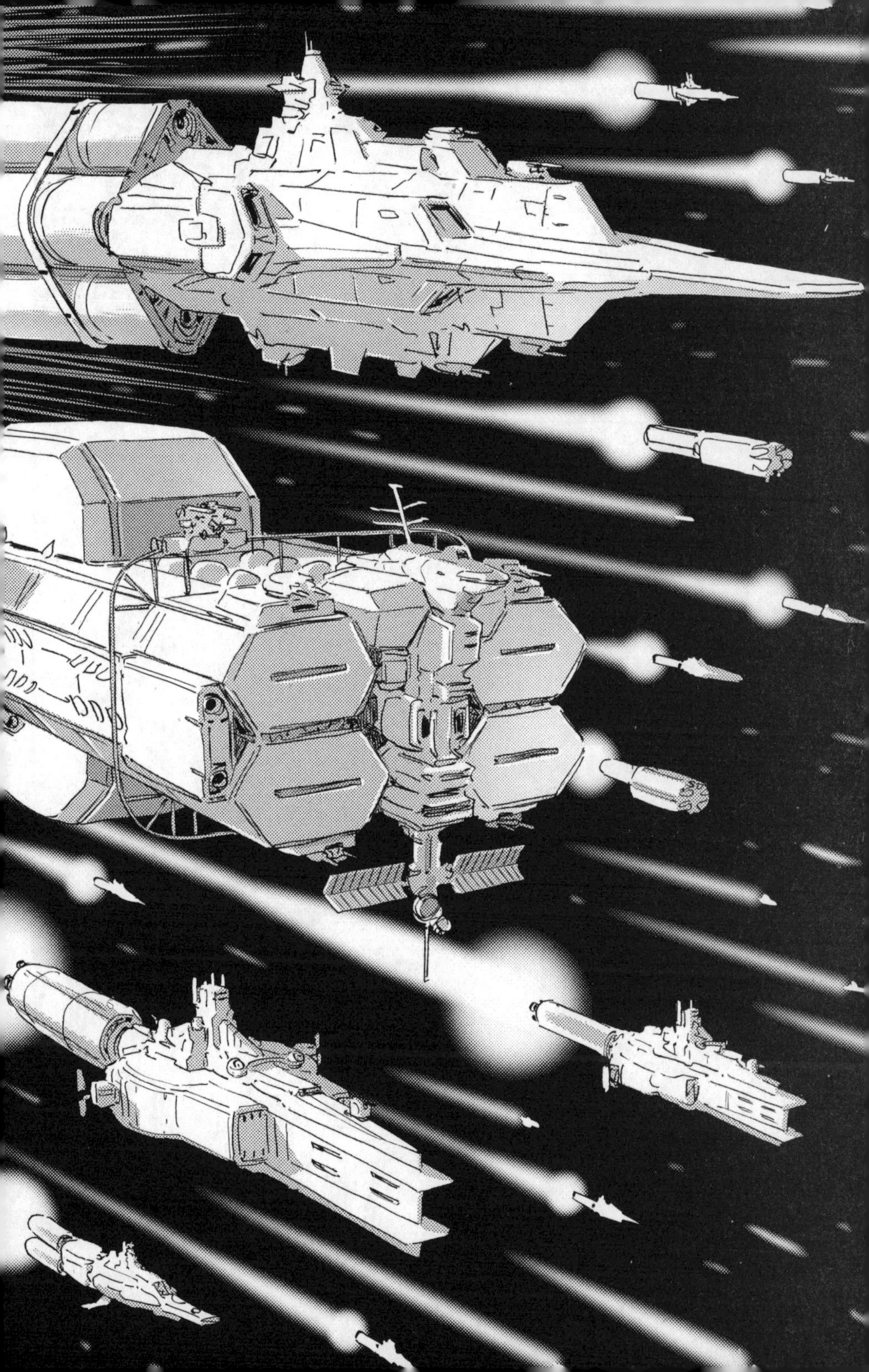

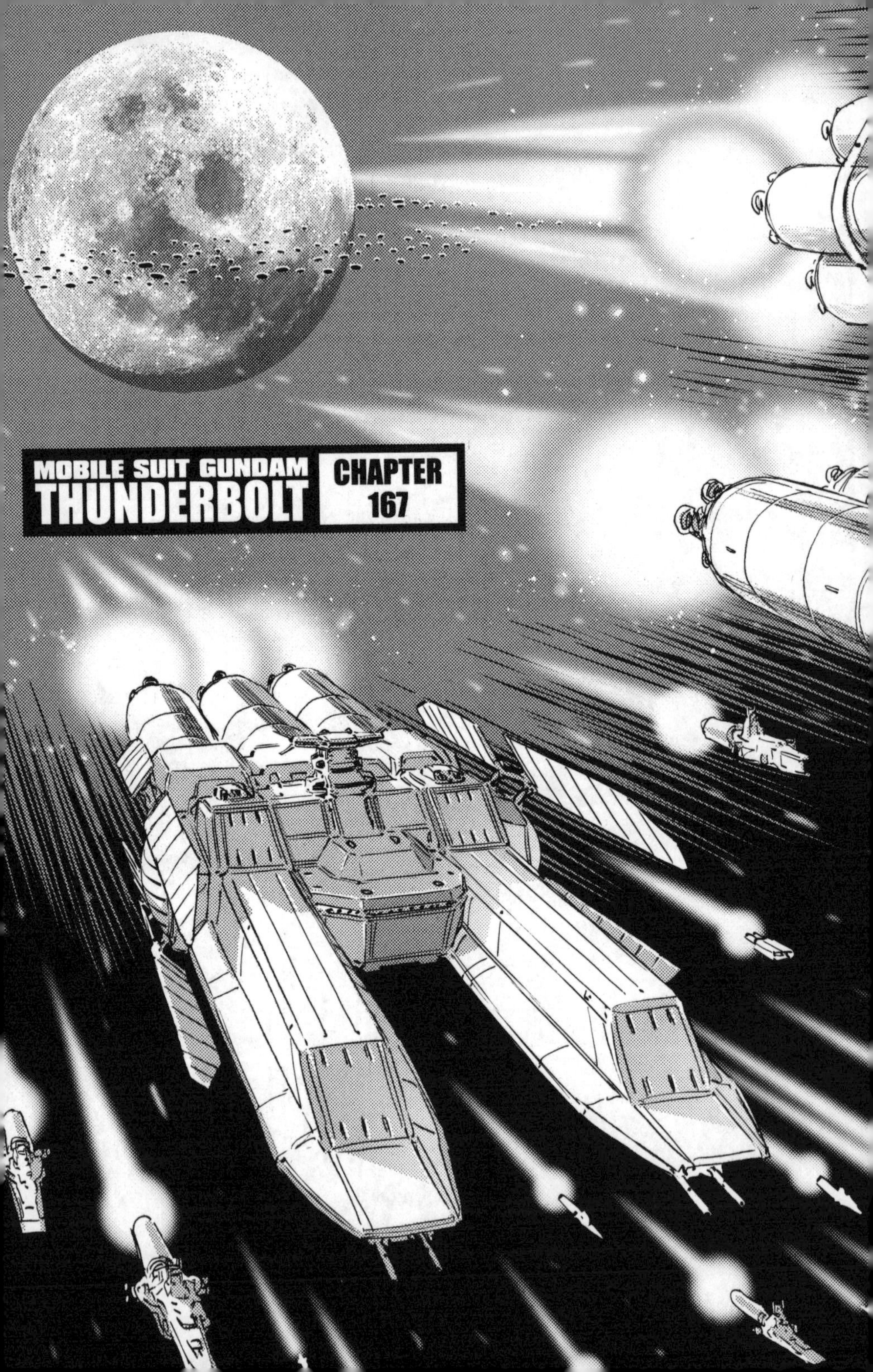
MOBILE SUIT GUNDAM
THUNDERBOLT
CHAPTER
167

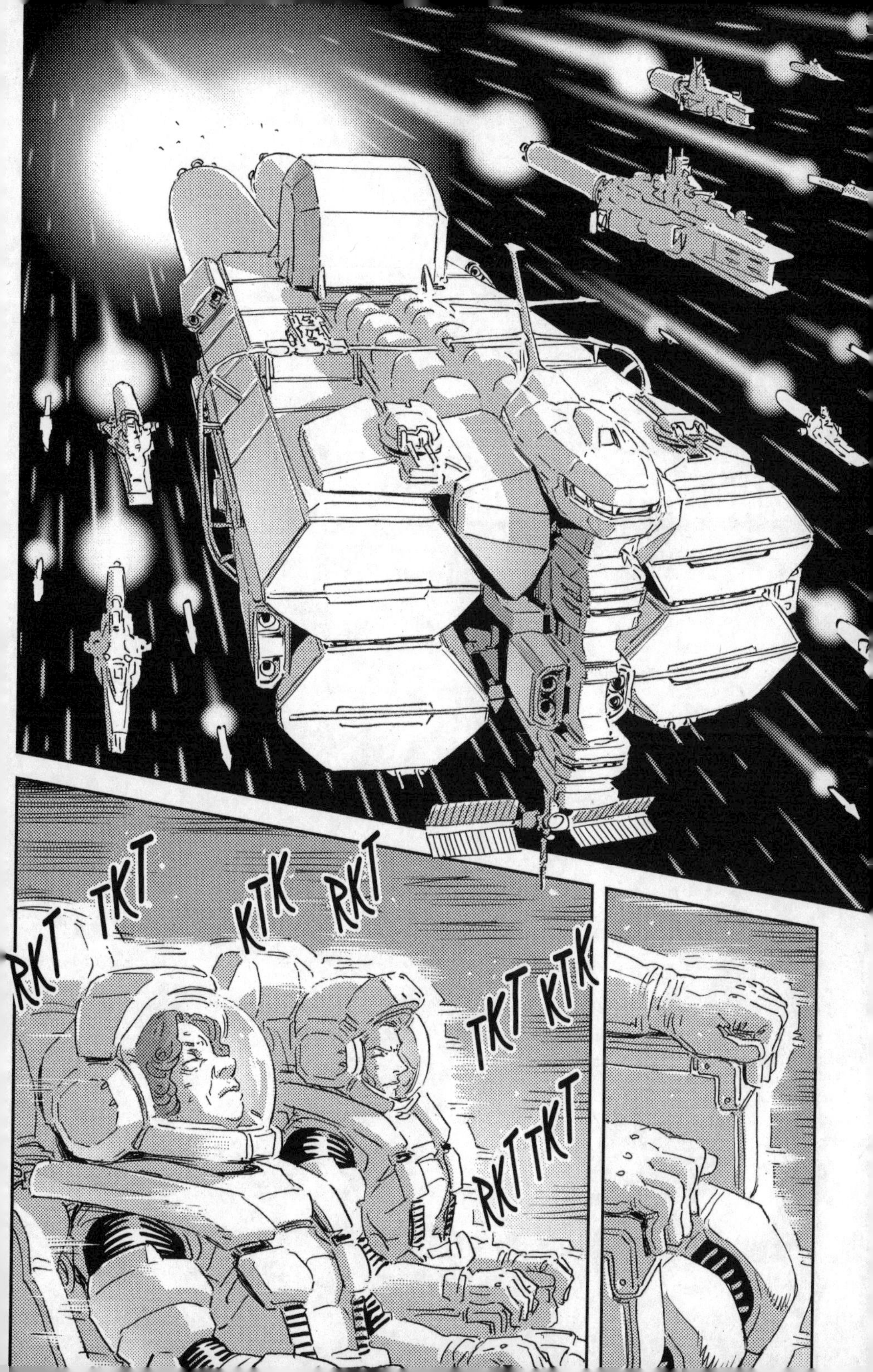
RKT
KTK
TKT
RKT
TKT KTK
RKTTKT

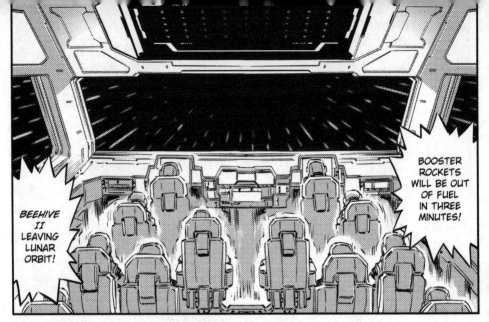

BOOSTER ROCKETS WILL BE OUT OF FUEL IN THREE MINUTES!
BEEHIVE II LEAVING LUNAR ORBIT!
ON COURSE FOR KONPEI ISLAND AT MAXIMUM THRUST!
URGH ...
KONPEITO
MOON

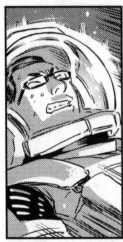

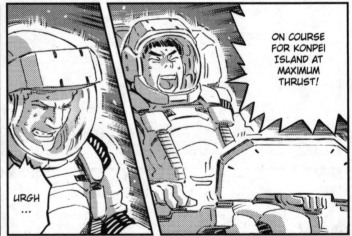

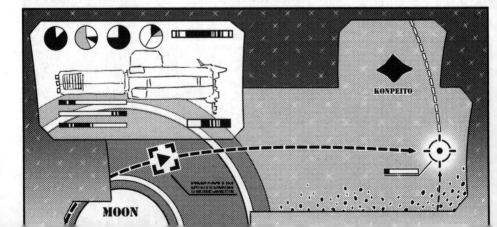

VWOOOO

RKT

TKT

KTK KTK

DIRECTOR HUMPHREY! ARE YOU ALL RIGHT?!

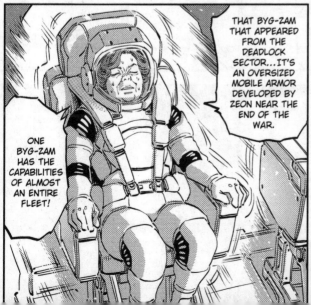

THAT BYG-ZAM THAT APPEARED FROM THE DEADLOCK SECTOR...IT'S AN OVERSIZED MOBILE ARMOR DEVELOPED BY ZEON NEAR THE END OF THE WAR.

ONE BYG-ZAM HAS THE CAPABILITIES OF ALMOST AN ENTIRE FLEET!

MONICA ...!

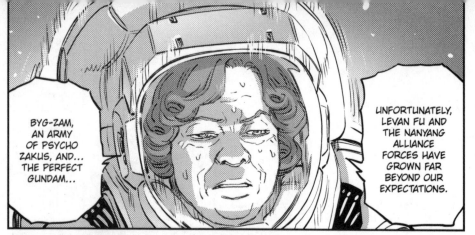

UNFORTUNATELY, LEVAN FU AND THE NANYANG ALLIANCE FORCES HAVE GROWN FAR BEYOND OUR EXPECTATIONS.
BYG-ZAM, AN ARMY OF PSYCHO ZAKUS, AND... THE PERFECT GUNDAM...
THEY'RE NOT EVEN TRYING TO HIDE THE BYG-ZAM. IS THAT...A DECLARATION OF WAR?
LEVAN FU ISN'T AIMING FOR MASS DEATH OR AN INDISCRIM-INATE TERRORIST ACT.
HE'S GIVEN THE REPUBLIC OF ZEON TIME TO EVACUATE ITS CITIZENS.

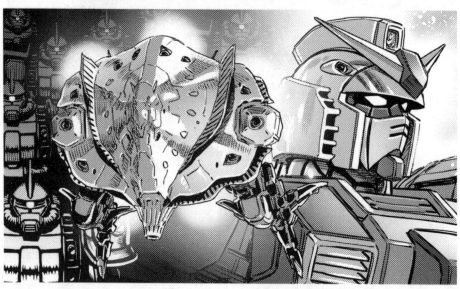

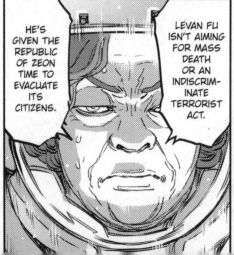

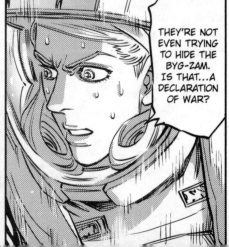

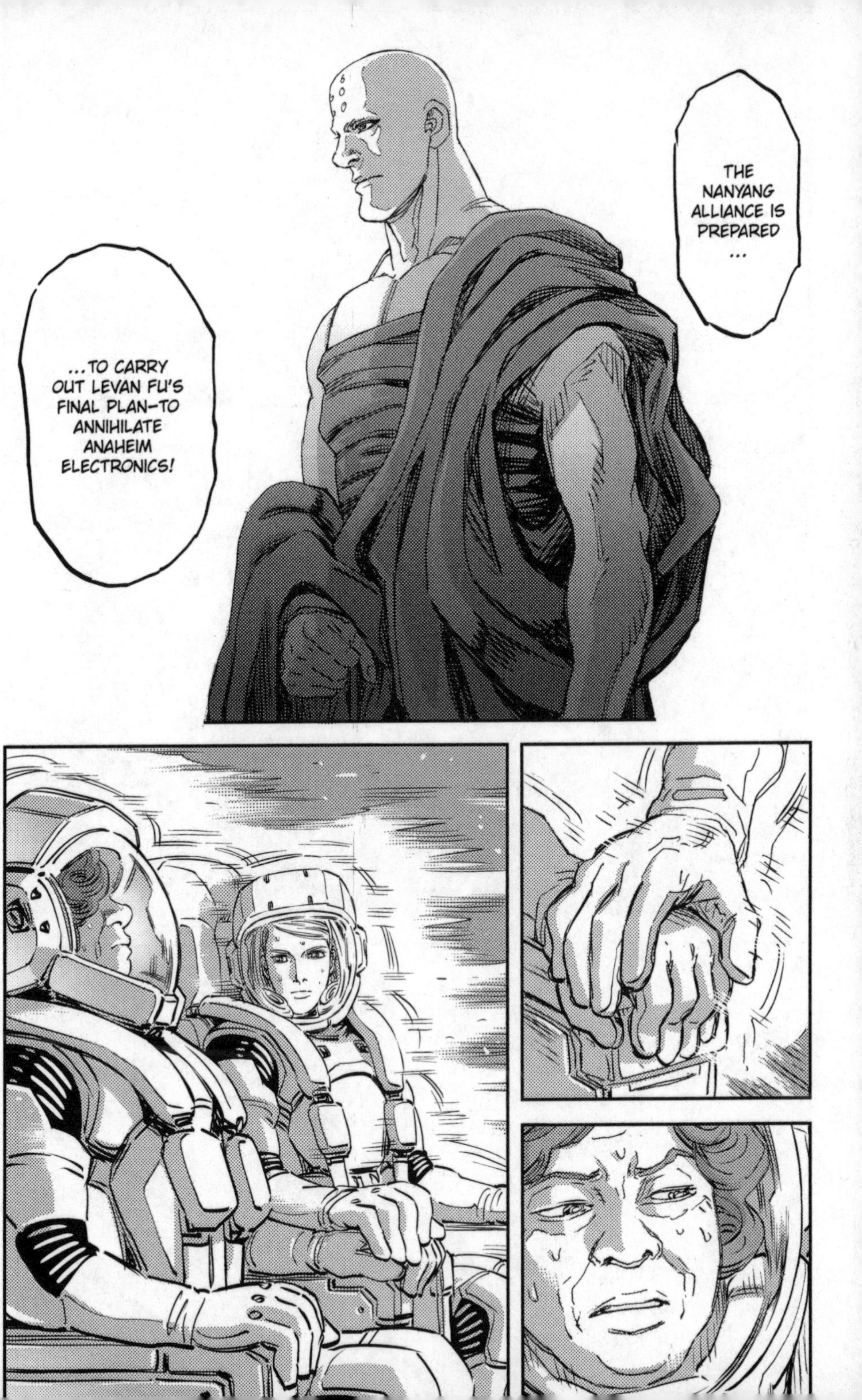
THE NANYANG ALLIANCE IS PREPARED ...
...TO CARRY OUT LEVAN FU'S FINAL PLAN—TO ANNIHILATE ANAHEIM ELECTRONICS!

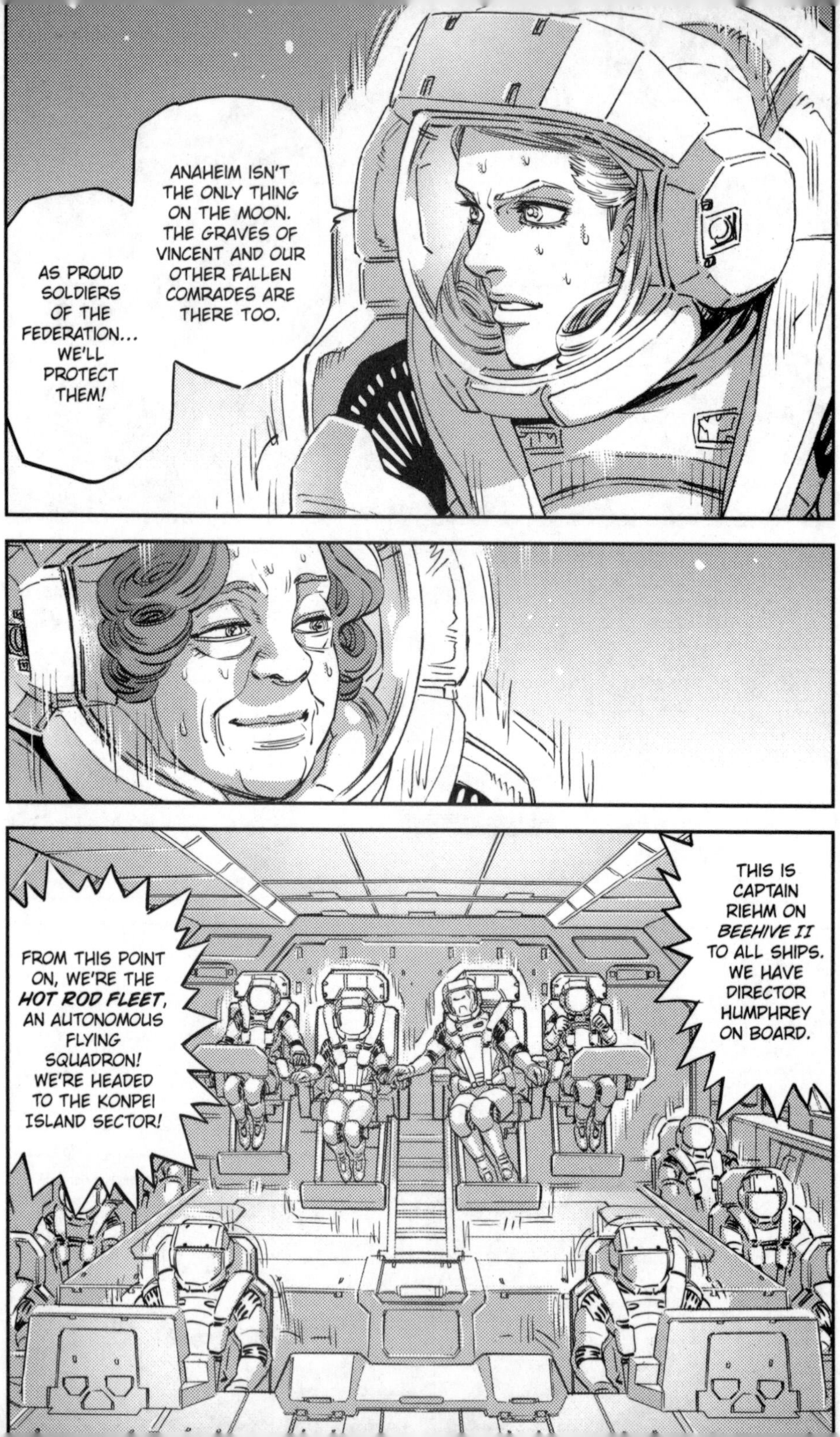
ANAHEIM ISN'T THE ONLY THING ON THE MOON. THE GRAVES OF VINCENT AND OUR OTHER FALLEN COMRADES ARE THERE TOO.
AS PROUD SOLDIERS OF THE FEDERATION... WE'LL PROTECT THEM!
THIS IS CAPTAIN RIEHM ON *BEEHIVE II* TO ALL SHIPS. WE HAVE DIRECTOR HUMPHREY ON BOARD.
FROM THIS POINT ON, WE'RE THE ***HOT ROD FLEET***, AN AUTONOMOUS FLYING SQUADRON! WE'RE HEADED TO THE KONPEI ISLAND SECTOR!

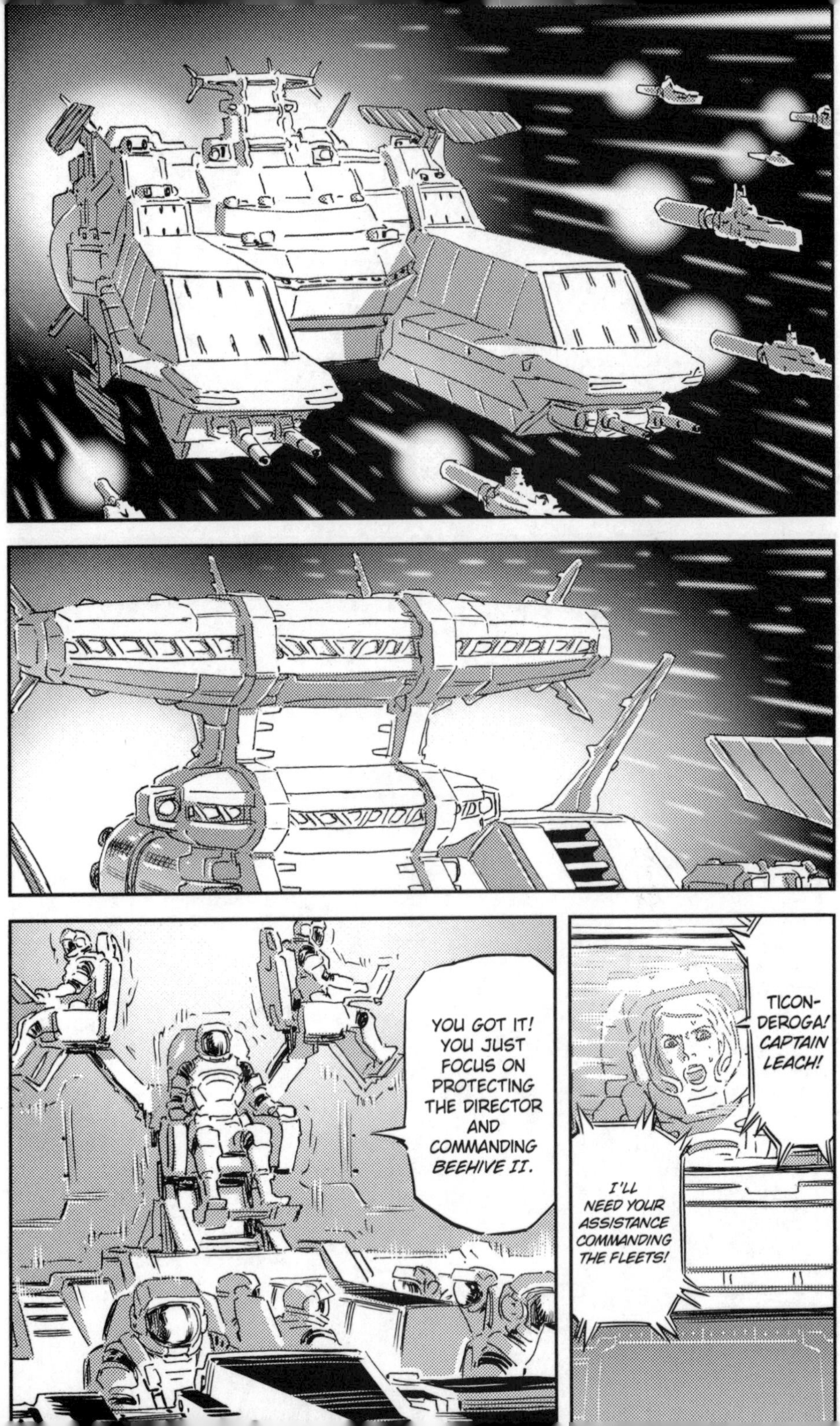
TICON-DEROGA! CAPTAIN LEACH!
I'LL NEED YOUR ASSISTANCE COMMANDING THE FLEETS!
YOU GOT IT! YOU JUST FOCUS ON PROTECTING THE DIRECTOR AND COMMANDING *BEEHIVE II*.

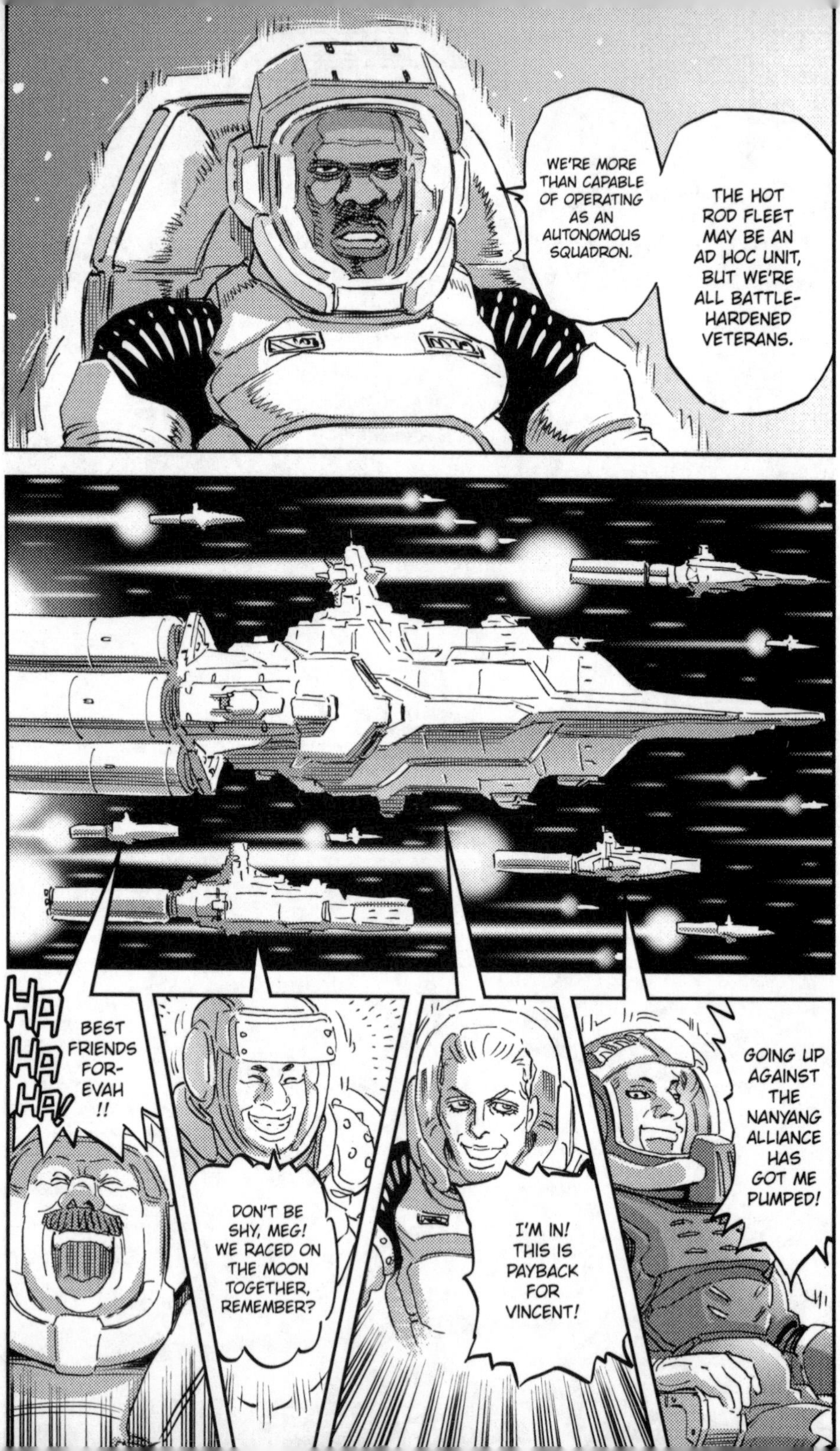
THE HOT ROD FLEET MAY BE AN AD HOC UNIT, BUT WE'RE ALL BATTLE-HARDENED VETERANS.
WE'RE MORE THAN CAPABLE OF OPERATING AS AN AUTONOMOUS SQUADRON.
GOING UP AGAINST THE NANYANG ALLIANCE HAS GOT ME PUMPED!
I'M IN! THIS IS PAYBACK FOR VINCENT!
DON'T BE SHY, MEG! WE RACED ON THE MOON TOGETHER, REMEMBER?
BEST FRIENDS FOR-EVAH!!
HA HA HA!

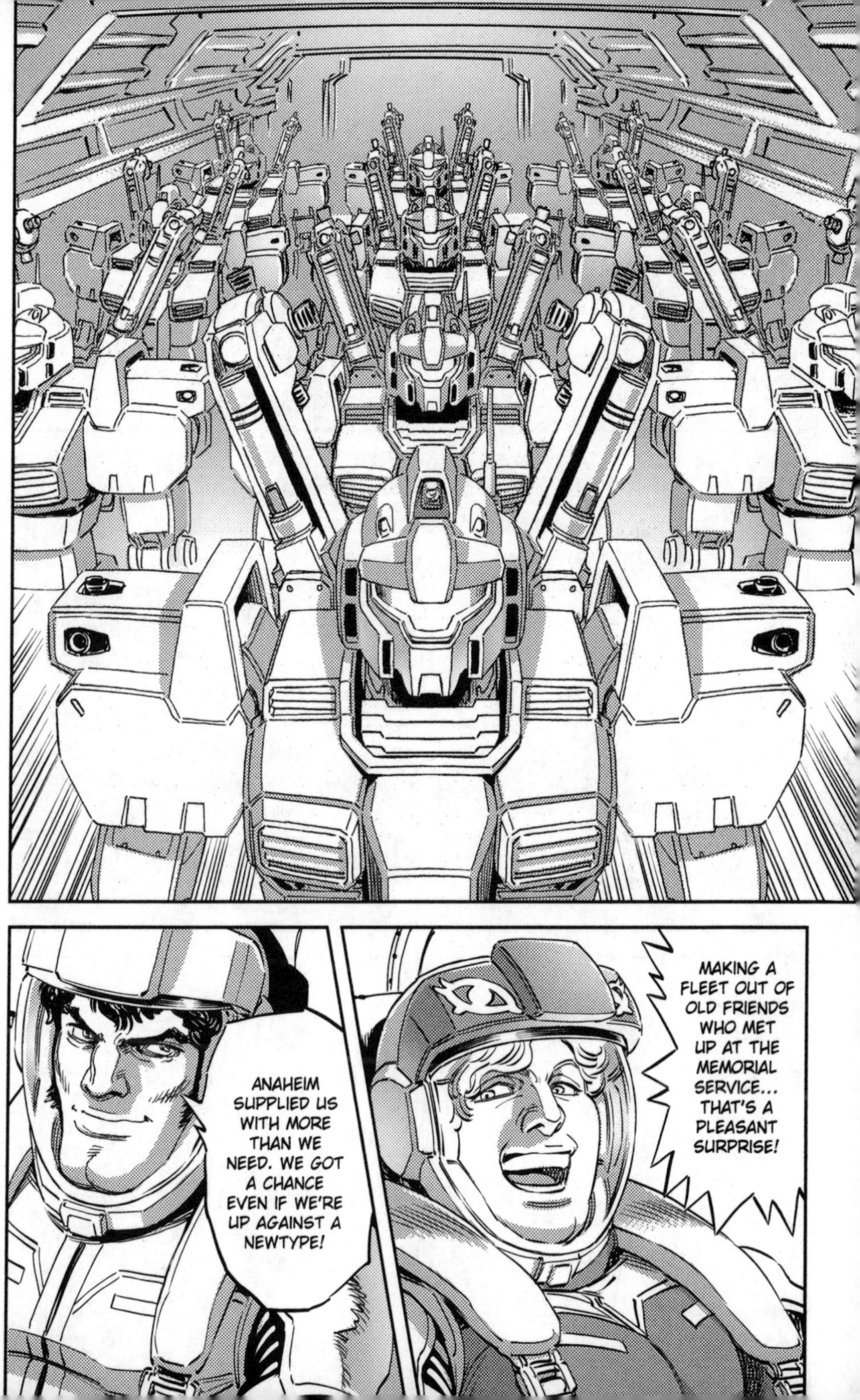
MAKING A FLEET OUT OF OLD FRIENDS WHO MET UP AT THE MEMORIAL SERVICE... THAT'S A PLEASANT SURPRISE!
ANAHEIM SUPPLIED US WITH MORE THAN WE NEED. WE GOT A CHANCE EVEN IF WE'RE UP AGAINST A NEWTYPE!

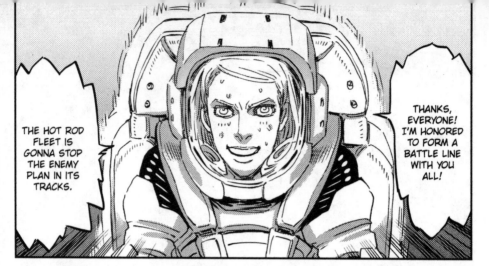

THANKS, EVERYONE! I'M HONORED TO FORM A BATTLE LINE WITH YOU ALL!
THE HOT ROD FLEET IS GONNA STOP THE ENEMY PLAN IN ITS TRACKS.
THIS IS THE ENGINE ROOM! WHEN THE BOOSTERS ARE OUT OF FUEL, WE'RE FIRING UP THE MAIN ENGINE, SO PREPARE YOURSELVES!
DETACHING BOOSTER ROCKETS!

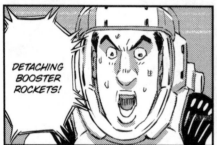

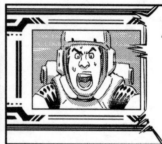

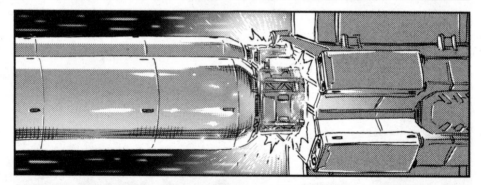

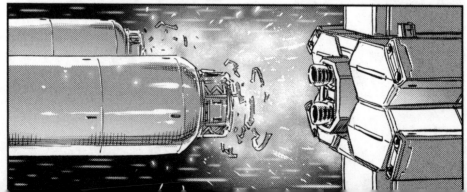

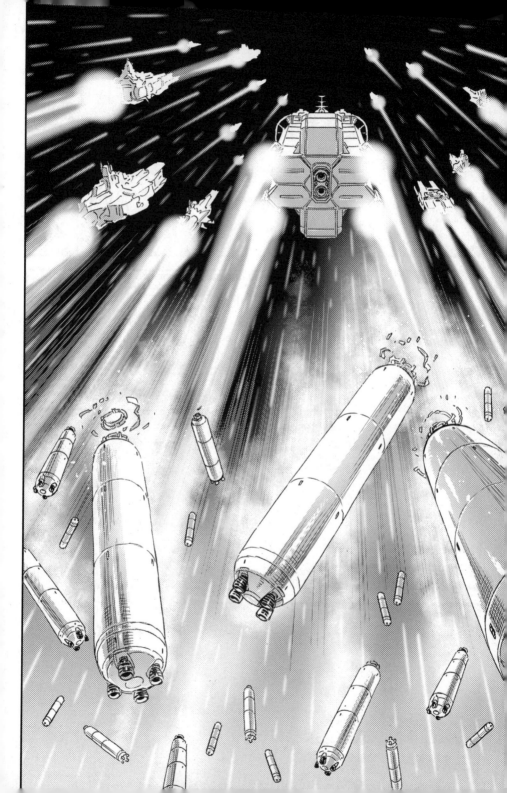

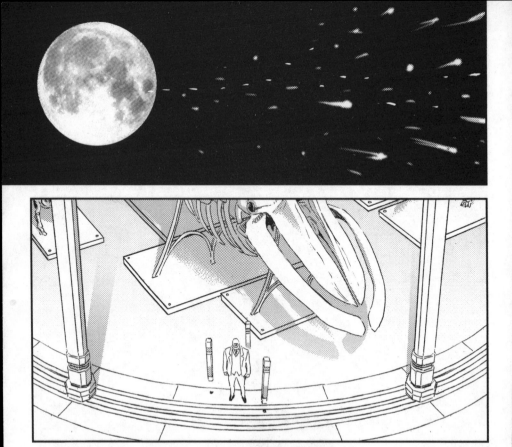

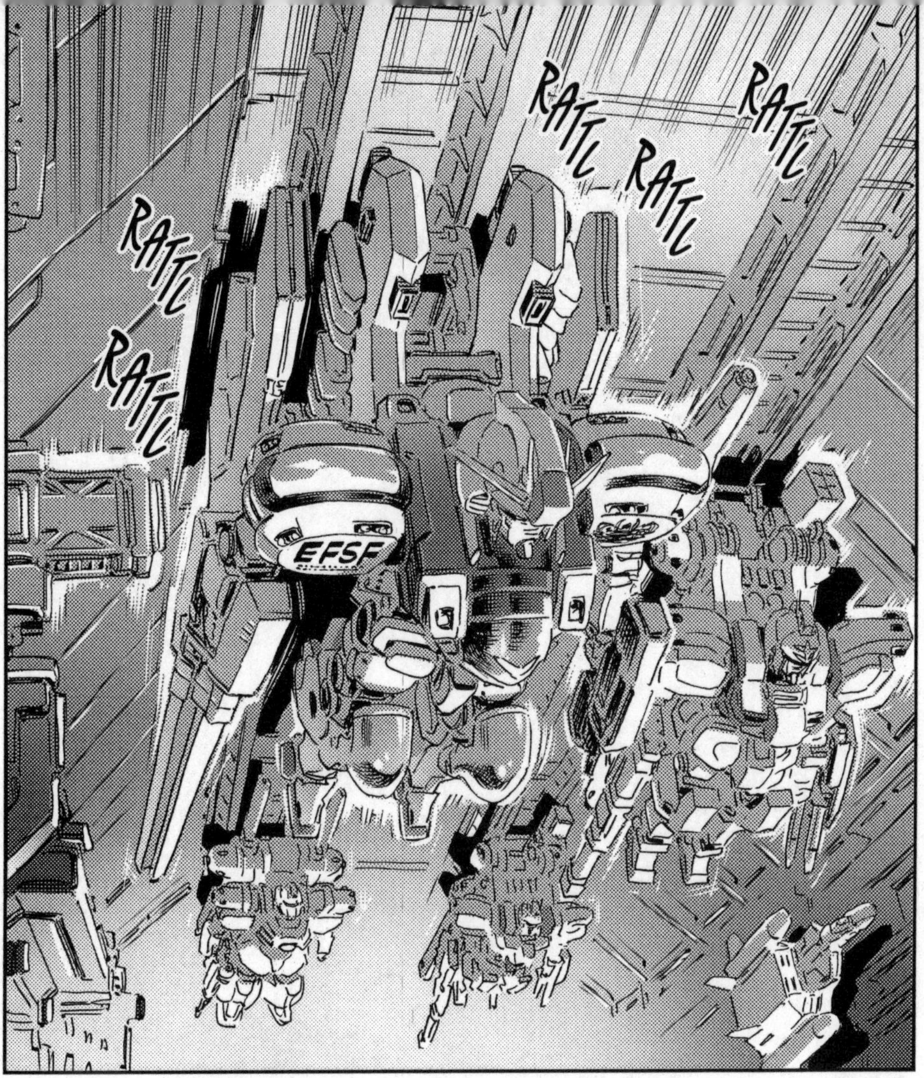
RATTL
RATTL
RATTL
RATTL
RATTL
EFSF
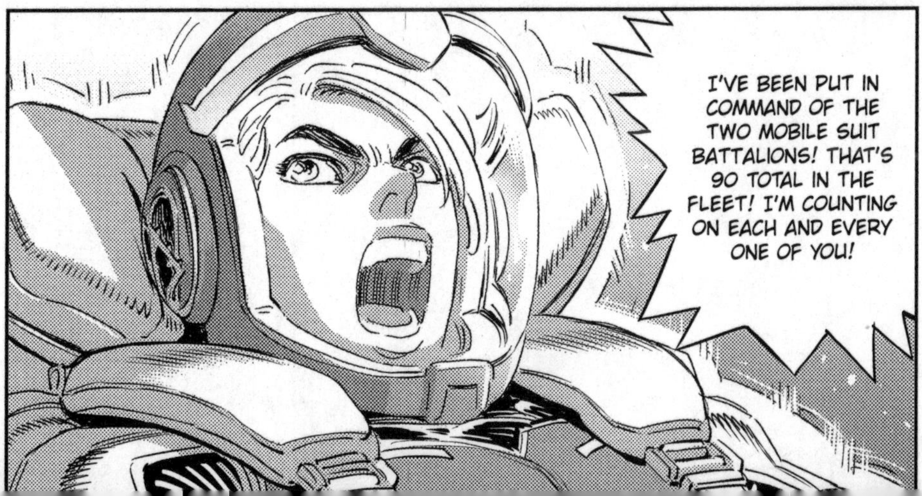
I'VE BEEN PUT IN COMMAND OF THE TWO MOBILE SUIT BATTALIONS! THAT'S 90 TOTAL IN THE FLEET! I'M COUNTING ON EACH AND EVERY ONE OF YOU!

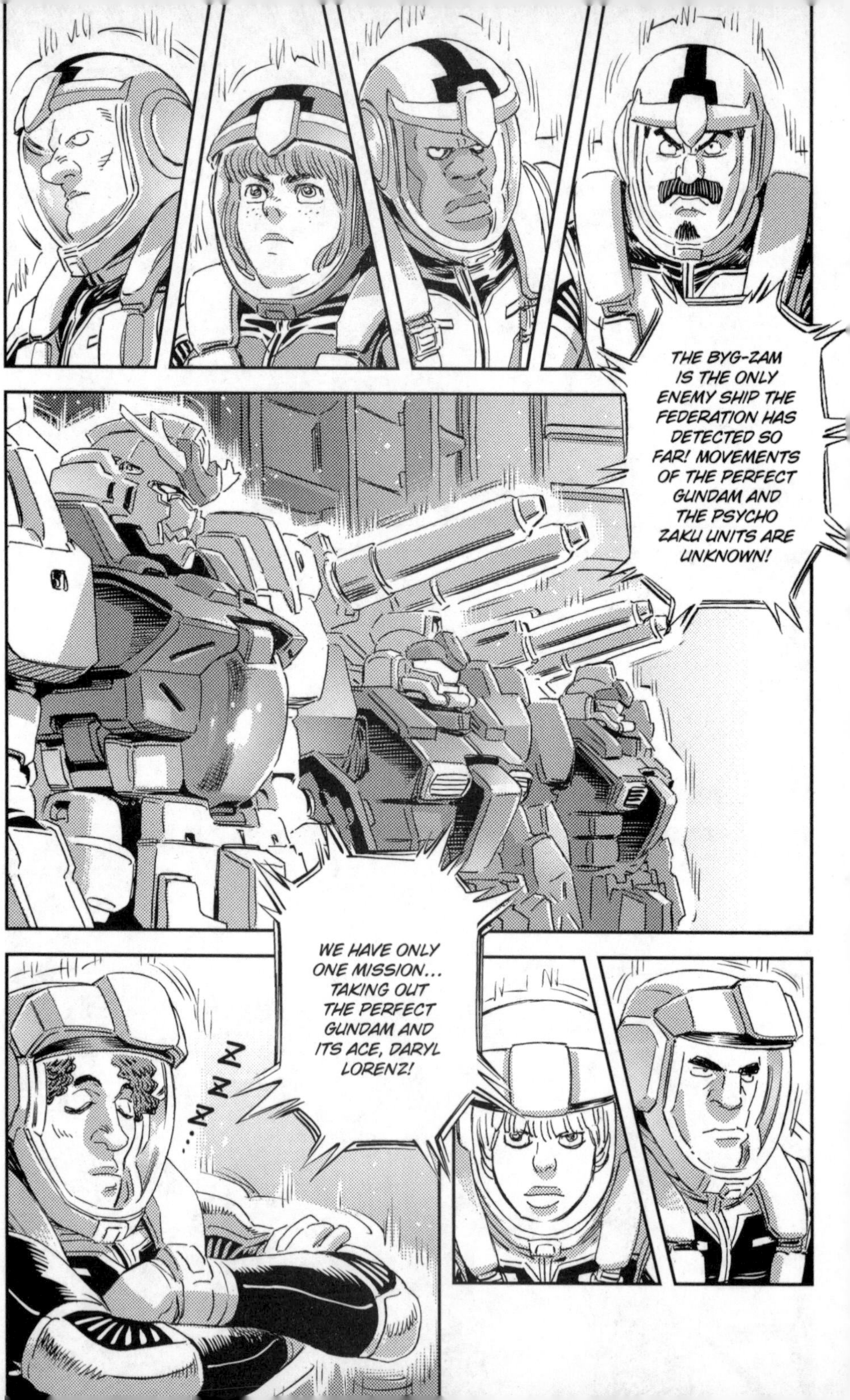
THE BYG-ZAM IS THE ONLY ENEMY SHIP THE FEDERATION HAS DETECTED SO FAR! MOVEMENTS OF THE PERFECT GUNDAM AND THE PSYCHO ZAKU UNITS ARE UNKNOWN!
WE HAVE ONLY ONE MISSION... TAKING OUT THE PERFECT GUNDAM AND ITS ACE, DARYL LORENZ!
...ZZZ

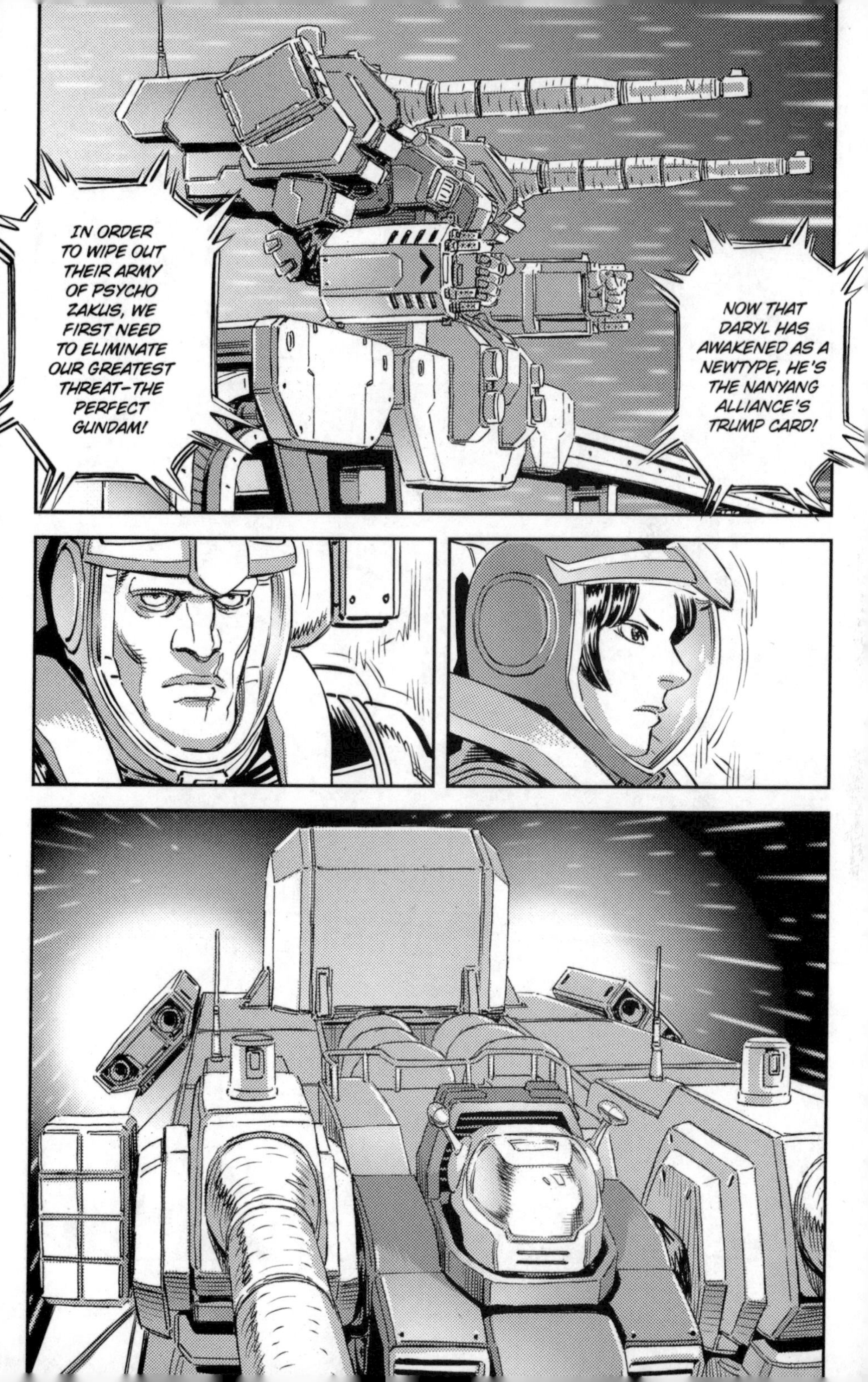
NOW THAT DARYL HAS AWAKENED AS A NEWTYPE, HE'S THE NANYANG ALLIANCE'S TRUMP CARD!
IN ORDER TO WIPE OUT THEIR ARMY OF PSYCHO ZAKUS, WE FIRST NEED TO ELIMINATE OUR GREATEST THREAT—THE PERFECT GUNDAM!

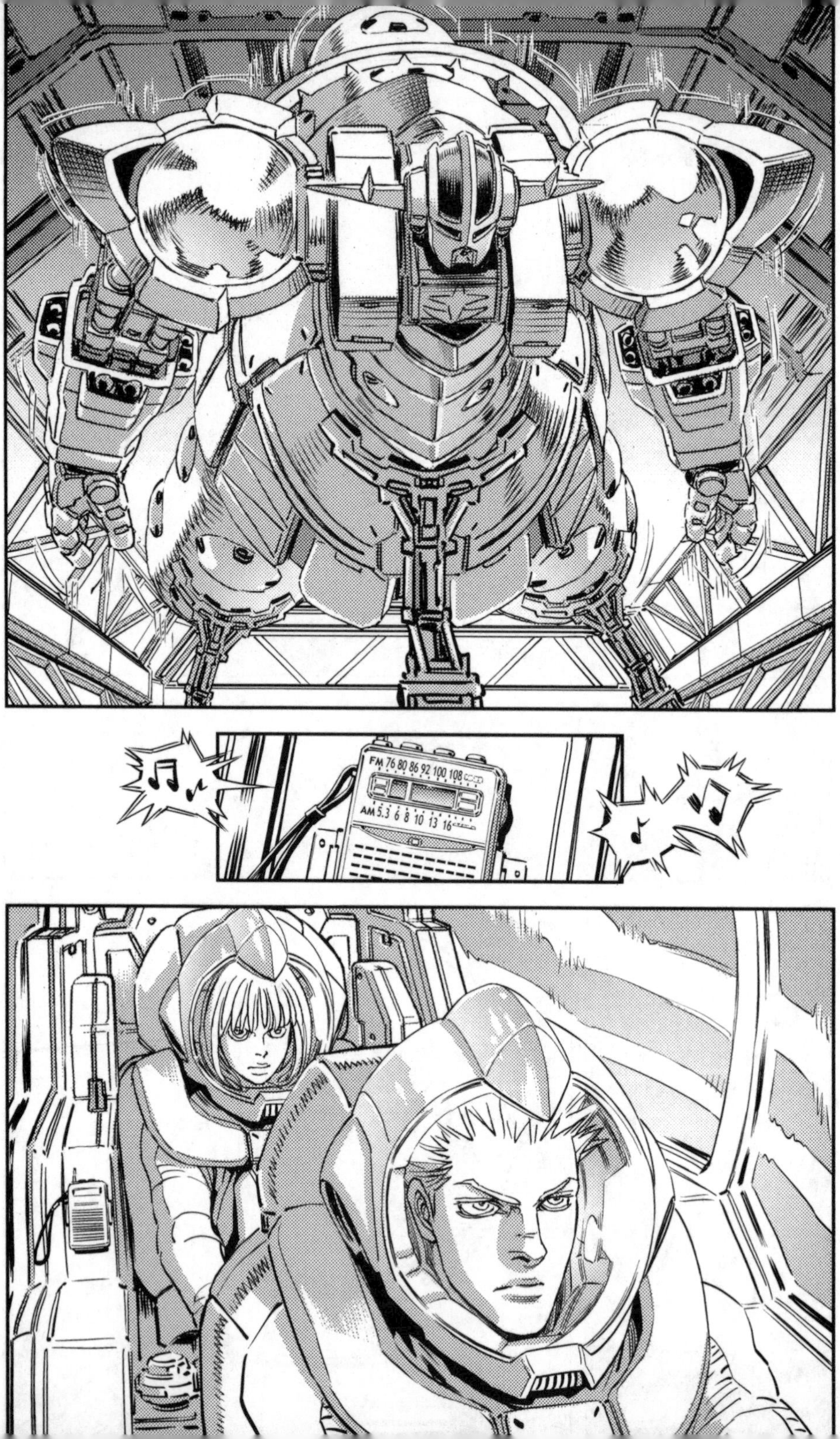
FM 76 80 86 92 100 108
AM 5.3 6 8 10 13 16

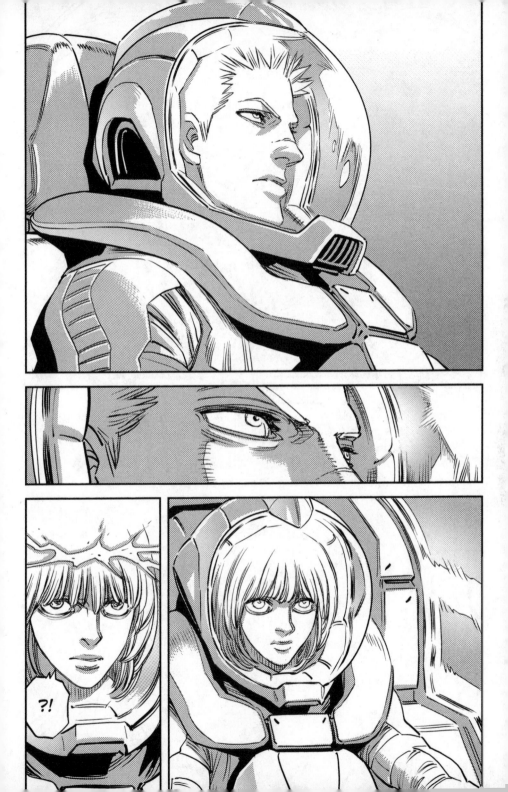

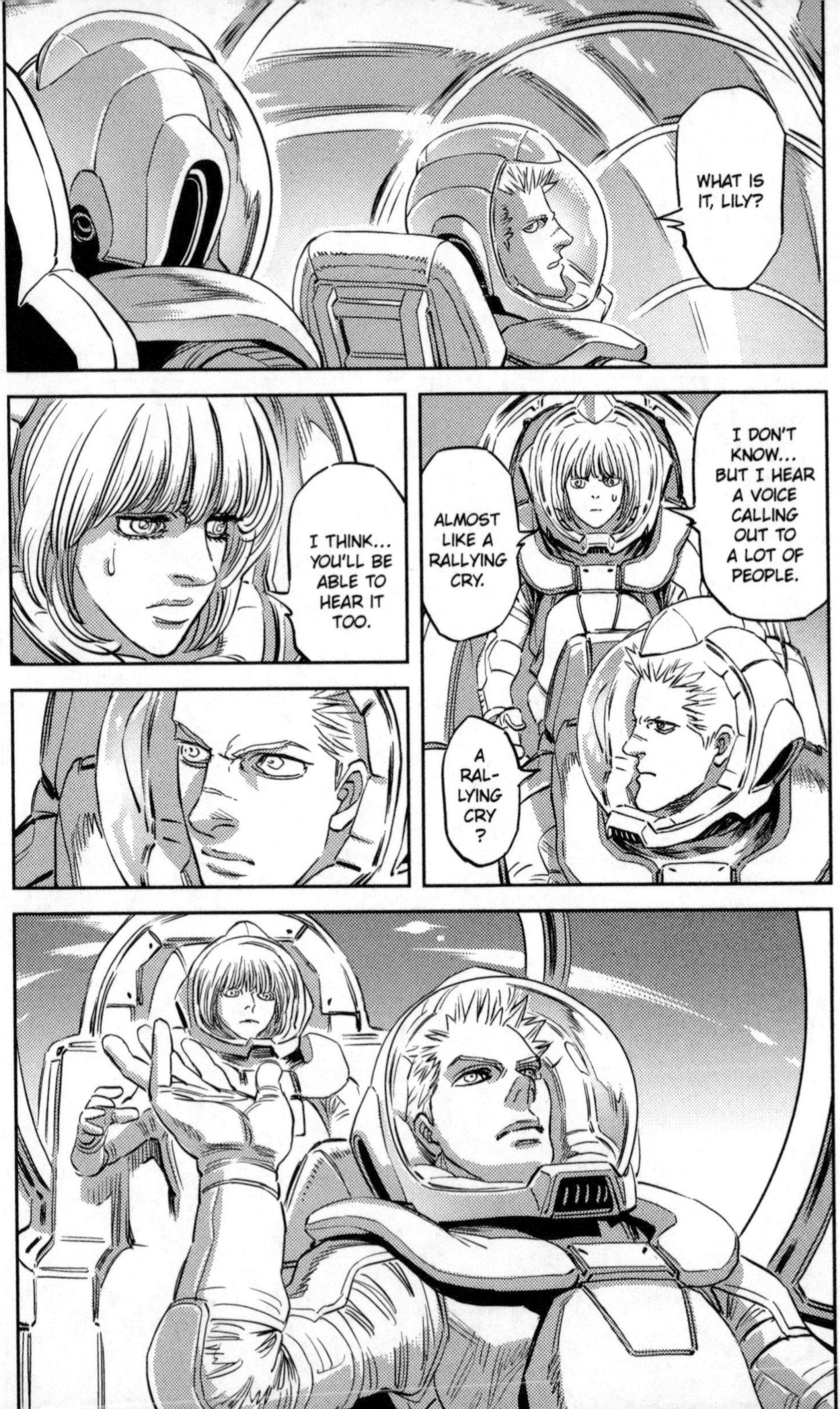
WHAT IS IT, LILY?
I DON'T KNOW... BUT I HEAR A VOICE CALLING OUT TO A LOT OF PEOPLE.
ALMOST LIKE A RALLYING CRY.
A RAL-LYING CRY?
I THINK... YOU'LL BE ABLE TO HEAR IT TOO.

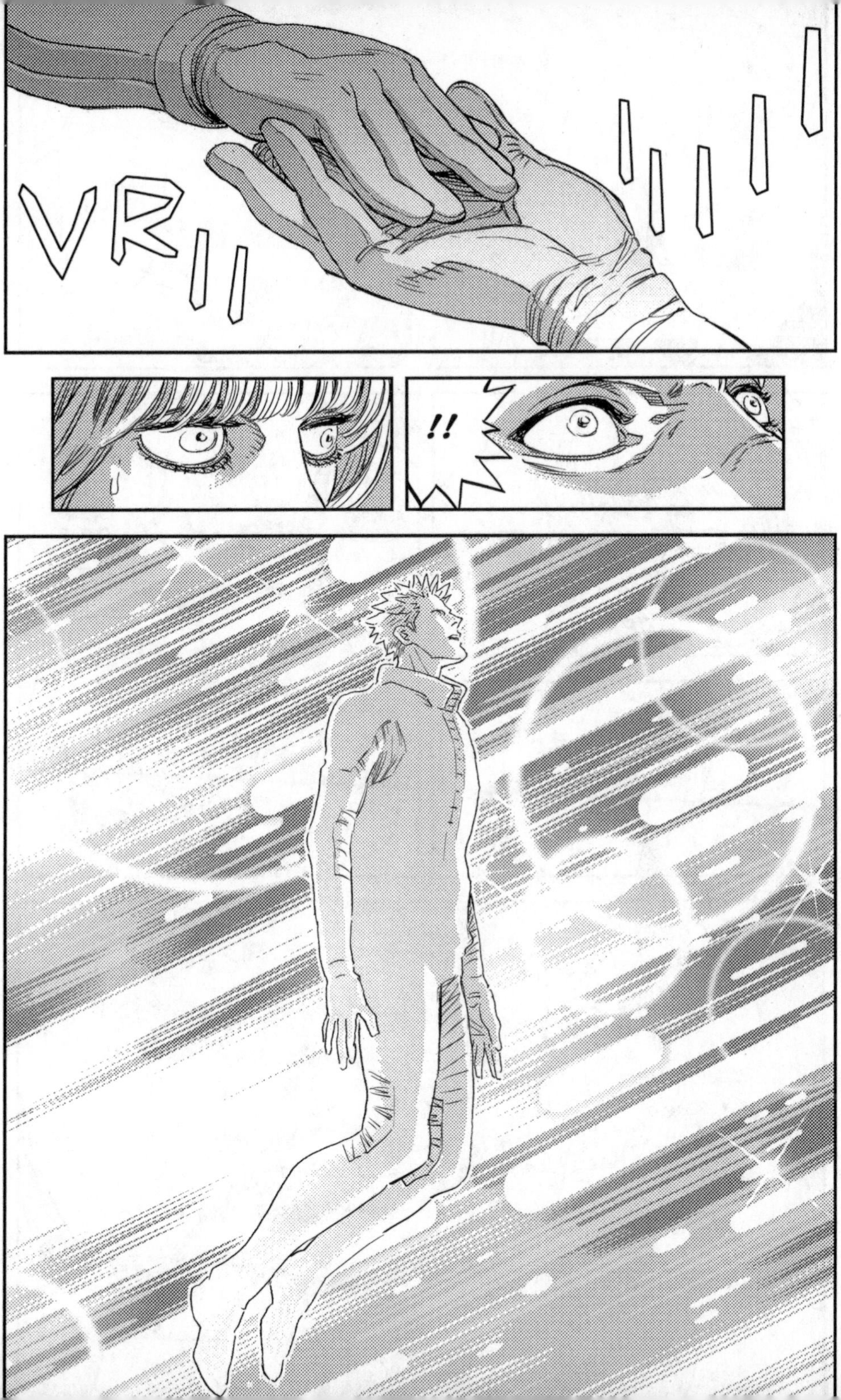

VRII
!!

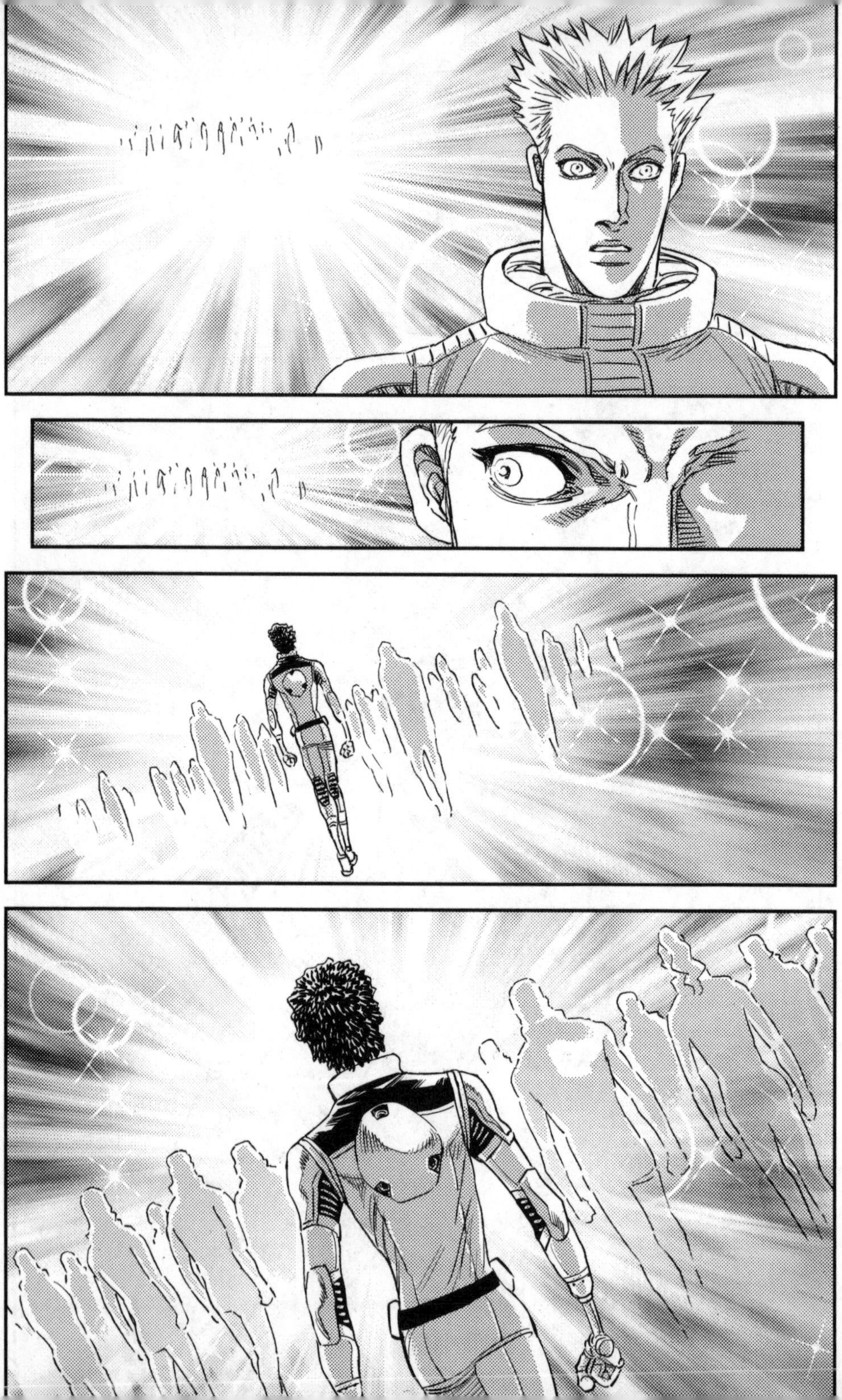

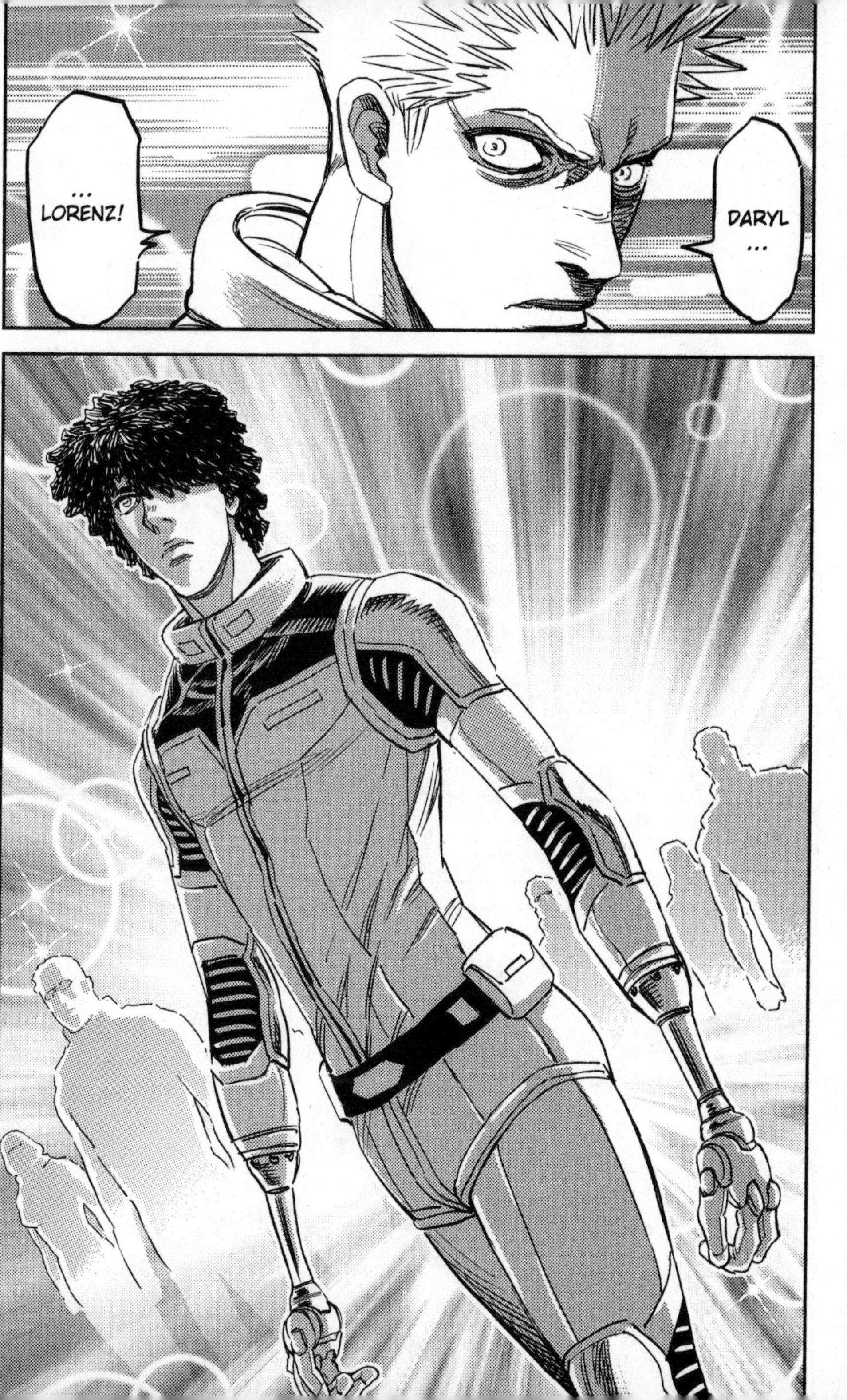
DARYL ...
... LORENZ!

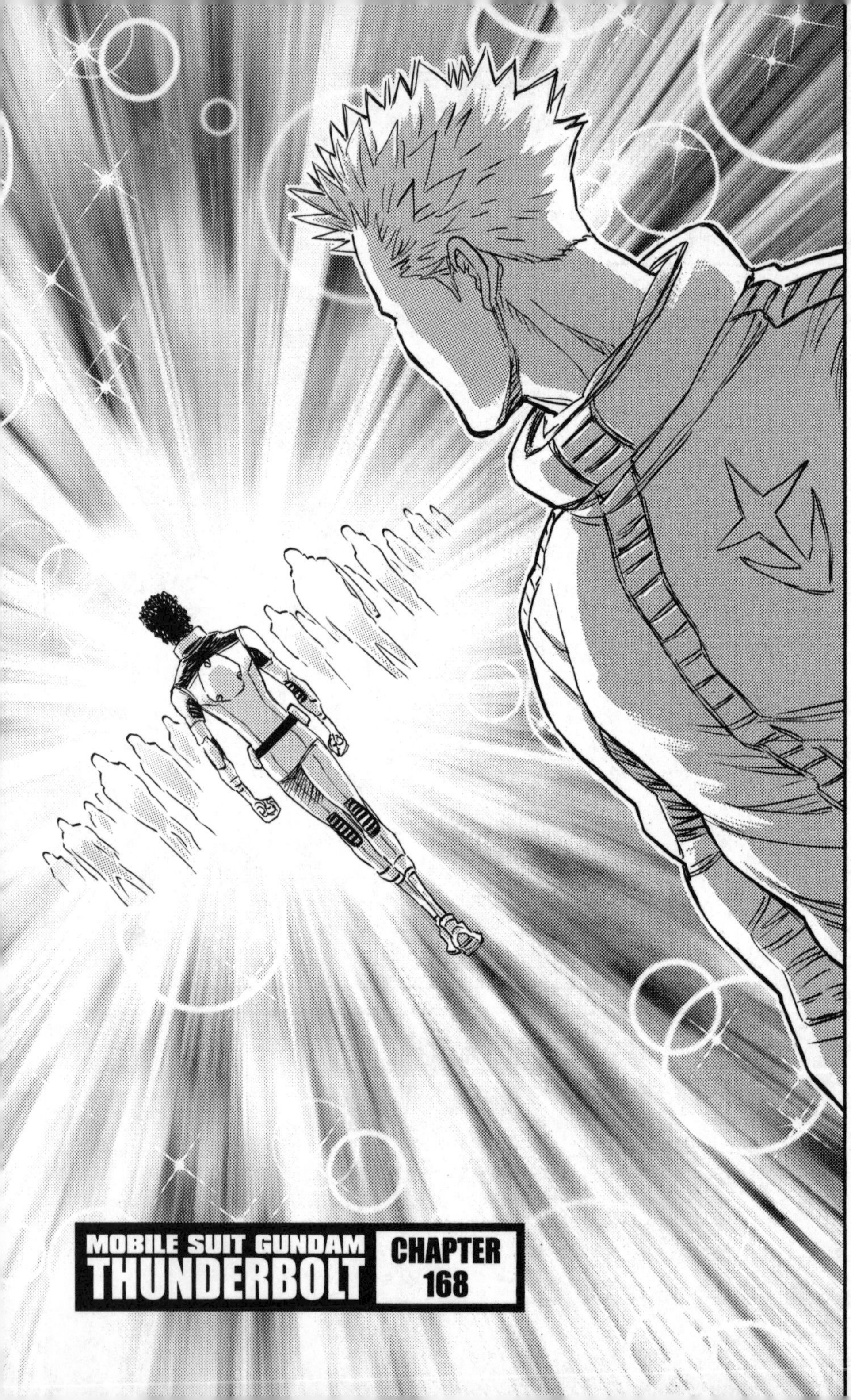
MOBILE SUIT GUNDAM
THUNDERBOLT
CHAPTER
168

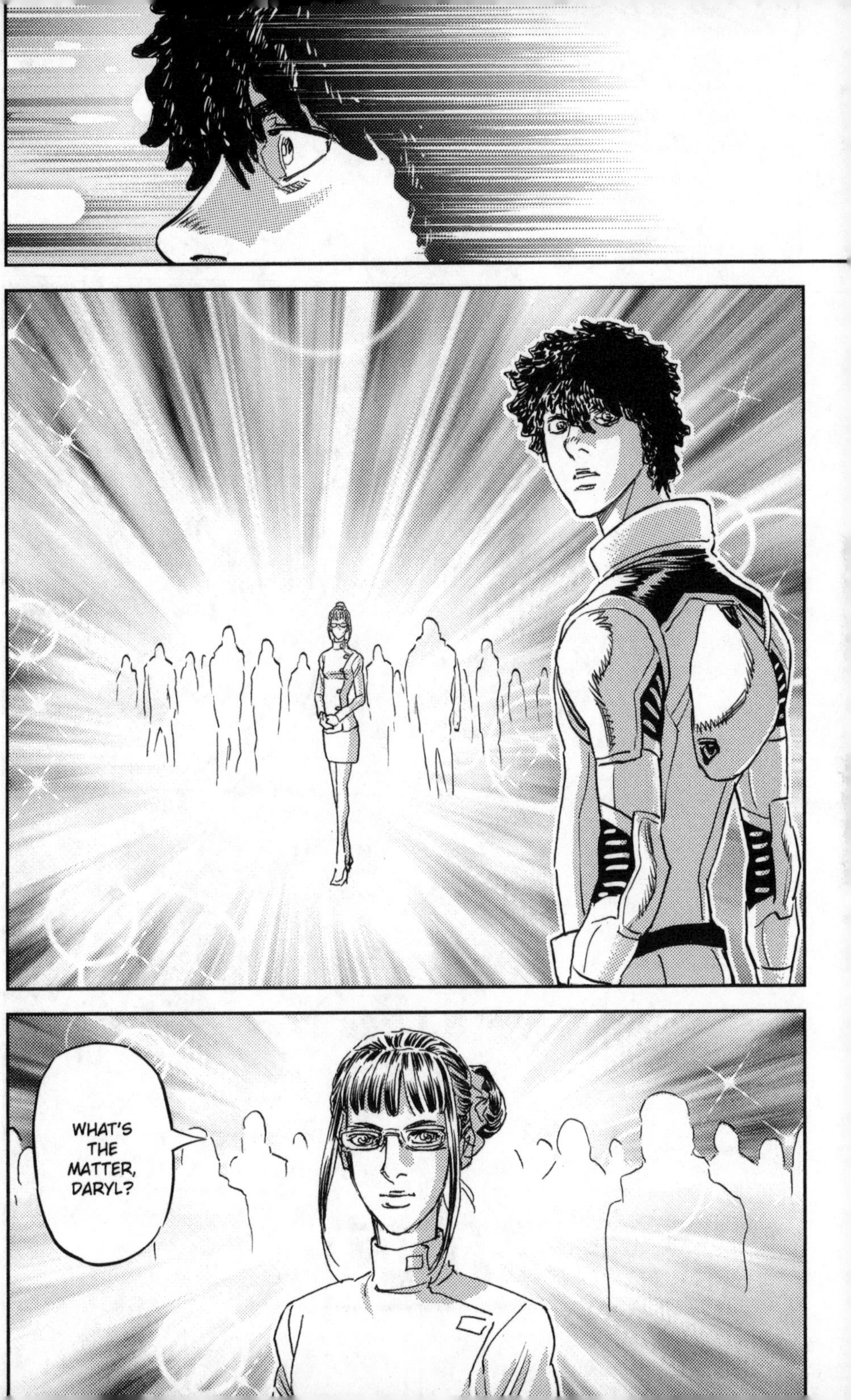
WHAT'S THE MATTER, DARYL?

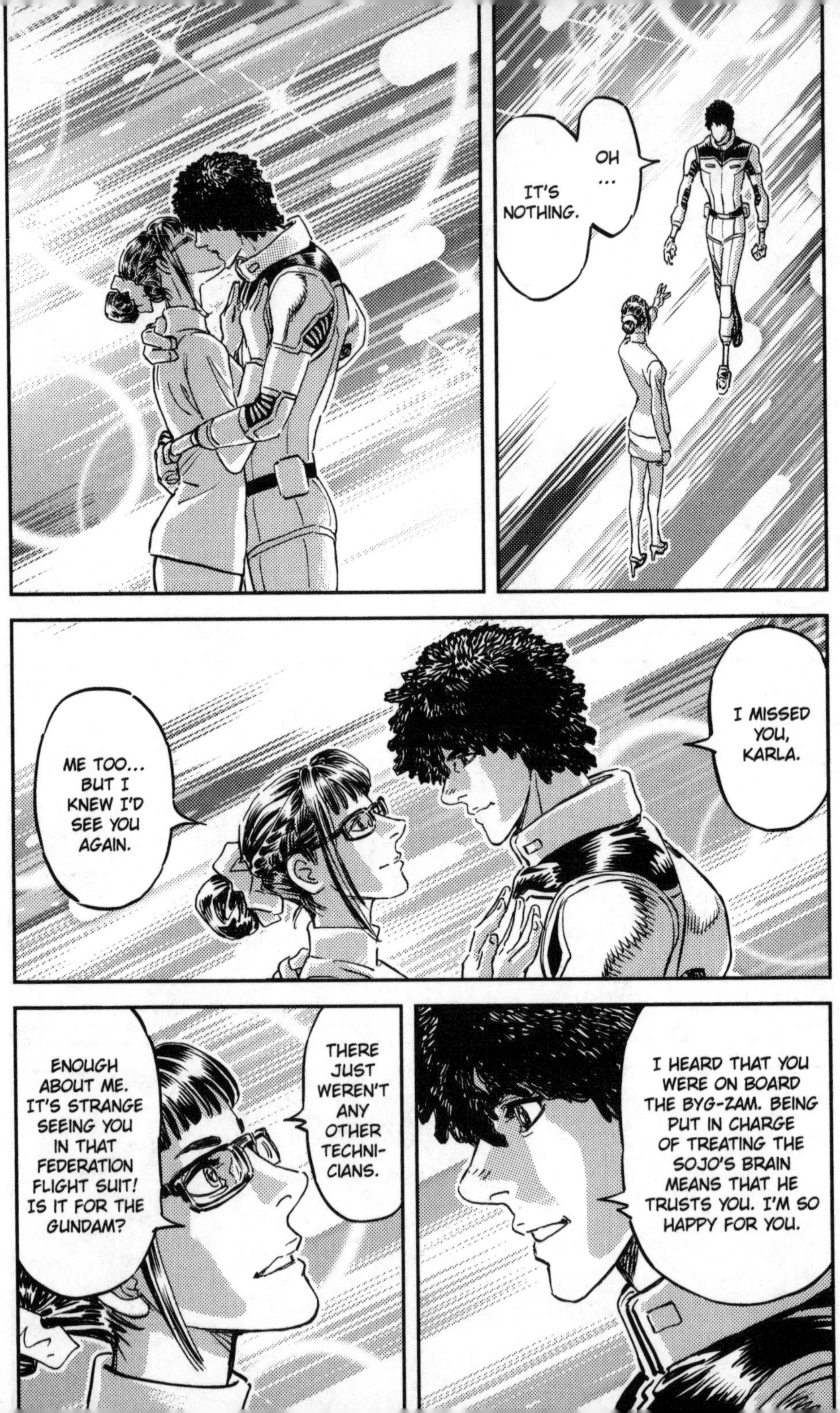
OH ... IT'S NOTHING.
I MISSED YOU, KARLA.
ME TOO... BUT I KNEW I'D SEE YOU AGAIN.
I HEARD THAT YOU WERE ON BOARD THE BYG-ZAM. BEING PUT IN CHARGE OF TREATING THE SOJO'S BRAIN MEANS THAT HE TRUSTS YOU. I'M SO HAPPY FOR YOU.
THERE JUST WEREN'T ANY OTHER TECHNICIANS.
ENOUGH ABOUT ME. IT'S STRANGE SEEING YOU IN THAT FEDERATION FLIGHT SUIT! IS IT FOR THE GUNDAM?

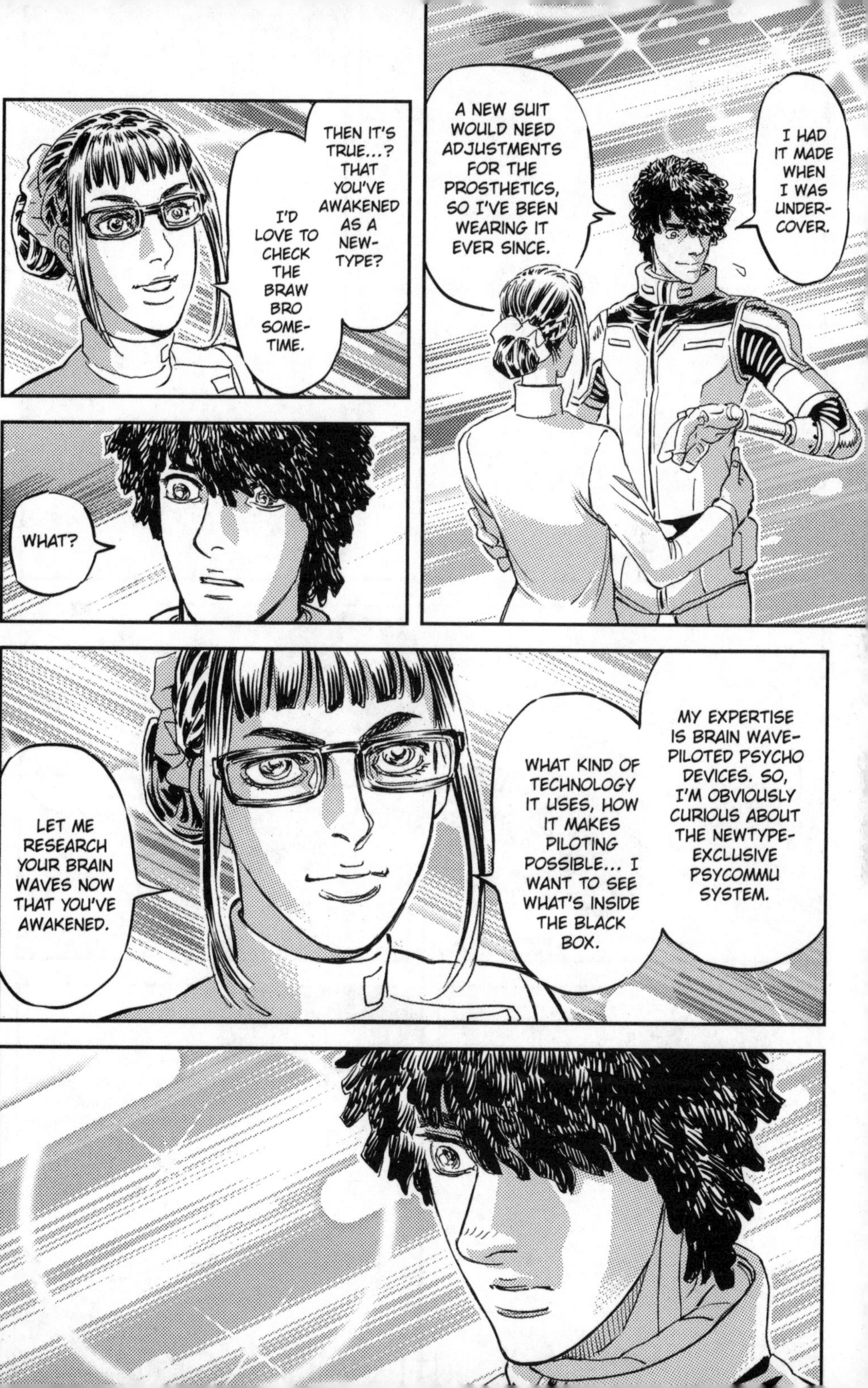
I HAD IT MADE WHEN I WAS UNDER-COVER.
A NEW SUIT WOULD NEED ADJUSTMENTS FOR THE PROSTHETICS, SO I'VE BEEN WEARING IT EVER SINCE.
THEN IT'S TRUE...? THAT YOU'VE AWAKENED AS A NEW-TYPE?
I'D LOVE TO CHECK THE BRAW BRO SOME-TIME.
WHAT?
MY EXPERTISE IS BRAIN WAVE-PILOTED PSYCHO DEVICES. SO, I'M OBVIOUSLY CURIOUS ABOUT THE NEWTYPE-EXCLUSIVE PSYCOMMU SYSTEM.
WHAT KIND OF TECHNOLOGY IT USES, HOW IT MAKES PILOTING POSSIBLE... I WANT TO SEE WHAT'S INSIDE THE BLACK BOX.
LET ME RESEARCH YOUR BRAIN WAVES NOW THAT YOU'VE AWAKENED.

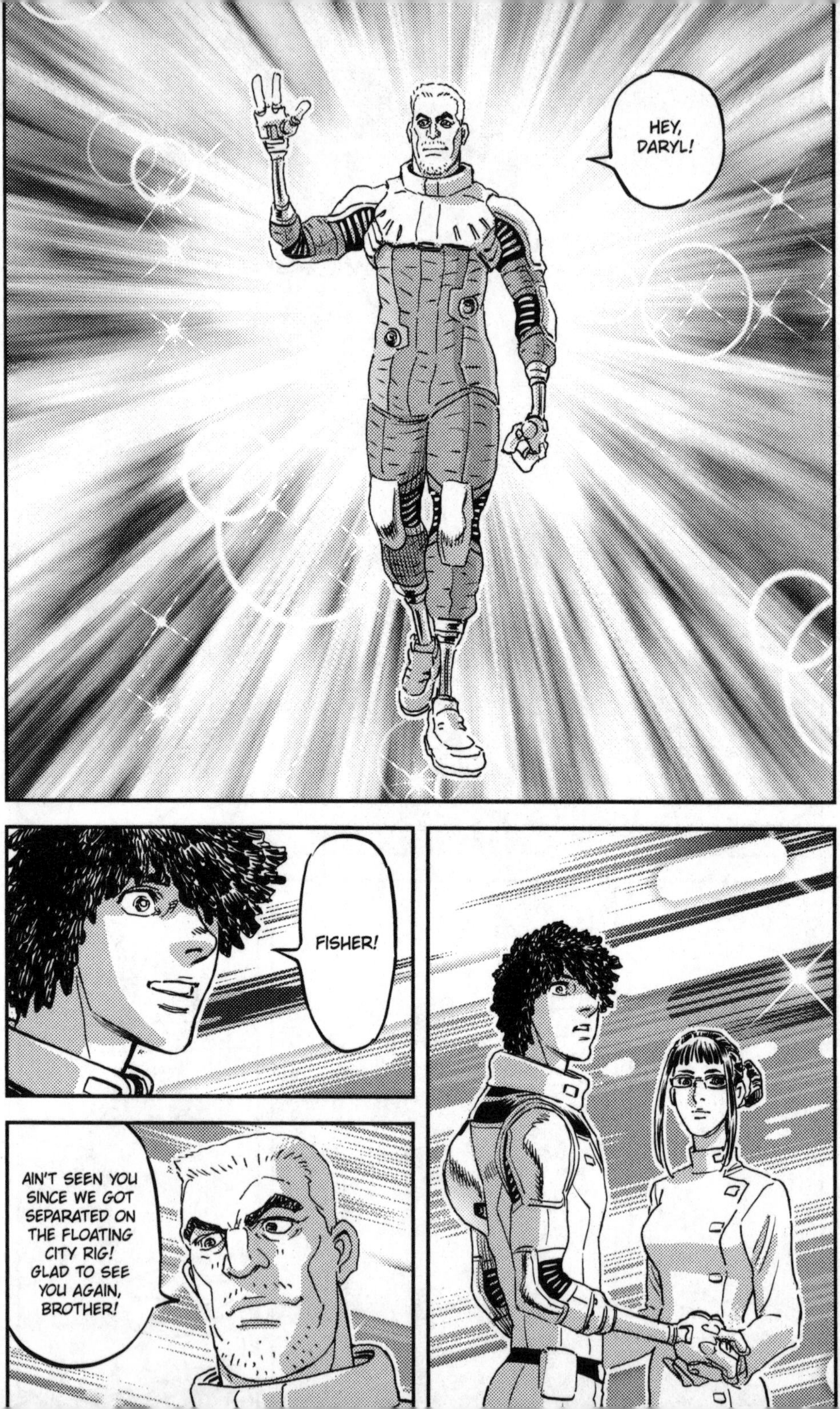
HEY, DARYL!
FISHER!
AIN'T SEEN YOU SINCE WE GOT SEPARATED ON THE FLOATING CITY RIG! GLAD TO SEE YOU AGAIN, BROTHER!

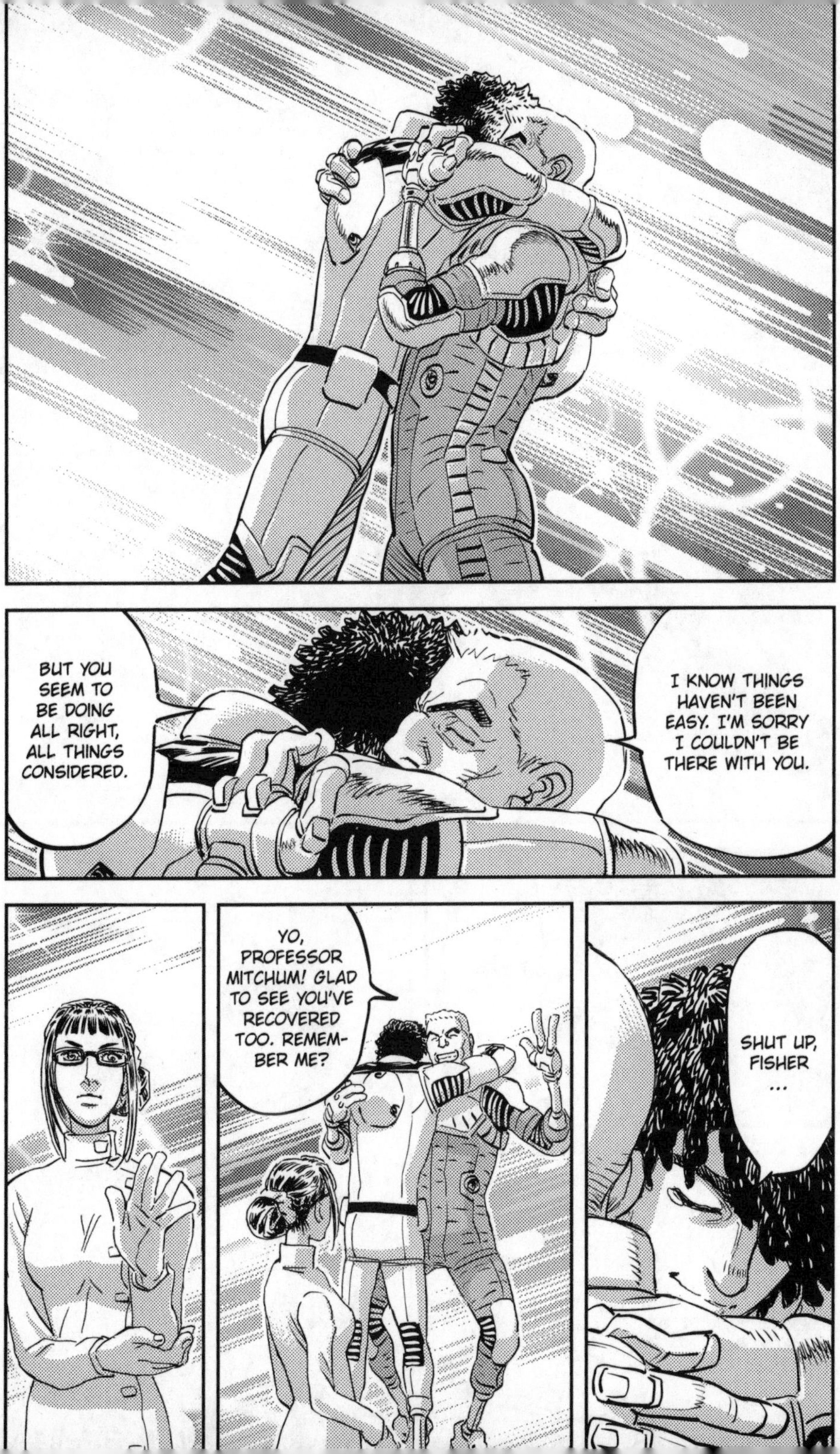
I KNOW THINGS HAVEN'T BEEN EASY. I'M SORRY I COULDN'T BE THERE WITH YOU.
BUT YOU SEEM TO BE DOING ALL RIGHT, ALL THINGS CONSIDERED.
SHUT UP, FISHER ...
YO, PROFESSOR MITCHUM! GLAD TO SEE YOU'VE RECOVERED TOO. REMEMBER ME?

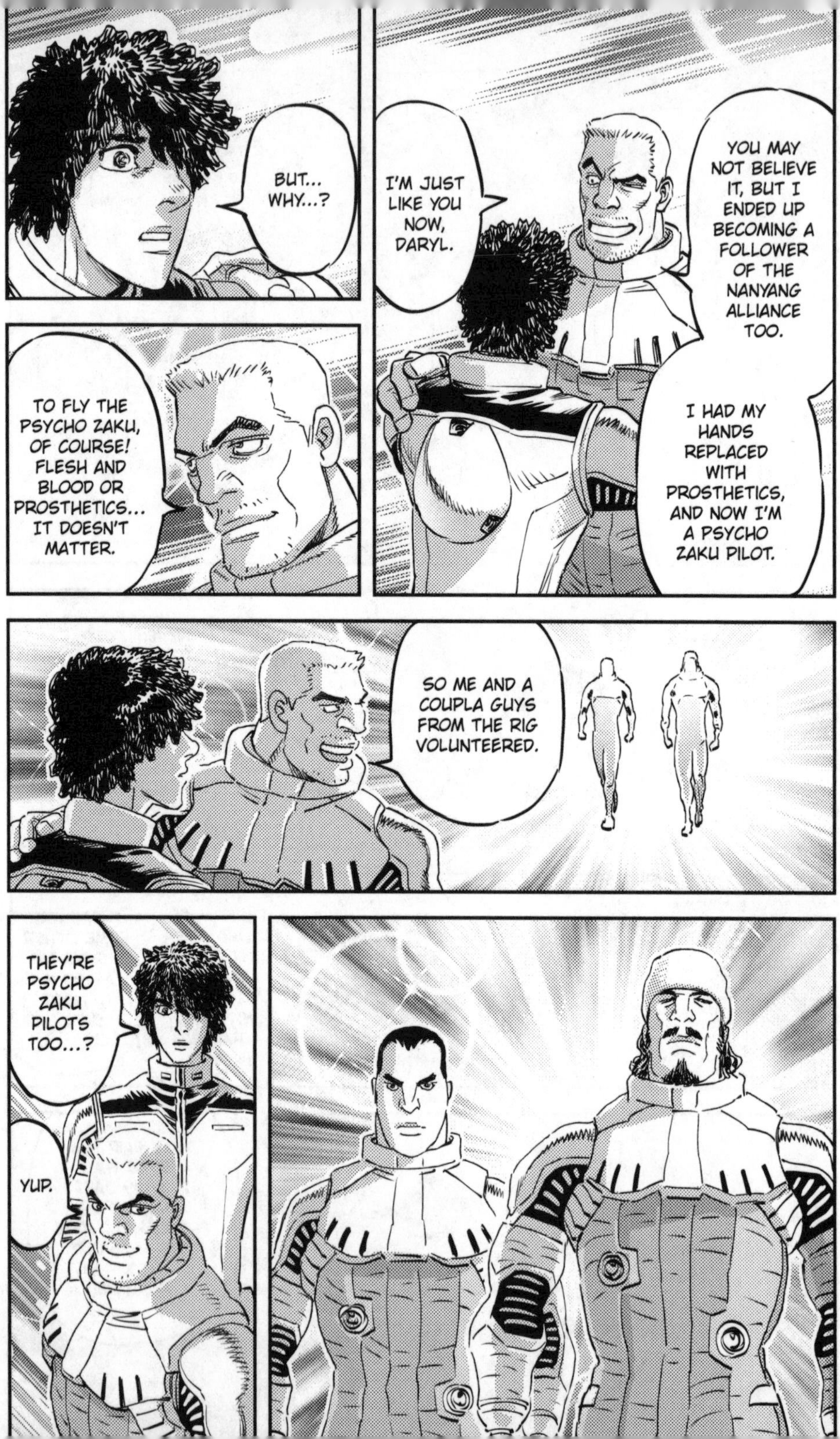
YOU MAY NOT BELIEVE IT, BUT I ENDED UP BECOMING A FOLLOWER OF THE NANYANG ALLIANCE TOO.
I'M JUST LIKE YOU NOW, DARYL.
I HAD MY HANDS REPLACED WITH PROSTHETICS, AND NOW I'M A PSYCHO ZAKU PILOT.
BUT... WHY...?
TO FLY THE PSYCHO ZAKU, OF COURSE! FLESH AND BLOOD OR PROSTHETICS... IT DOESN'T MATTER.
SO ME AND A COUPLA GUYS FROM THE RIG VOLUNTEERED.
THEY'RE PSYCHO ZAKU PILOTS TOO...?
YUP.

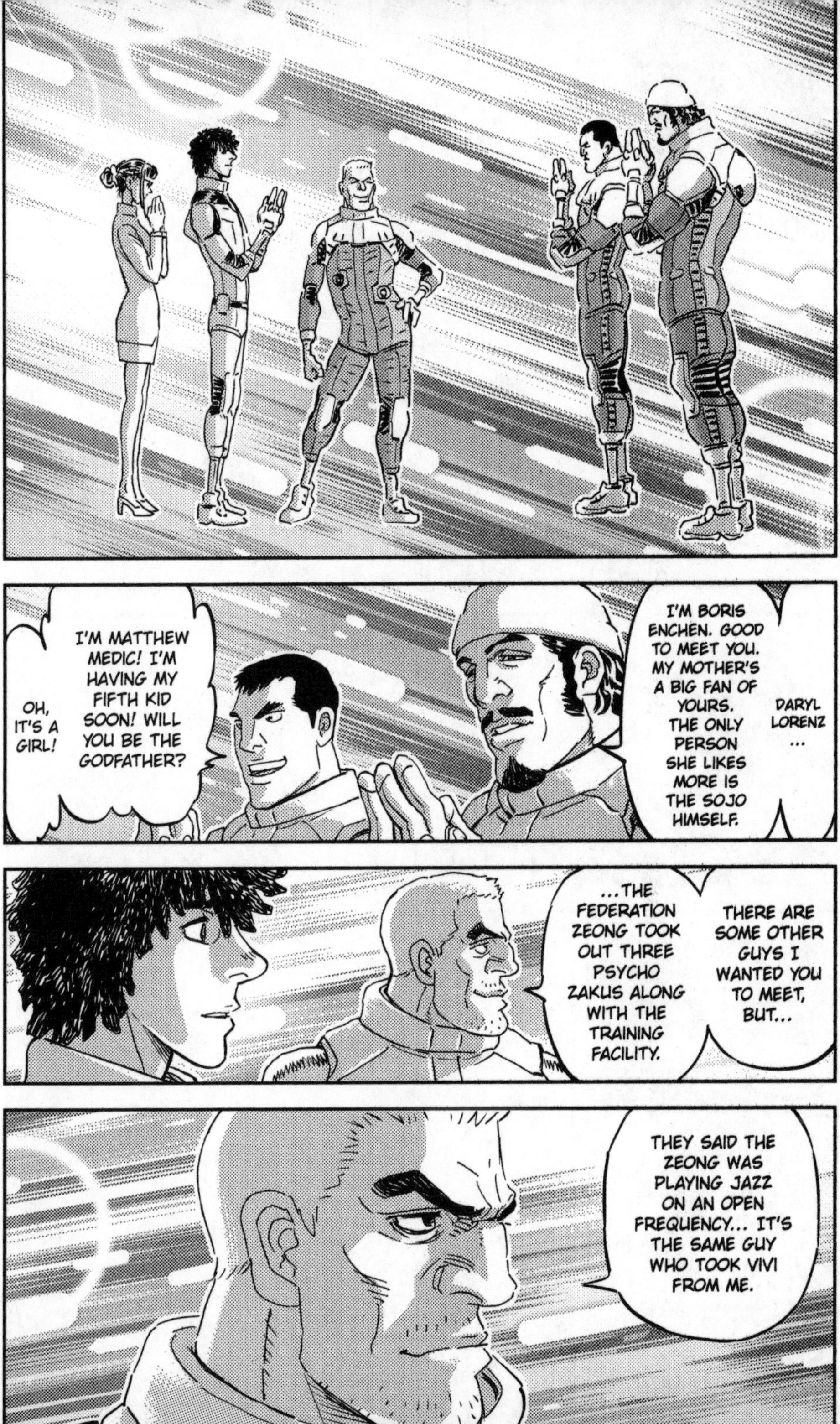
DARYL LORENZ...
I'M BORIS ENCHEN. GOOD TO MEET YOU. MY MOTHER'S A BIG FAN OF YOURS. THE ONLY PERSON SHE LIKES MORE IS THE SOJO HIMSELF.
I'M MATTHEW MEDIC! I'M HAVING MY FIFTH KID SOON! WILL YOU BE THE GODFATHER?
OH, IT'S A GIRL!
THERE ARE SOME OTHER GUYS I WANTED YOU TO MEET, BUT...
...THE FEDERATION ZEONG TOOK OUT THREE PSYCHO ZAKUS ALONG WITH THE TRAINING FACILITY.
THEY SAID THE ZEONG WAS PLAYING JAZZ ON AN OPEN FREQUENCY... IT'S THE SAME GUY WHO TOOK VIVI FROM ME.

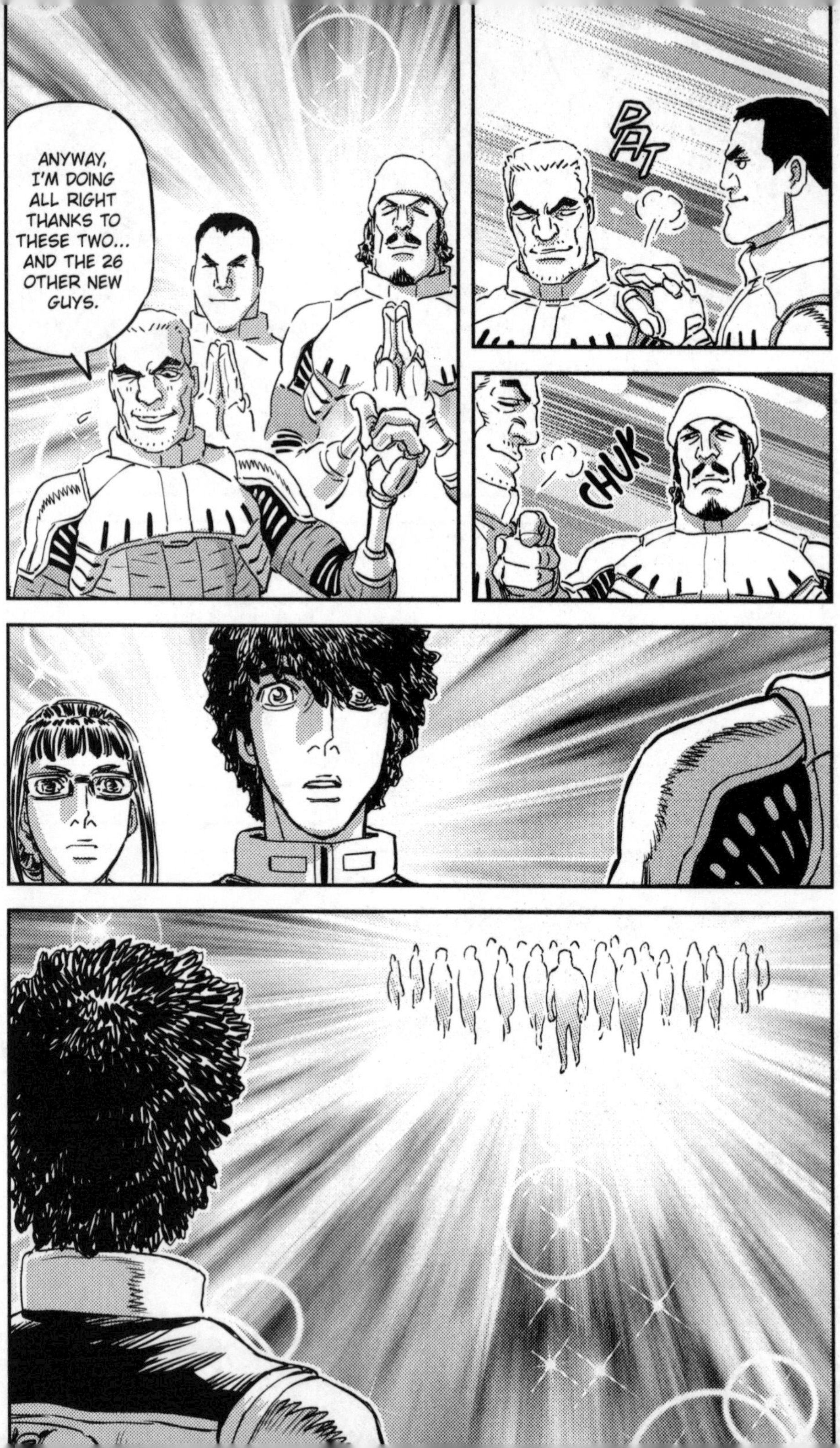
PAT
CHUK
ANYWAY, I'M DOING ALL RIGHT THANKS TO THESE TWO... AND THE 26 OTHER NEW GUYS.

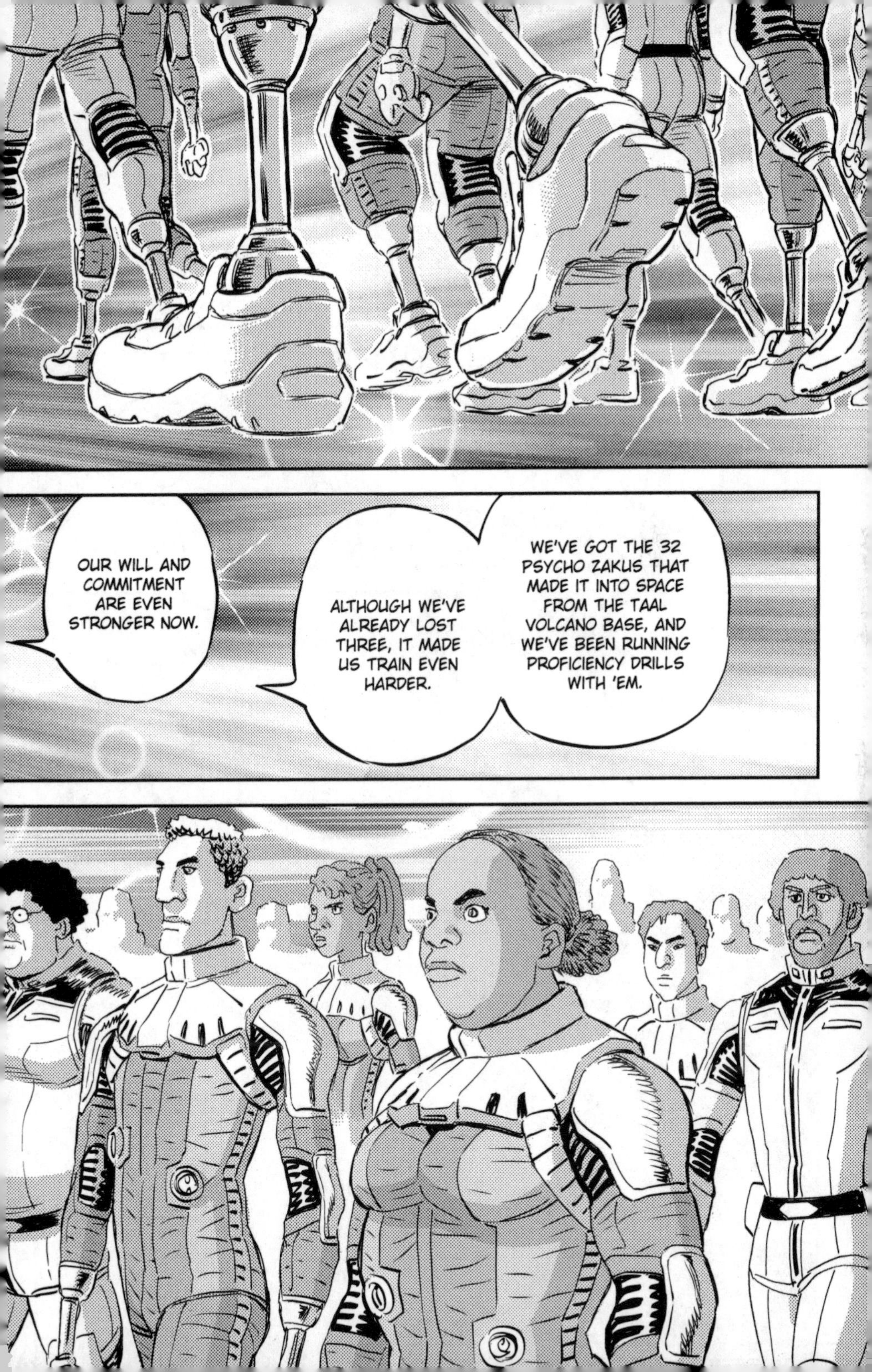
WE'VE GOT THE 32 PSYCHO ZAKUS THAT MADE IT INTO SPACE FROM THE TAAL VOLCANO BASE, AND WE'VE BEEN RUNNING PROFICIENCY DRILLS WITH 'EM.
ALTHOUGH WE'VE ALREADY LOST THREE, IT MADE US TRAIN EVEN HARDER.
OUR WILL AND COMMITMENT ARE EVEN STRONGER NOW.

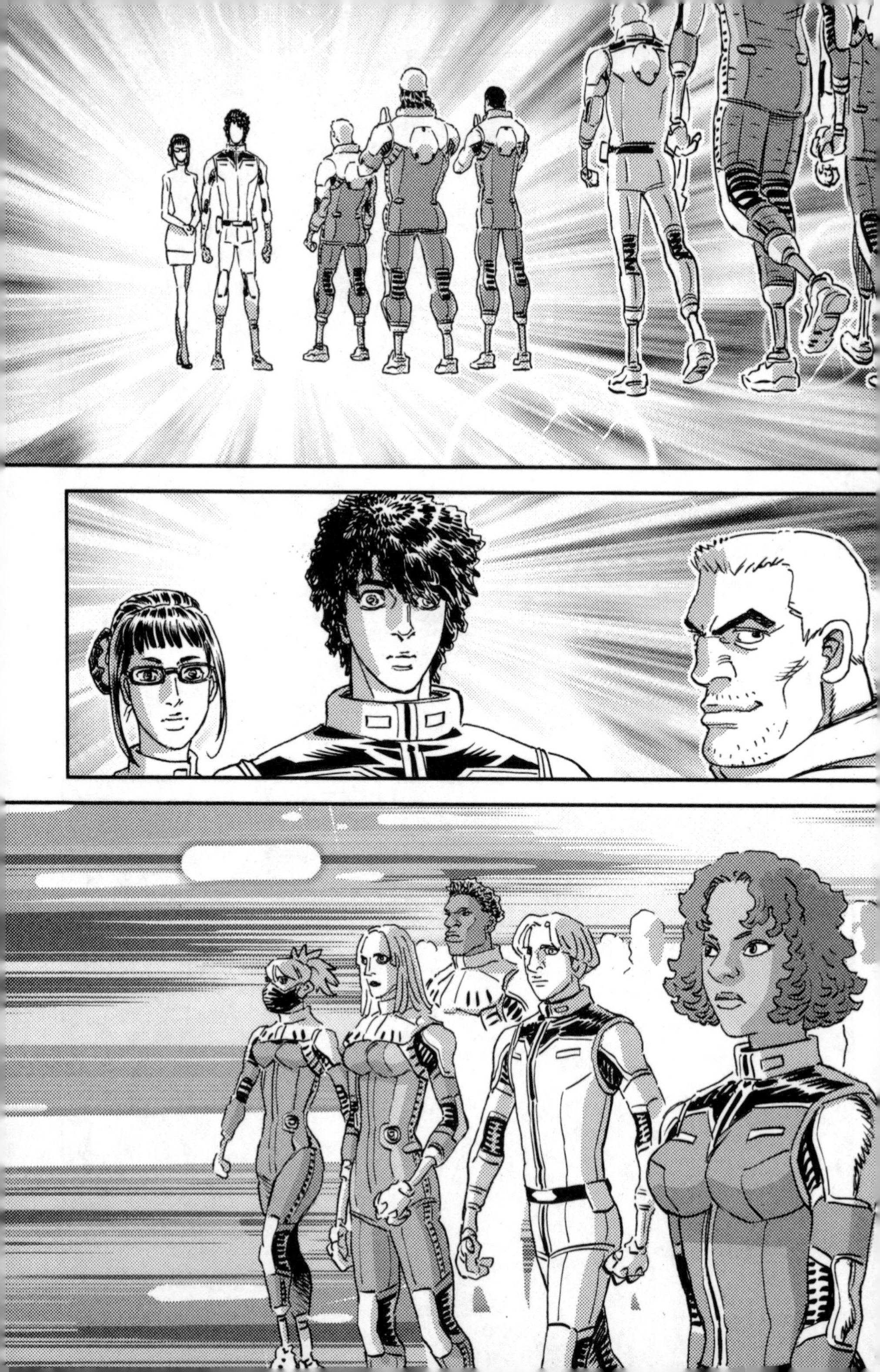

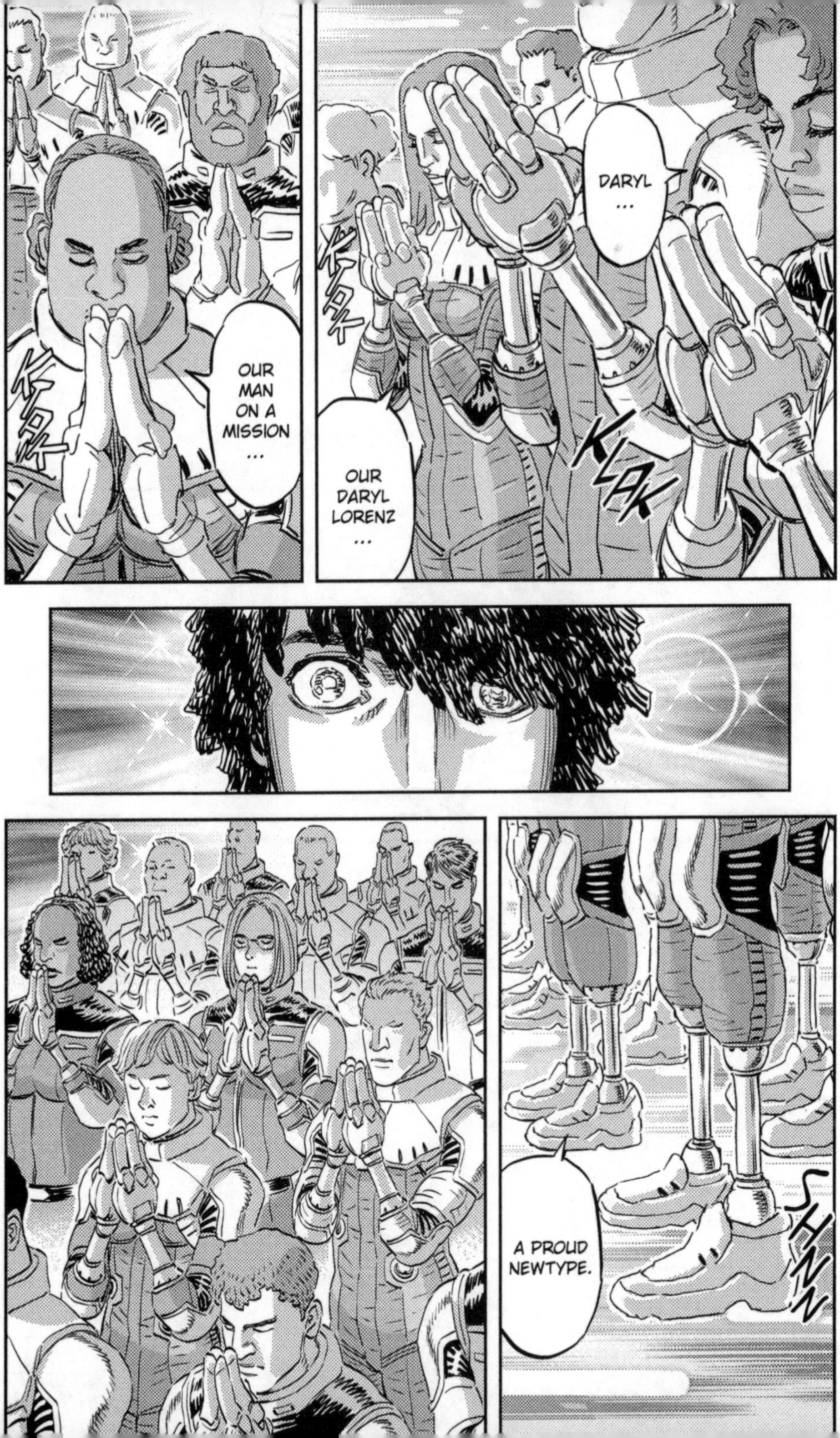
DARYL ...
KLAK
OUR DARYL LORENZ ...
KLAK
OUR MAN ON A MISSION ...
KLAK
SHNN
A PROUD NEWTYPE.

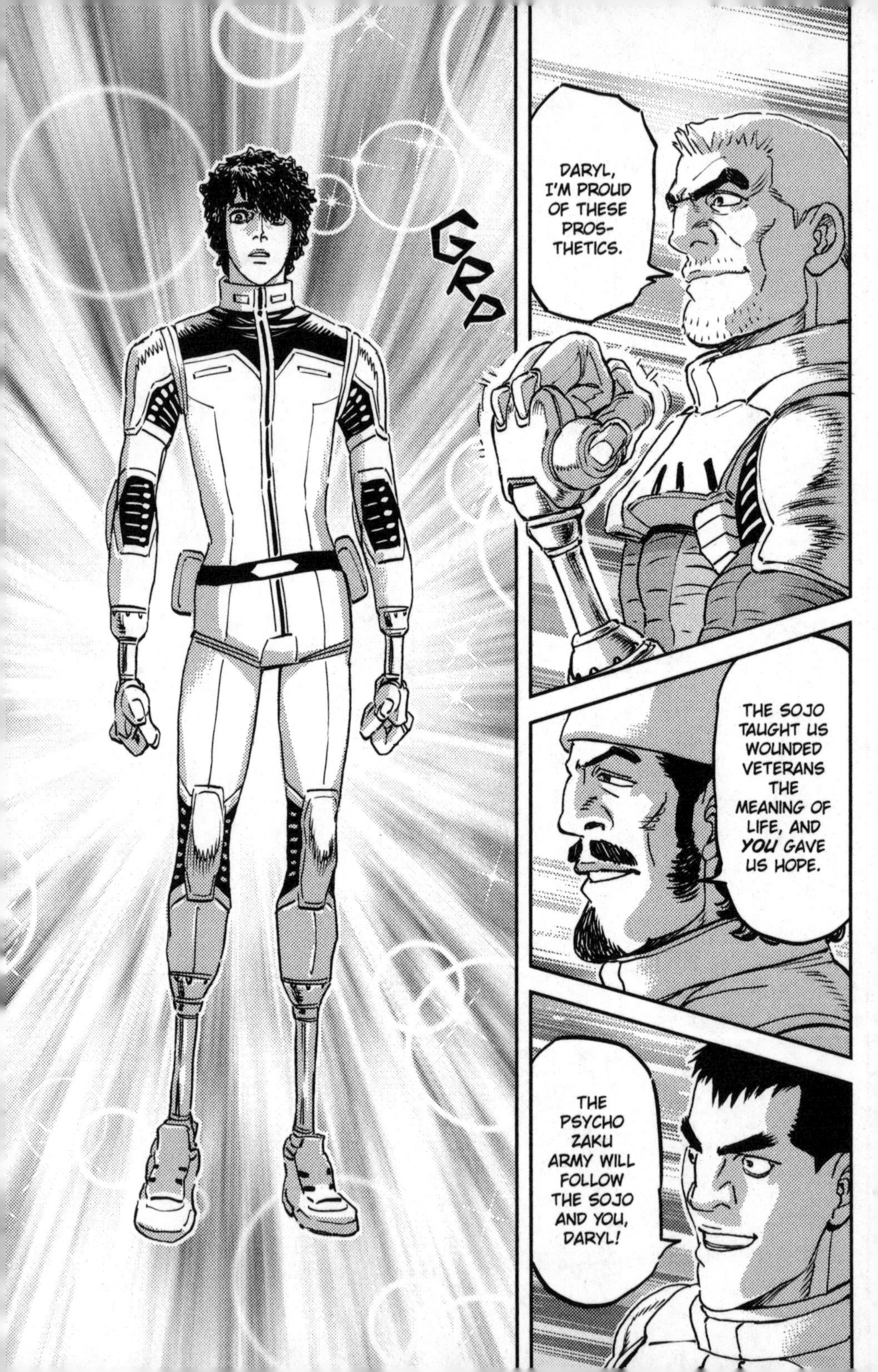
DARYL, I'M PROUD OF THESE PROS- THETICS.
GRP
THE SOJO TAUGHT US WOUNDED VETERANS THE MEANING OF LIFE, AND *YOU* GAVE US HOPE.
THE PSYCHO ZAKU ARMY WILL FOLLOW THE SOJO AND YOU, DARYL!

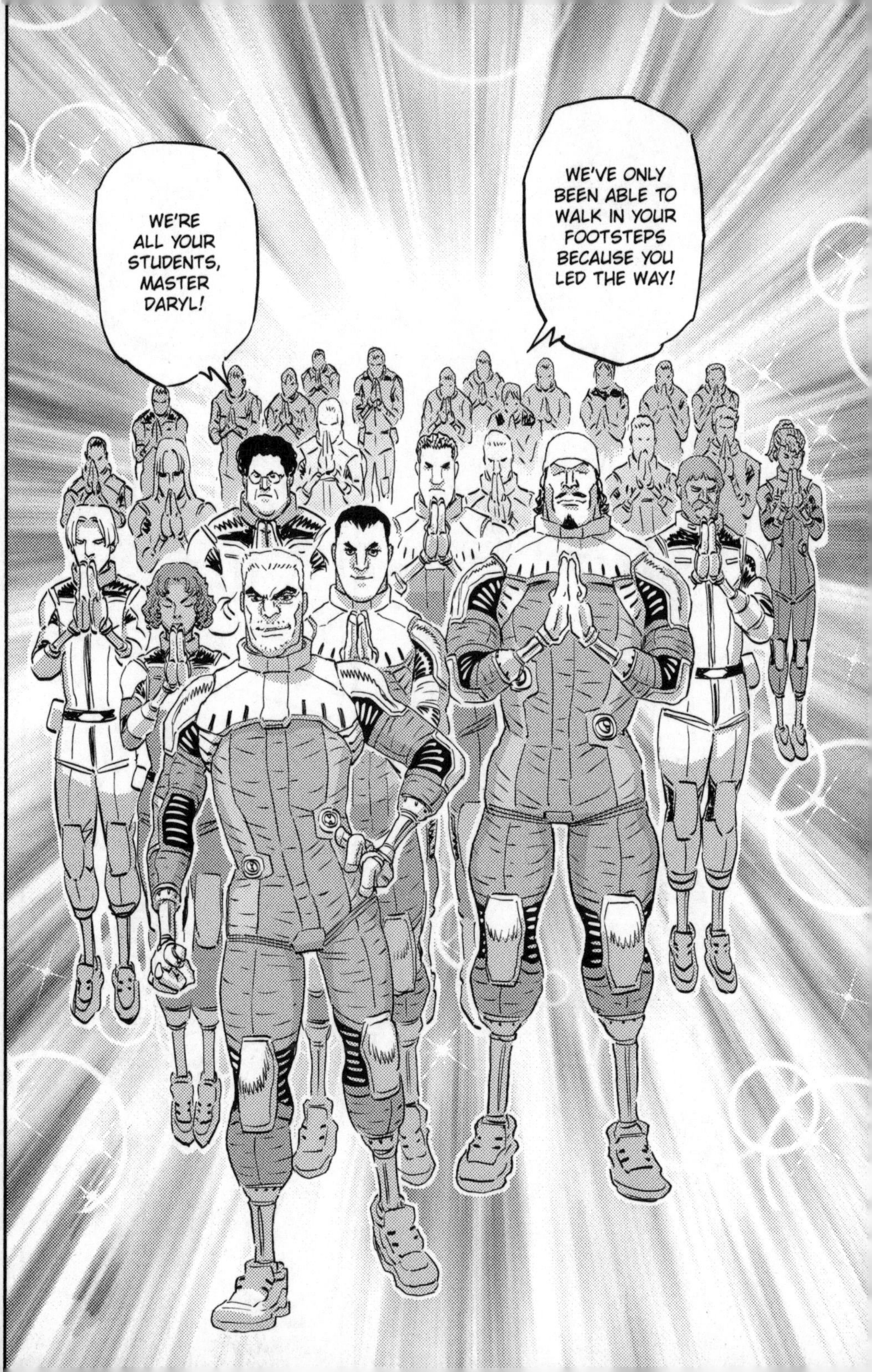
WE'VE ONLY BEEN ABLE TO WALK IN YOUR FOOTSTEPS BECAUSE YOU LED THE WAY!
WE'RE ALL YOUR STUDENTS, MASTER DARYL!

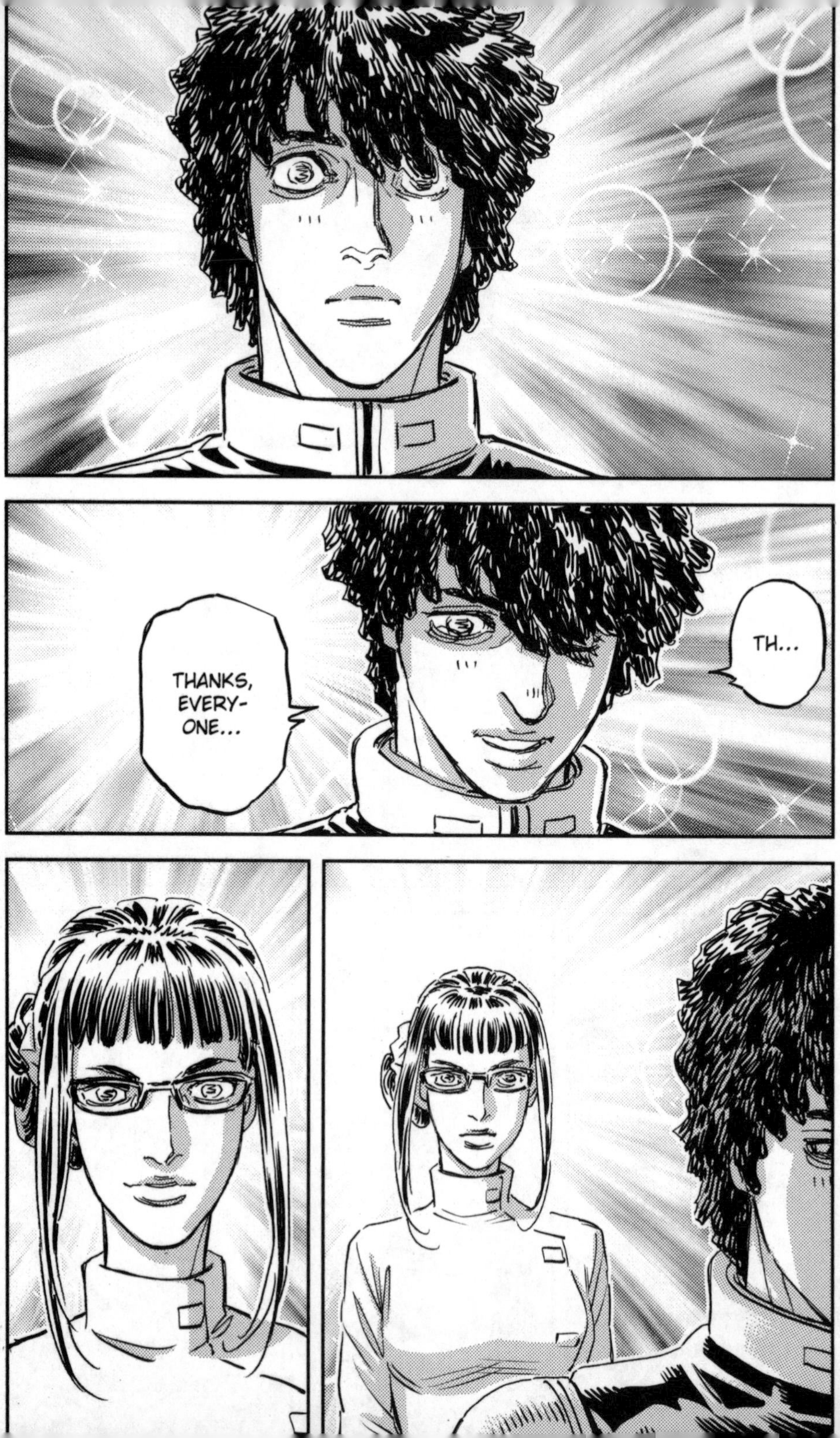
TH...
THANKS, EVERY-ONE...

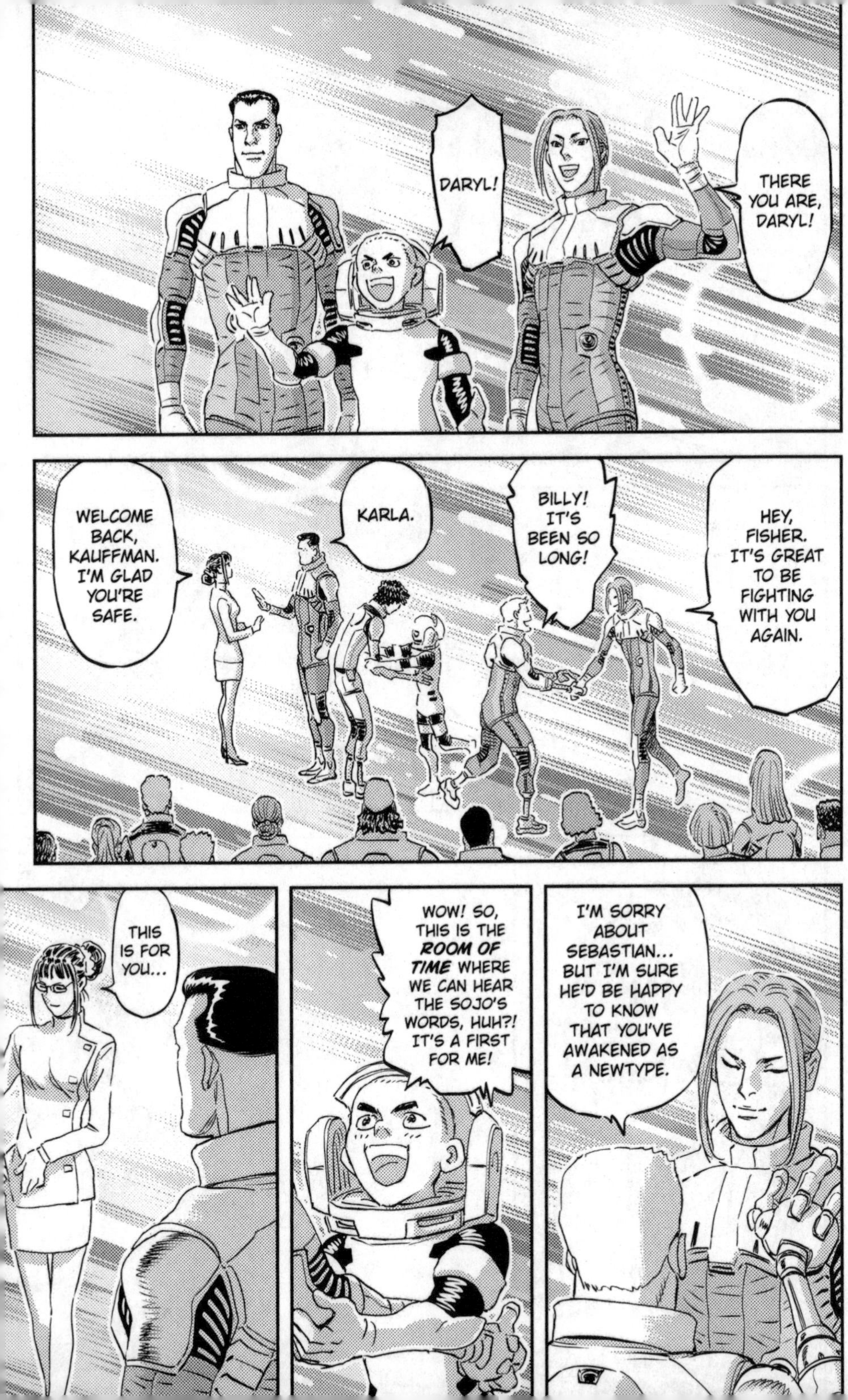
THERE YOU ARE, DARYL!
DARYL!
HEY, FISHER. IT'S GREAT TO BE FIGHTING WITH YOU AGAIN.
BILLY! IT'S BEEN SO LONG!
KARLA.
WELCOME BACK, KAUFFMAN. I'M GLAD YOU'RE SAFE.
I'M SORRY ABOUT SEBASTIAN... BUT I'M SURE HE'D BE HAPPY TO KNOW THAT YOU'VE AWAKENED AS A NEWTYPE.
WOW! SO, THIS IS THE ***ROOM OF TIME*** WHERE WE CAN HEAR THE SOJO'S WORDS, HUH?! IT'S A FIRST FOR ME!
THIS IS FOR YOU...

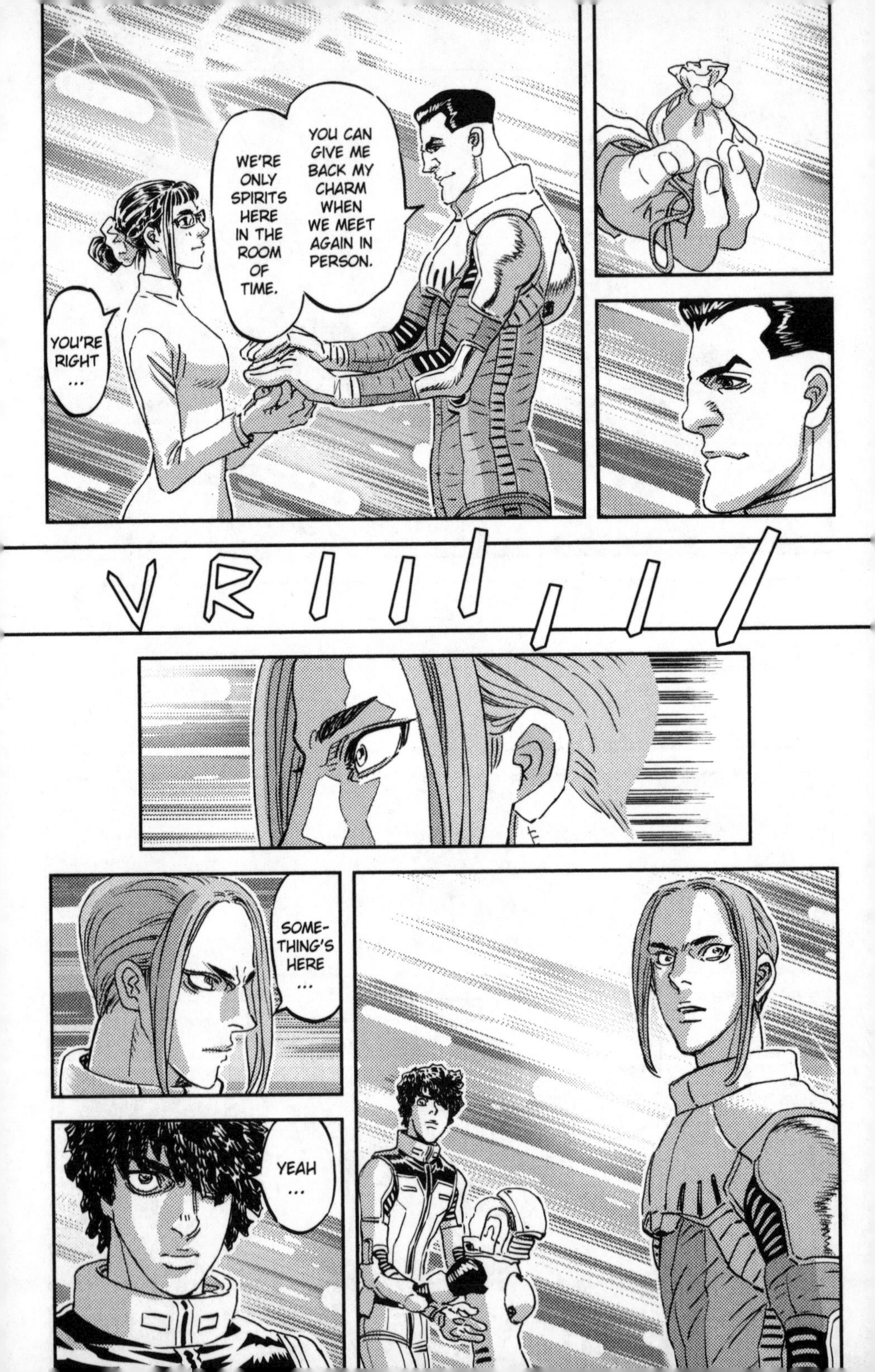
YOU CAN GIVE ME BACK MY CHARM WHEN WE MEET AGAIN IN PERSON.
WE'RE ONLY SPIRITS HERE IN THE ROOM OF TIME.
YOU'RE RIGHT ...
VRIIIIII
SOME-THING'S HERE ...
YEAH ...

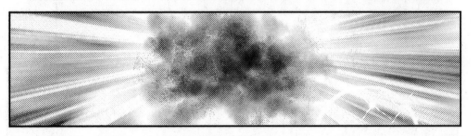

WHAT IS THAT?!

WHAT ...

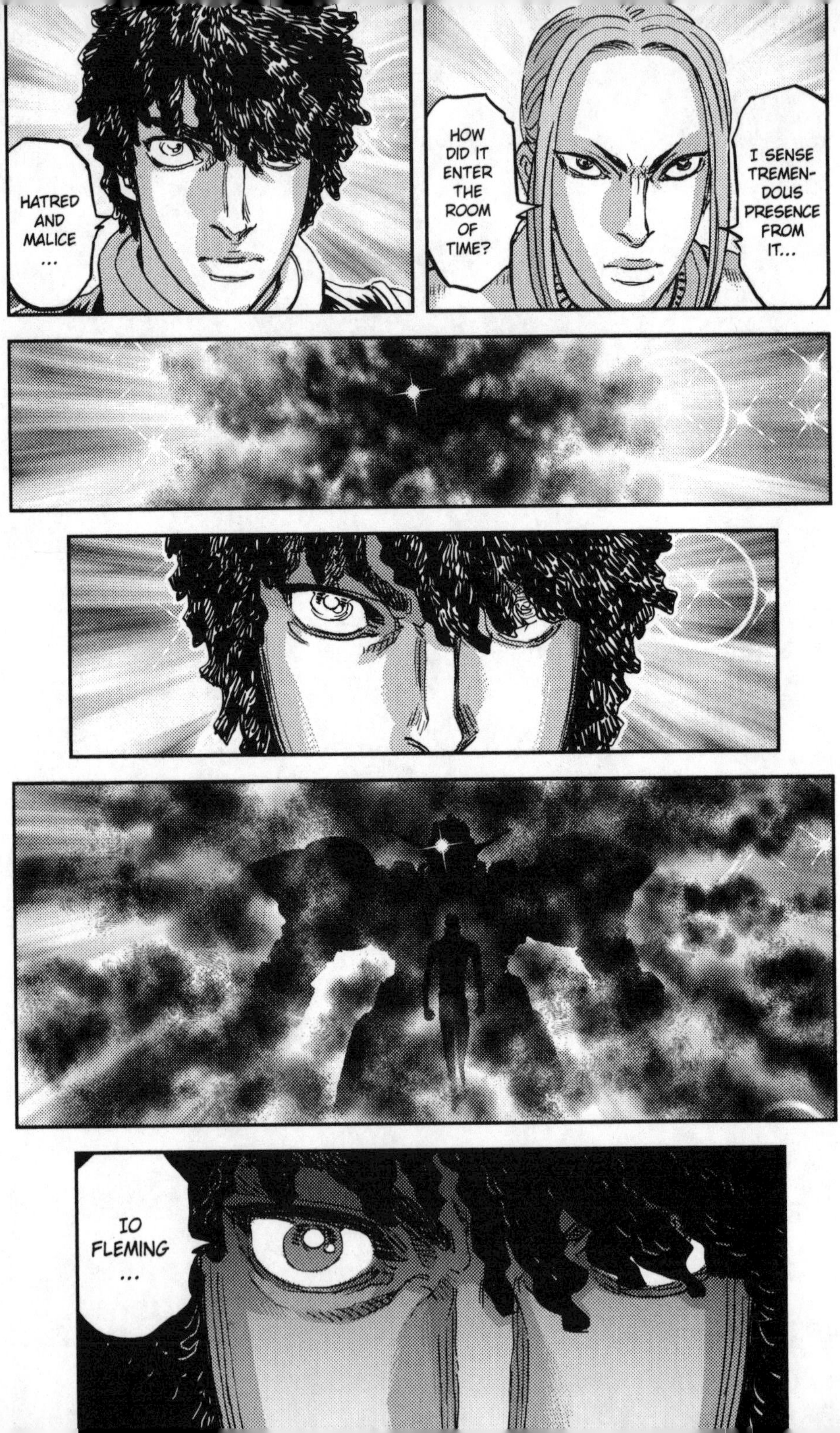
I SENSE TREMEN-DOUS PRESENCE FROM IT...
HOW DID IT ENTER THE ROOM OF TIME?
HATRED AND MALICE ...
IO FLEMING ...

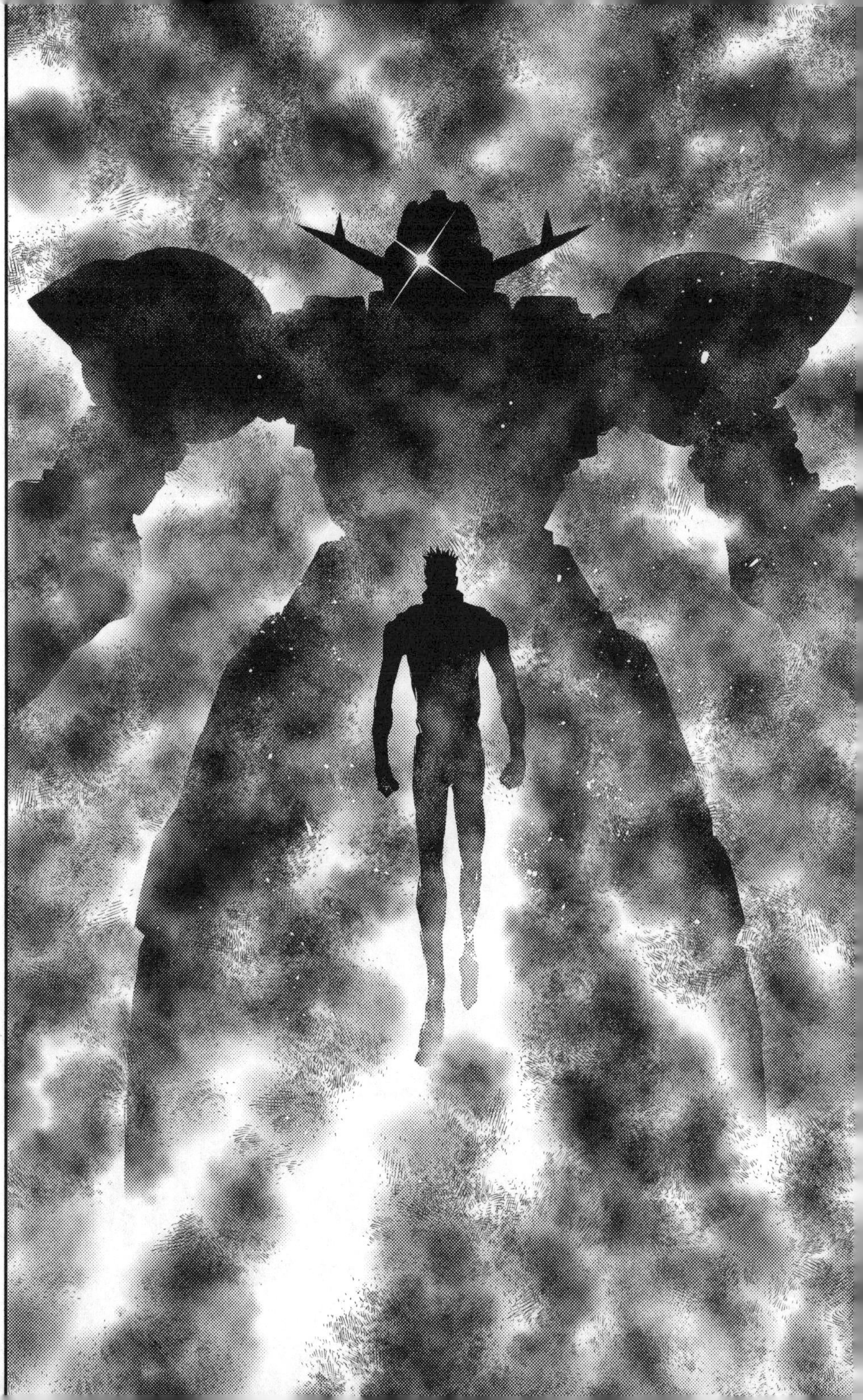

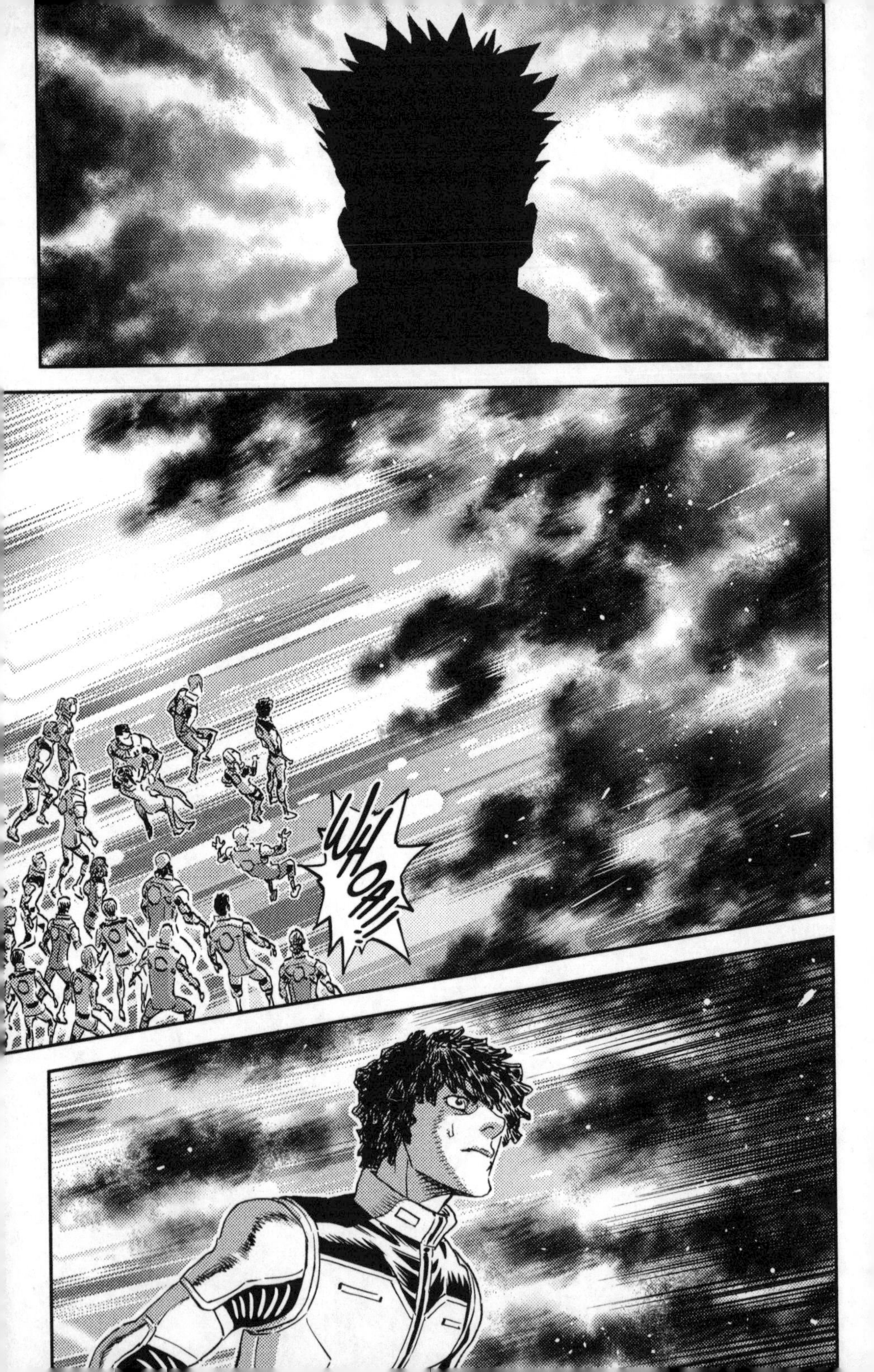
WHOA!!

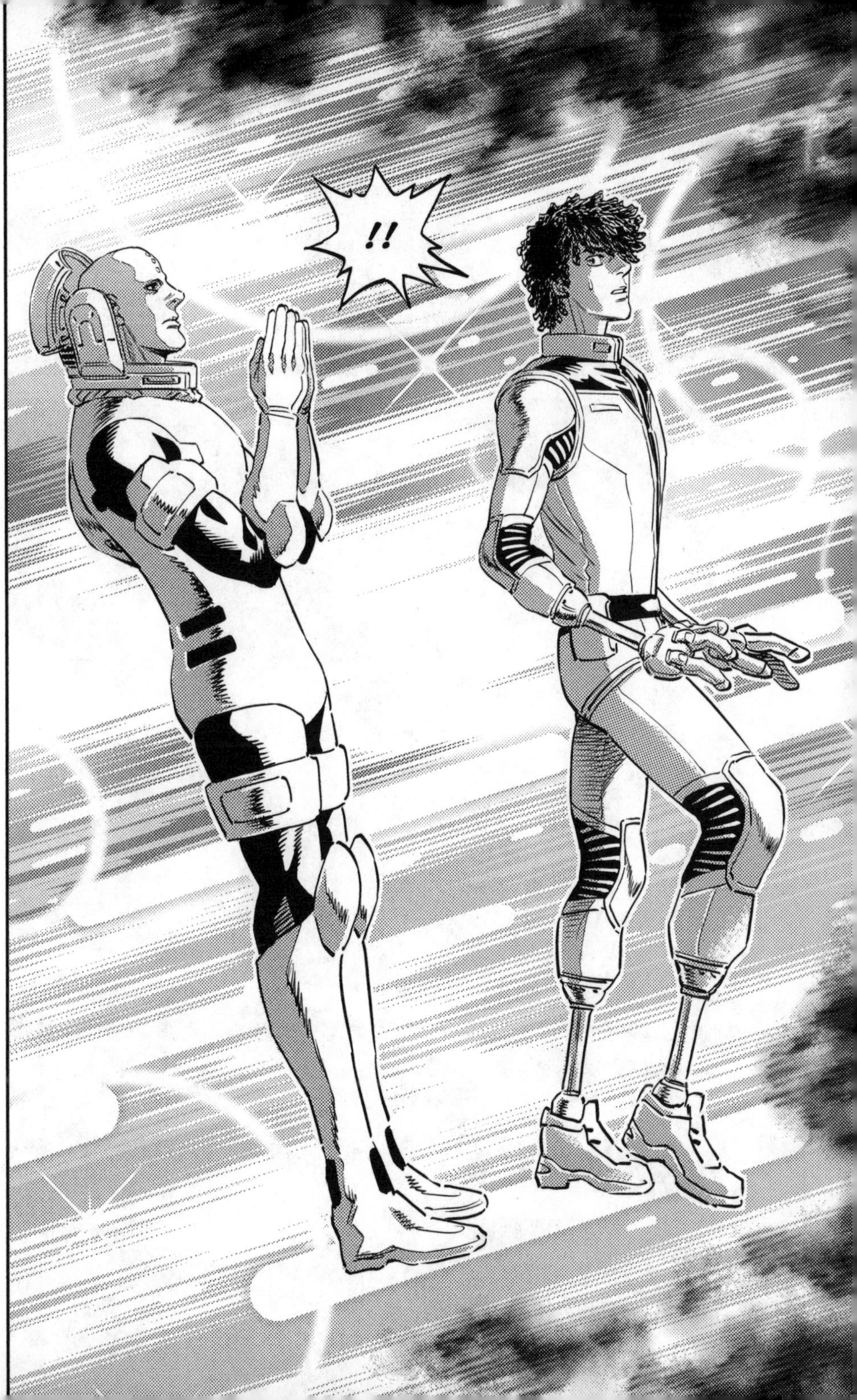
!!

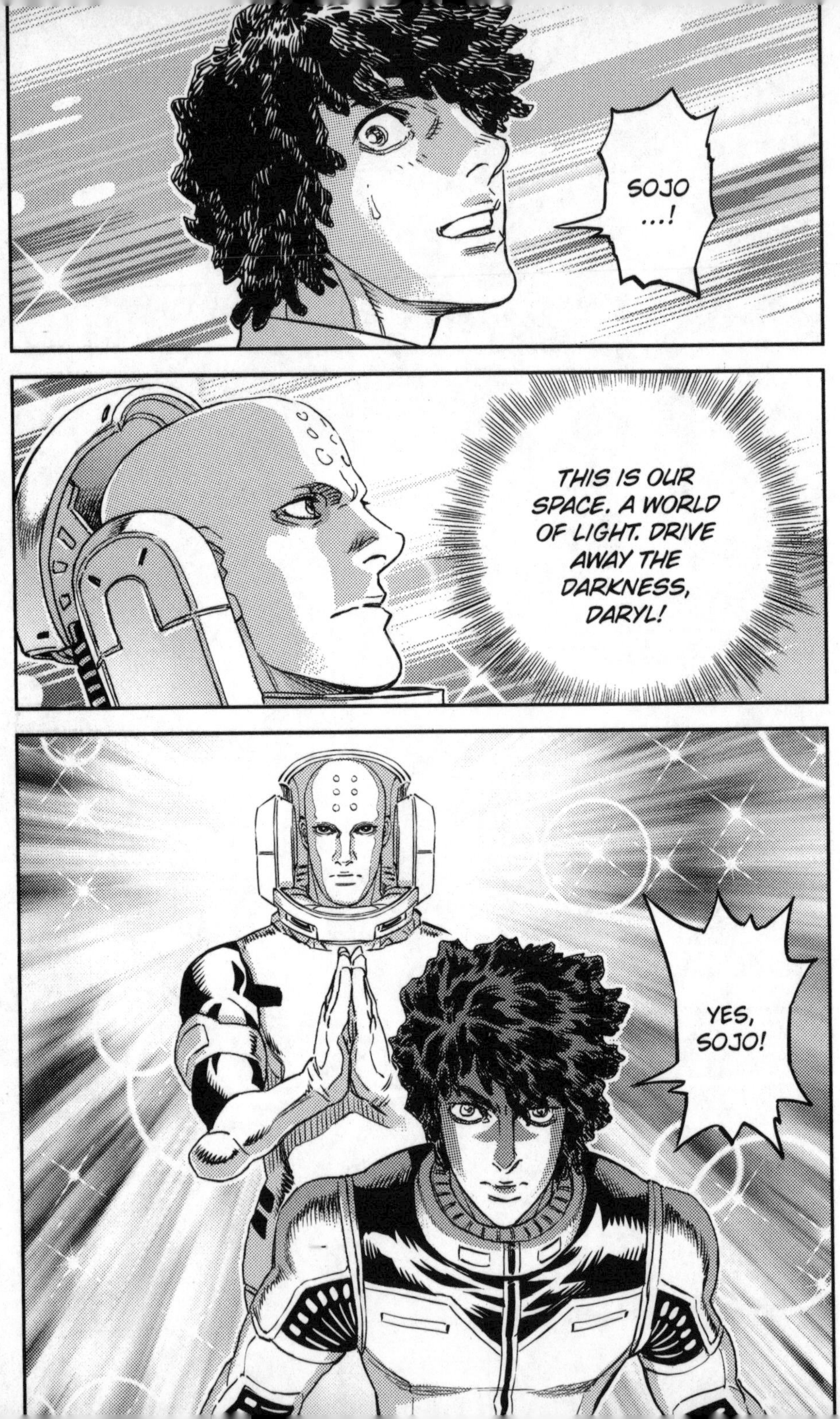
SOJO ...!
THIS IS OUR SPACE. A WORLD OF LIGHT. DRIVE AWAY THE DARKNESS, DARYL!
YES, SOJO!

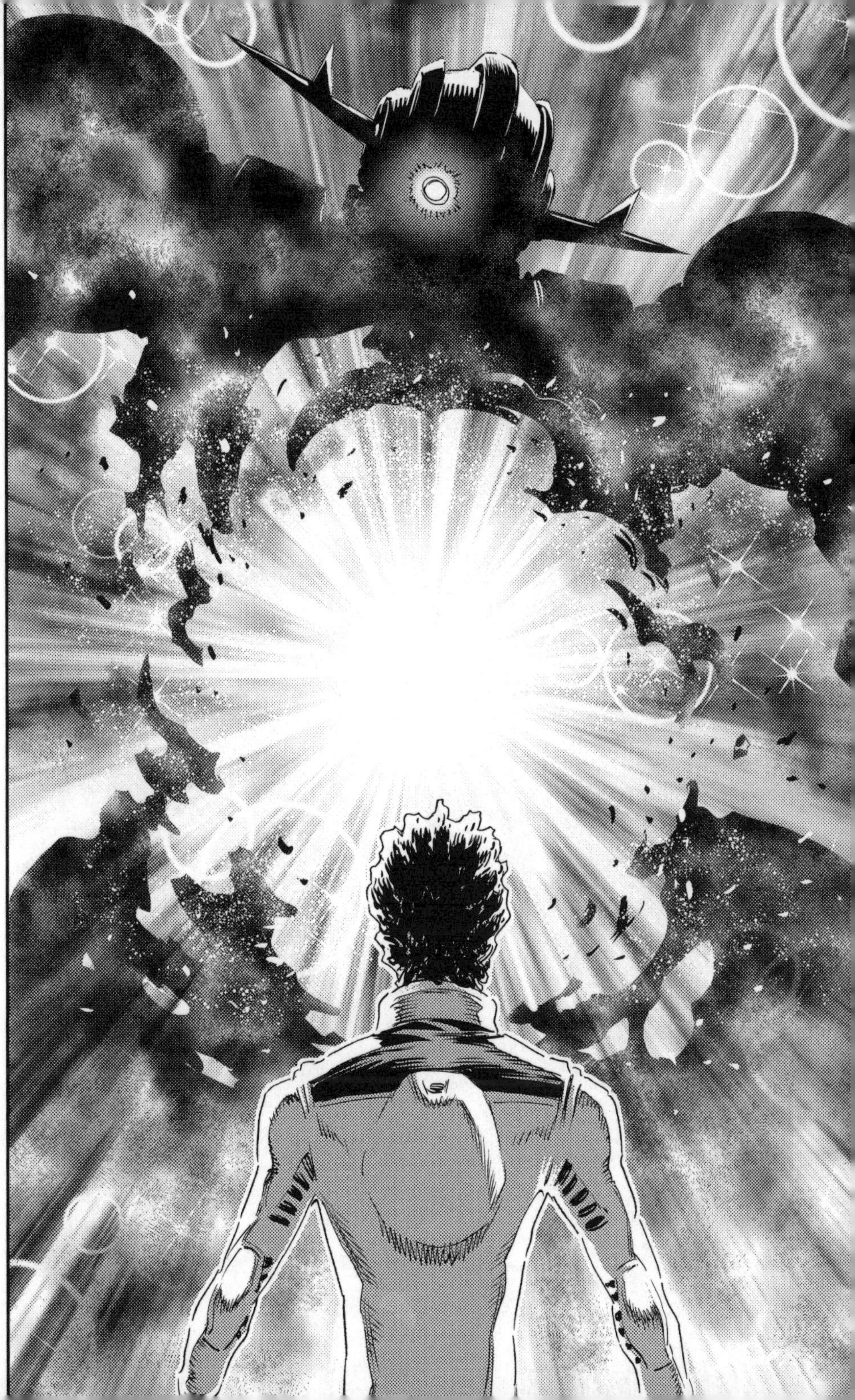

MOBILE SUIT GUNDAM
THUNDERBOLT

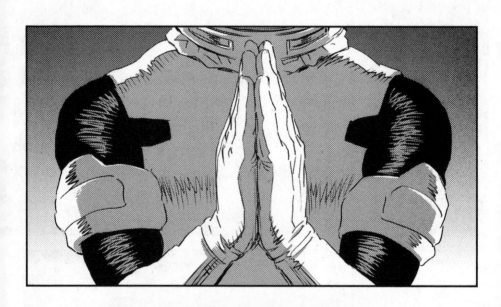

MOBILE SUIT GUNDAM THUNDERBOLT **CHAPTER 169**

68
142 97
99
DIP
DIP
DIP

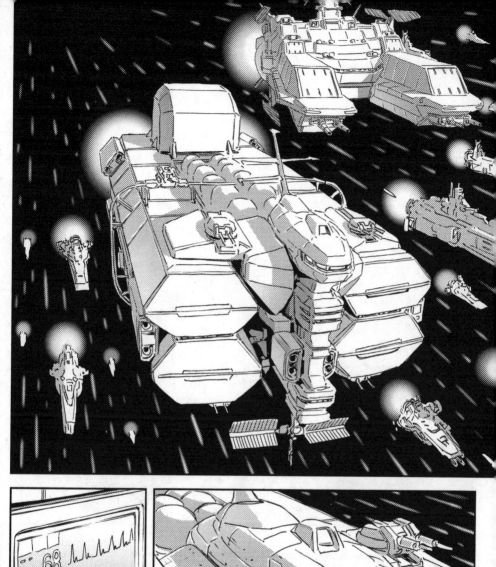

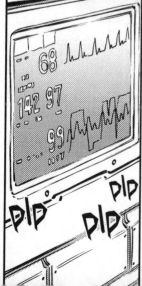

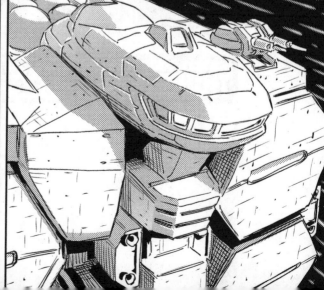

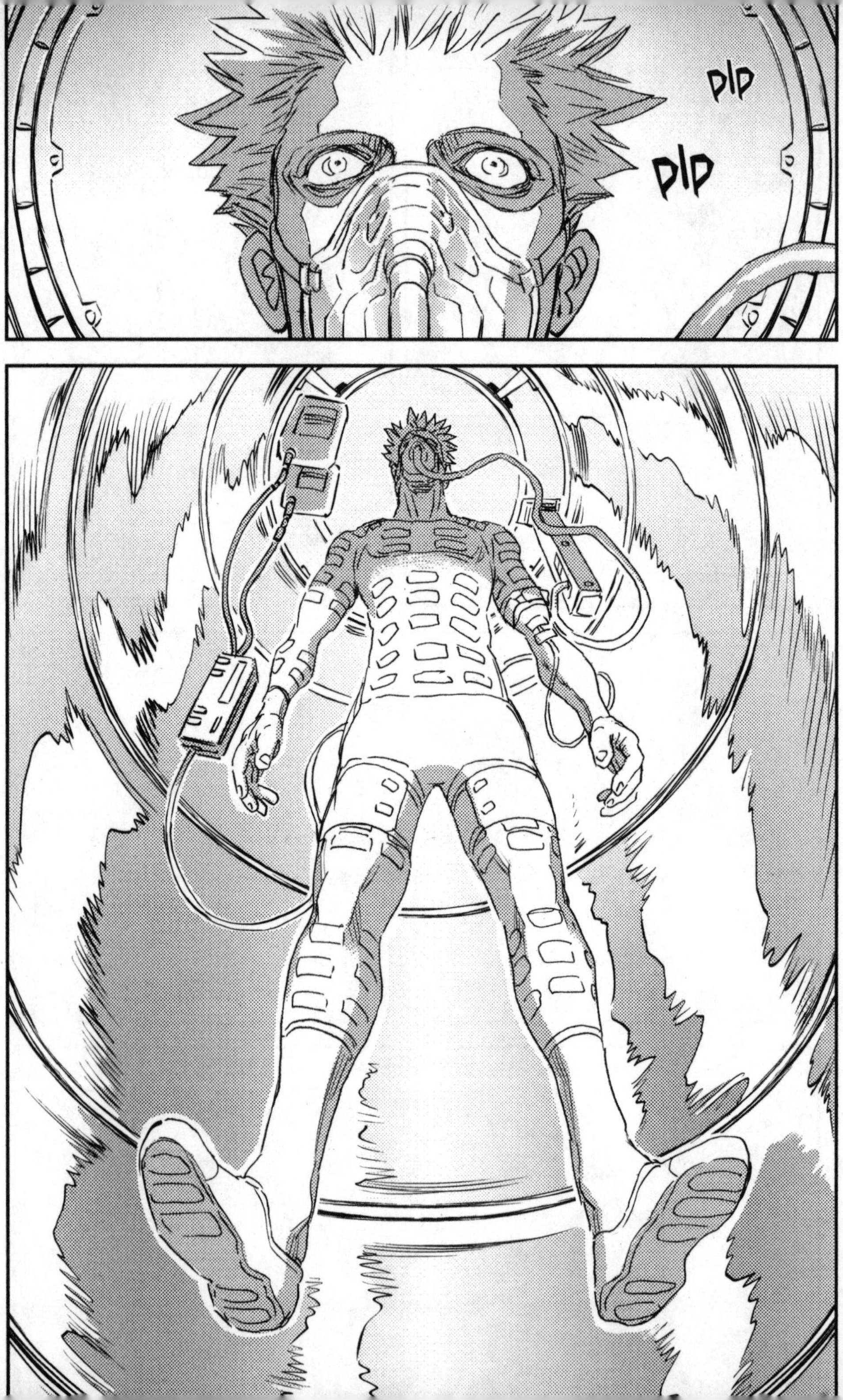
DIP
DIP

I'M GLAD YOU'RE BOTH ALL RIGHT, BUT THAT WAS A FOOLISH THING TO DO.

IO...

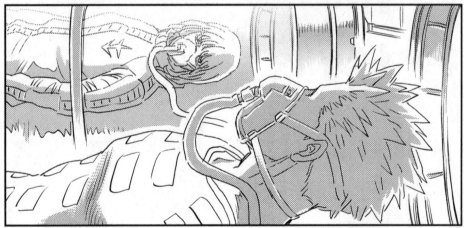

I'M SORRY, IO. ALL I COULD DO WAS TRY TO ESCAPE FROM THEIR THOUGHTS...

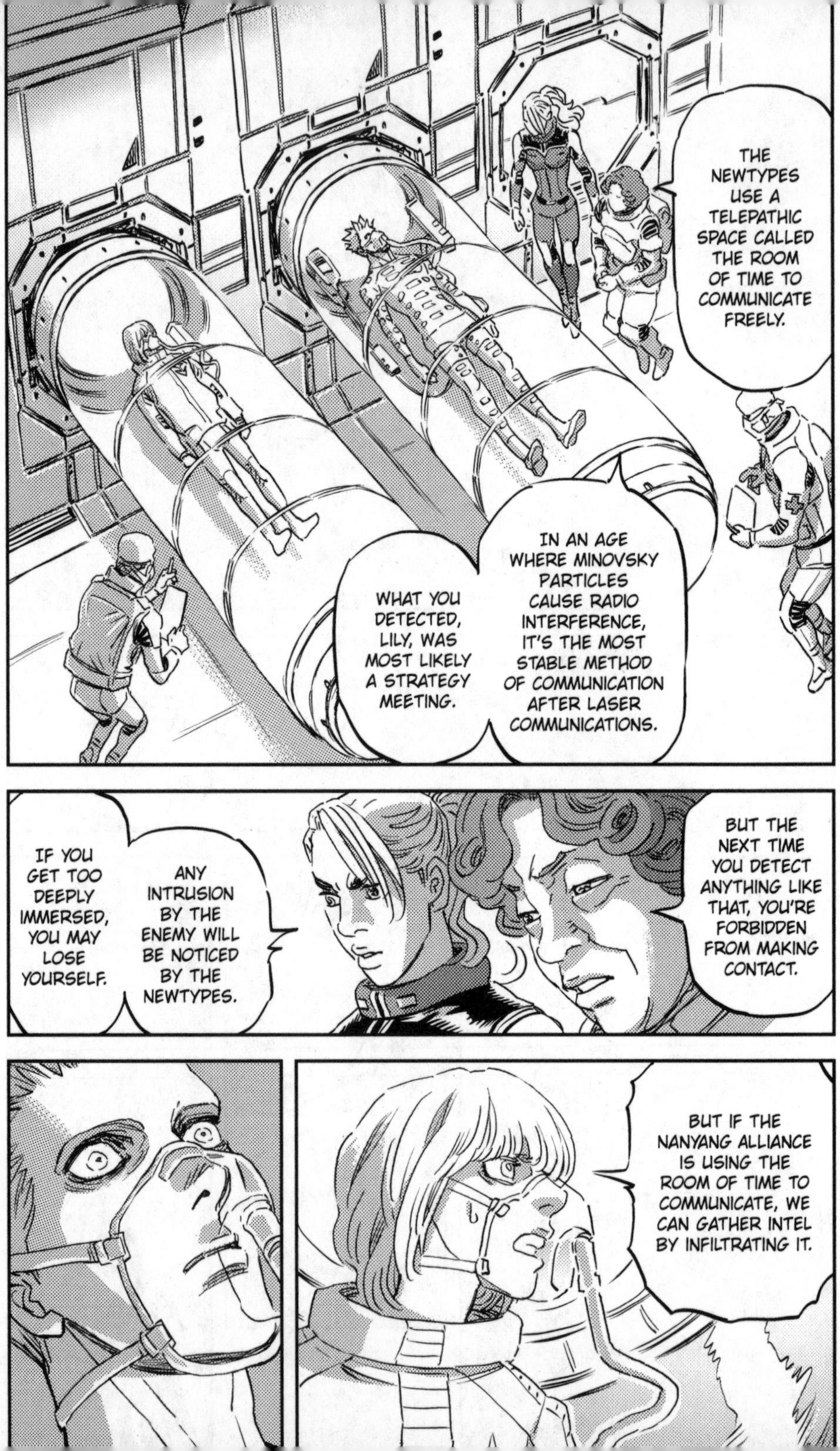
THE NEWTYPES USE A TELEPATHIC SPACE CALLED THE ROOM OF TIME TO COMMUNICATE FREELY.
IN AN AGE WHERE MINOVSKY PARTICLES CAUSE RADIO INTERFERENCE, IT'S THE MOST STABLE METHOD OF COMMUNICATION AFTER LASER COMMUNICATIONS.
WHAT YOU DETECTED, LILY, WAS MOST LIKELY A STRATEGY MEETING.
BUT THE NEXT TIME YOU DETECT ANYTHING LIKE THAT, YOU'RE FORBIDDEN FROM MAKING CONTACT.
ANY INTRUSION BY THE ENEMY WILL BE NOTICED BY THE NEWTYPES.
IF YOU GET TOO DEEPLY IMMERSED, YOU MAY LOSE YOURSELF.
BUT IF THE NANYANG ALLIANCE IS USING THE ROOM OF TIME TO COMMUNICATE, WE CAN GATHER INTEL BY INFILTRATING IT.

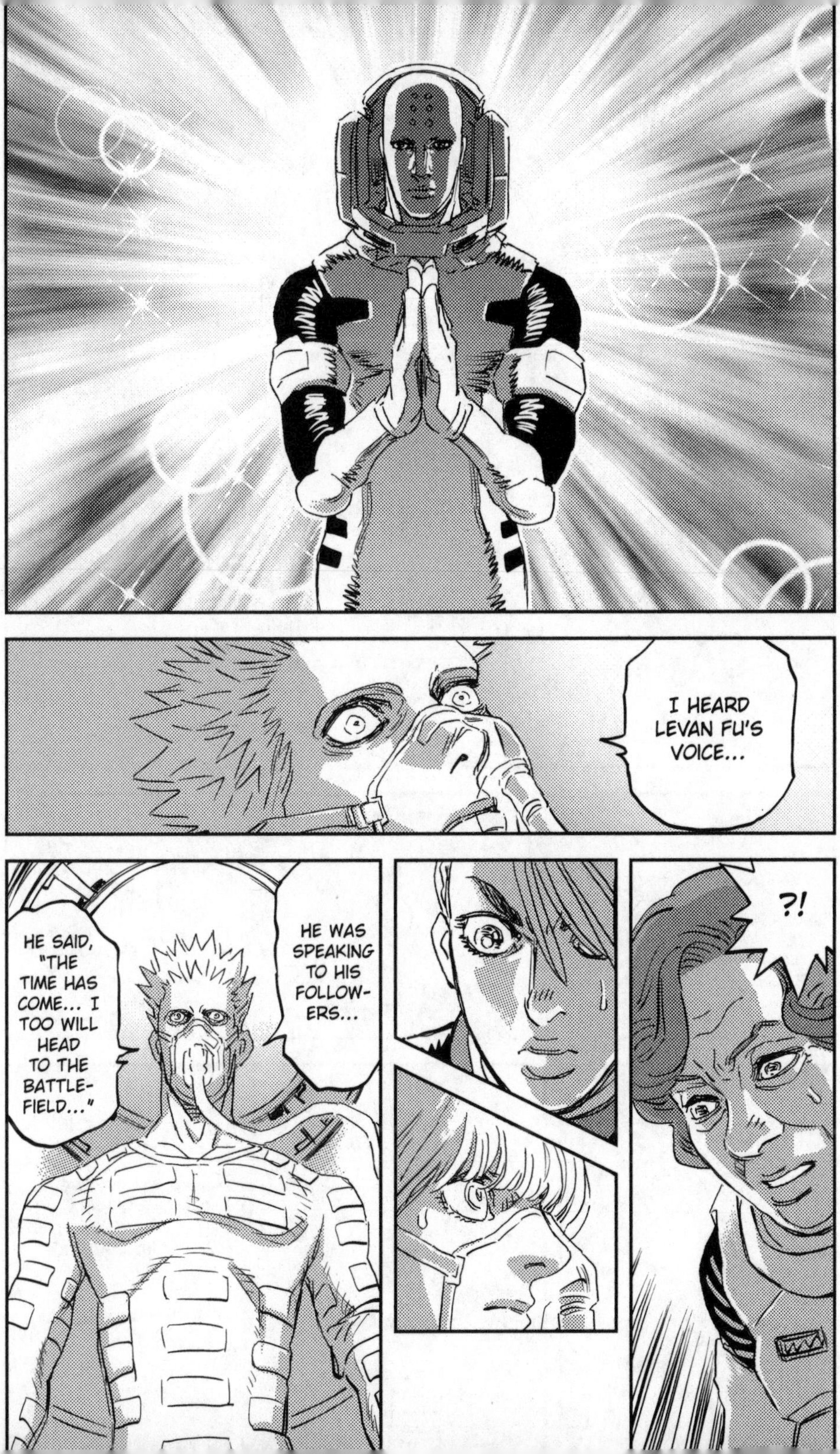
I HEARD LEVAN FU'S VOICE...
?!
HE WAS SPEAKING TO HIS FOLLOWERS...
HE SAID, "THE TIME HAS COME... I TOO WILL HEAD TO THE BATTLEFIELD..."

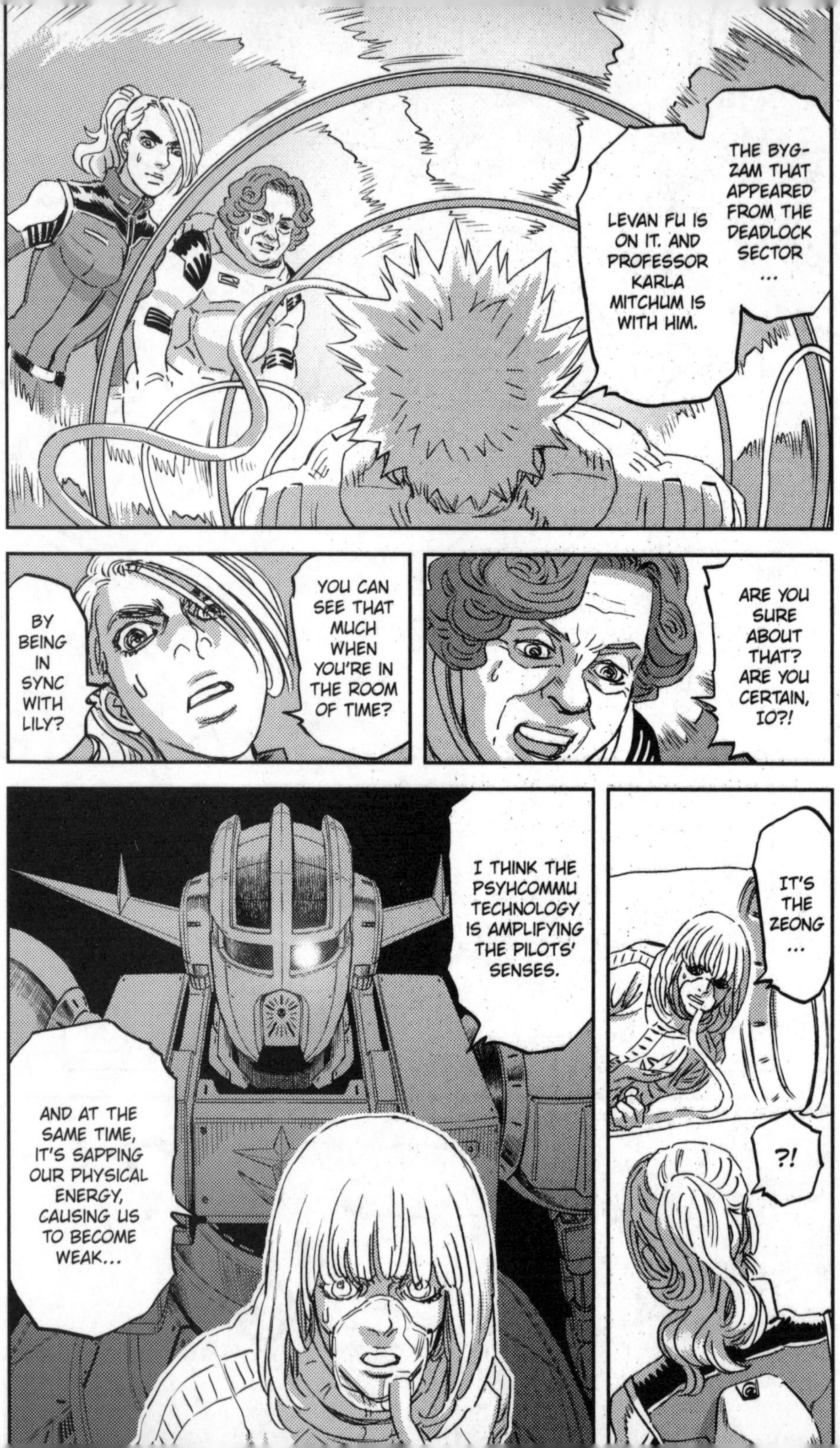
THE BYG-ZAM THAT APPEARED FROM THE DEADLOCK SECTOR ...
LEVAN FU IS ON IT. AND PROFESSOR KARLA MITCHUM IS WITH HIM.
ARE YOU SURE ABOUT THAT? ARE YOU CERTAIN, IO?!
YOU CAN SEE THAT MUCH WHEN YOU'RE IN THE ROOM OF TIME?
BY BEING IN SYNC WITH LILY?
IT'S THE ZEONG ...
?!
I THINK THE PSYHCOMMU TECHNOLOGY IS AMPLIFYING THE PILOTS' SENSES.
AND AT THE SAME TIME, IT'S SAPPING OUR PHYSICAL ENERGY, CAUSING US TO BECOME WEAK...

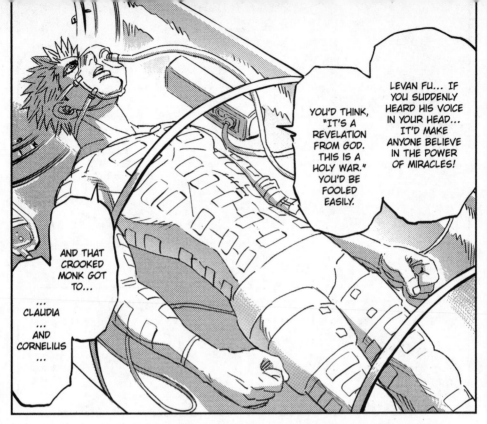

LEVAN FU... IF YOU SUDDENLY HEARD HIS VOICE IN YOUR HEAD... IT'D MAKE ANYONE BELIEVE IN THE POWER OF MIRACLES!

YOU'D THINK, "IT'S A REVELATION FROM GOD. THIS IS A HOLY WAR." YOU'D BE FOOLED EASILY.

AND THAT CROOKED MONK GOT TO...

... CLAUDIA ... AND CORNELIUS ...

GRIP

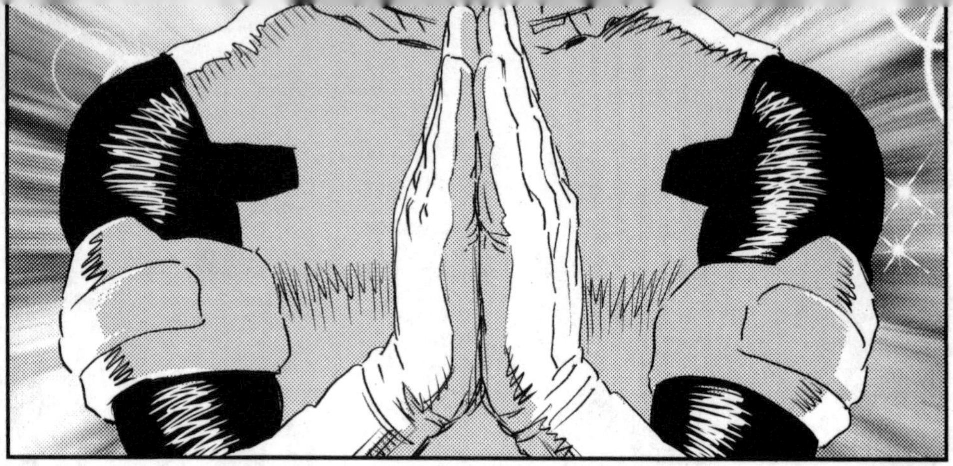
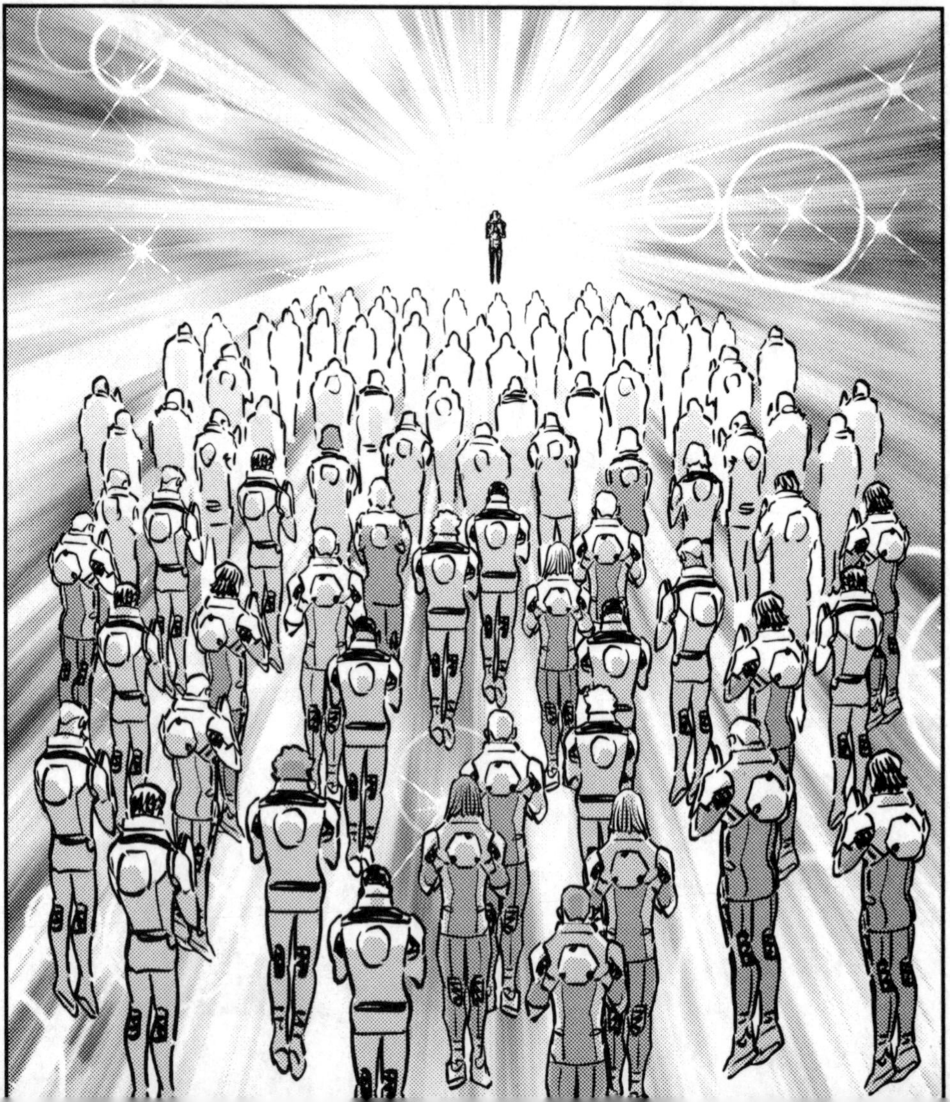

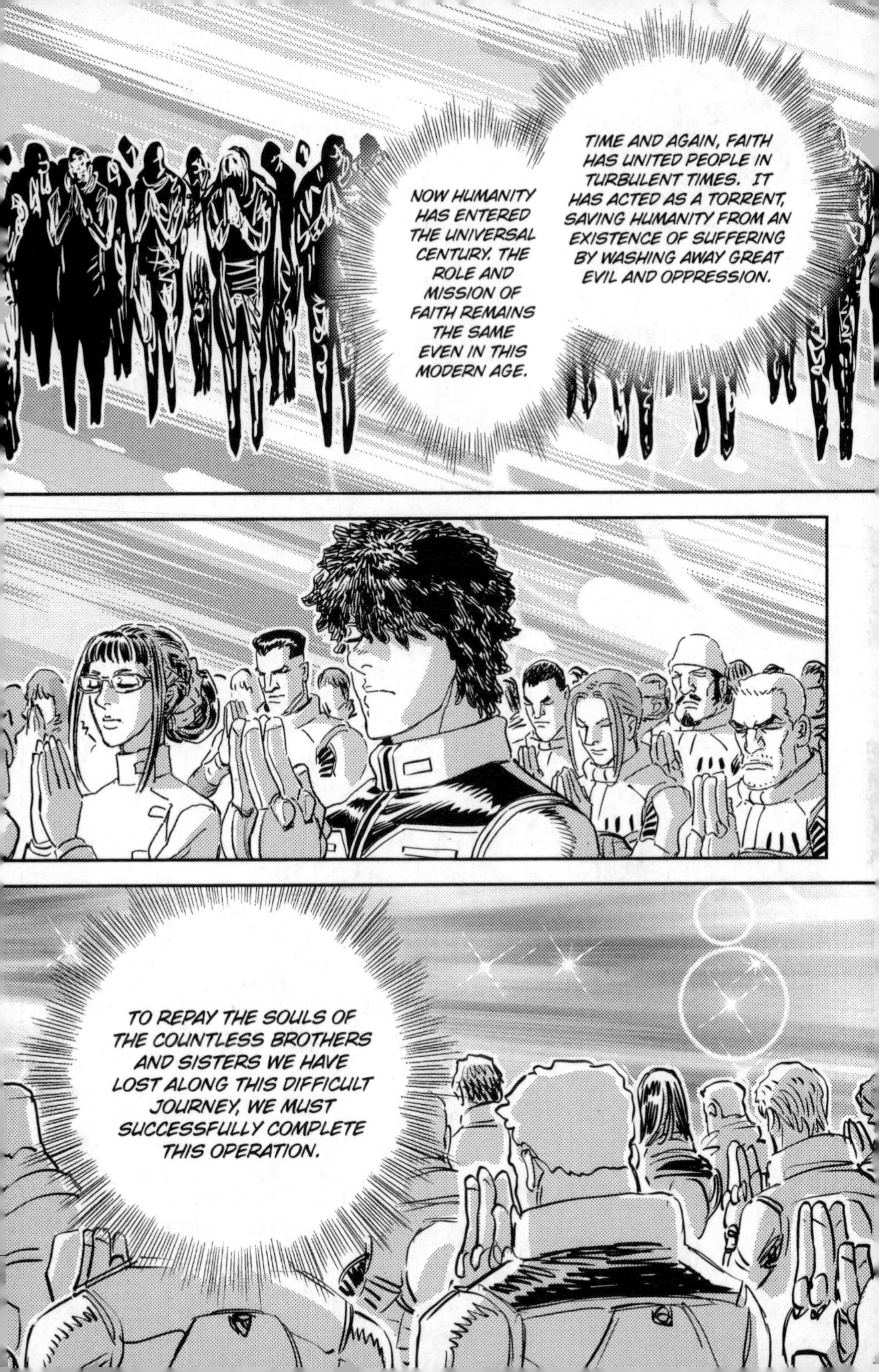
TIME AND AGAIN, FAITH HAS UNITED PEOPLE IN TURBULENT TIMES. IT HAS ACTED AS A TORRENT, SAVING HUMANITY FROM AN EXISTENCE OF SUFFERING BY WASHING AWAY GREAT EVIL AND OPPRESSION.
NOW HUMANITY HAS ENTERED THE UNIVERSAL CENTURY. THE ROLE AND MISSION OF FAITH REMAINS THE SAME EVEN IN THIS MODERN AGE.
TO REPAY THE SOULS OF THE COUNTLESS BROTHERS AND SISTERS WE HAVE LOST ALONG THIS DIFFICULT JOURNEY, WE MUST SUCCESSFULLY COMPLETE THIS OPERATION.

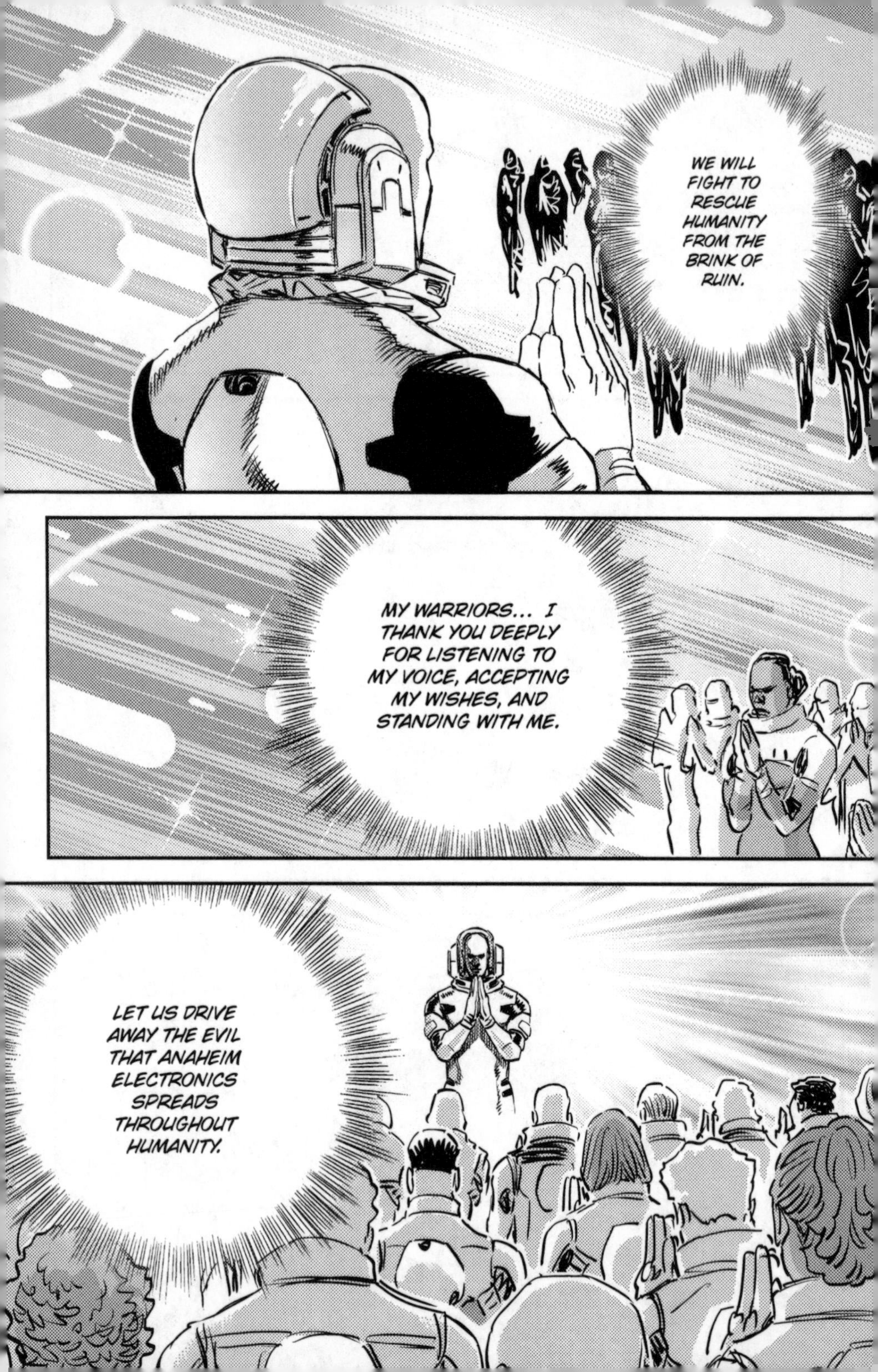
WE WILL FIGHT TO RESCUE HUMANITY FROM THE BRINK OF RUIN.
MY WARRIORS... I THANK YOU DEEPLY FOR LISTENING TO MY VOICE, ACCEPTING MY WISHES, AND STANDING WITH ME.
LET US DRIVE AWAY THE EVIL THAT ANAHEIM ELECTRONICS SPREADS THROUGHOUT HUMANITY.

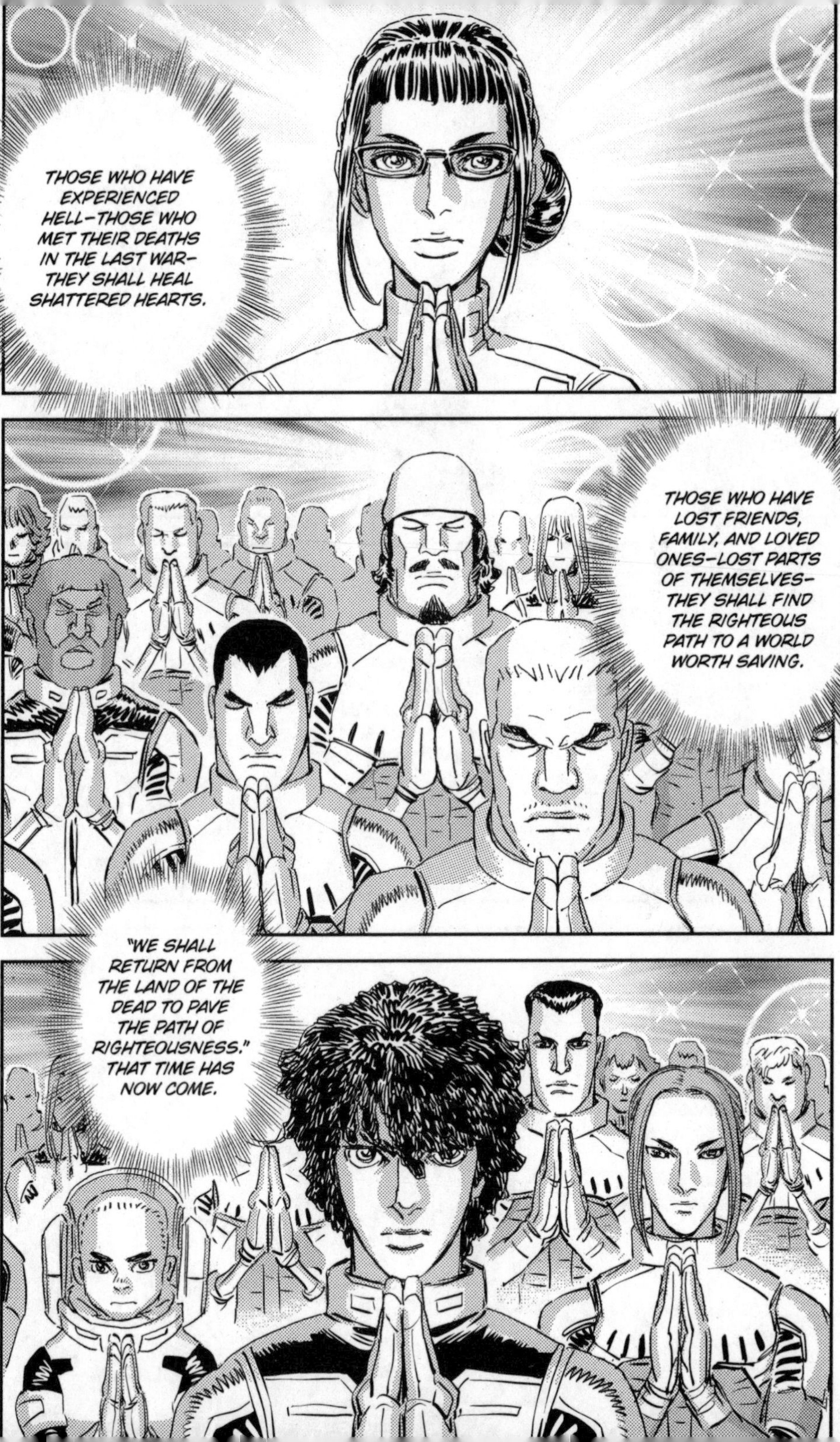
THOSE WHO HAVE EXPERIENCED HELL—THOSE WHO MET THEIR DEATHS IN THE LAST WAR—THEY SHALL HEAL SHATTERED HEARTS.
THOSE WHO HAVE LOST FRIENDS, FAMILY, AND LOVED ONES—LOST PARTS OF THEMSELVES—THEY SHALL FIND THE RIGHTEOUS PATH TO A WORLD WORTH SAVING.
"WE SHALL RETURN FROM THE LAND OF THE DEAD TO PAVE THE PATH OF RIGHTEOUSNESS." THAT TIME HAS NOW COME.

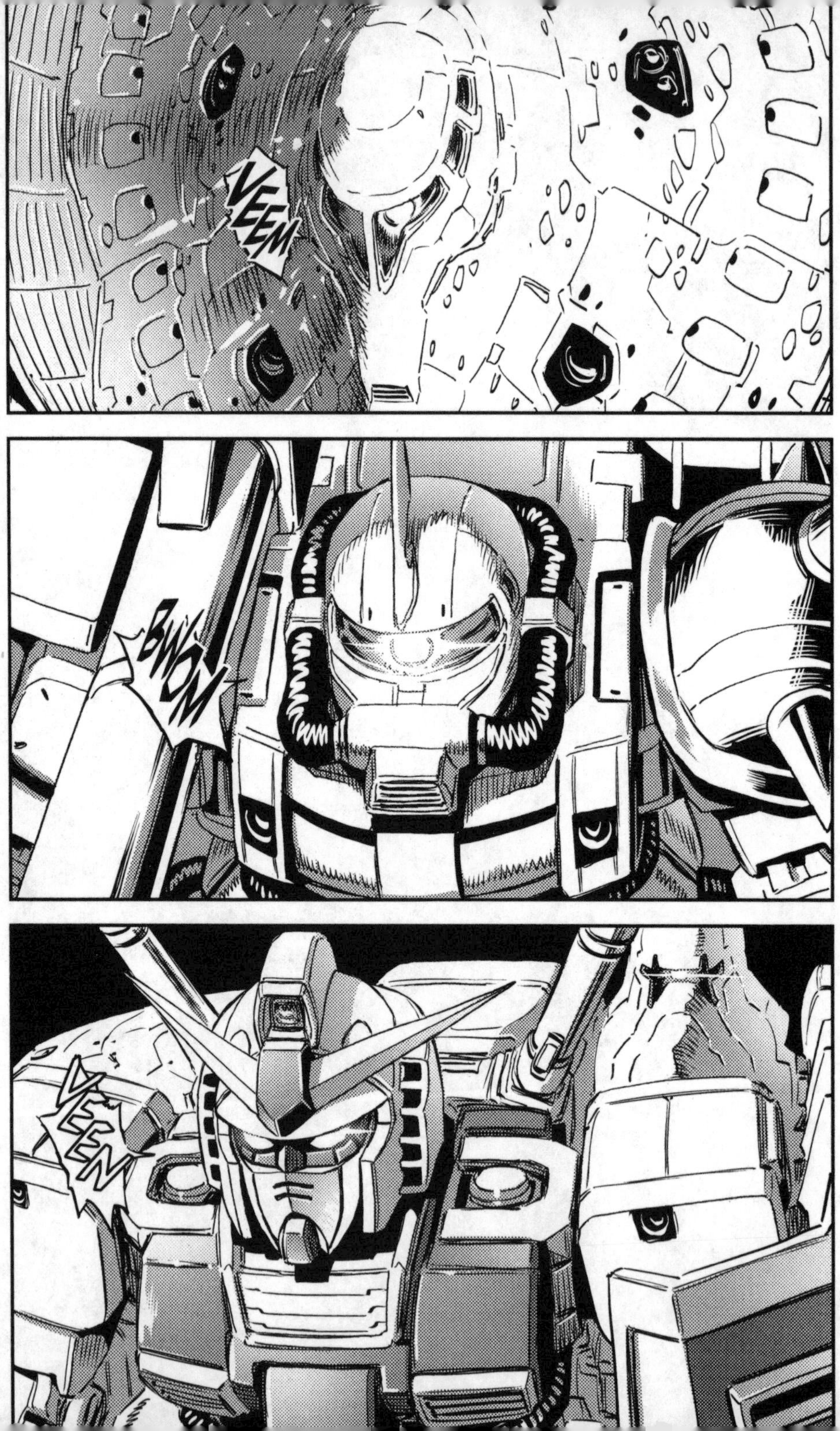
VEEM
BWOM
VEEN

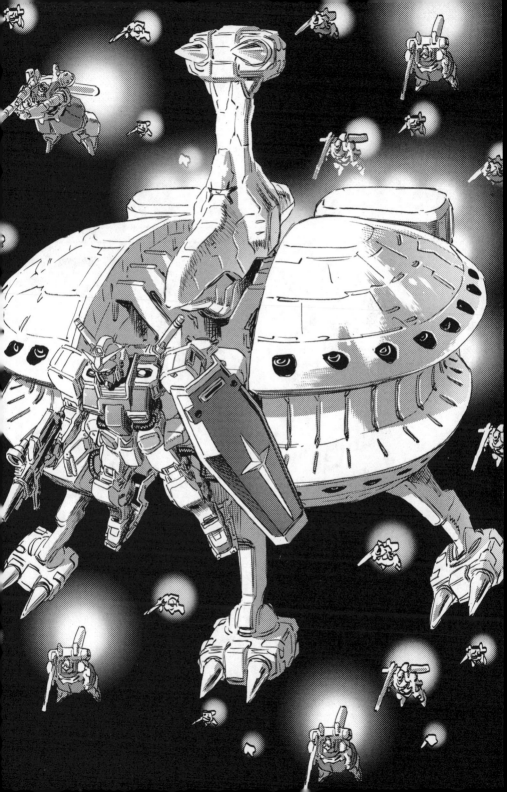

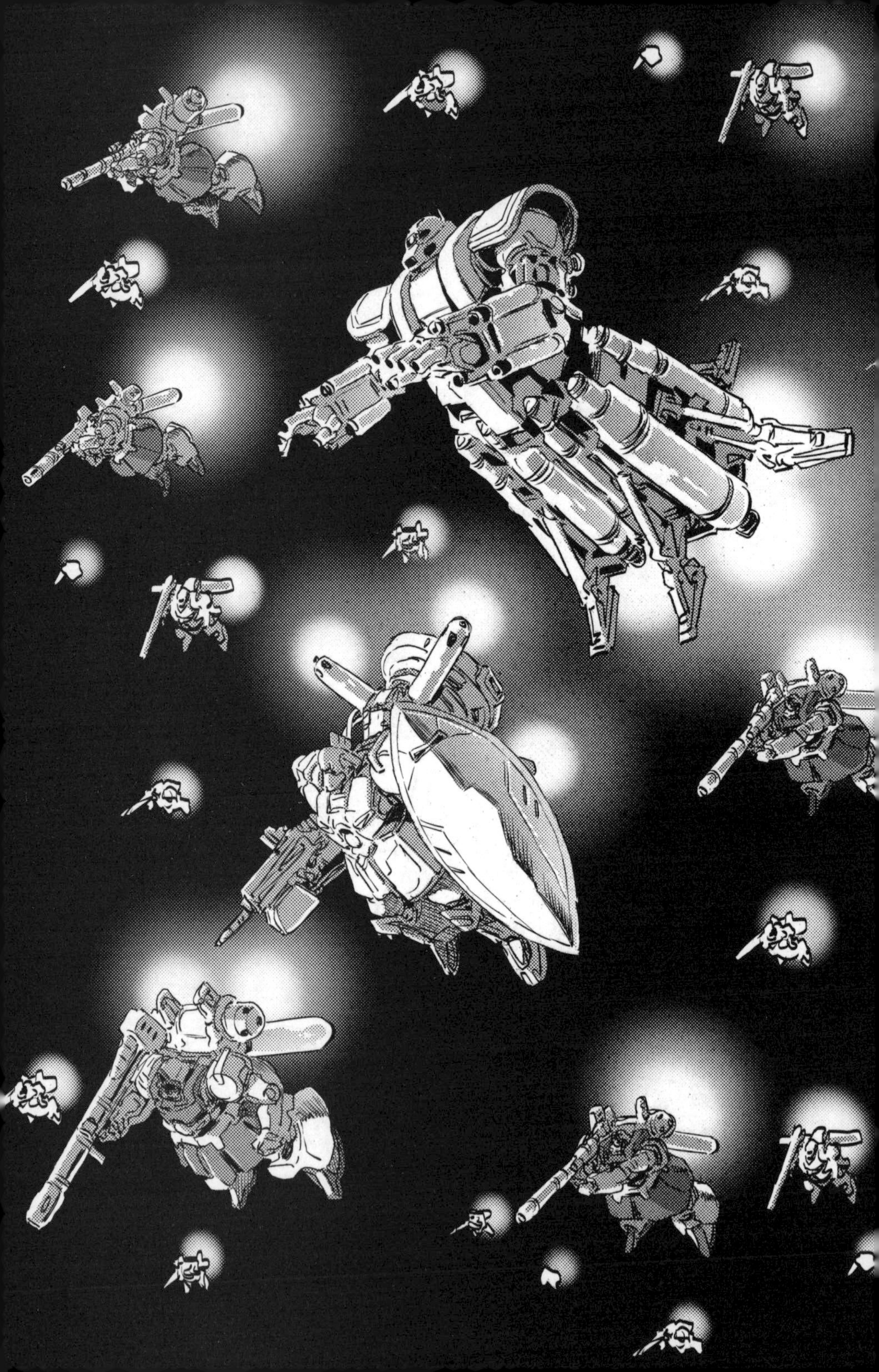

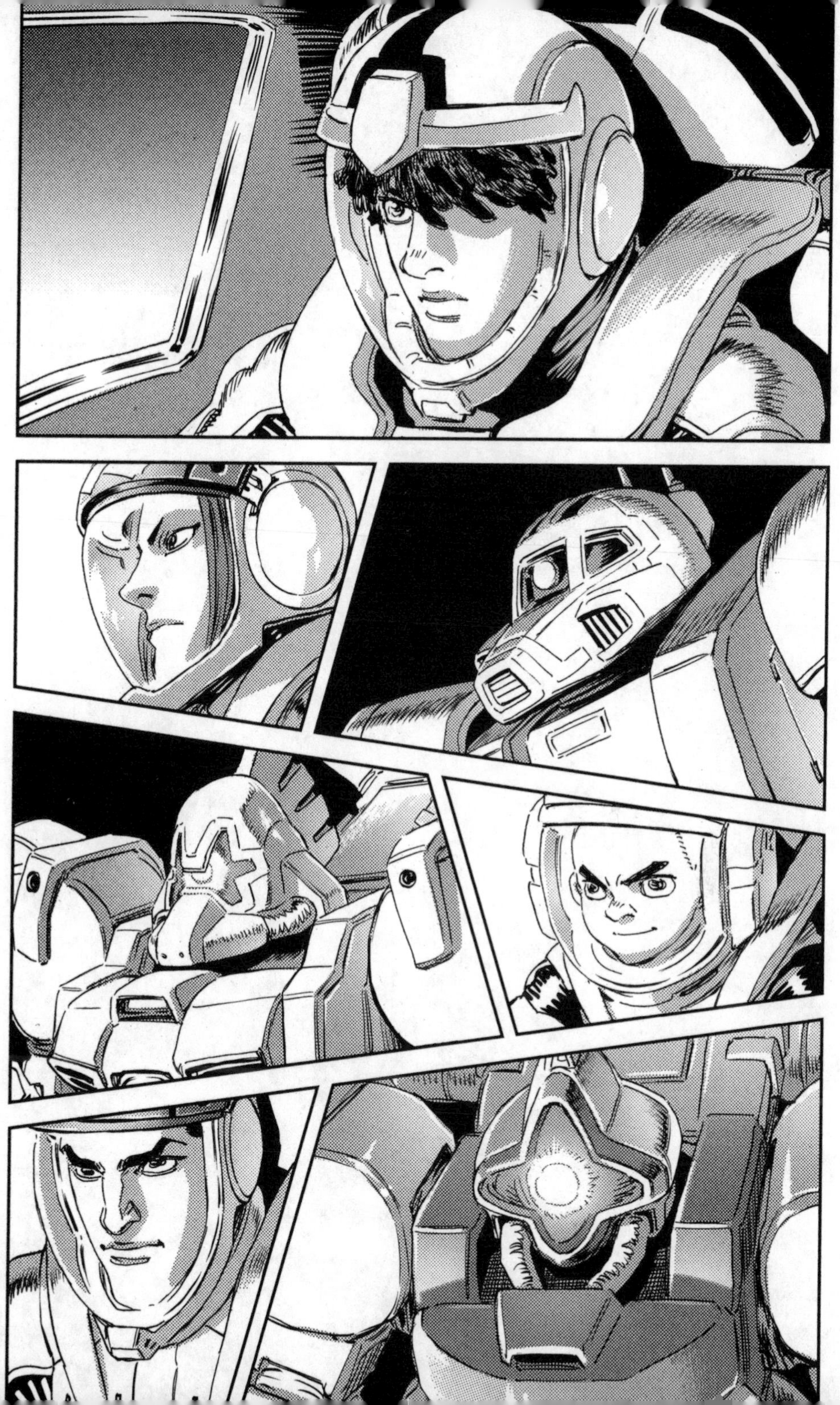

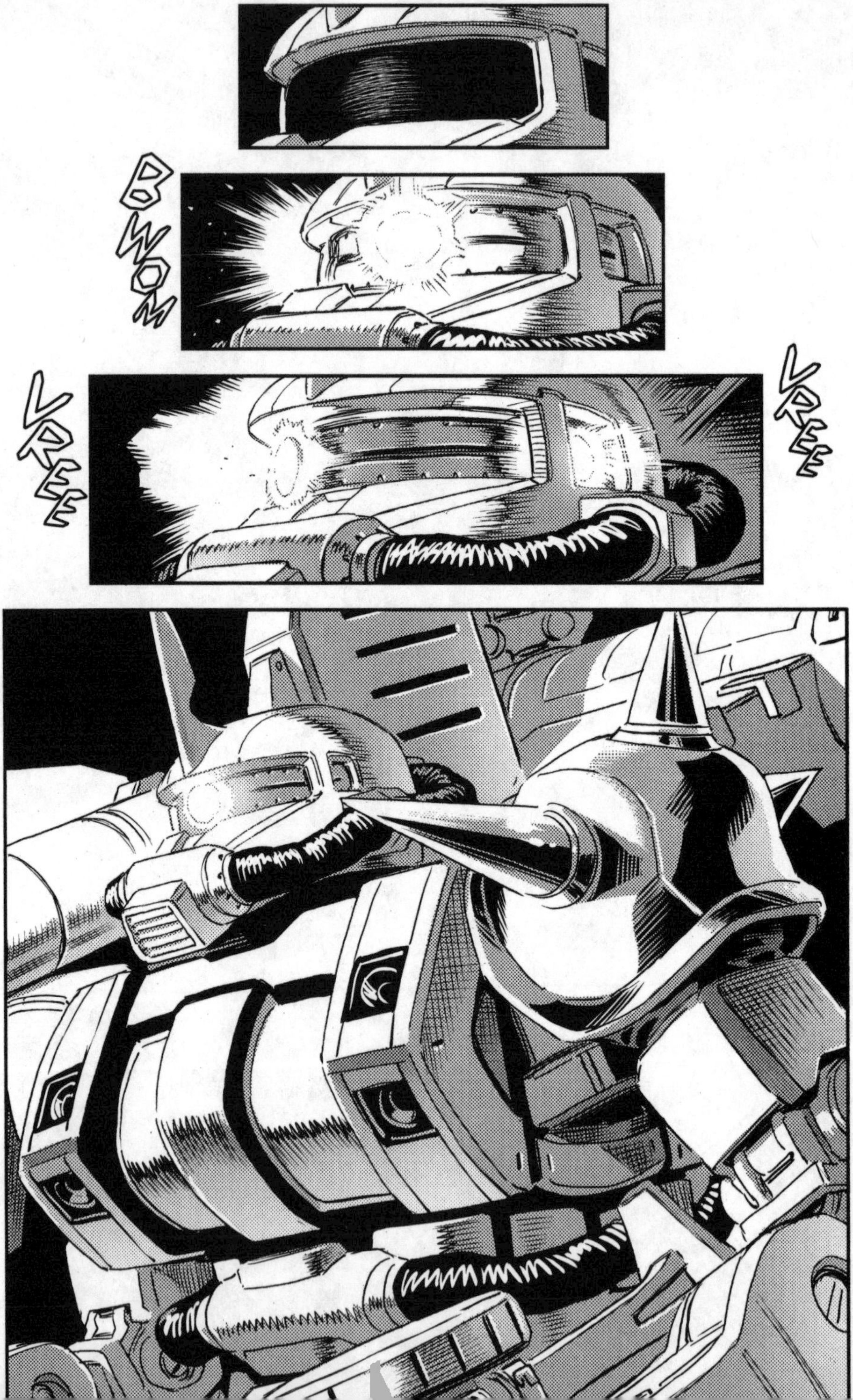
BWOM
VREE
VREE

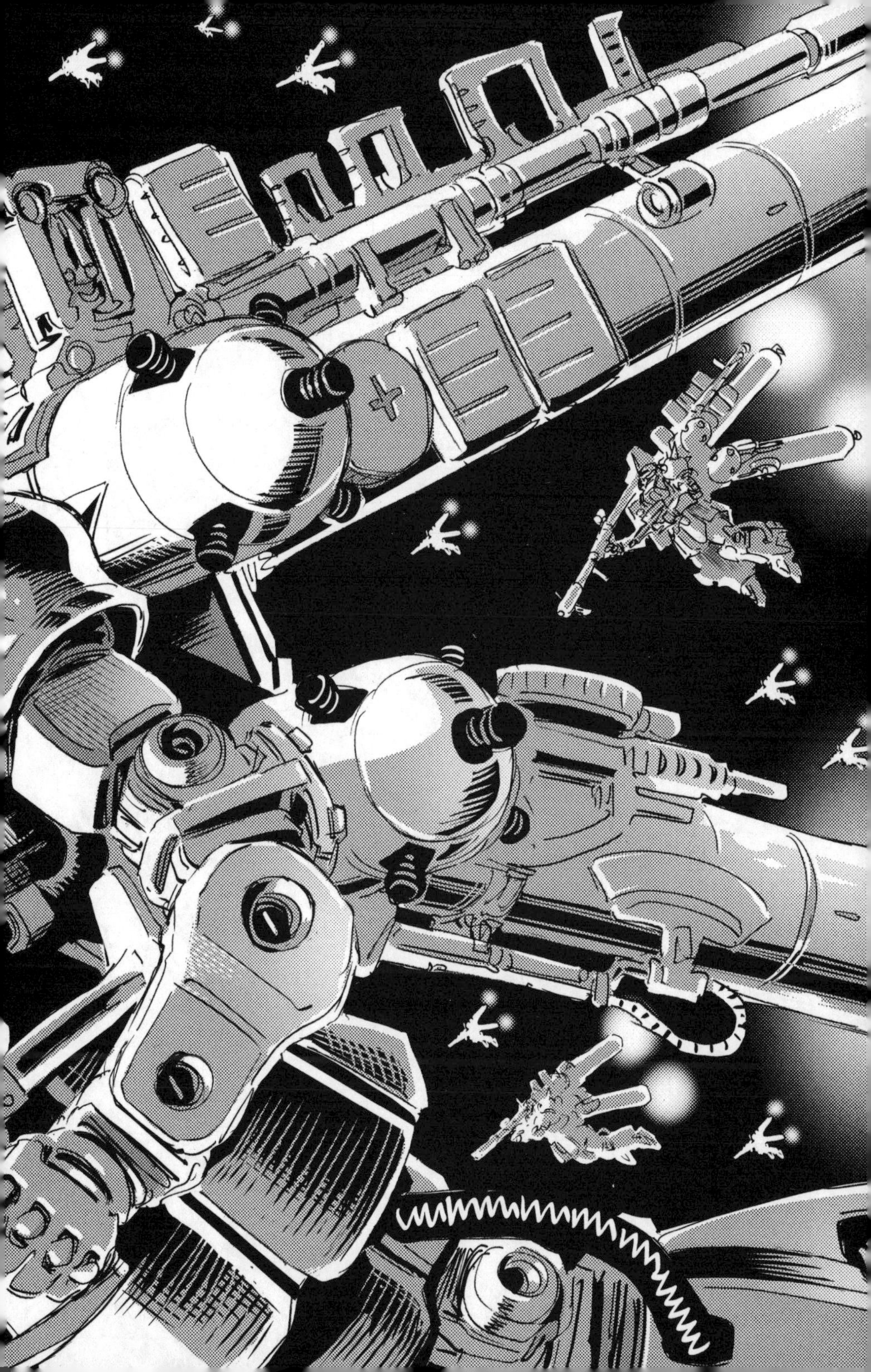

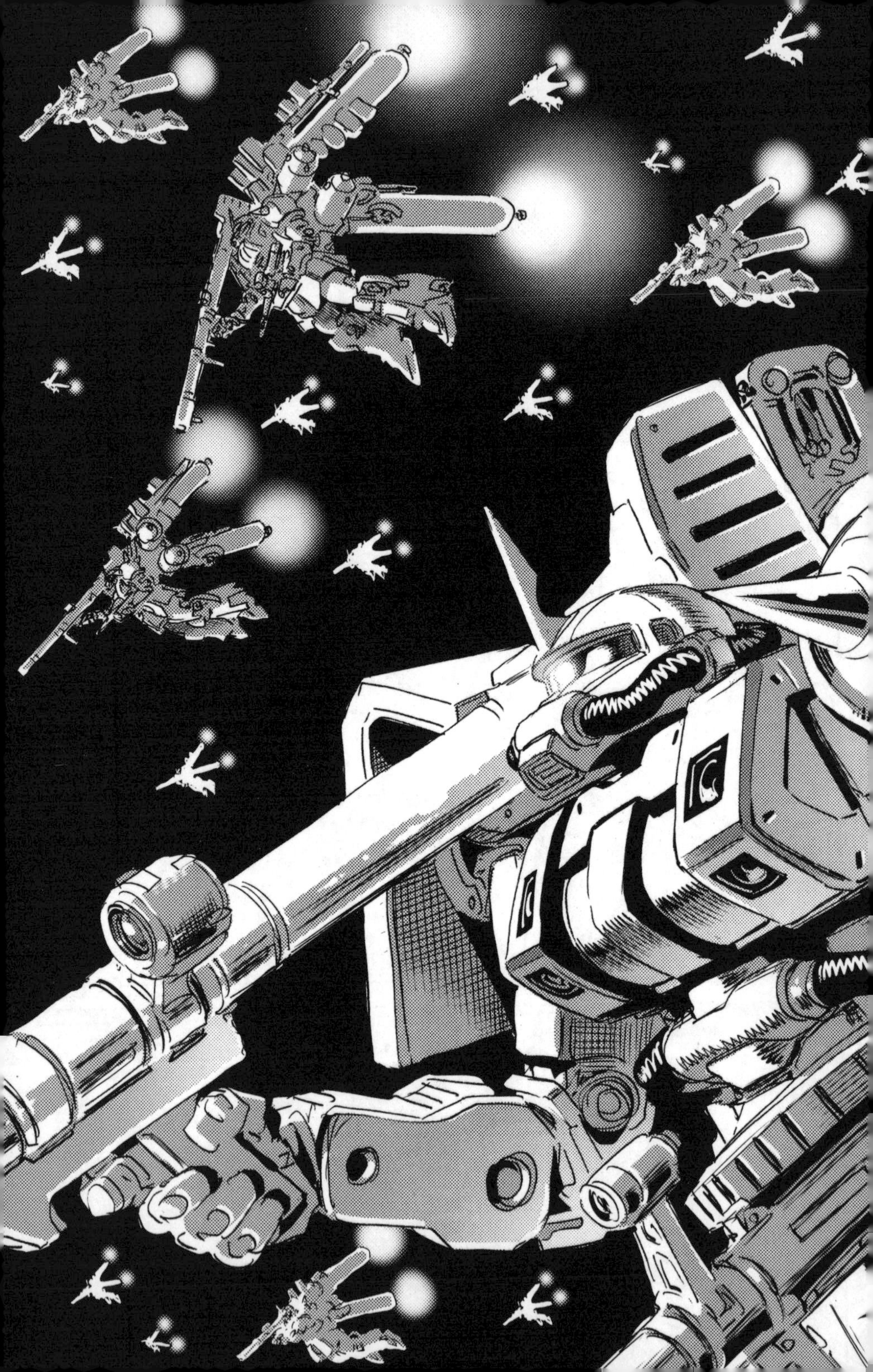

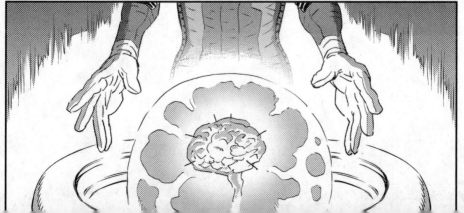

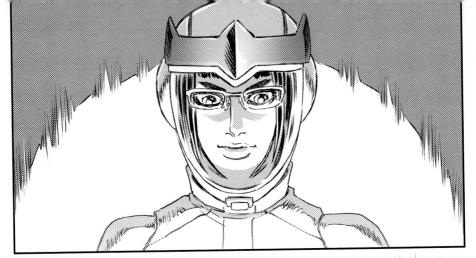

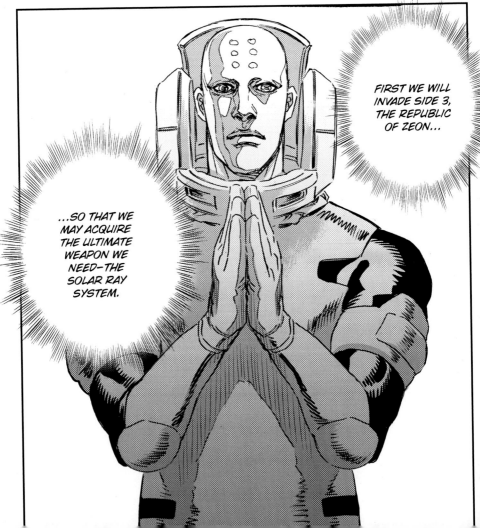

FIRST WE WILL INVADE SIDE 3, THE REPUBLIC OF ZEON...

...SO THAT WE MAY ACQUIRE THE ULTIMATE WEAPON WE NEED—THE SOLAR RAY SYSTEM.

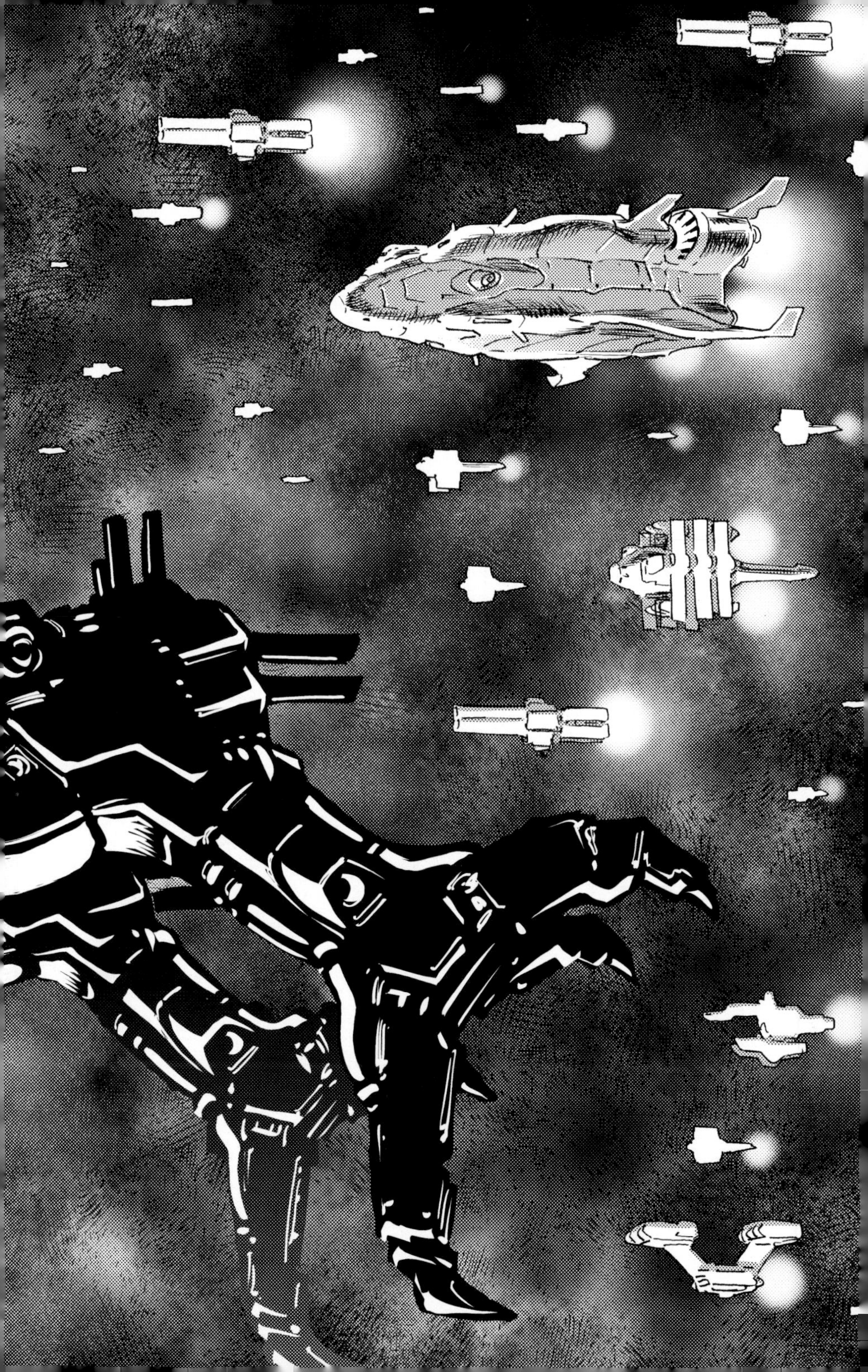

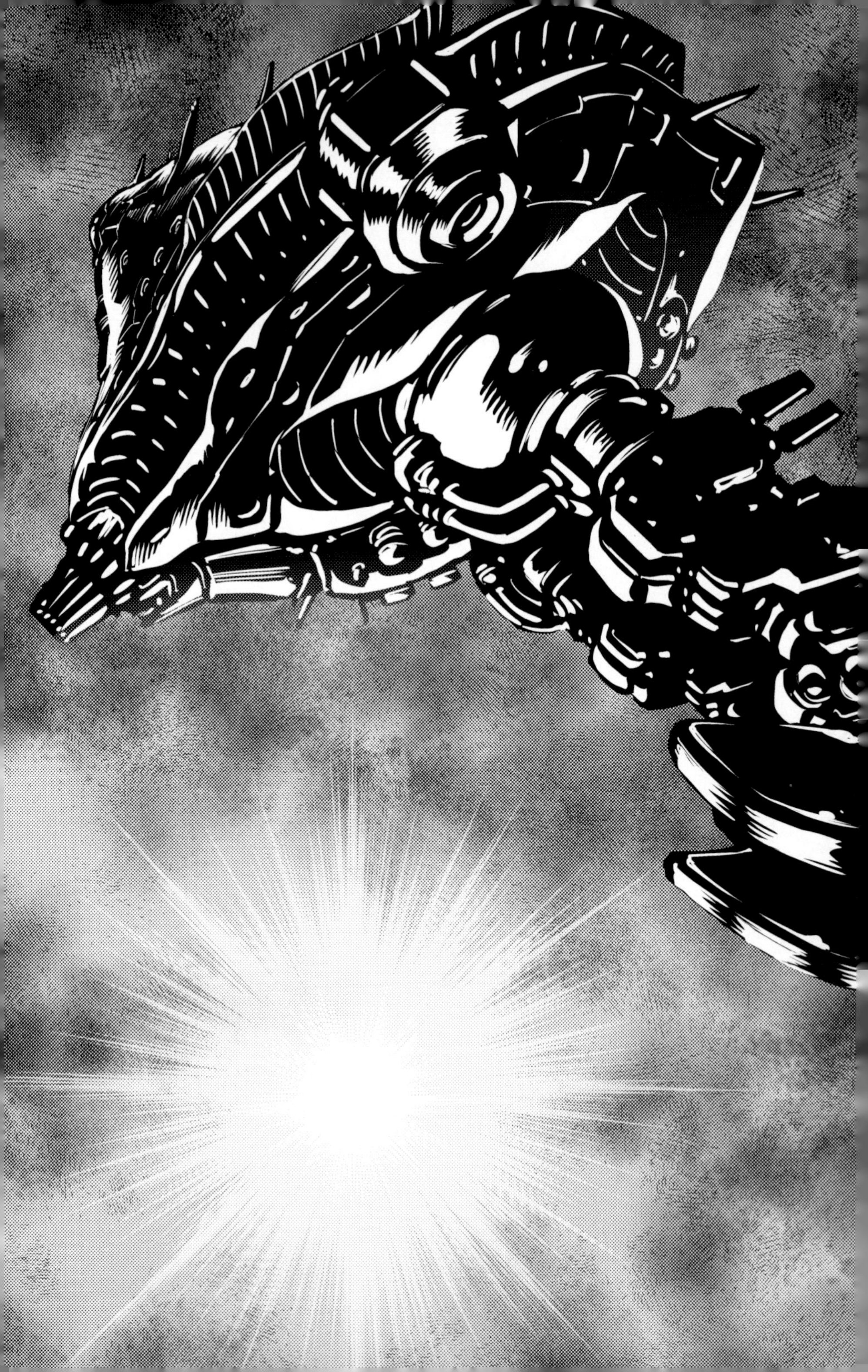

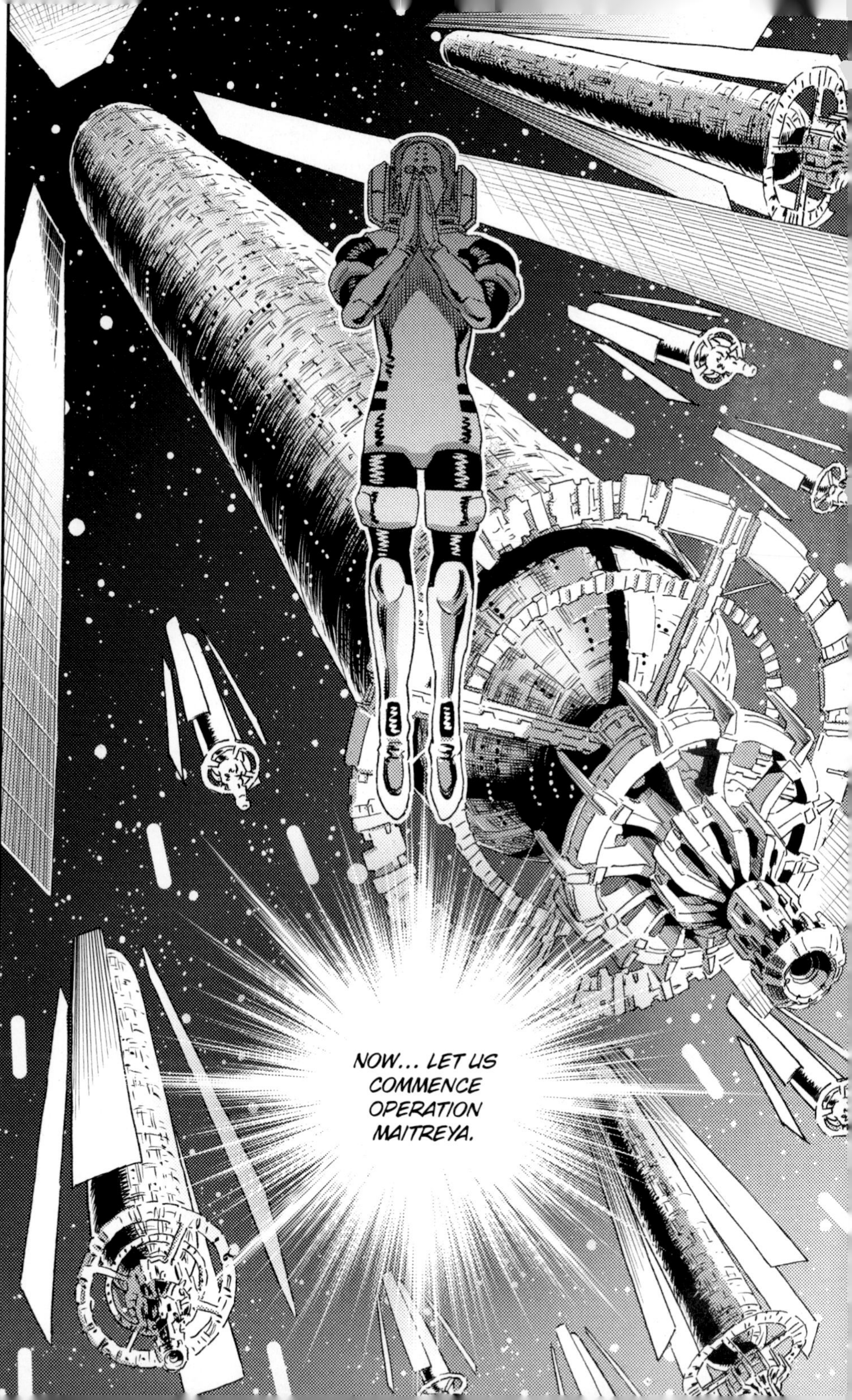
NOW... LET US COMMENCE OPERATION MAITREYA.

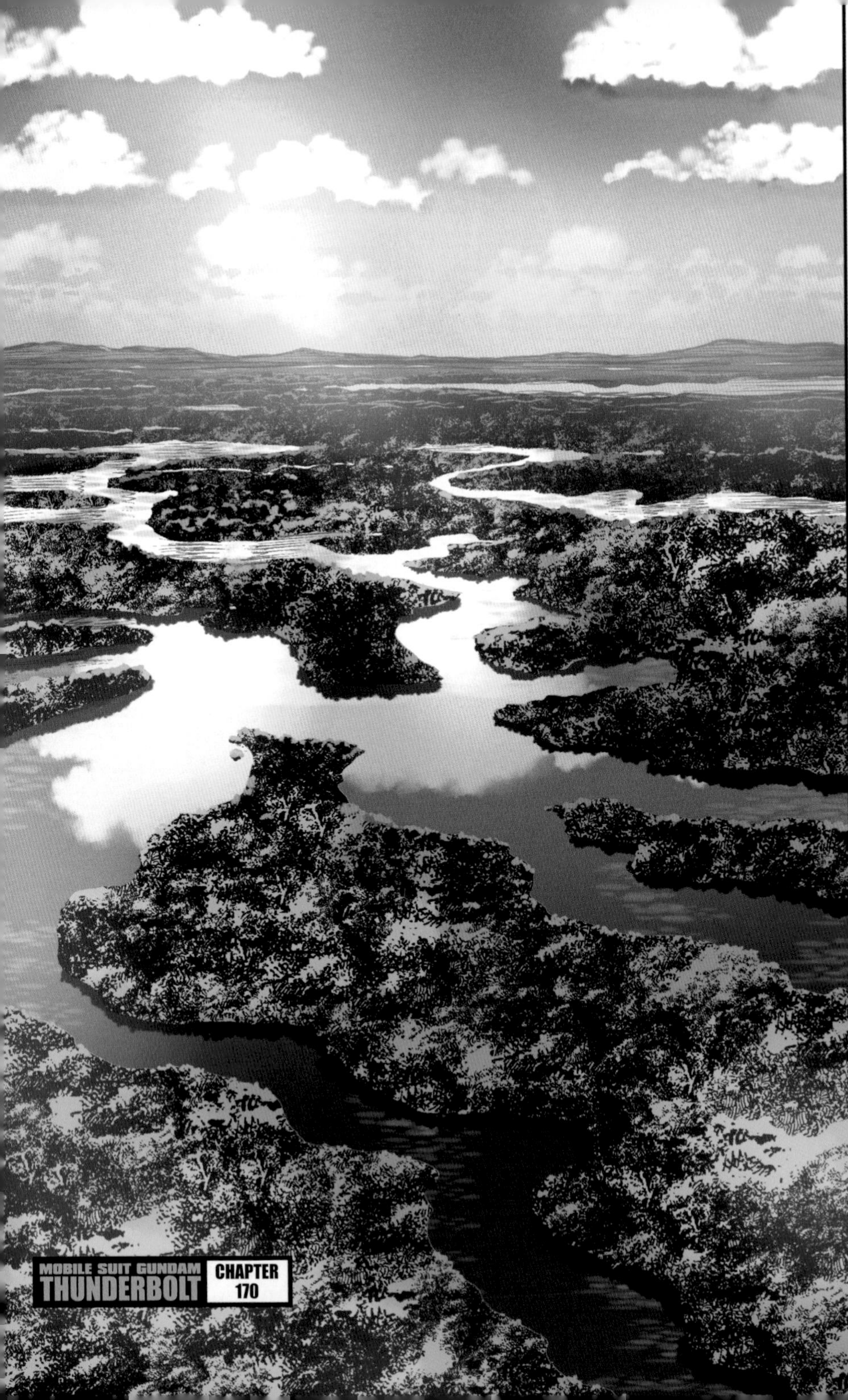
MOBILE SUIT GUNDAM
THUNDERBOLT
CHAPTER
170

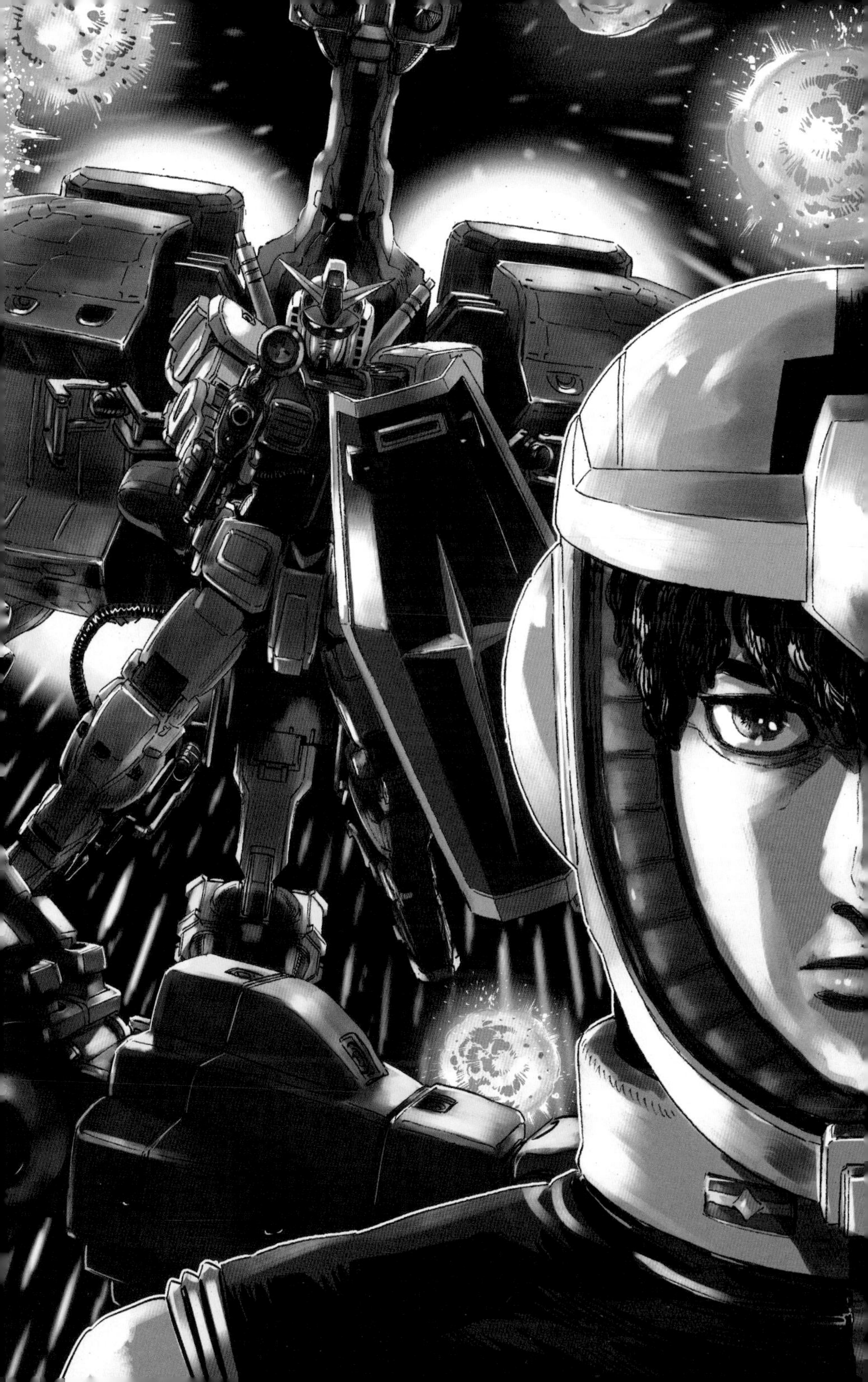

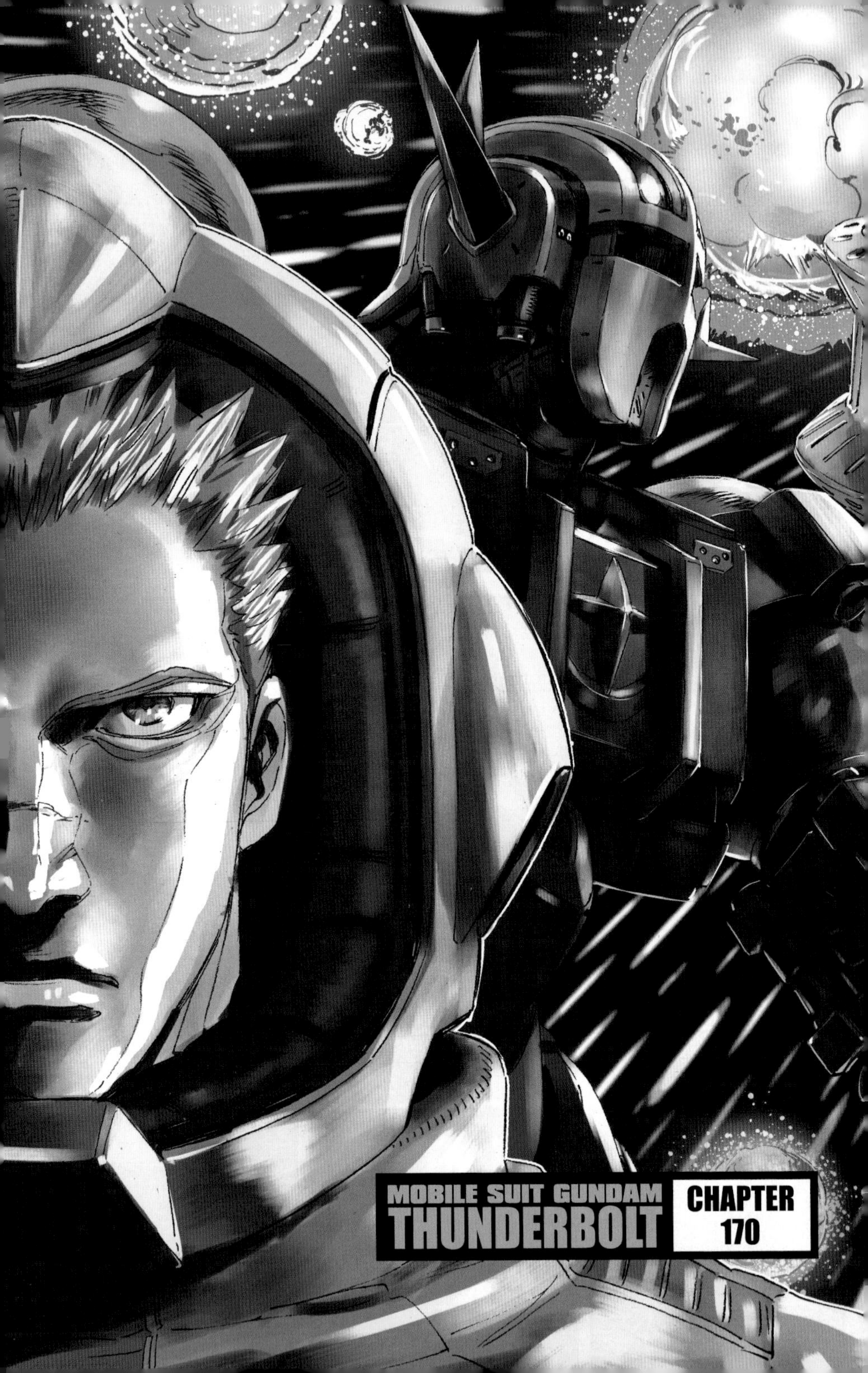
MOBILE SUIT GUNDAM
THUNDERBOLT
CHAPTER
170

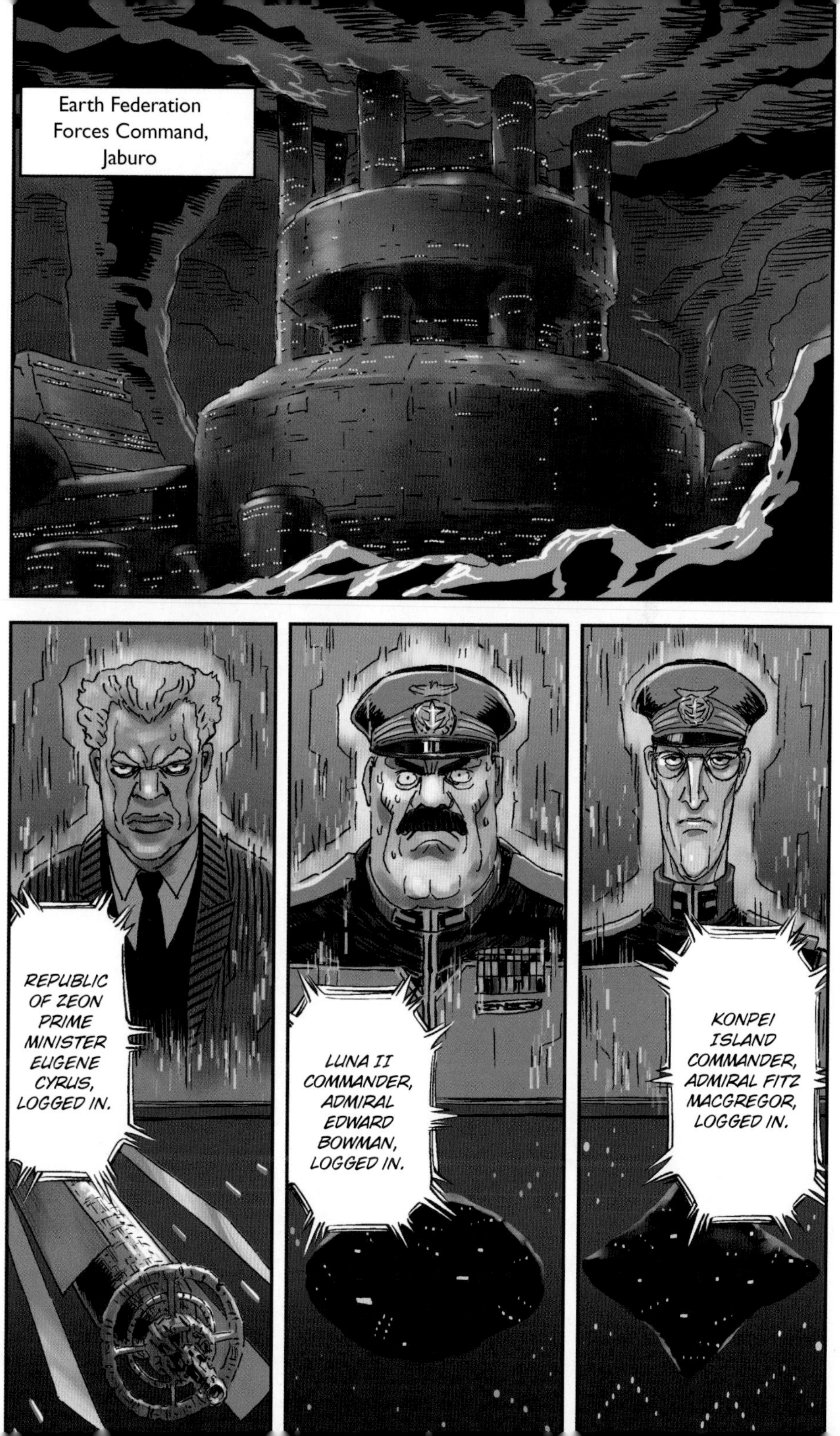
Earth Federation Forces Command, Jaburo
KONPEI ISLAND COMMANDER, ADMIRAL FITZ MACGREGOR, LOGGED IN.
LUNA II COMMANDER, ADMIRAL EDWARD BOWMAN, LOGGED IN.
REPUBLIC OF ZEON PRIME MINISTER EUGENE CYRUS, LOGGED IN.

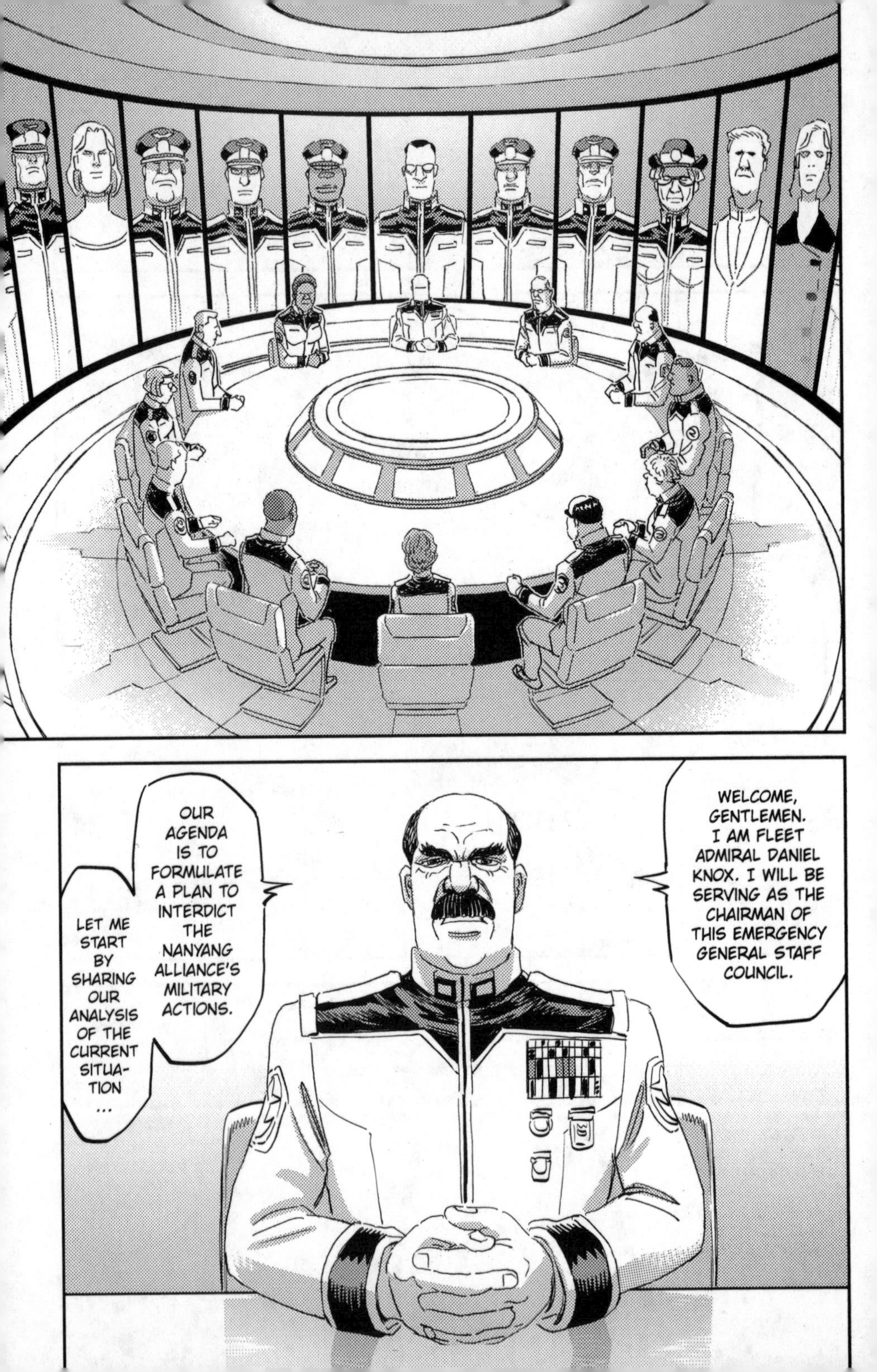
WELCOME, GENTLEMEN. I AM FLEET ADMIRAL DANIEL KNOX. I WILL BE SERVING AS THE CHAIRMAN OF THIS EMERGENCY GENERAL STAFF COUNCIL.
OUR AGENDA IS TO FORMULATE A PLAN TO INTERDICT THE NANYANG ALLIANCE'S MILITARY ACTIONS.
LET ME START BY SHARING OUR ANALYSIS OF THE CURRENT SITUATION...

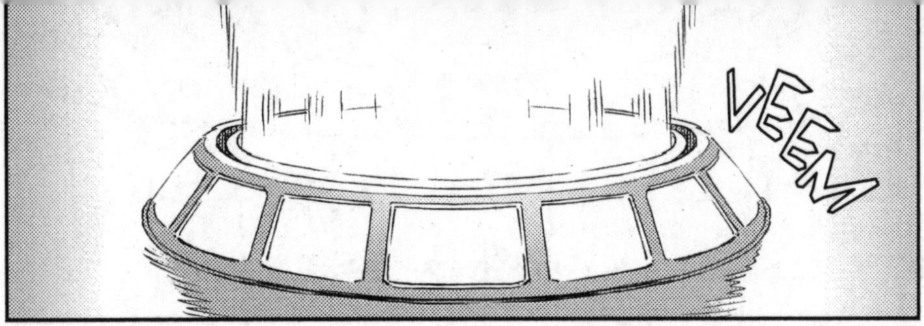
VEEM

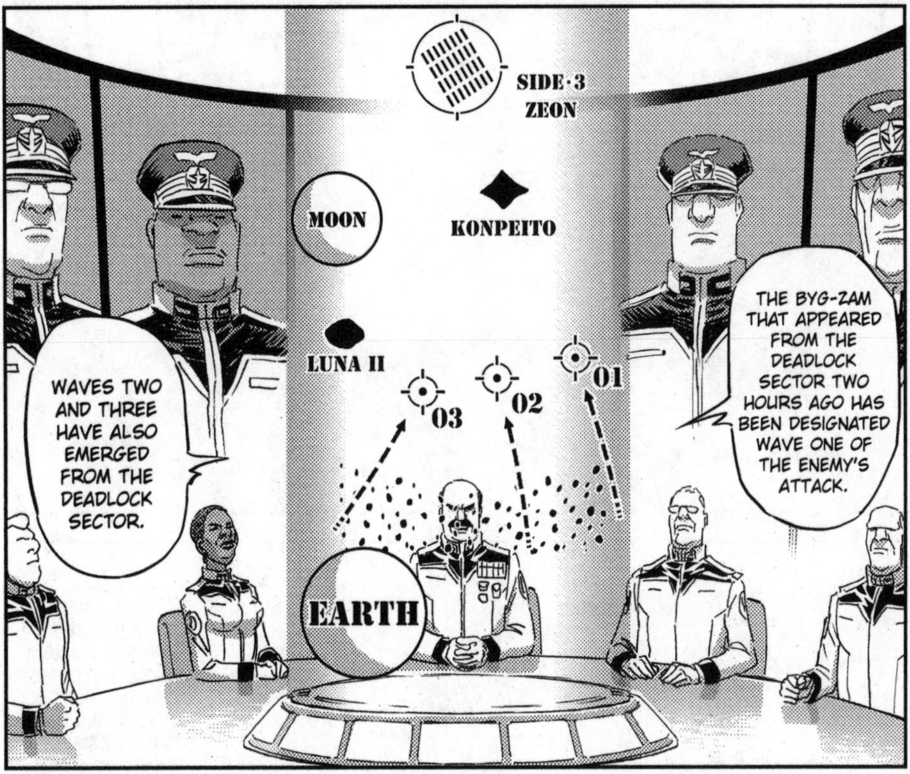
SIDE·3
ZEON
KONPEITO
MOON
THE BYG-ZAM THAT APPEARED FROM THE DEADLOCK SECTOR TWO HOURS AGO HAS BEEN DESIGNATED WAVE ONE OF THE ENEMY'S ATTACK.
LUNA II
01
02
03
WAVES TWO AND THREE HAVE ALSO EMERGED FROM THE DEADLOCK SECTOR.
EARTH

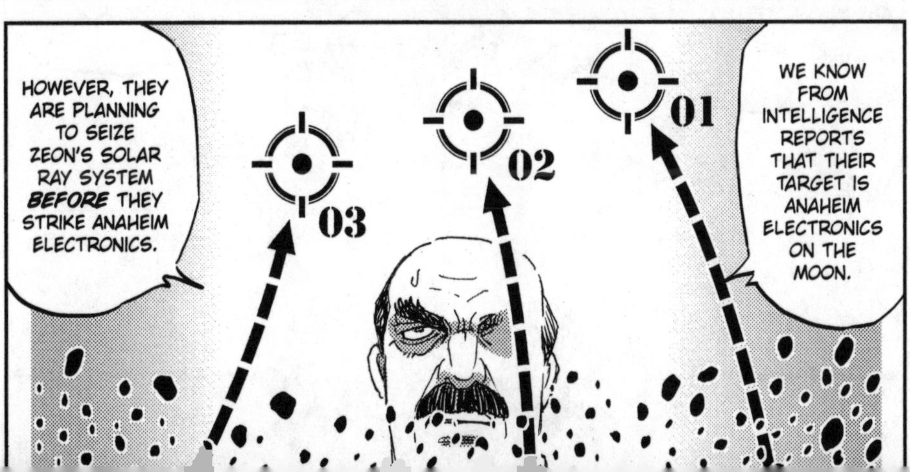
WE KNOW FROM INTELLIGENCE REPORTS THAT THEIR TARGET IS ANAHEIM ELECTRONICS ON THE MOON.
01
02
03
HOWEVER, THEY ARE PLANNING TO SEIZE ZEON'S SOLAR RAY SYSTEM *BEFORE* THEY STRIKE ANAHEIM ELECTRONICS.

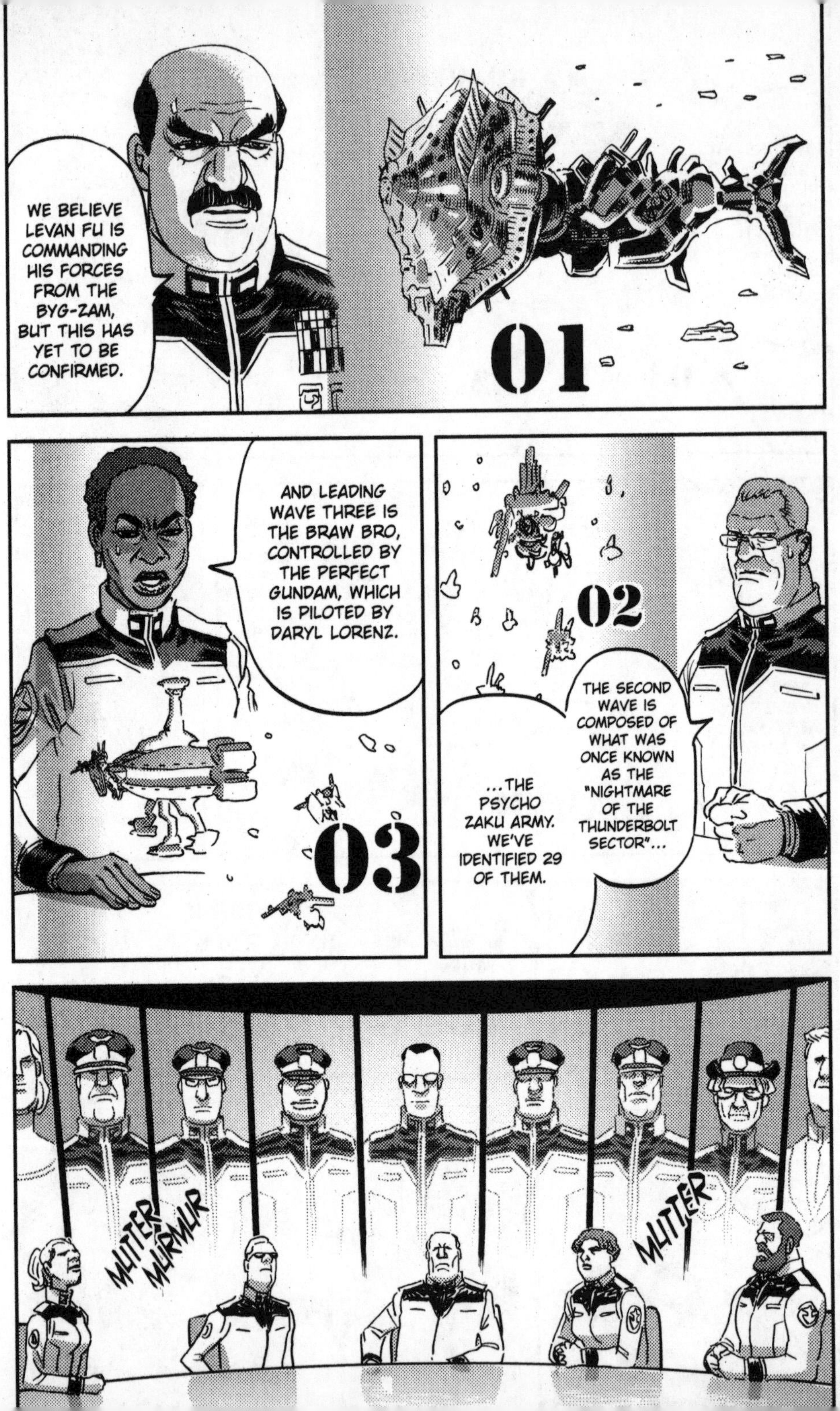

WE BELIEVE LEVAN FU IS COMMANDING HIS FORCES FROM THE BYG-ZAM, BUT THIS HAS YET TO BE CONFIRMED.
01
02
THE SECOND WAVE IS COMPOSED OF WHAT WAS ONCE KNOWN AS THE "NIGHTMARE OF THE THUNDERBOLT SECTOR"...
...THE PSYCHO ZAKU ARMY. WE'VE IDENTIFIED 29 OF THEM.
AND LEADING WAVE THREE IS THE BRAW BRO, CONTROLLED BY THE PERFECT GUNDAM, WHICH IS PILOTED BY DARYL LORENZ.
03
MUTTER
MUTTER-MURMUR

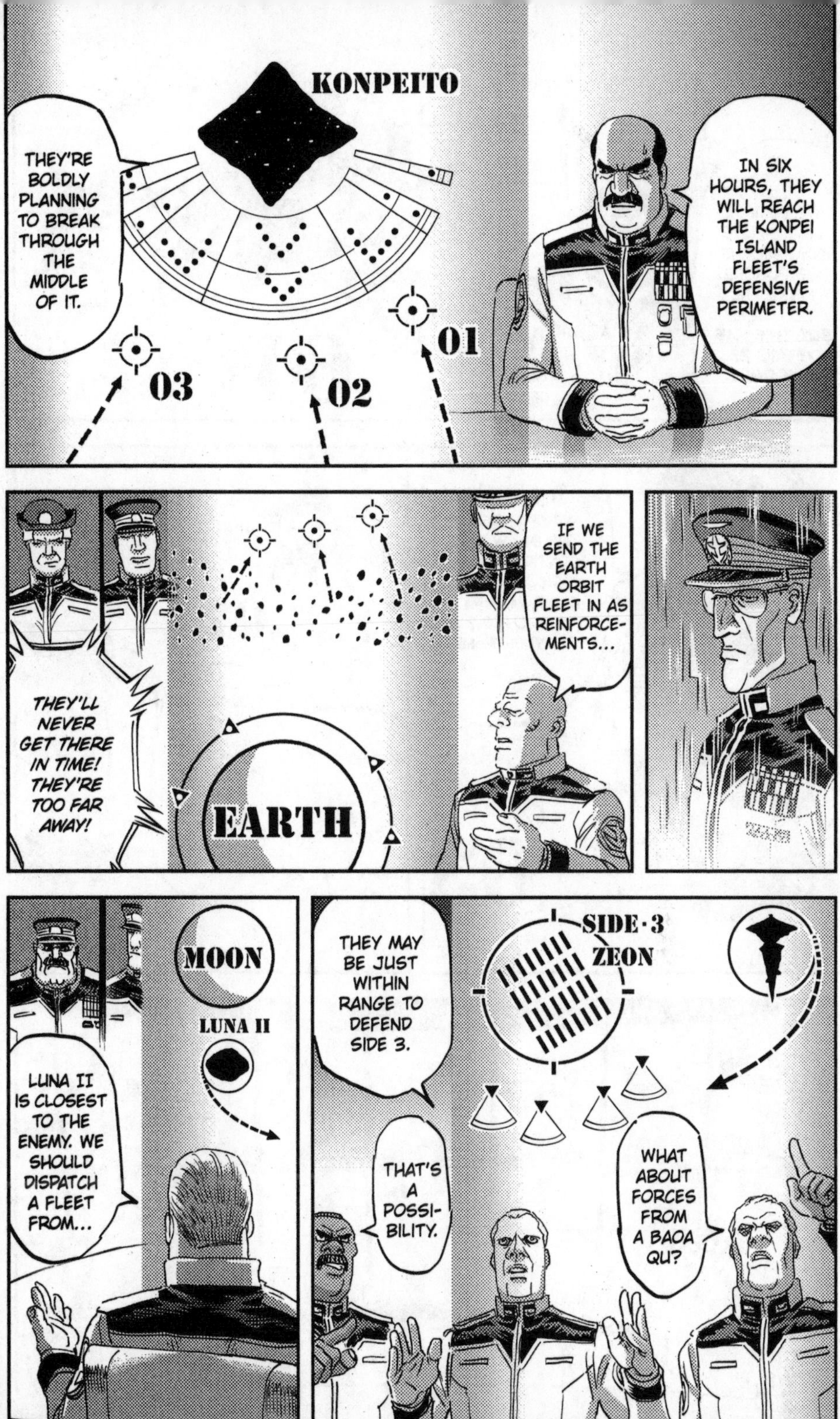
IN SIX HOURS, THEY WILL REACH THE KONPEI ISLAND FLEET'S DEFENSIVE PERIMETER.
KONPEITO
THEY'RE BOLDLY PLANNING TO BREAK THROUGH THE MIDDLE OF IT.
01
02
03
IF WE SEND THE EARTH ORBIT FLEET IN AS REINFORCE-MENTS...
THEY'LL NEVER GET THERE IN TIME! THEY'RE TOO FAR AWAY!
EARTH
SIDE·3
ZEON
WHAT ABOUT FORCES FROM A BAOA QU?
THAT'S A POSSI-BILITY.
THEY MAY BE JUST WITHIN RANGE TO DEFEND SIDE 3.
MOON
LUNA II
LUNA II IS CLOSEST TO THE ENEMY. WE SHOULD DISPATCH A FLEET FROM...

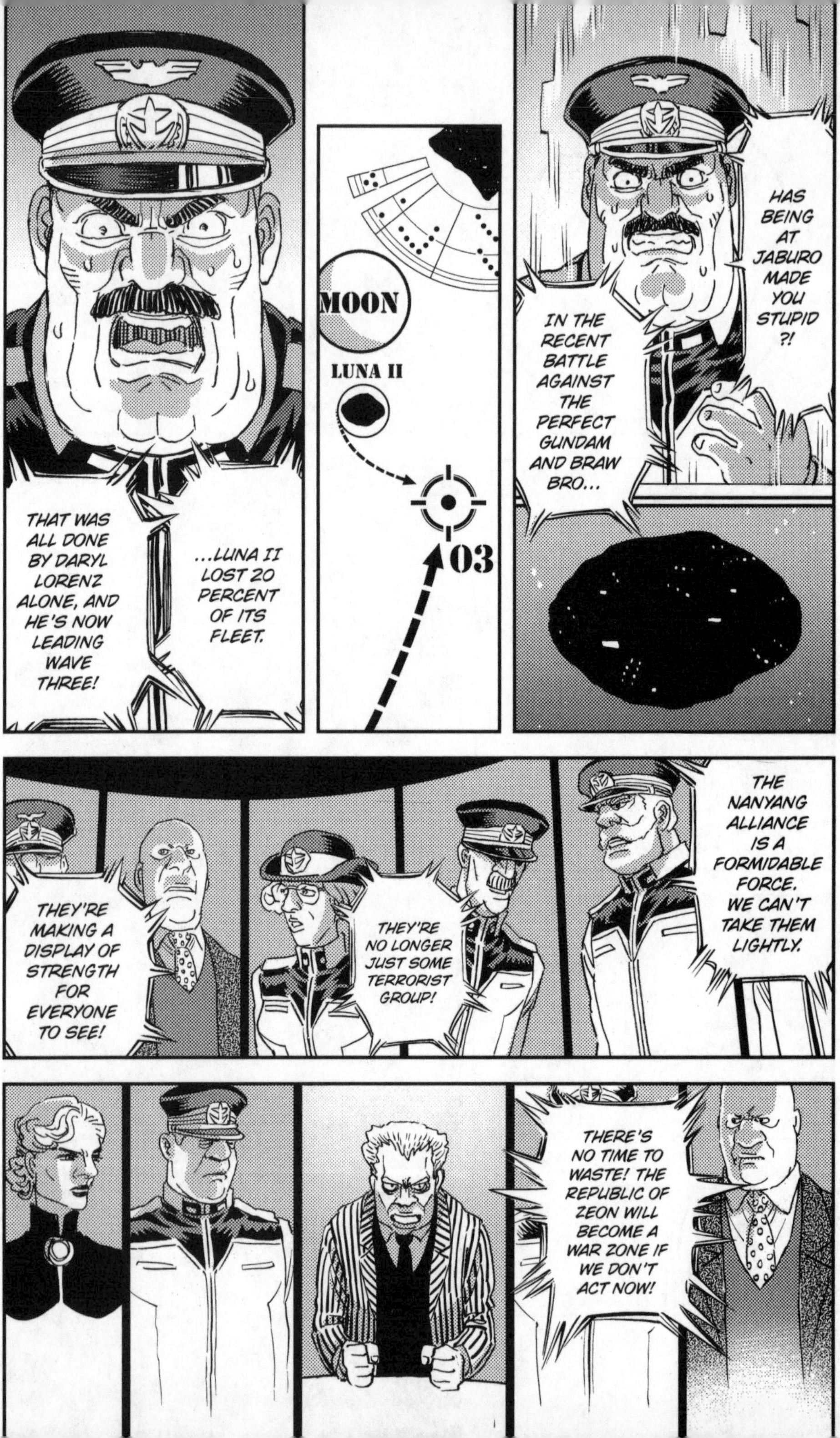
HAS BEING AT JABURO MADE YOU STUPID ?!
IN THE RECENT BATTLE AGAINST THE PERFECT GUNDAM AND BRAW BRO...
MOON
LUNA II
03
...LUNA II LOST 20 PERCENT OF ITS FLEET.
THAT WAS ALL DONE BY DARYL LORENZ ALONE, AND HE'S NOW LEADING WAVE THREE!
THE NANYANG ALLIANCE IS A FORMIDABLE FORCE. WE CAN'T TAKE THEM LIGHTLY.
THEY'RE NO LONGER JUST SOME TERRORIST GROUP!
THEY'RE MAKING A DISPLAY OF STRENGTH FOR EVERYONE TO SEE!
THERE'S NO TIME TO WASTE! THE REPUBLIC OF ZEON WILL BECOME A WAR ZONE IF WE DON'T ACT NOW!

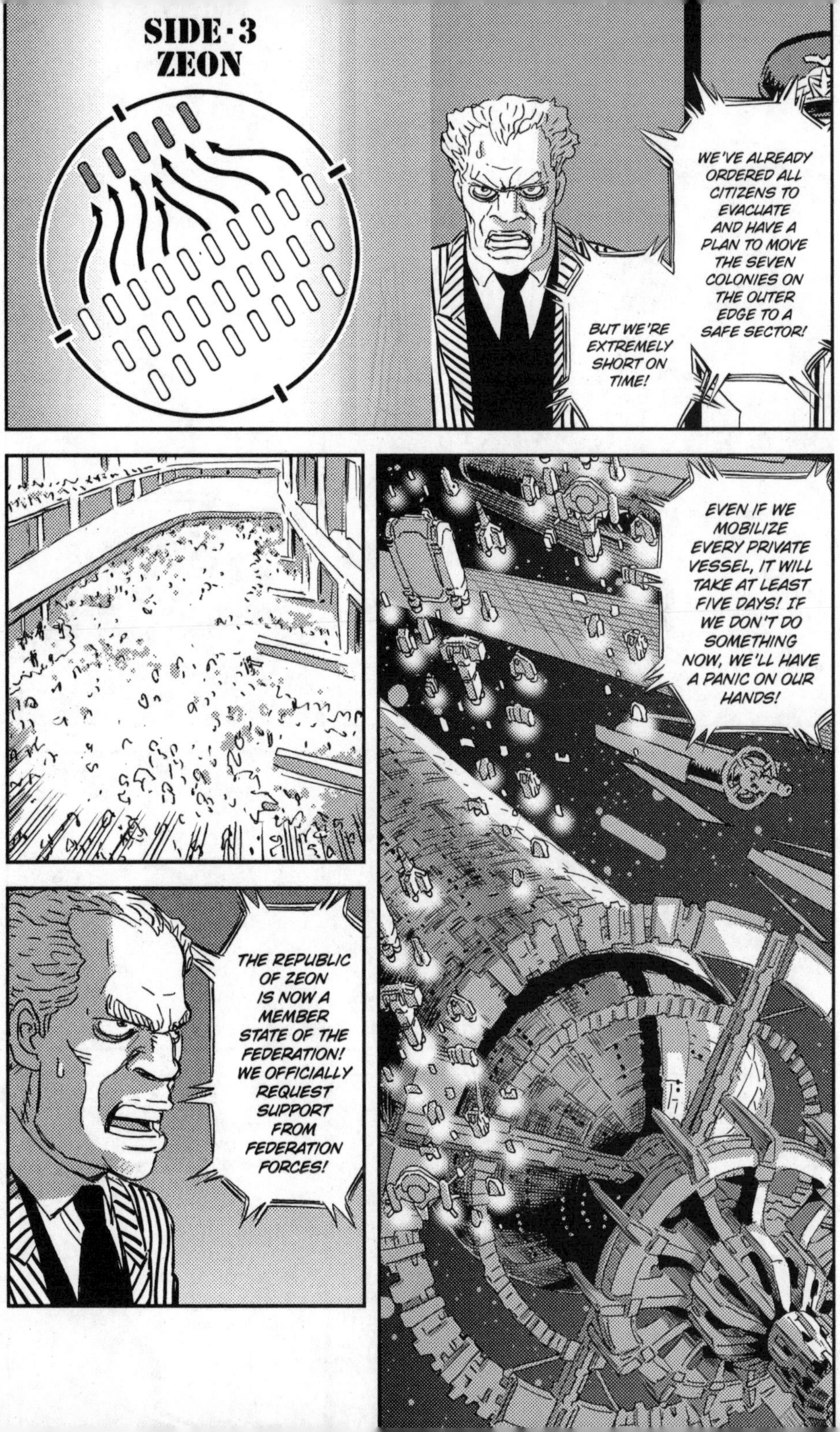
WE'VE ALREADY ORDERED ALL CITIZENS TO EVACUATE AND HAVE A PLAN TO MOVE THE SEVEN COLONIES ON THE OUTER EDGE TO A SAFE SECTOR!
BUT WE'RE EXTREMELY SHORT ON TIME!
SIDE·3
ZEON
EVEN IF WE MOBILIZE EVERY PRIVATE VESSEL, IT WILL TAKE AT LEAST FIVE DAYS! IF WE DON'T DO SOMETHING NOW, WE'LL HAVE A PANIC ON OUR HANDS!
THE REPUBLIC OF ZEON IS NOW A MEMBER STATE OF THE FEDERATION! WE OFFICIALLY REQUEST SUPPORT FROM FEDERATION FORCES!

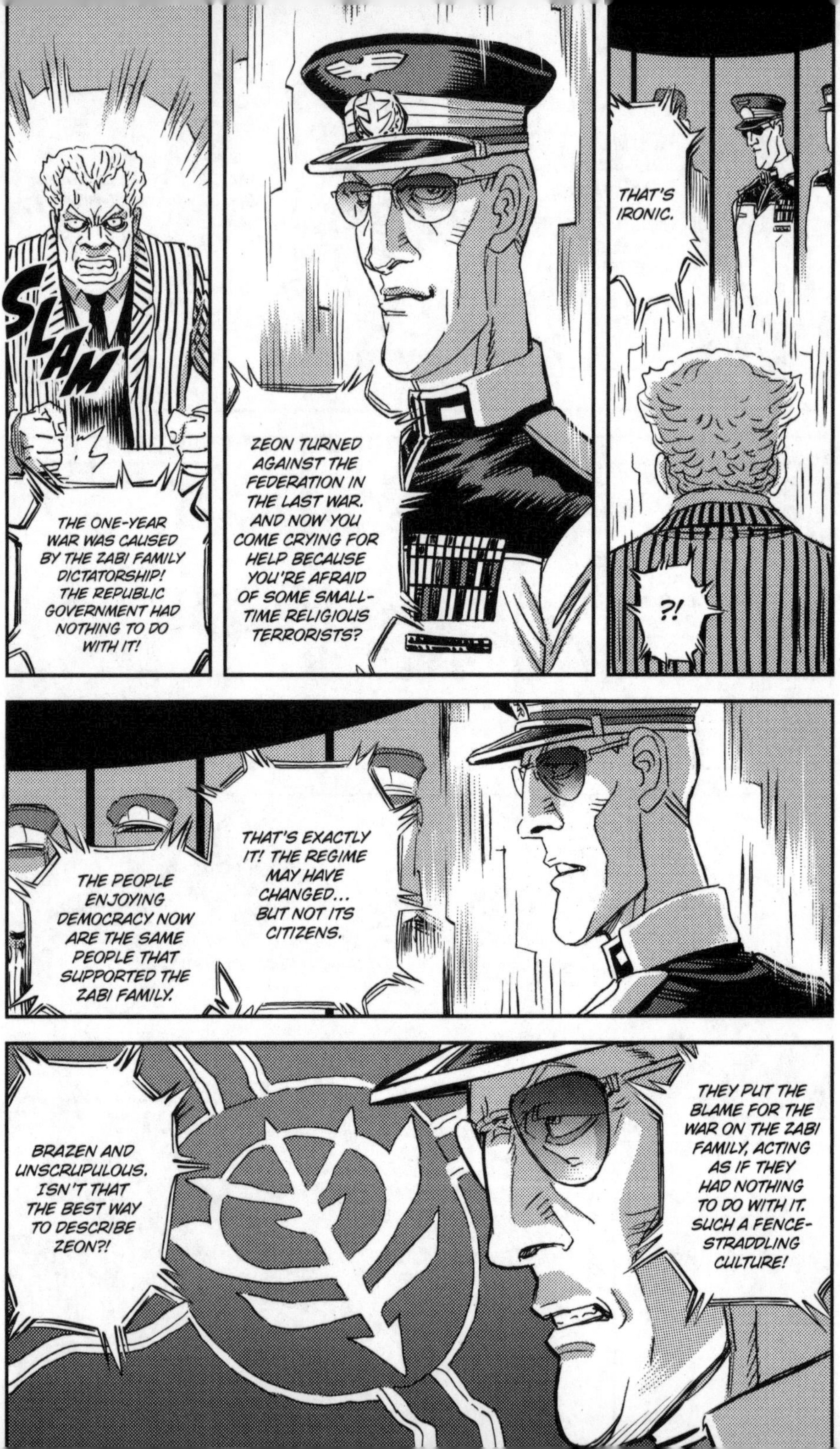
THAT'S IRONIC.
?!
ZEON TURNED AGAINST THE FEDERATION IN THE LAST WAR. AND NOW YOU COME CRYING FOR HELP BECAUSE YOU'RE AFRAID OF SOME SMALL-TIME RELIGIOUS TERRORISTS?
SLAM
THE ONE-YEAR WAR WAS CAUSED BY THE ZABI FAMILY DICTATORSHIP! THE REPUBLIC GOVERNMENT HAD NOTHING TO DO WITH IT!
THAT'S EXACTLY IT! THE REGIME MAY HAVE CHANGED... BUT NOT ITS CITIZENS.
THE PEOPLE ENJOYING DEMOCRACY NOW ARE THE SAME PEOPLE THAT SUPPORTED THE ZABI FAMILY.
THEY PUT THE BLAME FOR THE WAR ON THE ZABI FAMILY, ACTING AS IF THEY HAD NOTHING TO DO WITH IT. SUCH A FENCE-STRADDLING CULTURE!
BRAZEN AND UNSCRUPULOUS. ISN'T THAT THE BEST WAY TO DESCRIBE ZEON?!

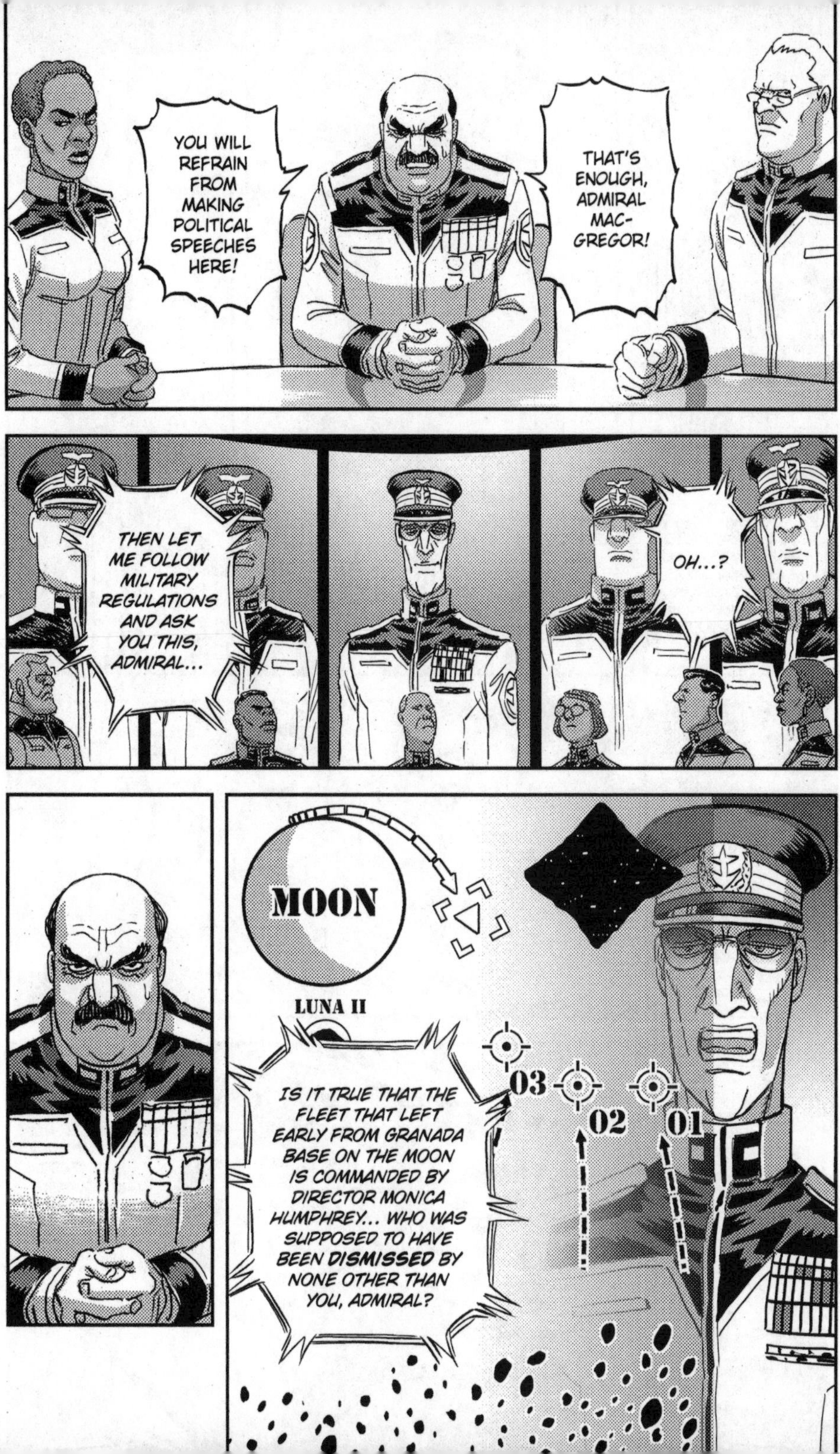
THAT'S ENOUGH, ADMIRAL MAC-GREGOR!
YOU WILL REFRAIN FROM MAKING POLITICAL SPEECHES HERE!
OH...?
THEN LET ME FOLLOW MILITARY REGULATIONS AND ASK YOU THIS, ADMIRAL...
MOON
LUNA II
03
02
01
IS IT TRUE THAT THE FLEET THAT LEFT EARLY FROM GRANADA BASE ON THE MOON IS COMMANDED BY DIRECTOR MONICA HUMPHREY... WHO WAS SUPPOSED TO HAVE BEEN **DISMISSED** BY NONE OTHER THAN YOU, ADMIRAL?

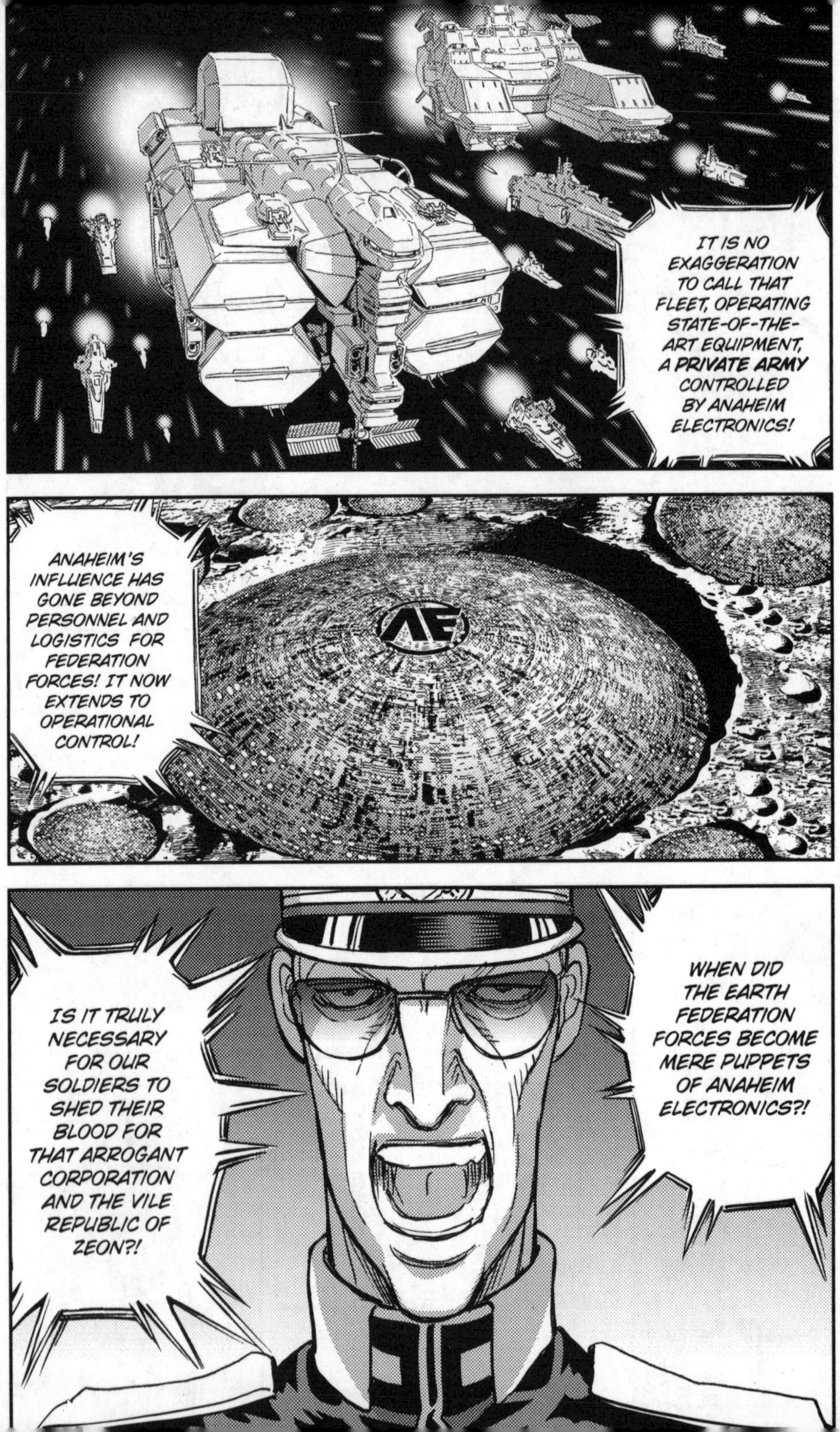
IT IS NO EXAGGERATION TO CALL THAT FLEET, OPERATING STATE-OF-THE-ART EQUIPMENT, **A PRIVATE ARMY** CONTROLLED BY ANAHEIM ELECTRONICS!
ANAHEIM'S INFLUENCE HAS GONE BEYOND PERSONNEL AND LOGISTICS FOR FEDERATION FORCES! IT NOW EXTENDS TO OPERATIONAL CONTROL!
WHEN DID THE EARTH FEDERATION FORCES BECOME MERE PUPPETS OF ANAHEIM ELECTRONICS?!
IS IT TRULY NECESSARY FOR OUR SOLDIERS TO SHED THEIR BLOOD FOR THAT ARROGANT CORPORATION AND THE VILE REPUBLIC OF ZEON?!

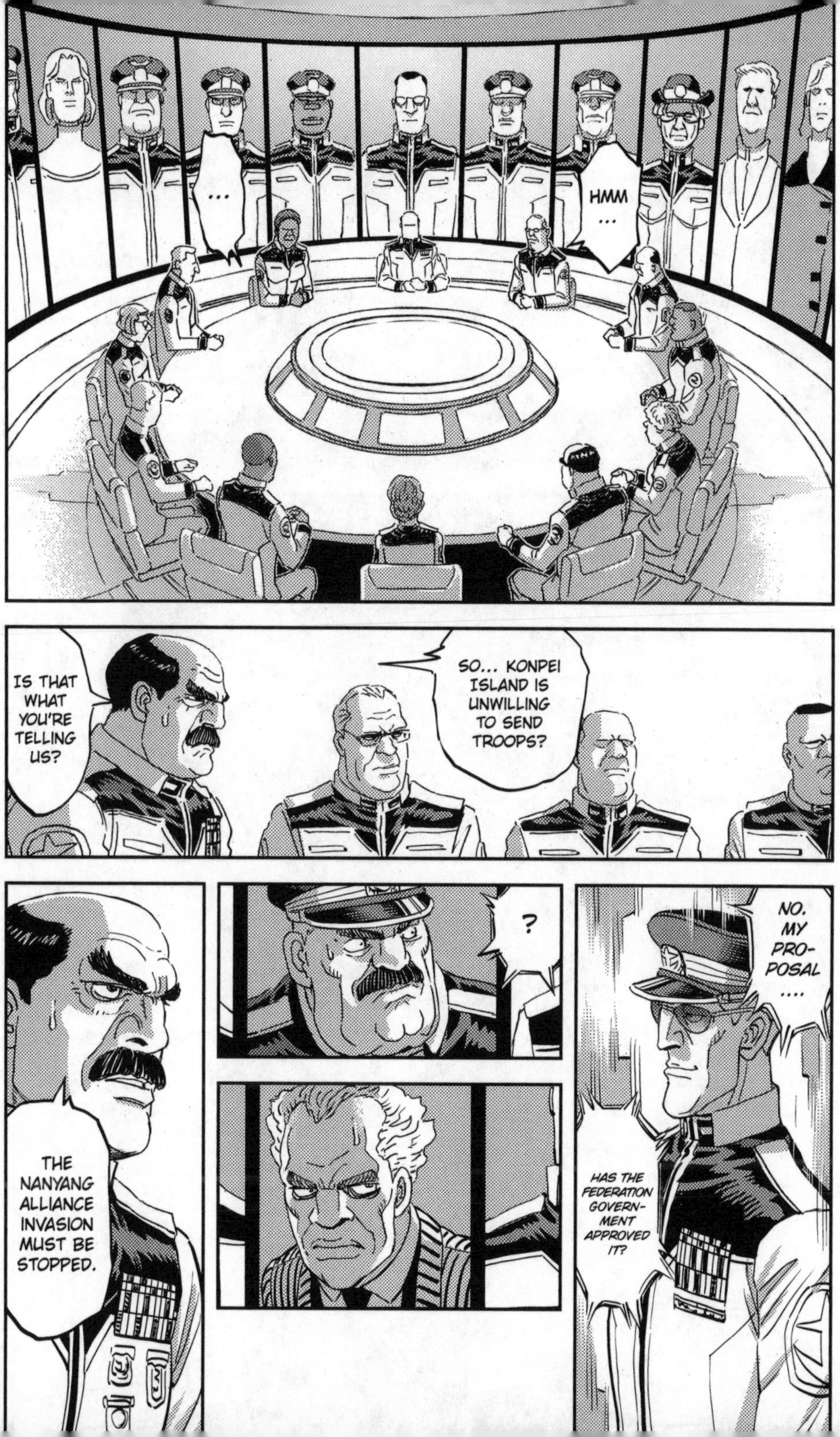
HMM ...
...
SO... KONPEI ISLAND IS UNWILLING TO SEND TROOPS?
IS THAT WHAT YOU'RE TELLING US?
NO. MY PRO-POSAL ....
HAS THE FEDERATION GOVERN-MENT APPROVED IT?
?
THE NANYANG ALLIANCE INVASION MUST BE STOPPED.

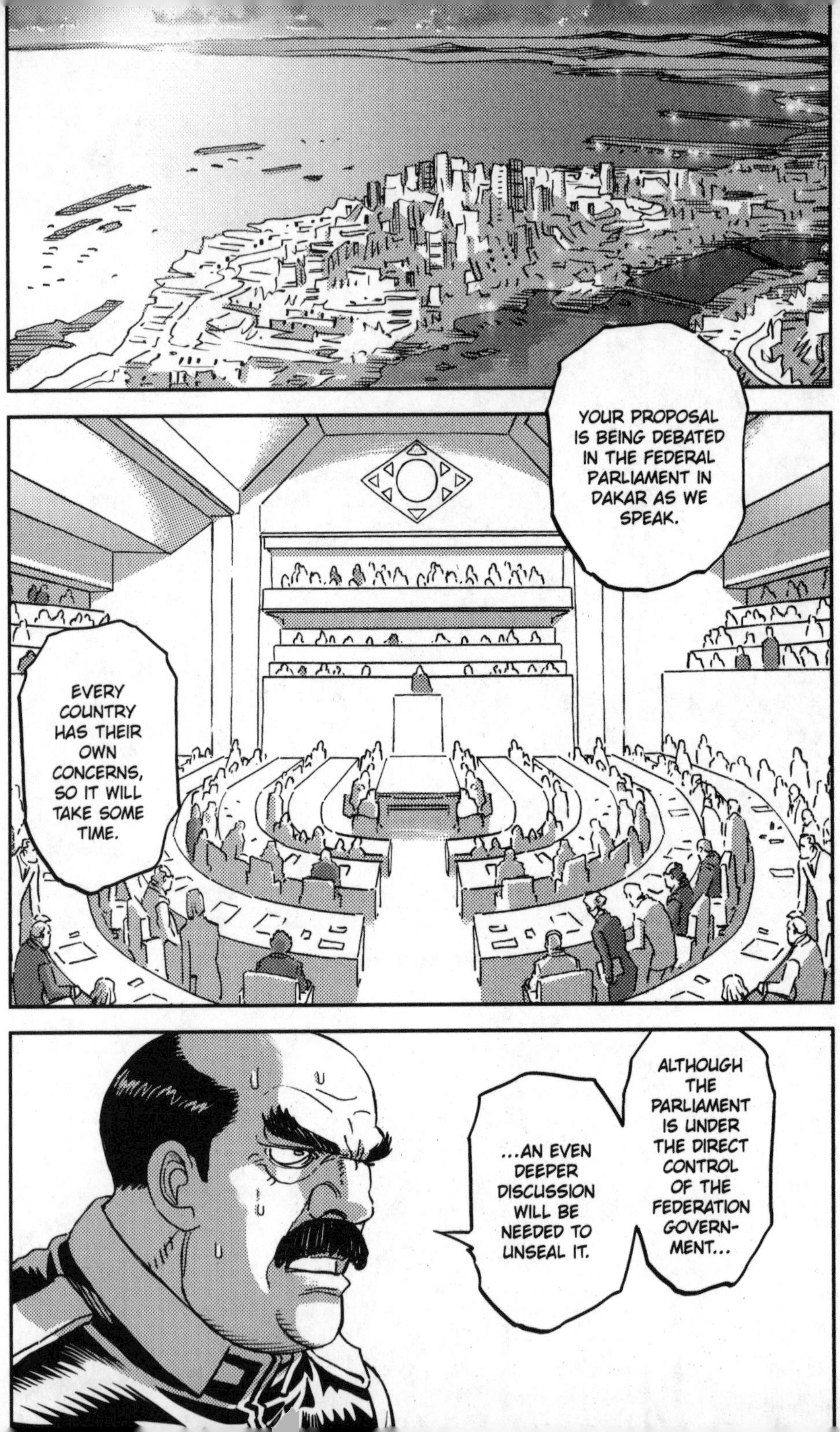
YOUR PROPOSAL IS BEING DEBATED IN THE FEDERAL PARLIAMENT IN DAKAR AS WE SPEAK.
EVERY COUNTRY HAS THEIR OWN CONCERNS, SO IT WILL TAKE SOME TIME.
ALTHOUGH THE PARLIAMENT IS UNDER THE DIRECT CONTROL OF THE FEDERATION GOVERN-MENT...
...AN EVEN DEEPER DISCUSSION WILL BE NEEDED TO UNSEAL IT.

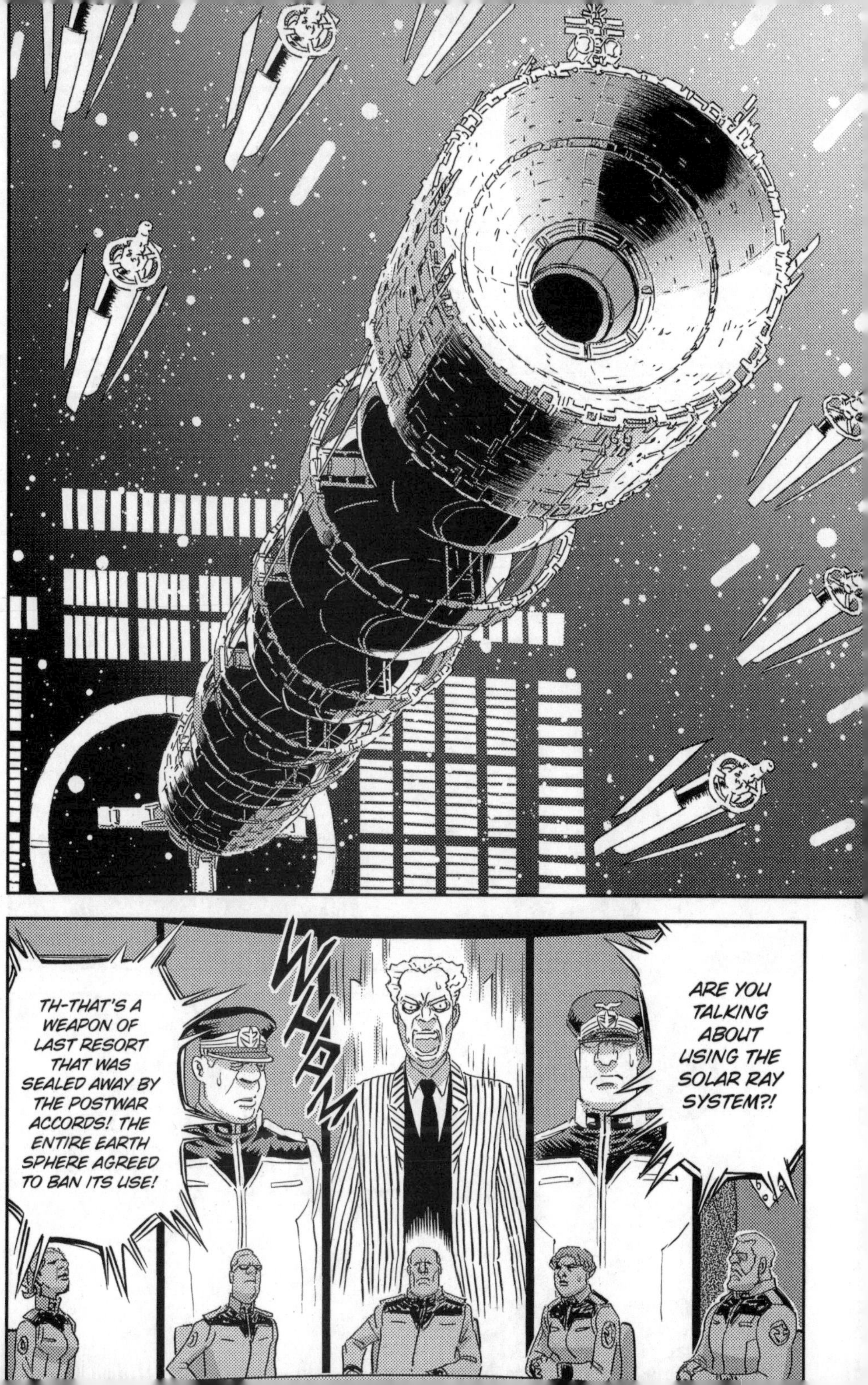
ARE YOU TALKING ABOUT USING THE SOLAR RAY SYSTEM?!
WHAM
TH-THAT'S A WEAPON OF LAST RESORT THAT WAS SEALED AWAY BY THE POSTWAR ACCORDS! THE ENTIRE EARTH SPHERE AGREED TO BAN ITS USE!

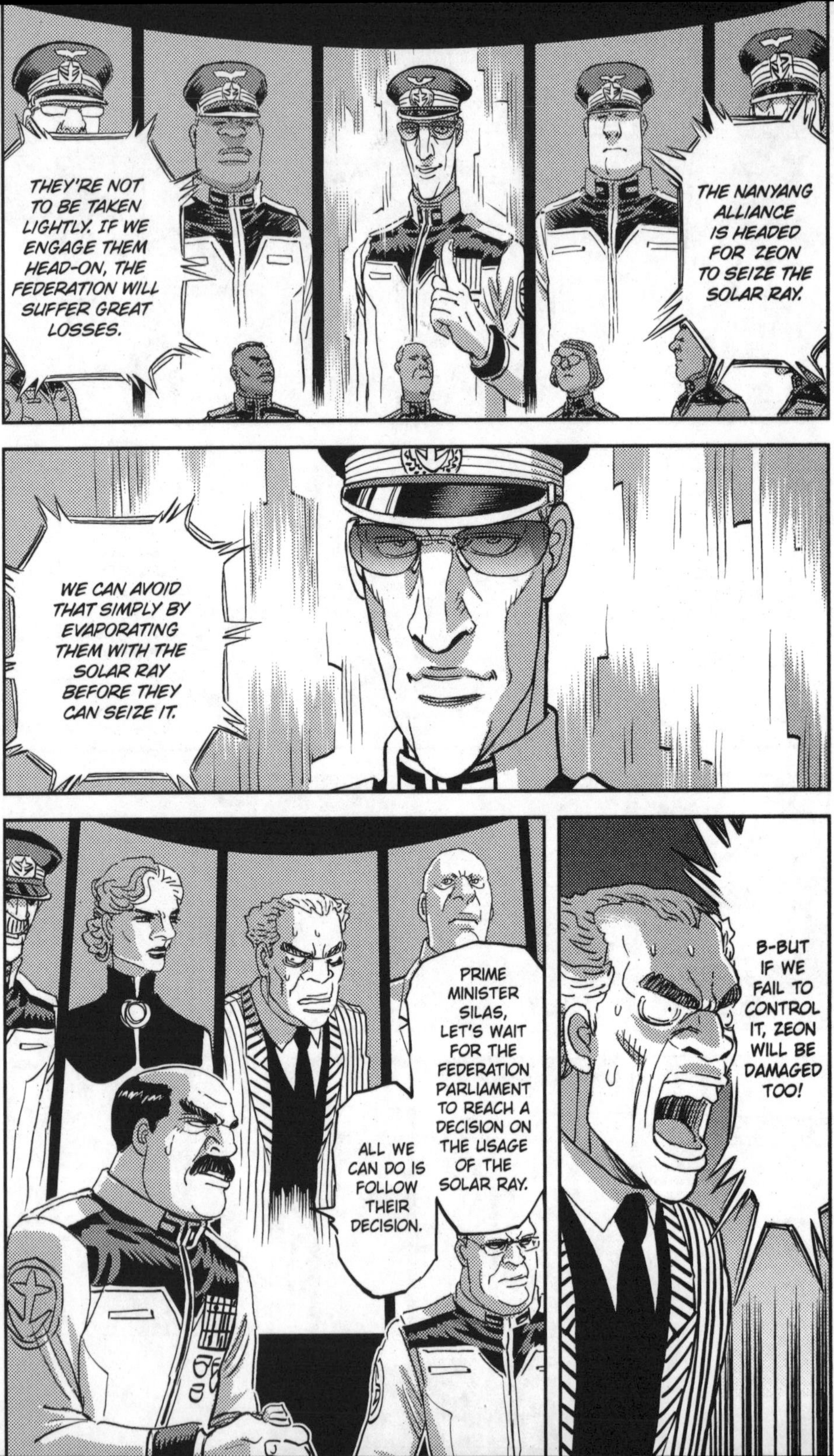
THE NANYANG ALLIANCE IS HEADED FOR ZEON TO SEIZE THE SOLAR RAY.
THEY'RE NOT TO BE TAKEN LIGHTLY. IF WE ENGAGE THEM HEAD-ON, THE FEDERATION WILL SUFFER GREAT LOSSES.
WE CAN AVOID THAT SIMPLY BY EVAPORATING THEM WITH THE SOLAR RAY BEFORE THEY CAN SEIZE IT.
B-BUT IF WE FAIL TO CONTROL IT, ZEON WILL BE DAMAGED TOO!
PRIME MINISTER SILAS, LET'S WAIT FOR THE FEDERATION PARLIAMENT TO REACH A DECISION ON THE USAGE OF THE SOLAR RAY.
ALL WE CAN DO IS FOLLOW THEIR DECISION.

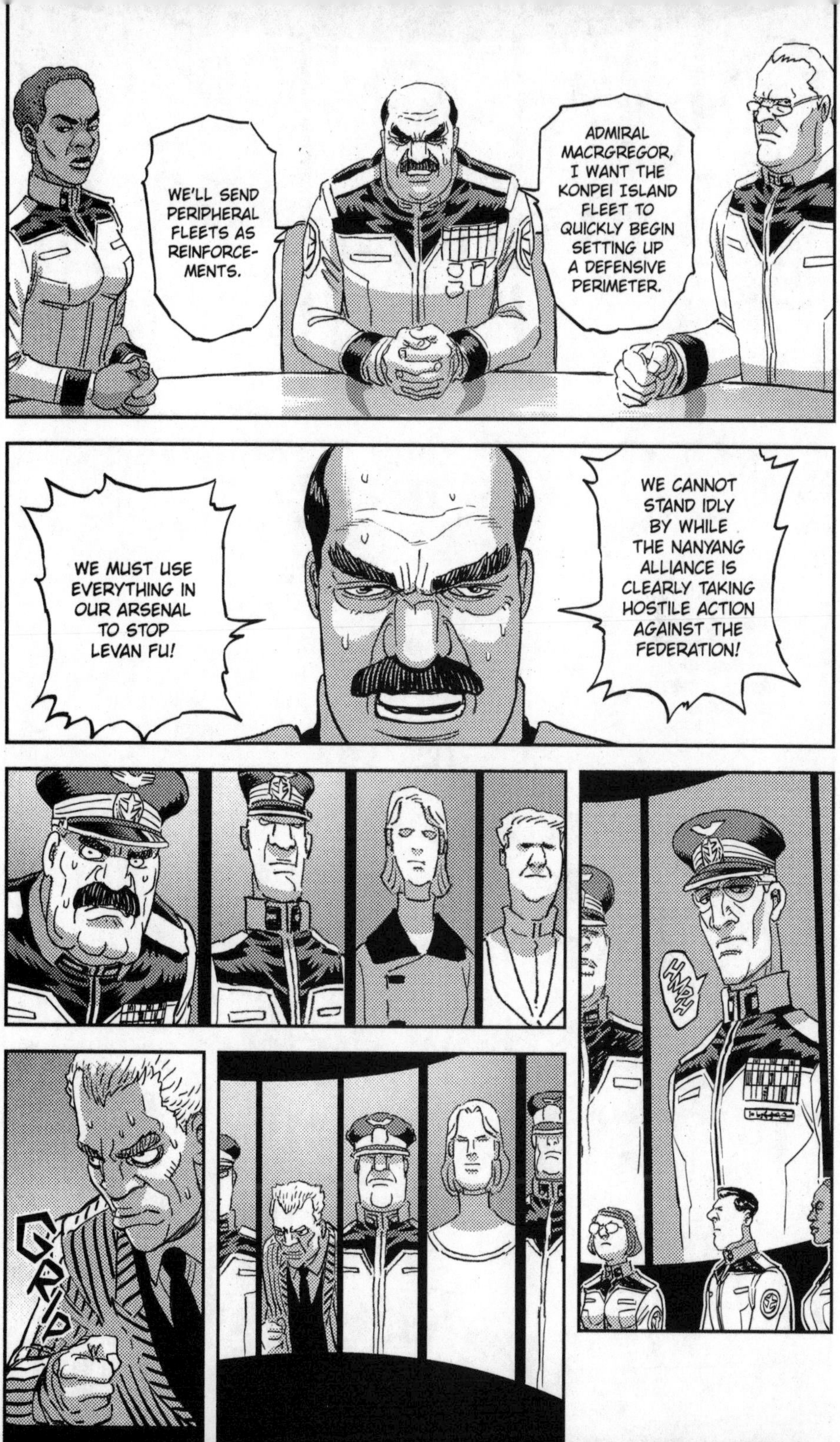
ADMIRAL MACRGREGOR, I WANT THE KONPEI ISLAND FLEET TO QUICKLY BEGIN SETTING UP A DEFENSIVE PERIMETER.
WE'LL SEND PERIPHERAL FLEETS AS REINFORCE-MENTS.
WE CANNOT STAND IDLY BY WHILE THE NANYANG ALLIANCE IS CLEARLY TAKING HOSTILE ACTION AGAINST THE FEDERATION!
WE MUST USE EVERYTHING IN OUR ARSENAL TO STOP LEVAN FU!
HMPH
GRIP

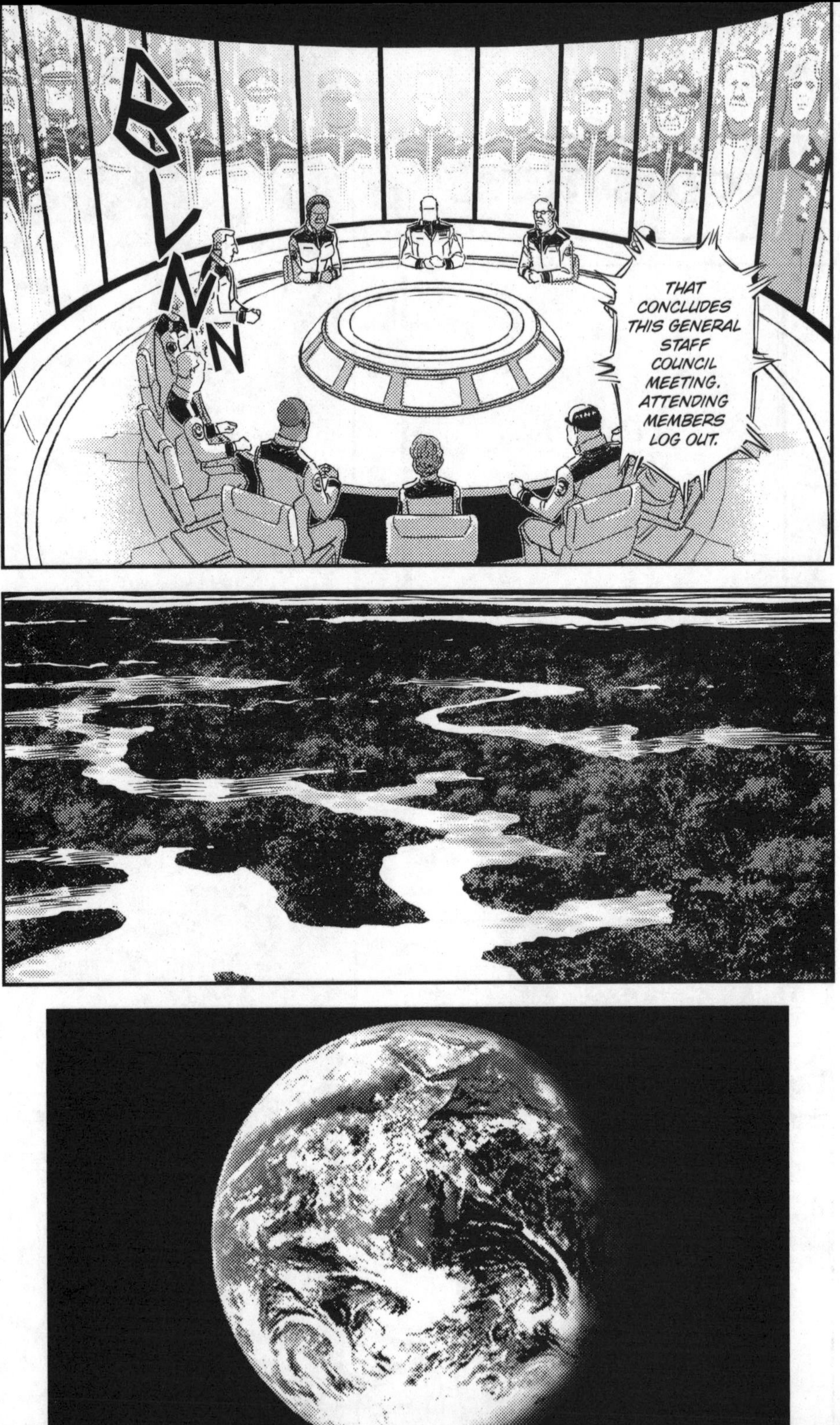
THAT CONCLUDES THIS GENERAL STAFF COUNCIL MEETING. ATTENDING MEMBERS LOG OUT.
BLNNN

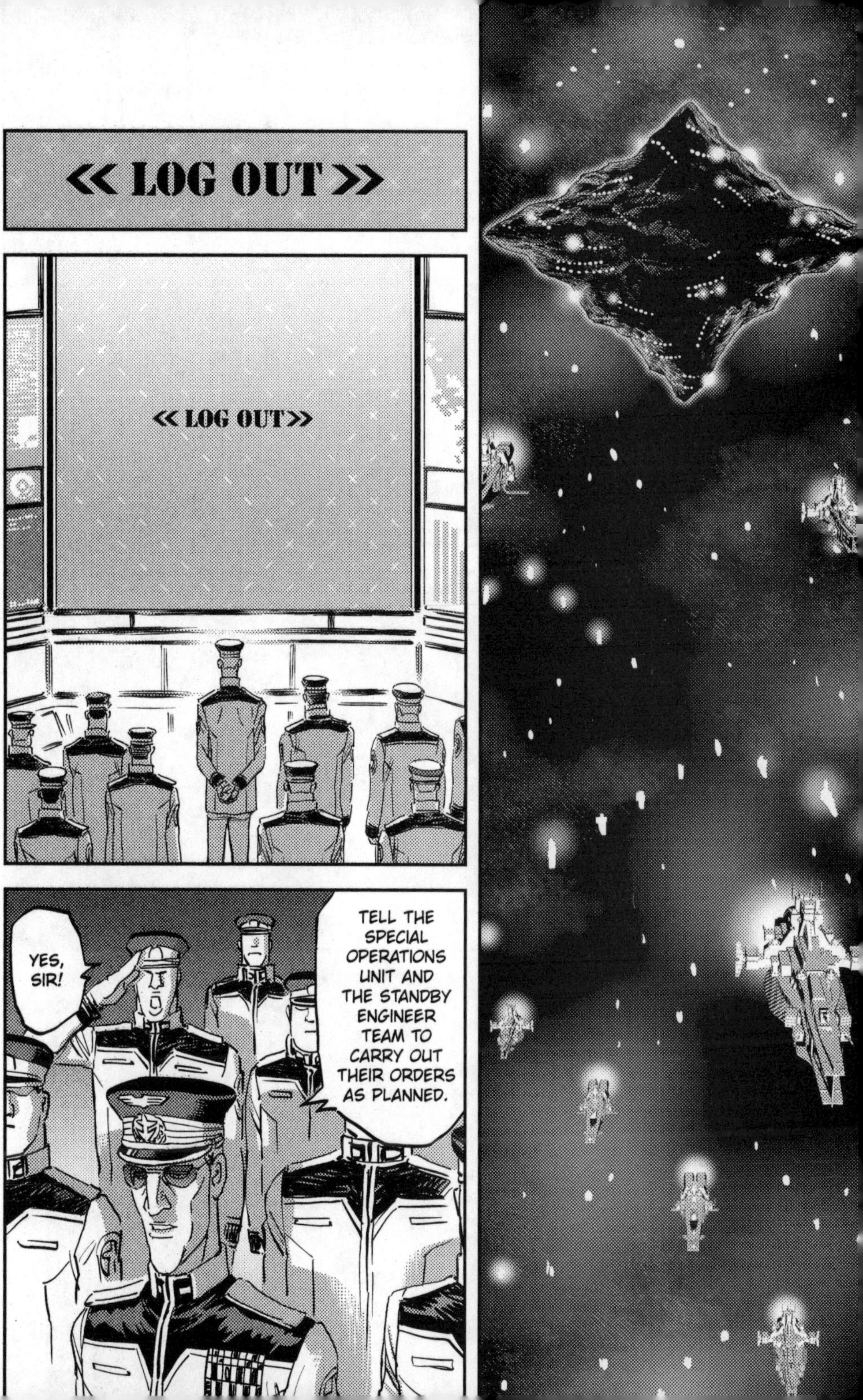
«LOG OUT»
«LOG OUT»
TELL THE SPECIAL OPERATIONS UNIT AND THE STANDBY ENGINEER TEAM TO CARRY OUT THEIR ORDERS AS PLANNED.
YES, SIR!

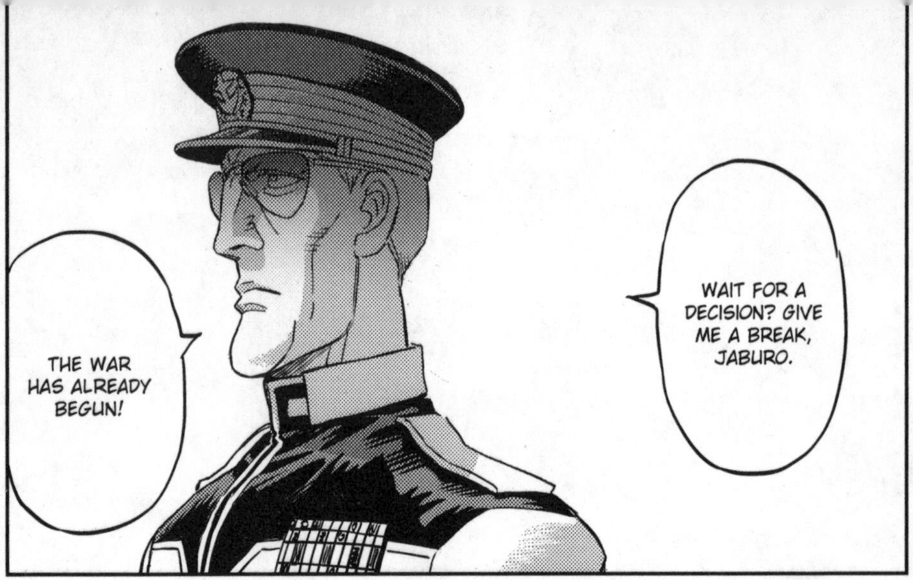
WAIT FOR A DECISION? GIVE ME A BREAK, JABURO.
THE WAR HAS ALREADY BEGUN!

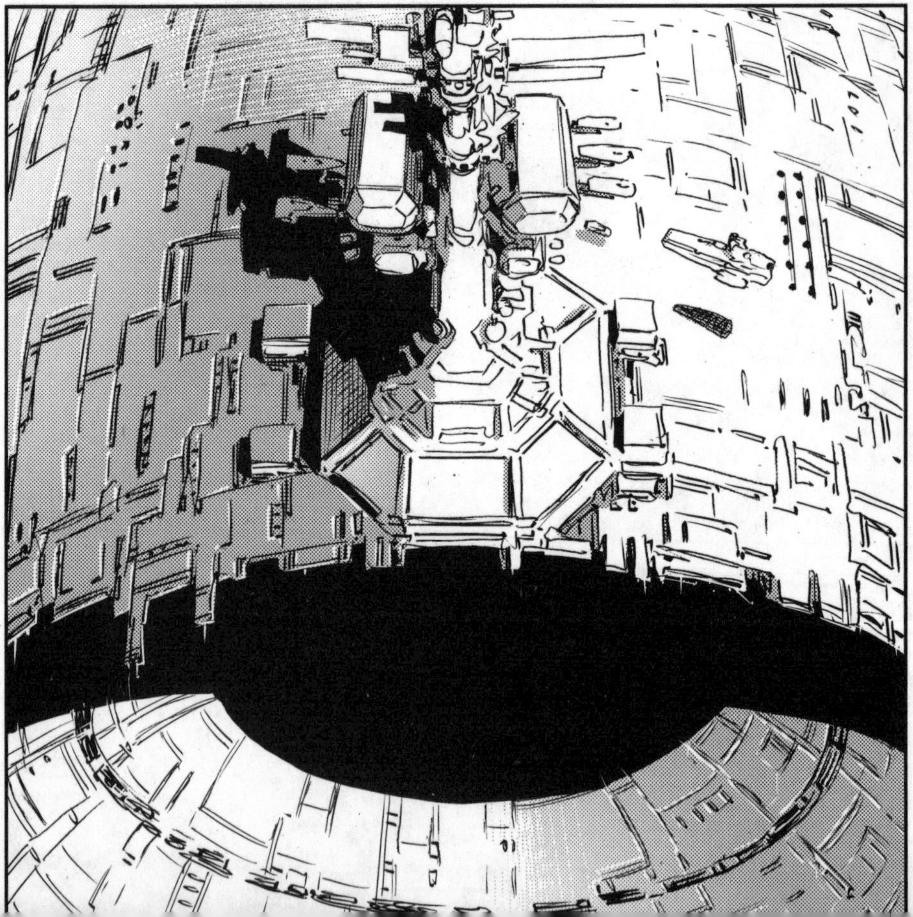

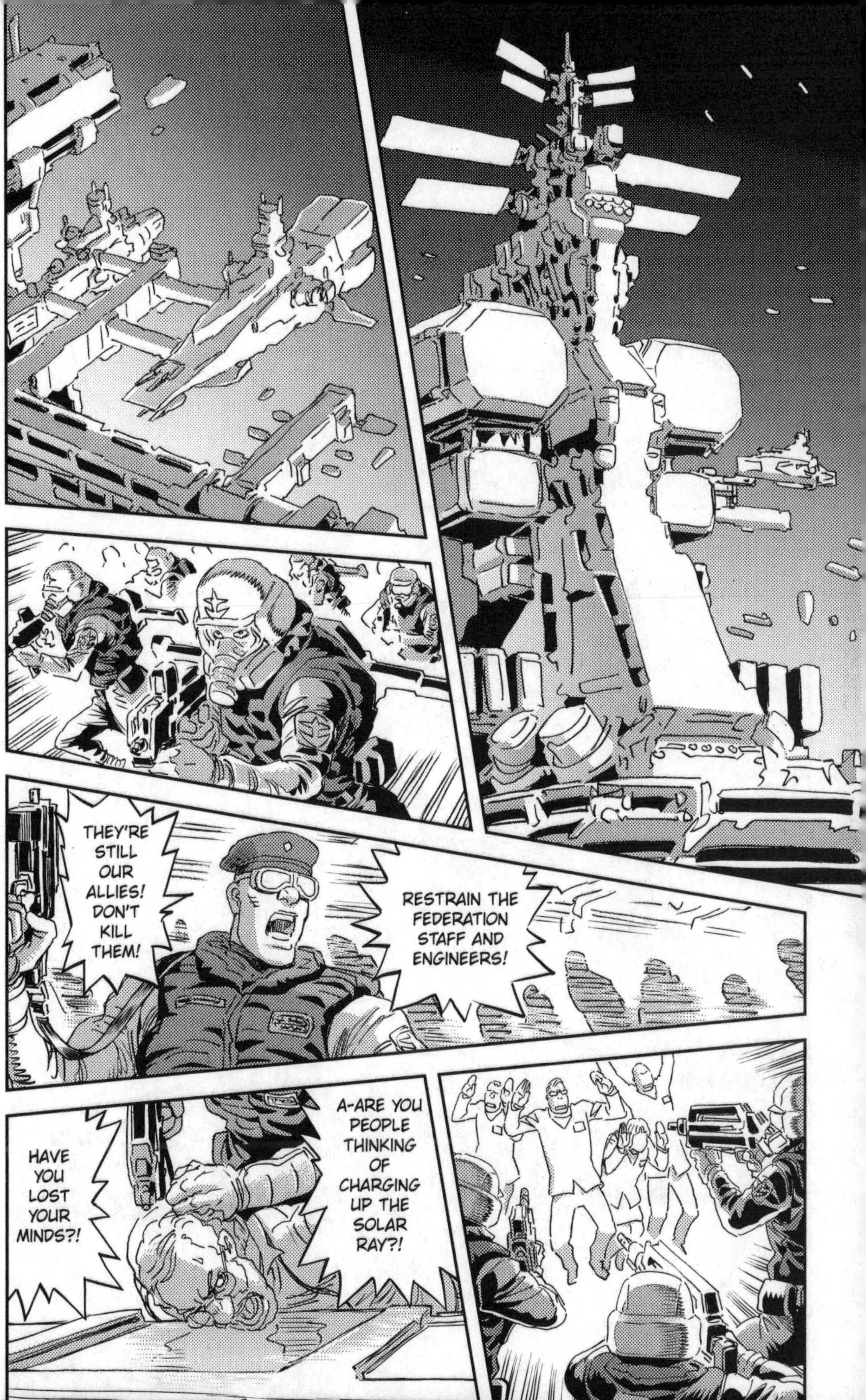
RESTRAIN THE FEDERATION STAFF AND ENGINEERS!
THEY'RE STILL OUR ALLIES! DON'T KILL THEM!
A-ARE YOU PEOPLE THINKING OF CHARGING UP THE SOLAR RAY?!
HAVE YOU LOST YOUR MINDS?!

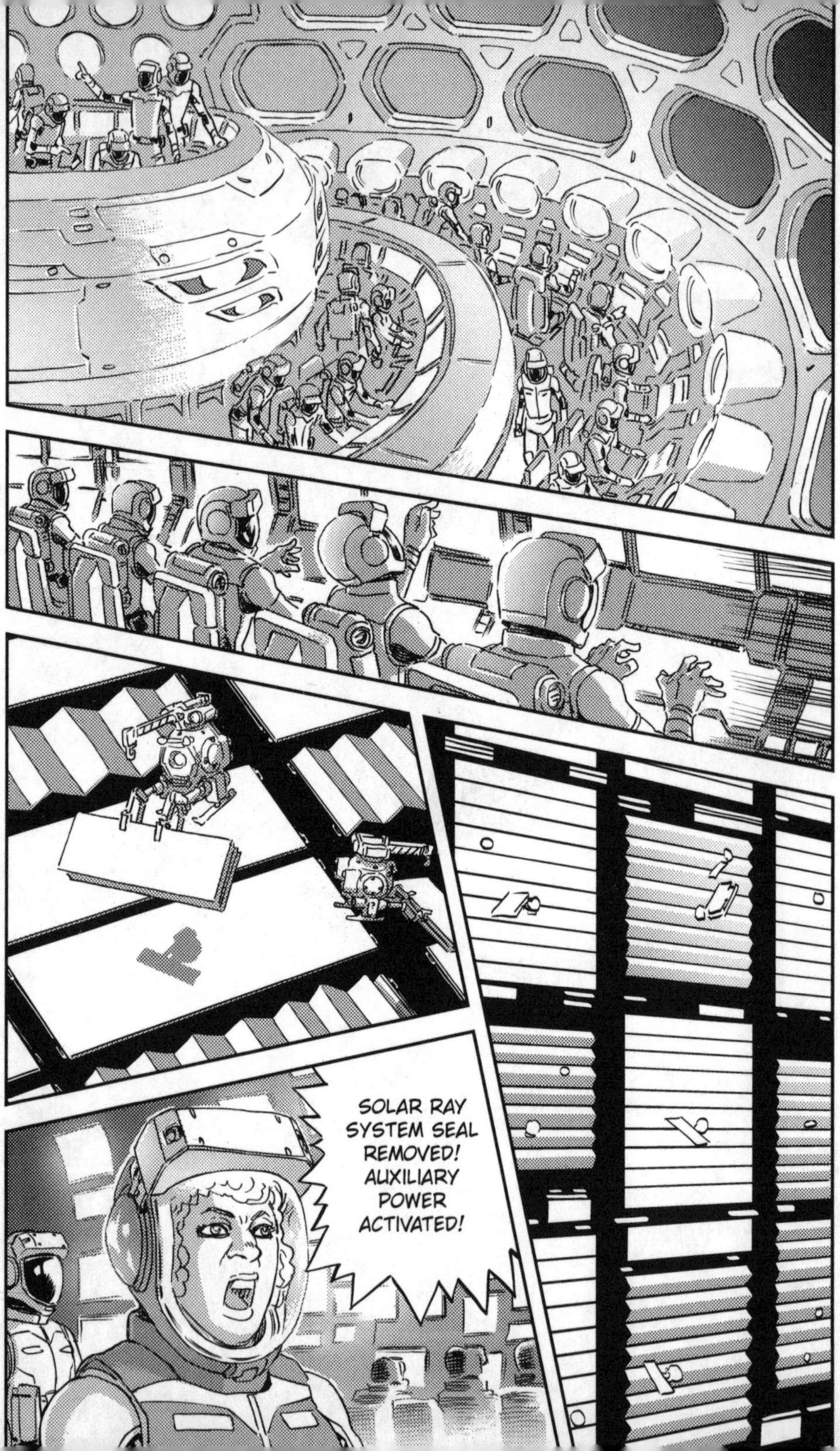
SOLAR RAY SYSTEM SEAL REMOVED! AUXILIARY POWER ACTIVATED!

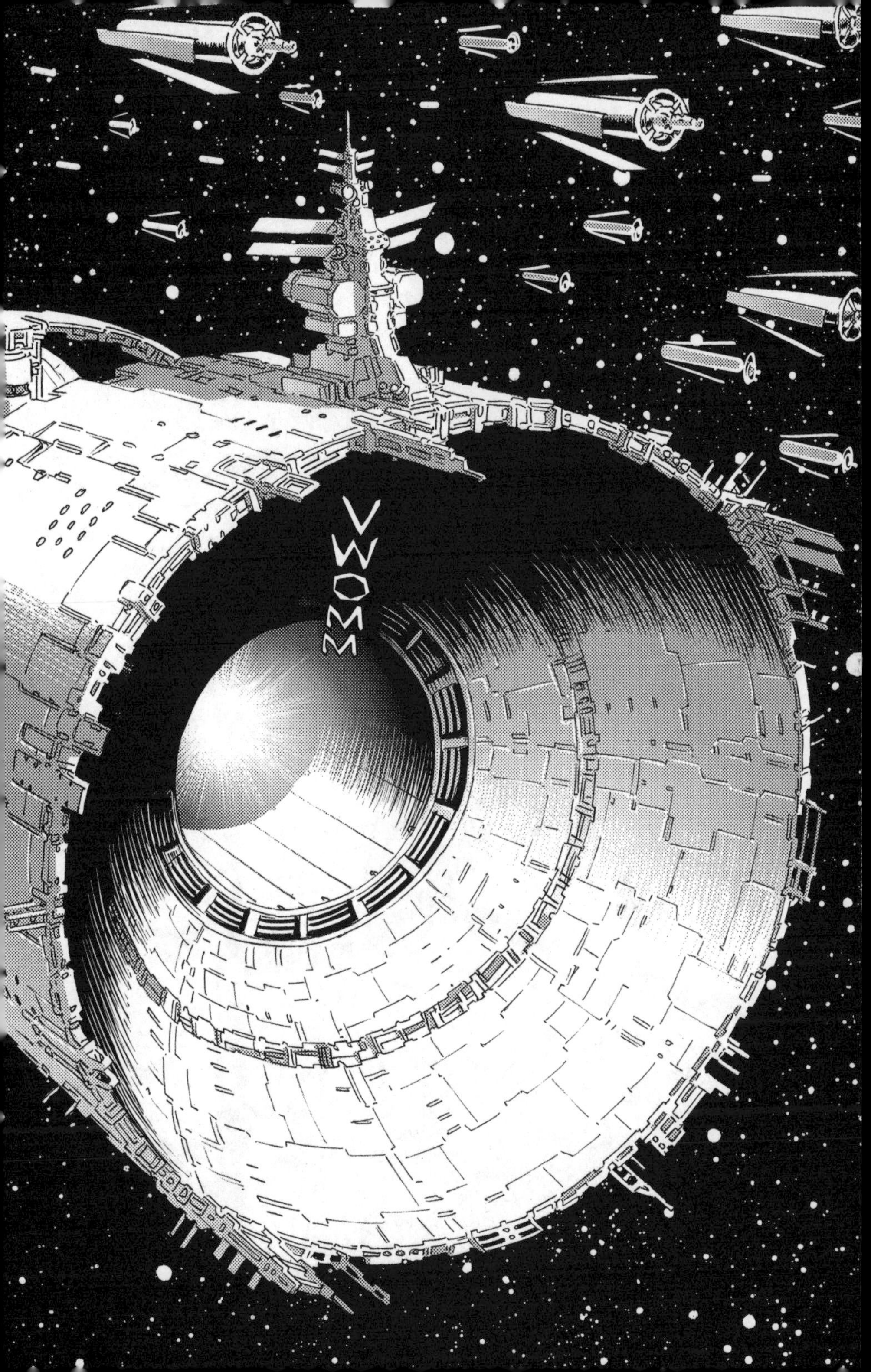
VWOMM

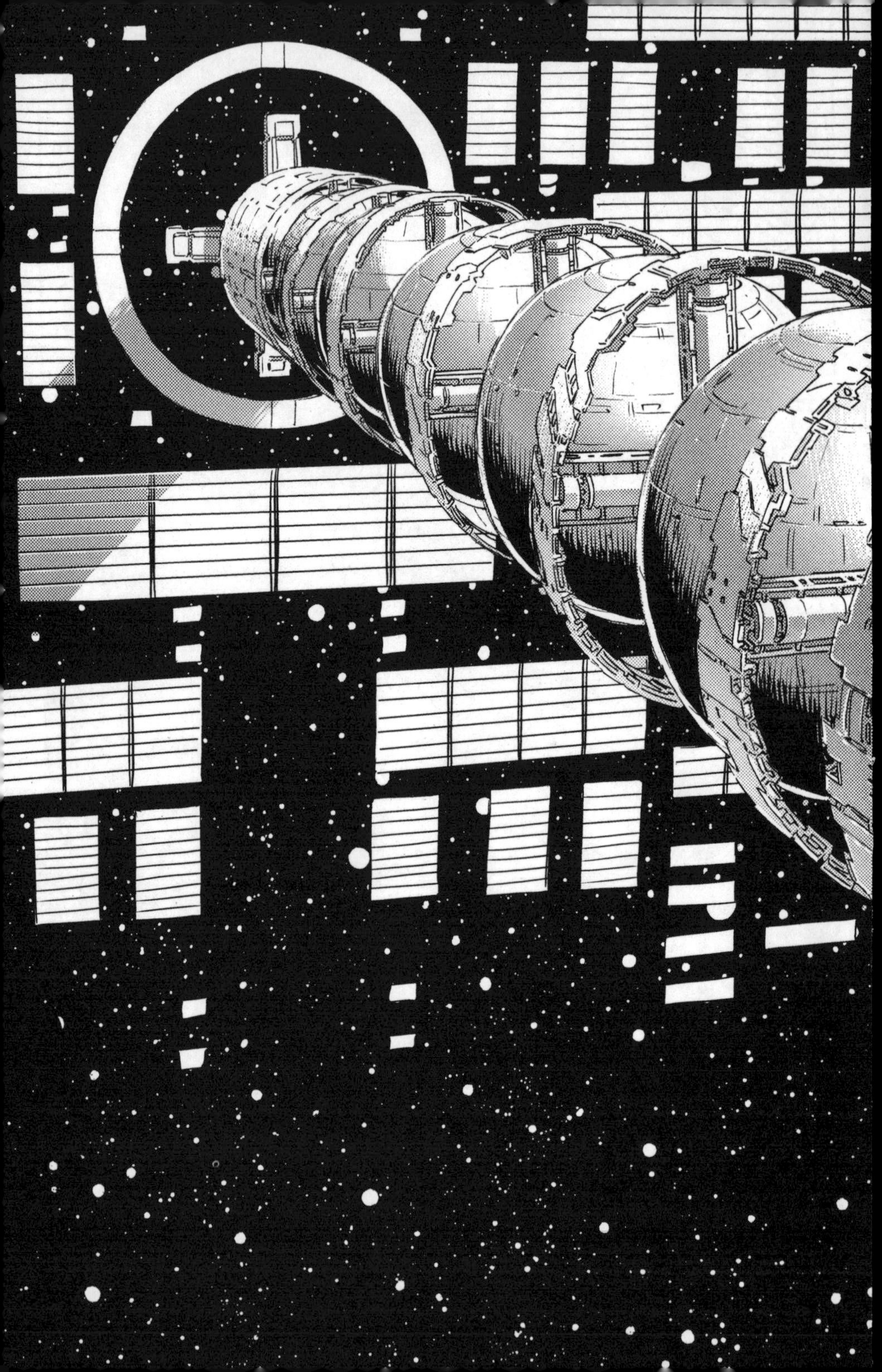

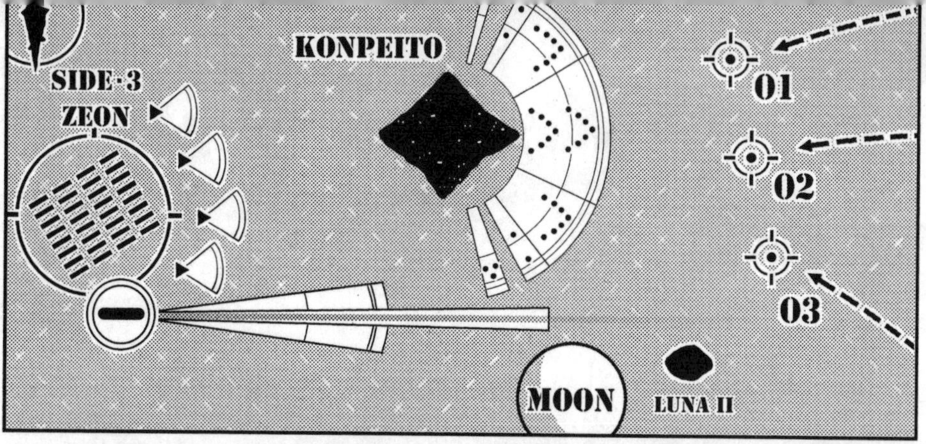
01
02
03
KONPEITO
SIDE-3
ZEON
LUNA II
MOON

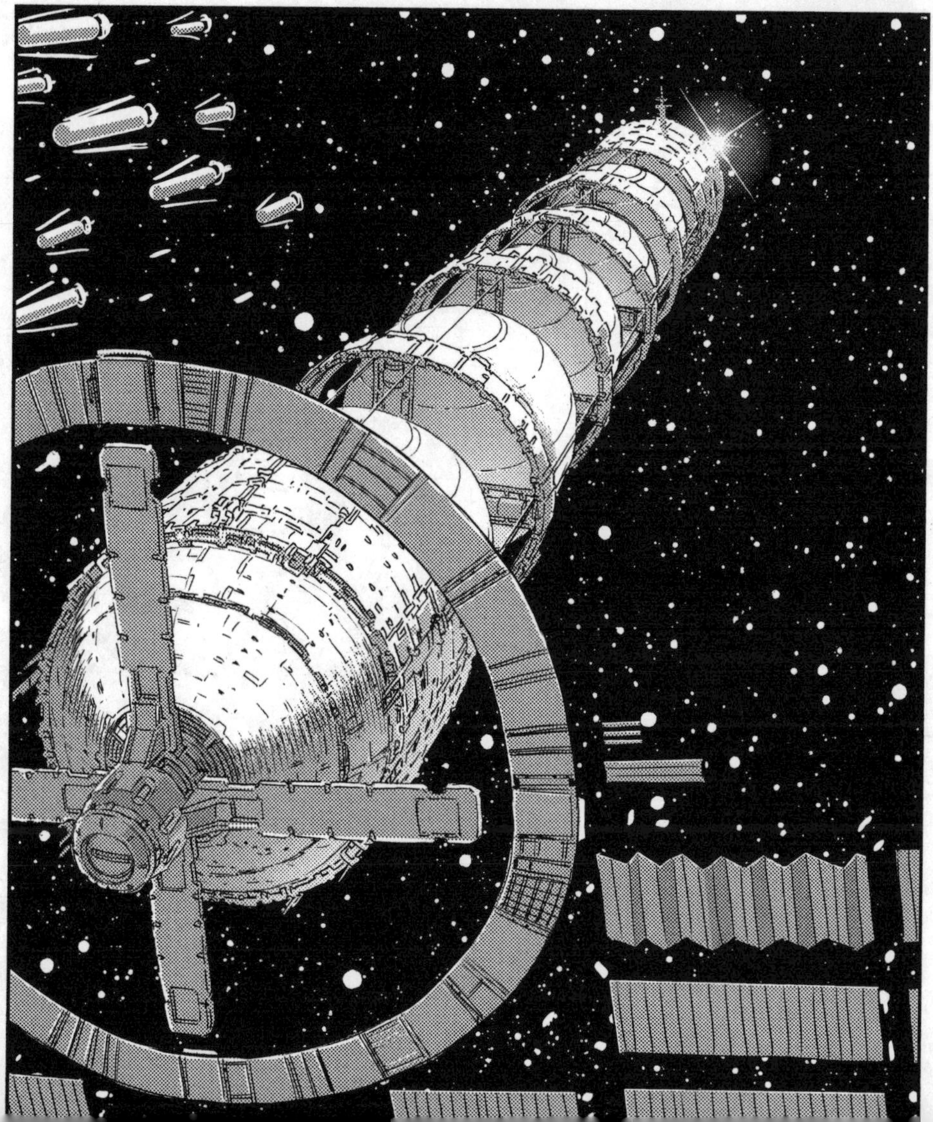

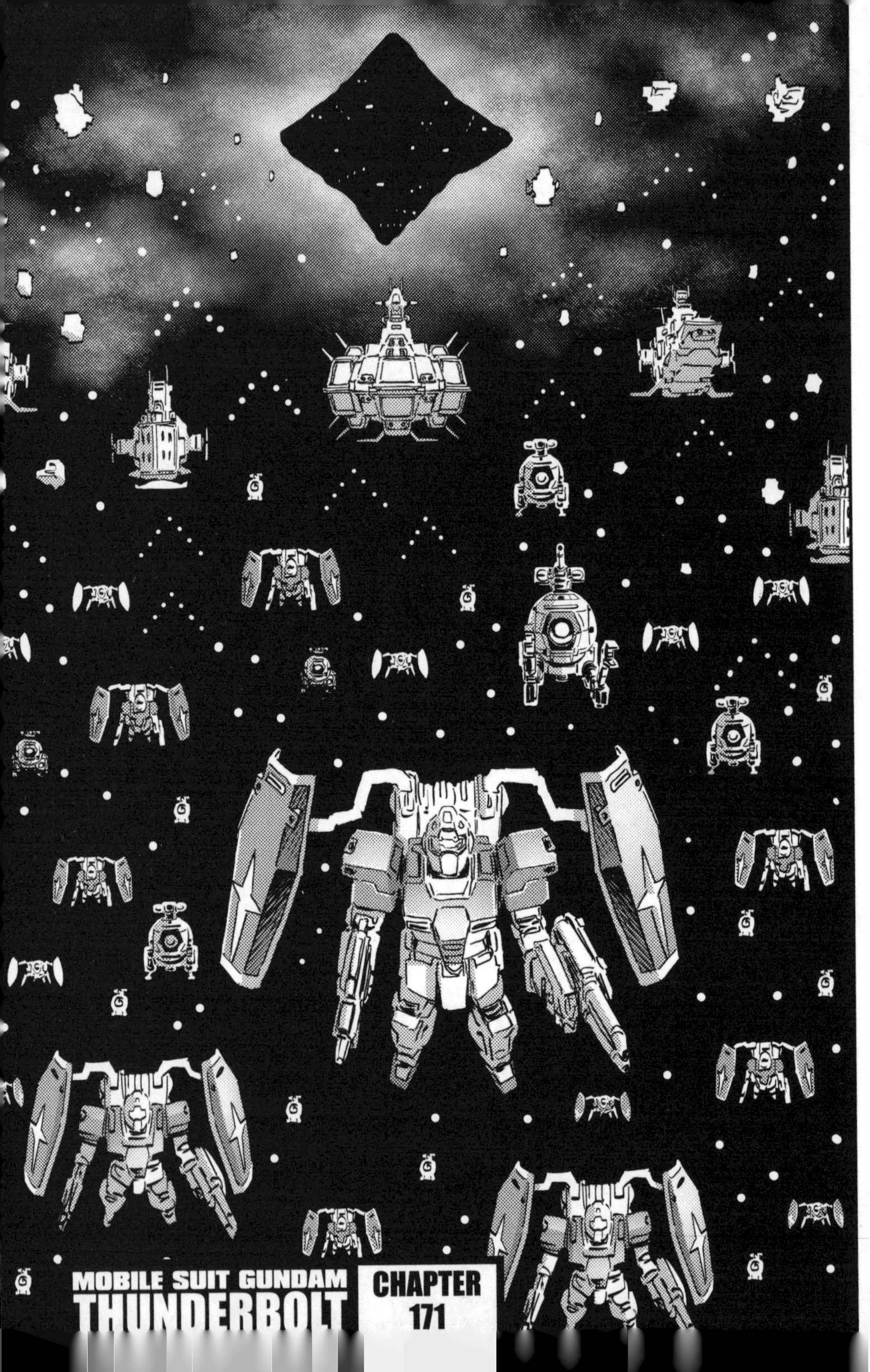
MOBILE SUIT GUNDAM
THUNDERBOLT
CHAPTER
171

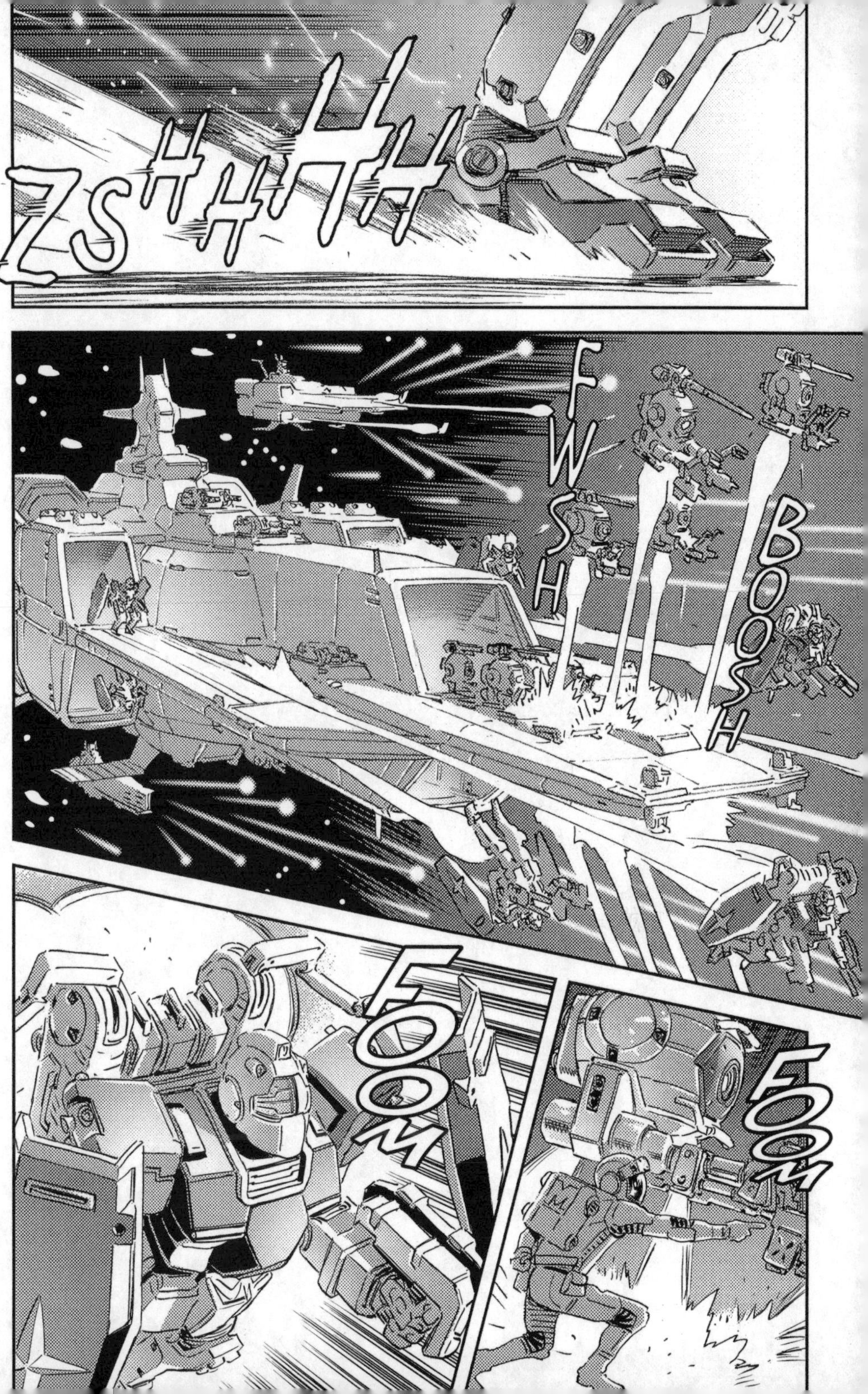
ZSHHHHH
BOOOSH
FWSH
FOOM
FOOM

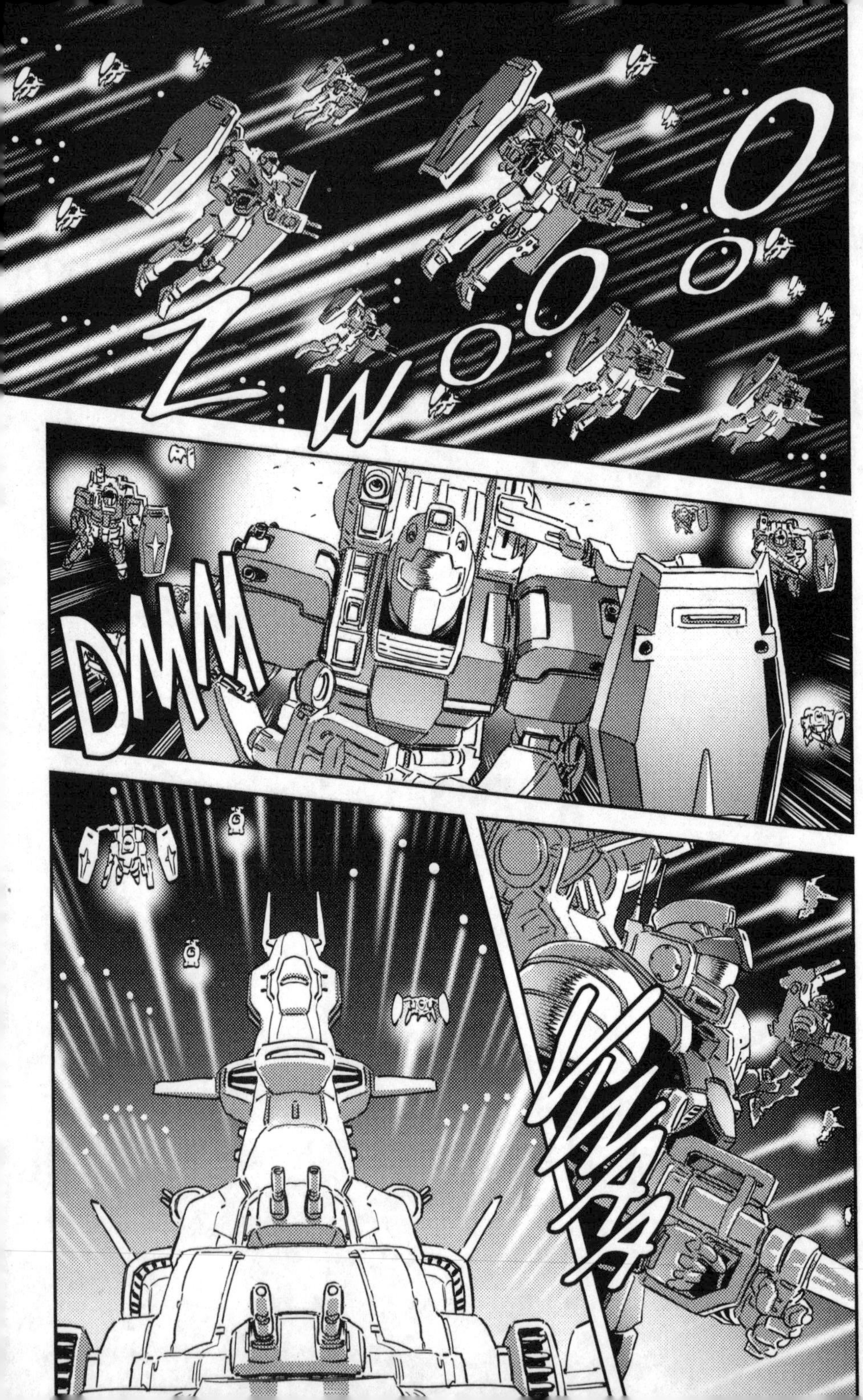
ZWOOOOO
DMM
VWAA

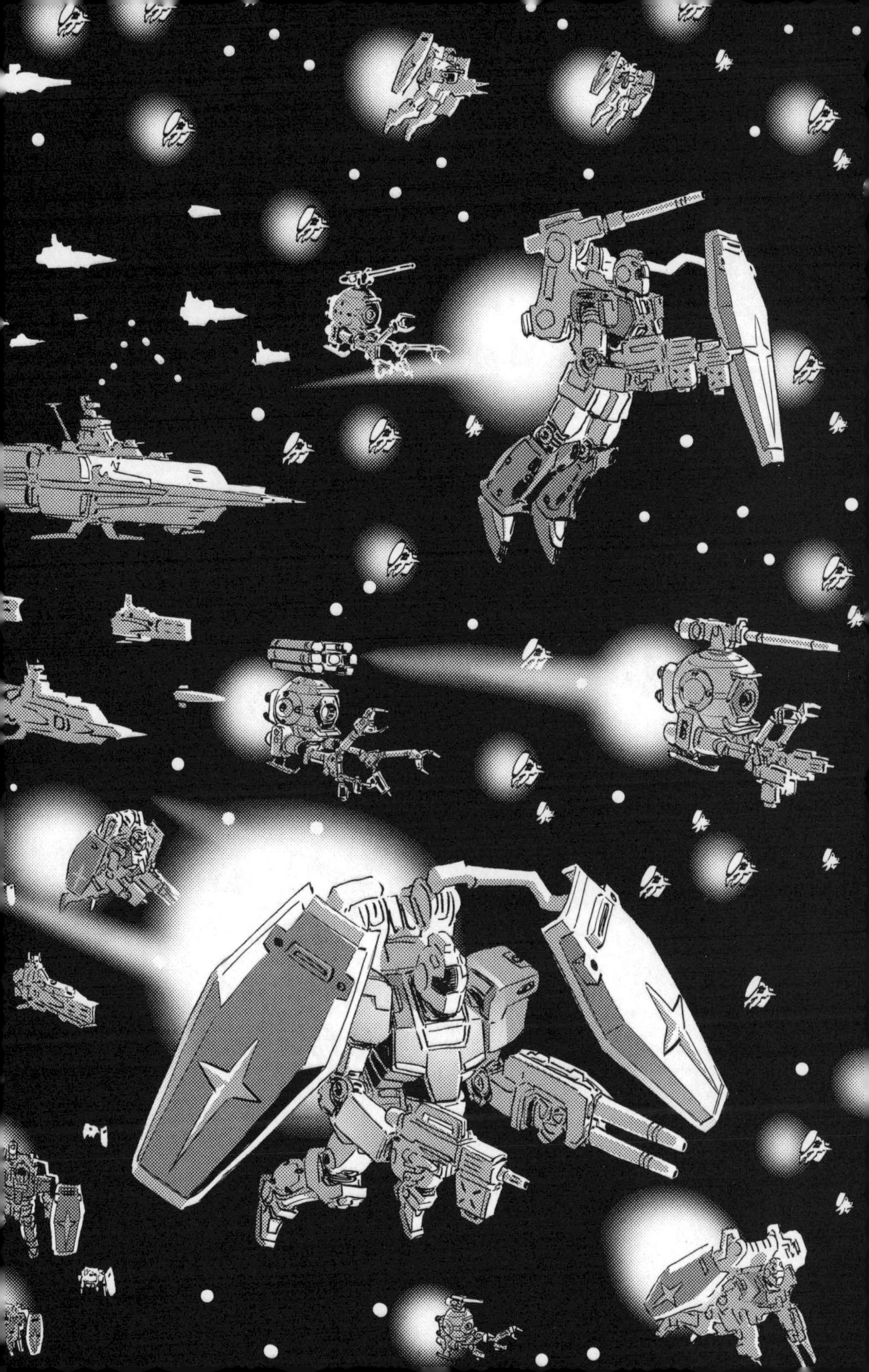

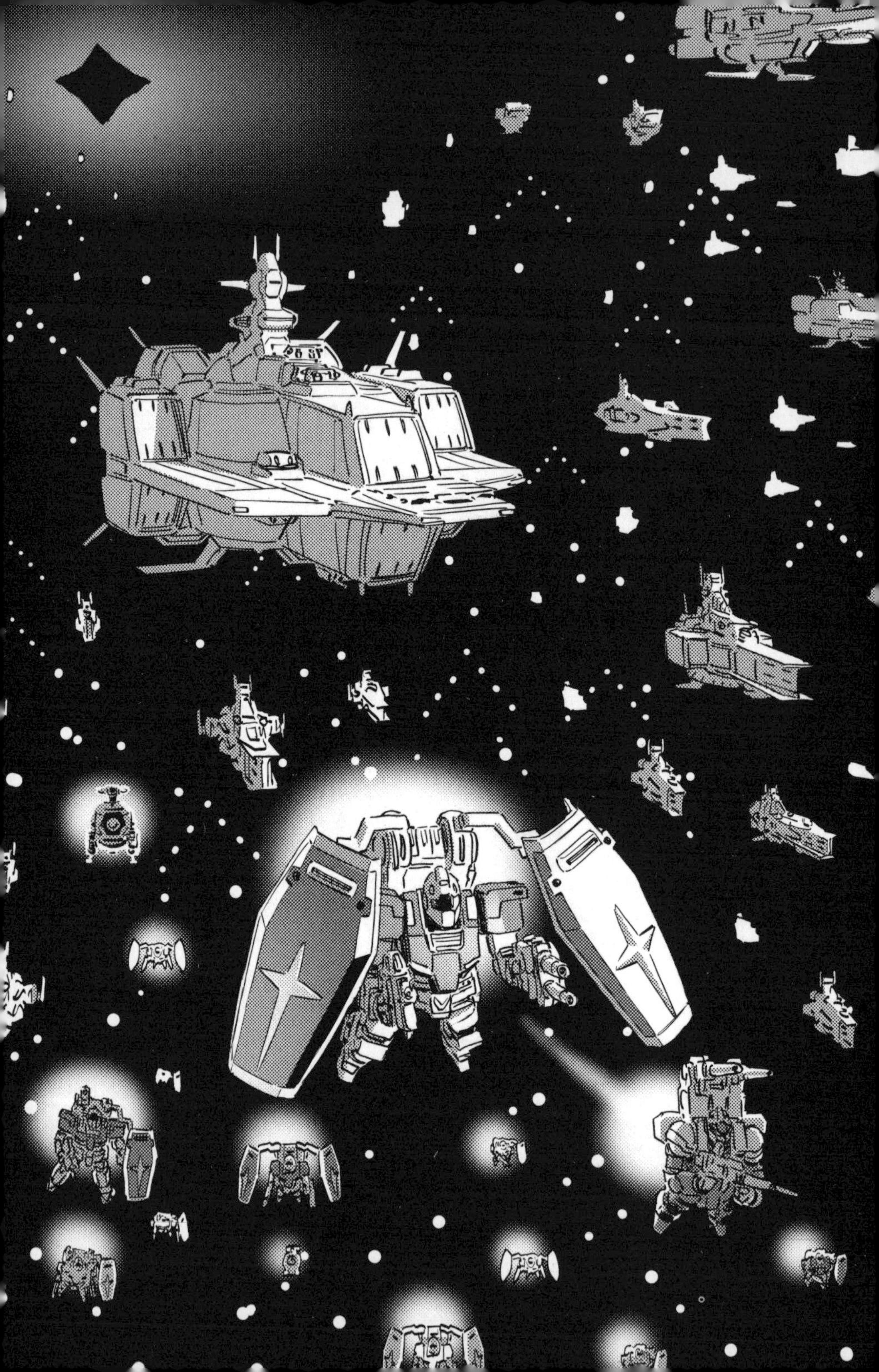

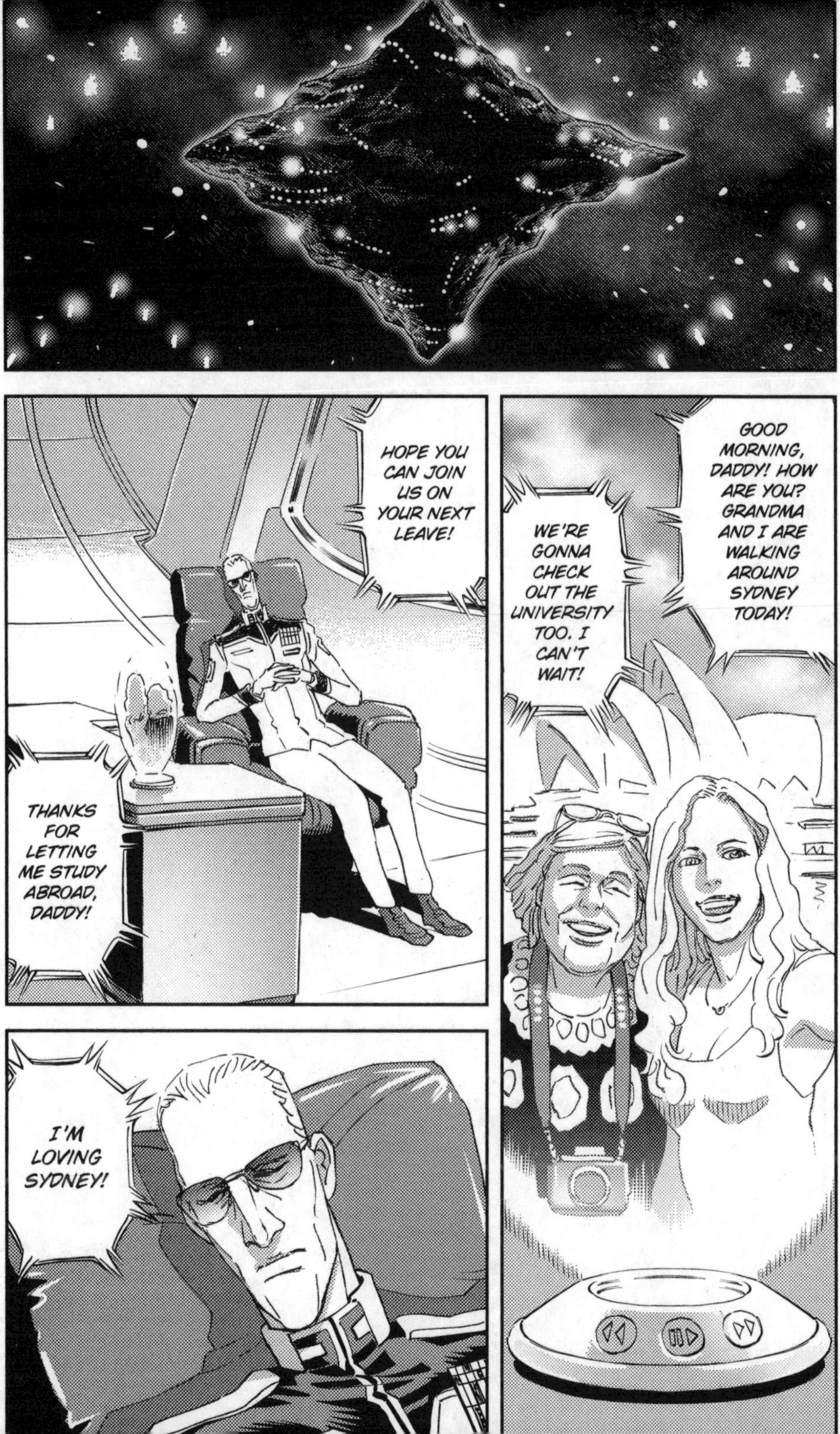
GOOD MORNING, DADDY! HOW ARE YOU? GRANDMA AND I ARE WALKING AROUND SYDNEY TODAY!
WE'RE GONNA CHECK OUT THE UNIVERSITY TOO. I CAN'T WAIT!
HOPE YOU CAN JOIN US ON YOUR NEXT LEAVE!
THANKS FOR LETTING ME STUDY ABROAD, DADDY!
I'M LOVING SYDNEY!

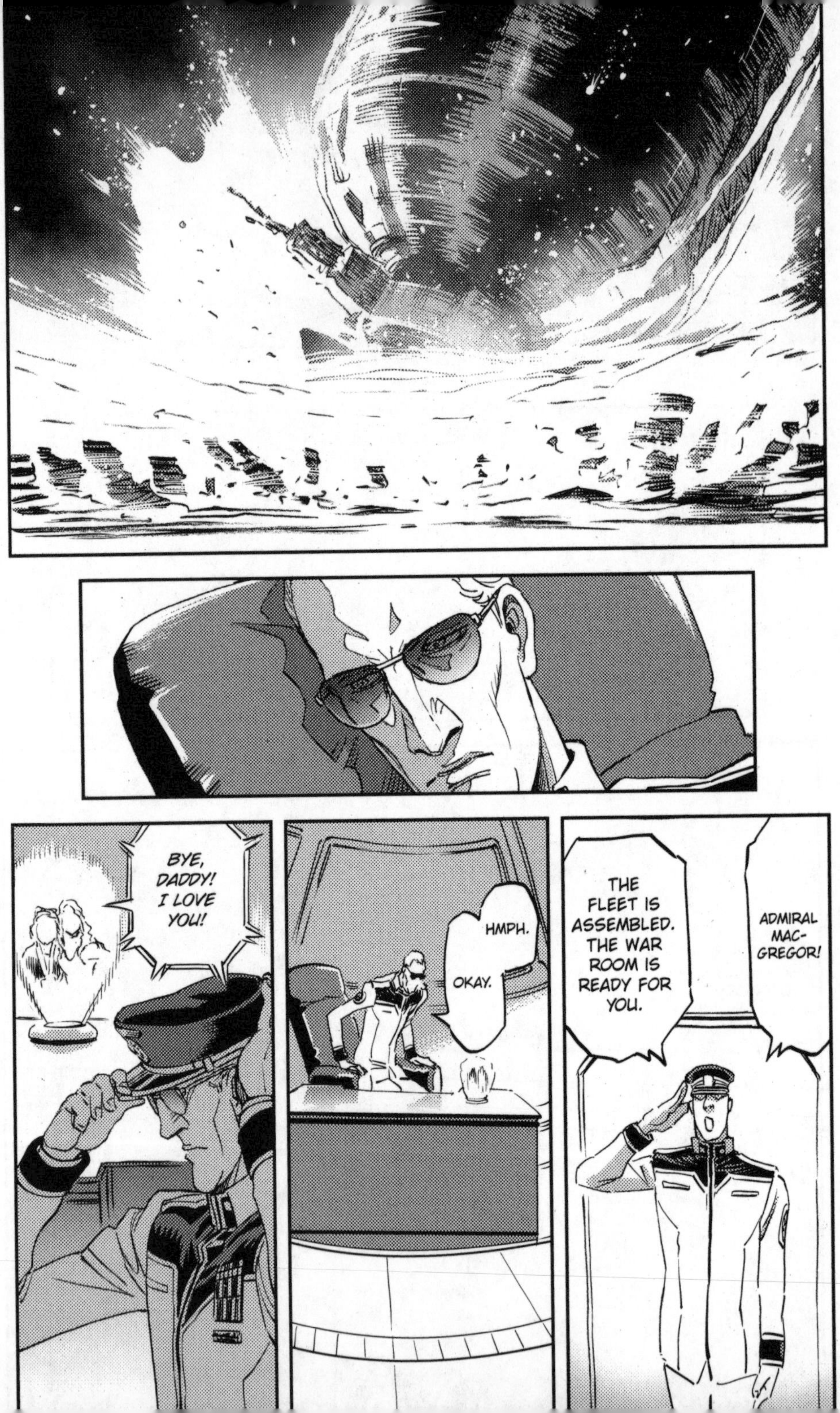
ADMIRAL MAC-GREGOR!
THE FLEET IS ASSEMBLED. THE WAR ROOM IS READY FOR YOU.
HMPH.
OKAY.
BYE, DADDY! I LOVE YOU!

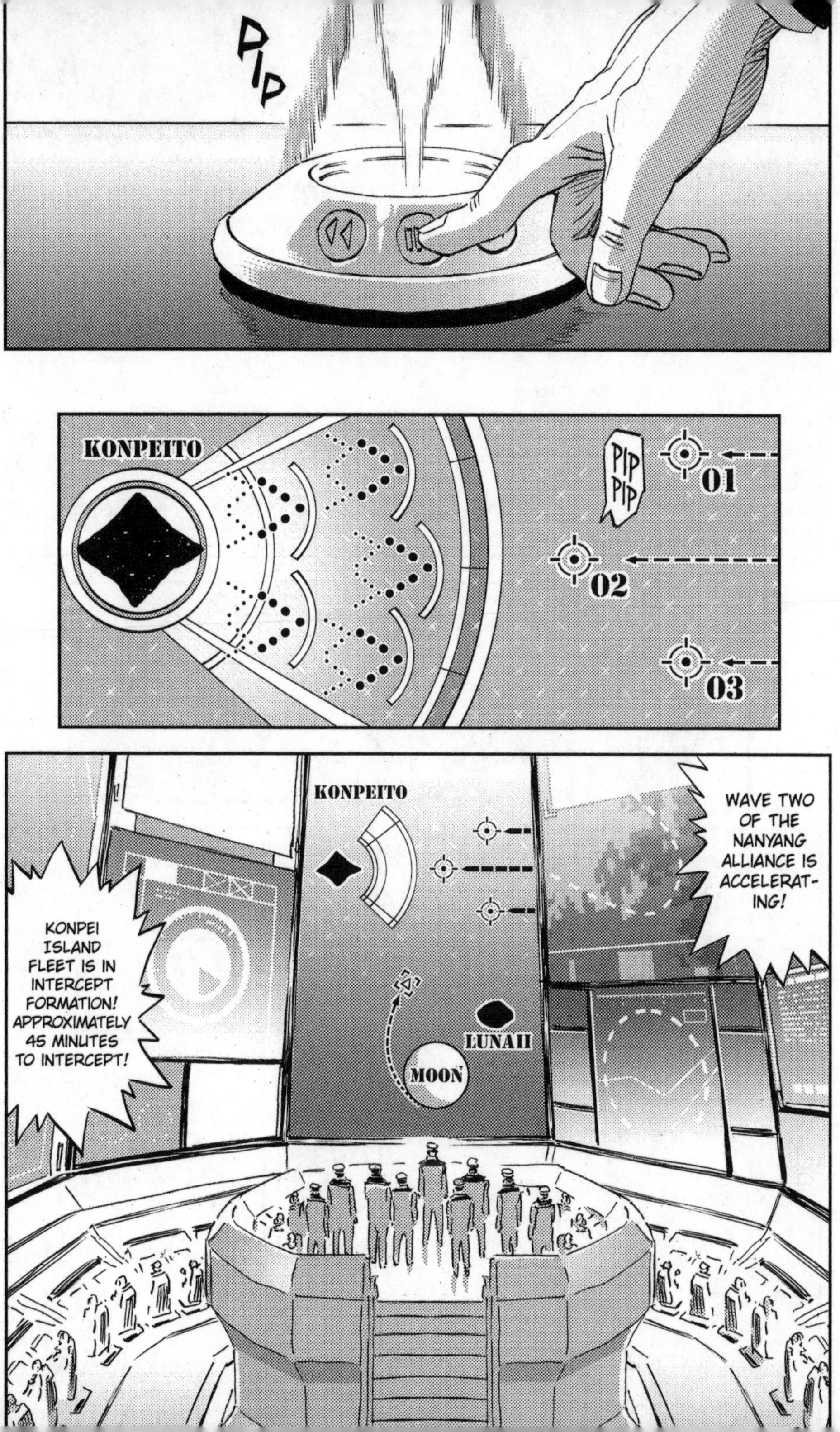
PIP
KONPEITO
PIP PIP
01
02
03
WAVE TWO OF THE NANYANG ALLIANCE IS ACCELERAT-ING!
KONPEITO
LUNAII
MOON
KONPEI ISLAND FLEET IS IN INTERCEPT FORMATION! APPROXIMATELY 45 MINUTES TO INTERCEPT!

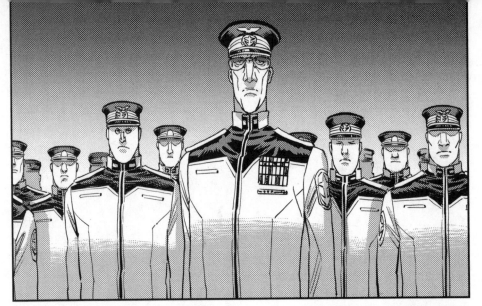

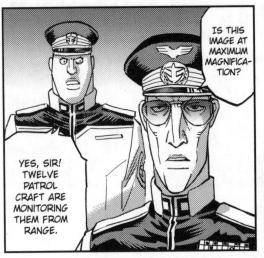

01
02
03
IS THIS IMAGE AT MAXIMUM MAGNIFICA-TION?
YES, SIR! TWELVE PATROL CRAFT ARE MONITORING THEM FROM RANGE.
THE BATTLE OF SOLOMON AT THE END OF THE WAR LEFT A LOT OF DEBRIS IN THIS AREA.
IT'S IDEAL FOR THE EAGLE EYE RECON TEAM TO STAY CONCEALED.

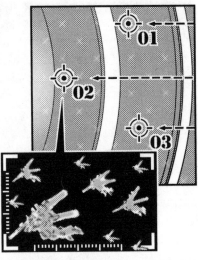

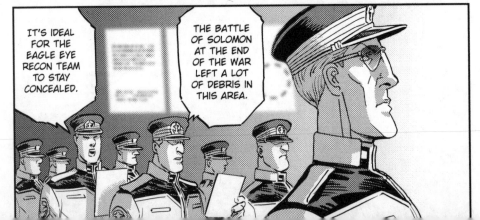

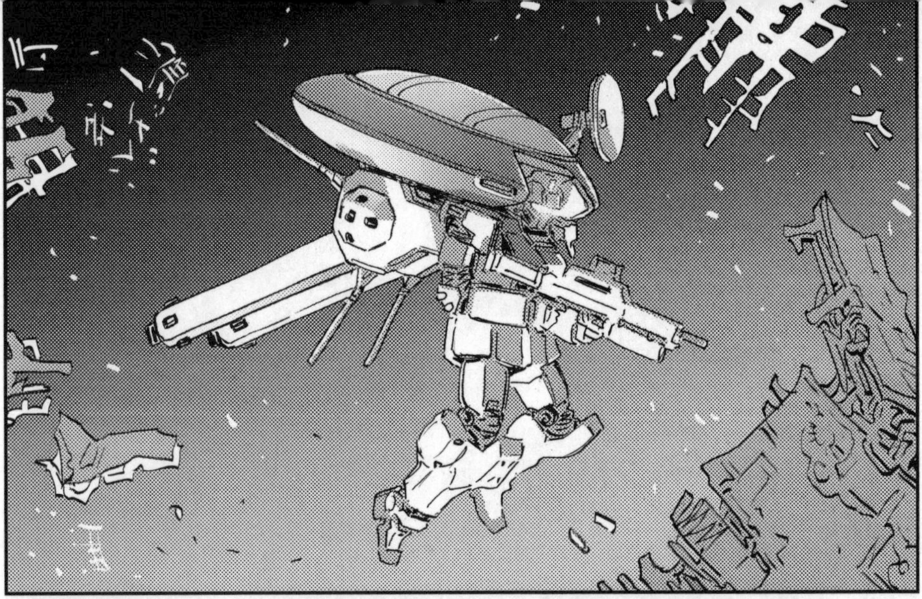

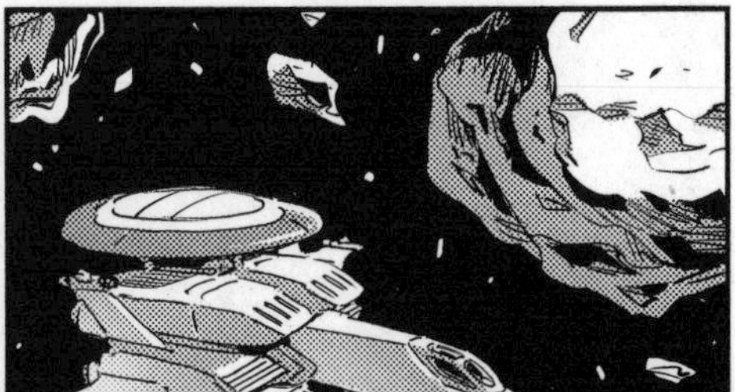

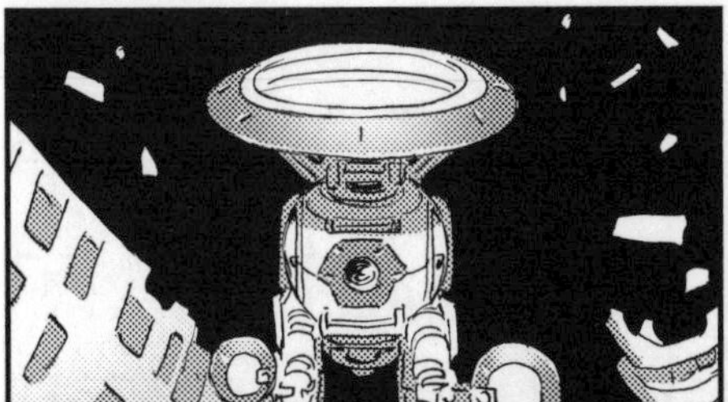

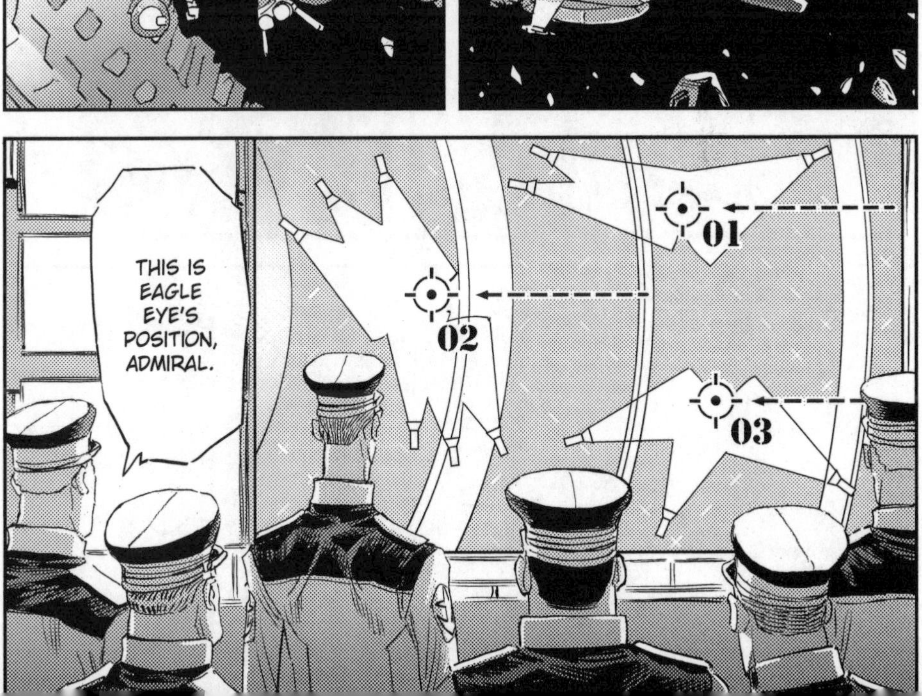
THIS IS EAGLE EYE'S POSITION, ADMIRAL.
01
02
03

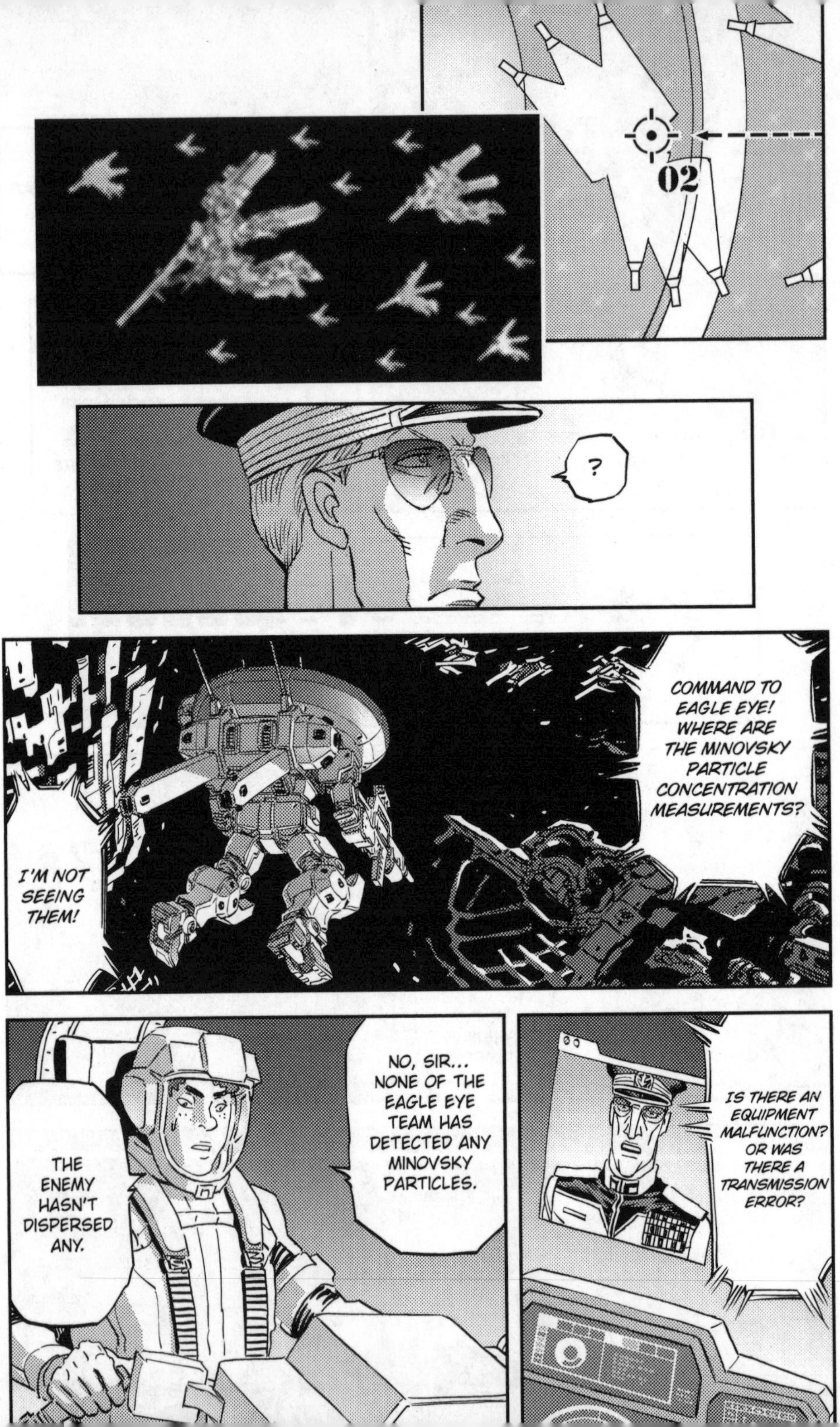
02
?
COMMAND TO EAGLE EYE! WHERE ARE THE MINOVSKY PARTICLE CONCENTRATION MEASUREMENTS?
I'M NOT SEEING THEM!
IS THERE AN EQUIPMENT MALFUNCTION? OR WAS THERE A TRANSMISSION ERROR?
NO, SIR... NONE OF THE EAGLE EYE TEAM HAS DETECTED ANY MINOVSKY PARTICLES.
THE ENEMY HASN'T DISPERSED ANY.

BZZ
BZZ
BZZ

WHAT?

IT SEEMS THEY HAVE NO INTENTION OF HIDING. BOTH RADAR DETECTION AND SENSOR TRACKING ARE POSSIBLE.

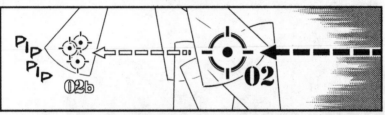

PIP
PIP

02b

02

!!

THREE MOBILE SUITS FROM WAVE TWO ARE ACCELERATING!

THEY'RE HEADED FOR THE KONPEI ISLAND DEFENSIVE PERIMETER!

02b

02

?!

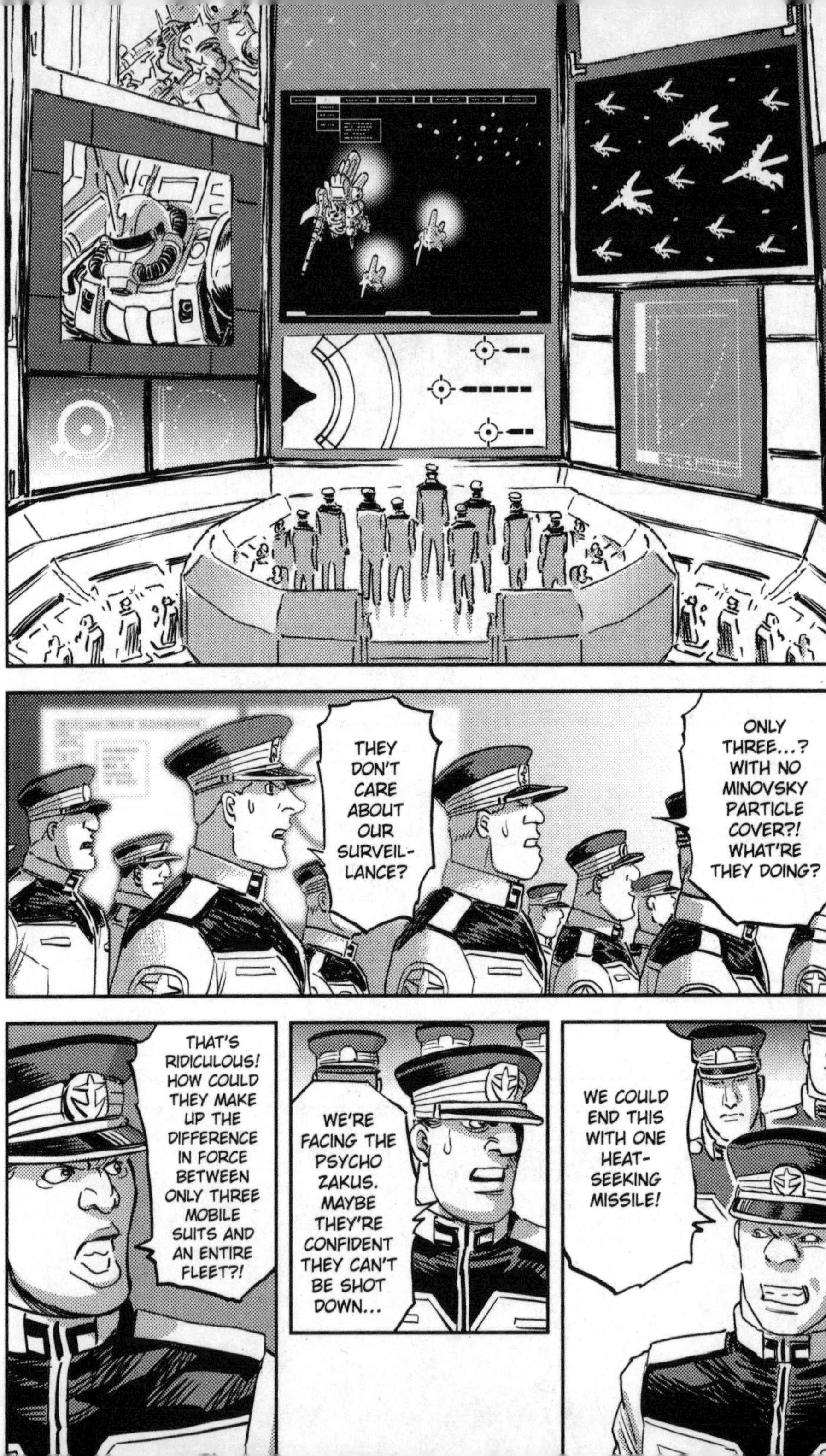
ONLY THREE...? WITH NO MINOVSKY PARTICLE COVER?! WHAT'RE THEY DOING?
THEY DON'T CARE ABOUT OUR SURVEIL-LANCE?
WE COULD END THIS WITH ONE HEAT-SEEKING MISSILE!
WE'RE FACING THE PSYCHO ZAKUS. MAYBE THEY'RE CONFIDENT THEY CAN'T BE SHOT DOWN...
THAT'S RIDICULOUS! HOW COULD THEY MAKE UP THE DIFFERENCE IN FORCE BETWEEN ONLY THREE MOBILE SUITS AND AN ENTIRE FLEET?!

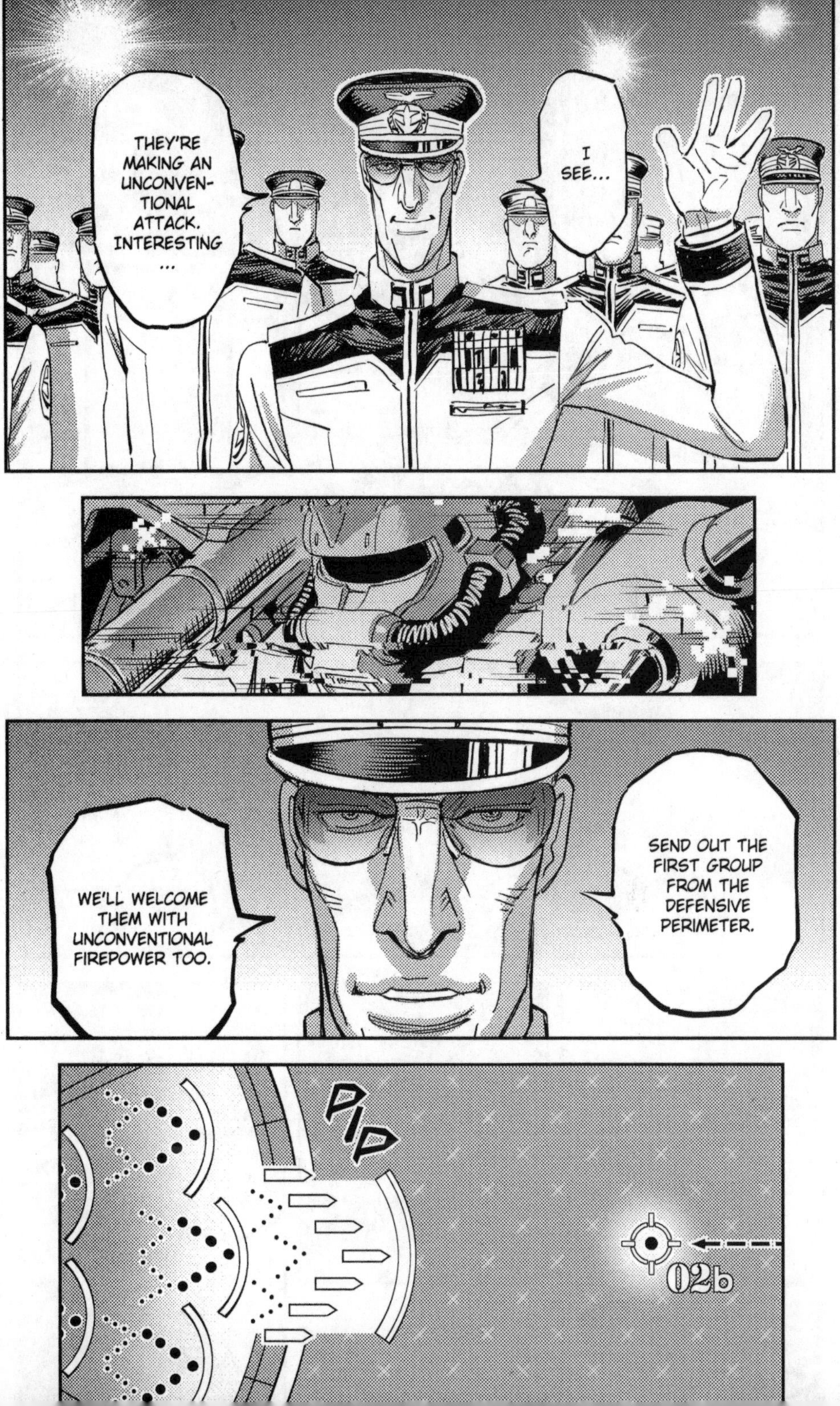
I SEE...
THEY'RE MAKING AN UNCONVENTIONAL ATTACK. INTERESTING...
SEND OUT THE FIRST GROUP FROM THE DEFENSIVE PERIMETER.
WE'LL WELCOME THEM WITH UNCONVENTIONAL FIREPOWER TOO.
PIP
02b

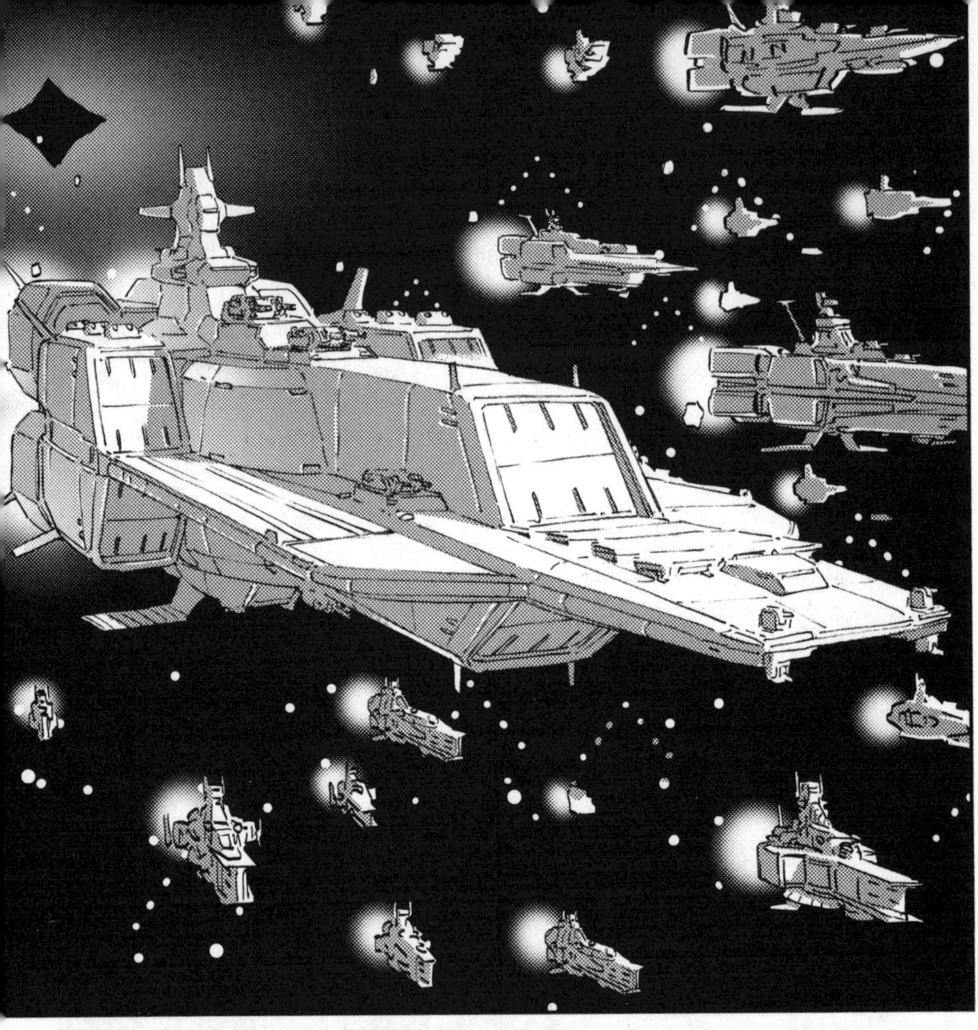

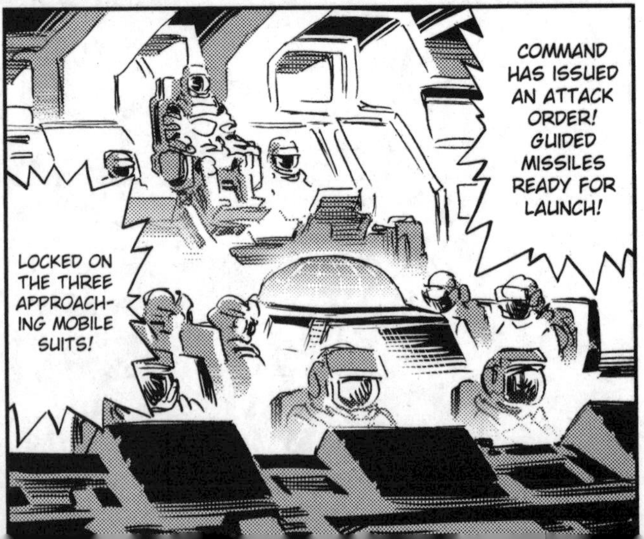
COMMAND HAS ISSUED AN ATTACK ORDER! GUIDED MISSILES READY FOR LAUNCH!
LOCKED ON THE THREE APPROACH-ING MOBILE SUITS!

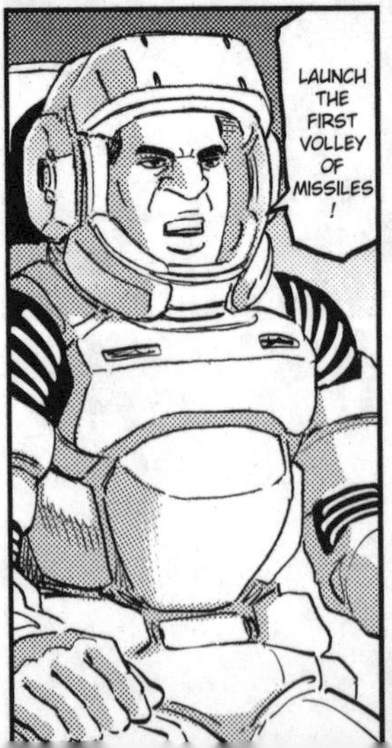
LAUNCH THE FIRST VOLLEY OF MISSILES!

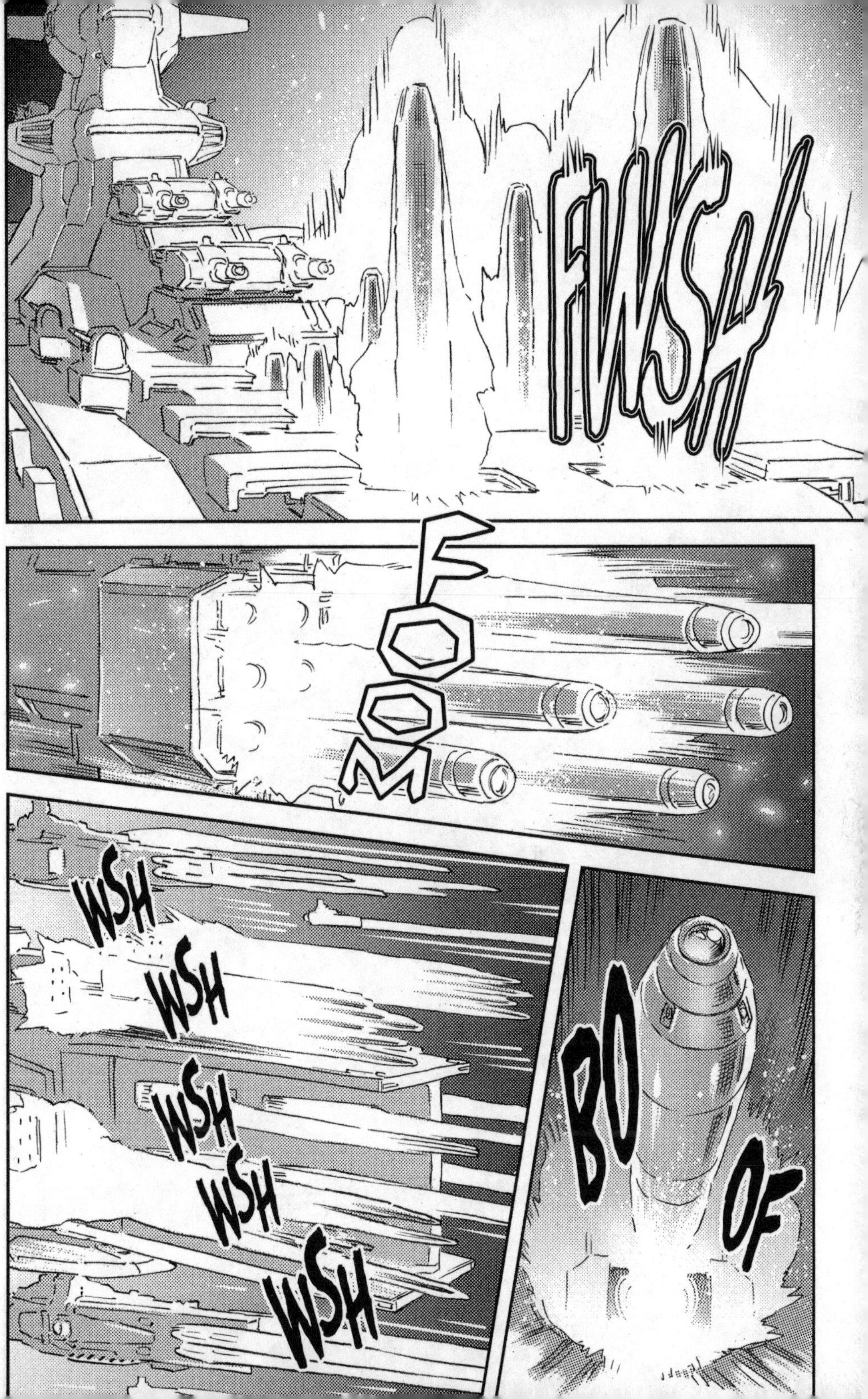
FWSH
FOOM
BOOF
WSH
WSH
WSH
WSH
WSH

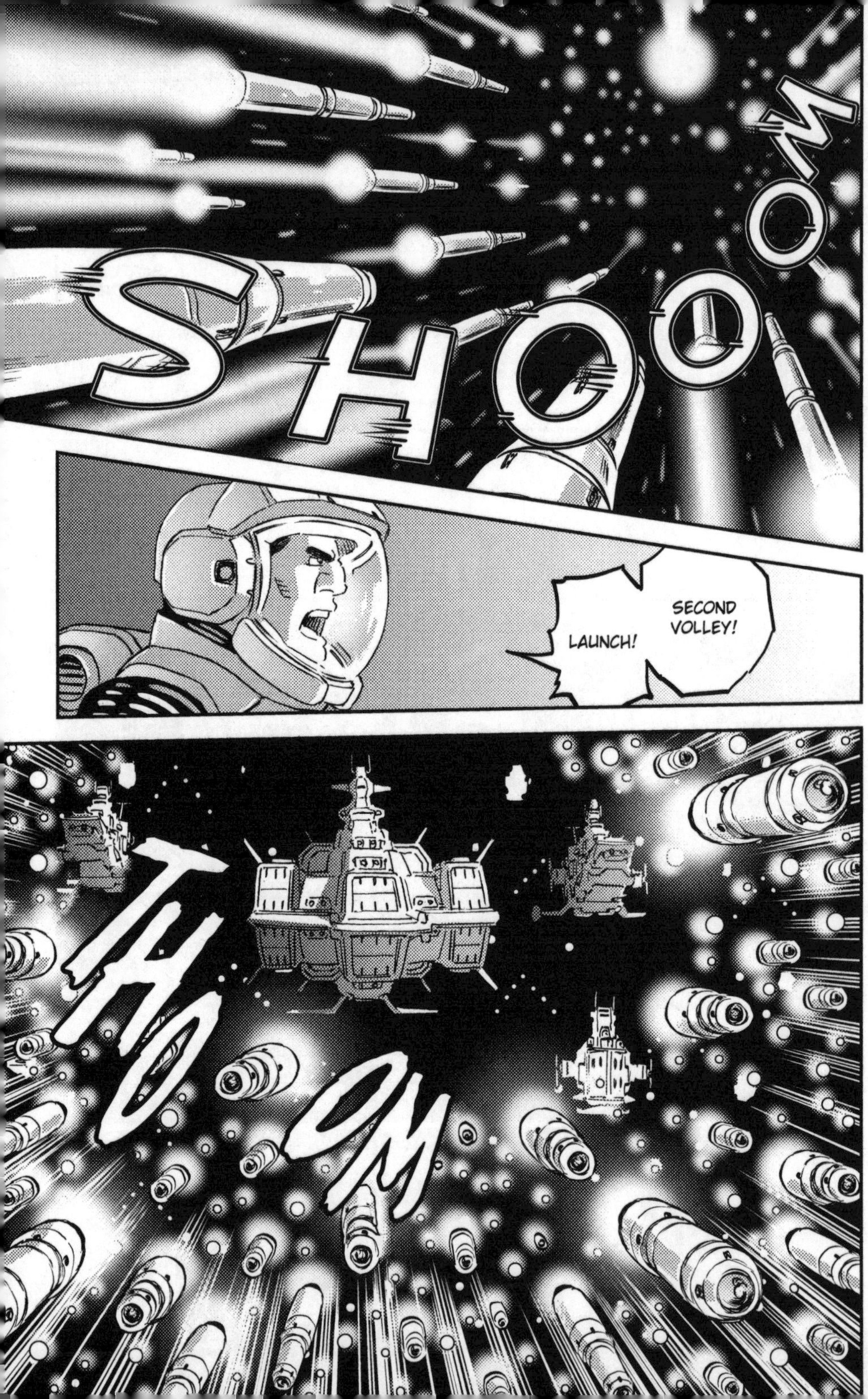
SHOOOM
SECOND VOLLEY!
LAUNCH!
THOOM

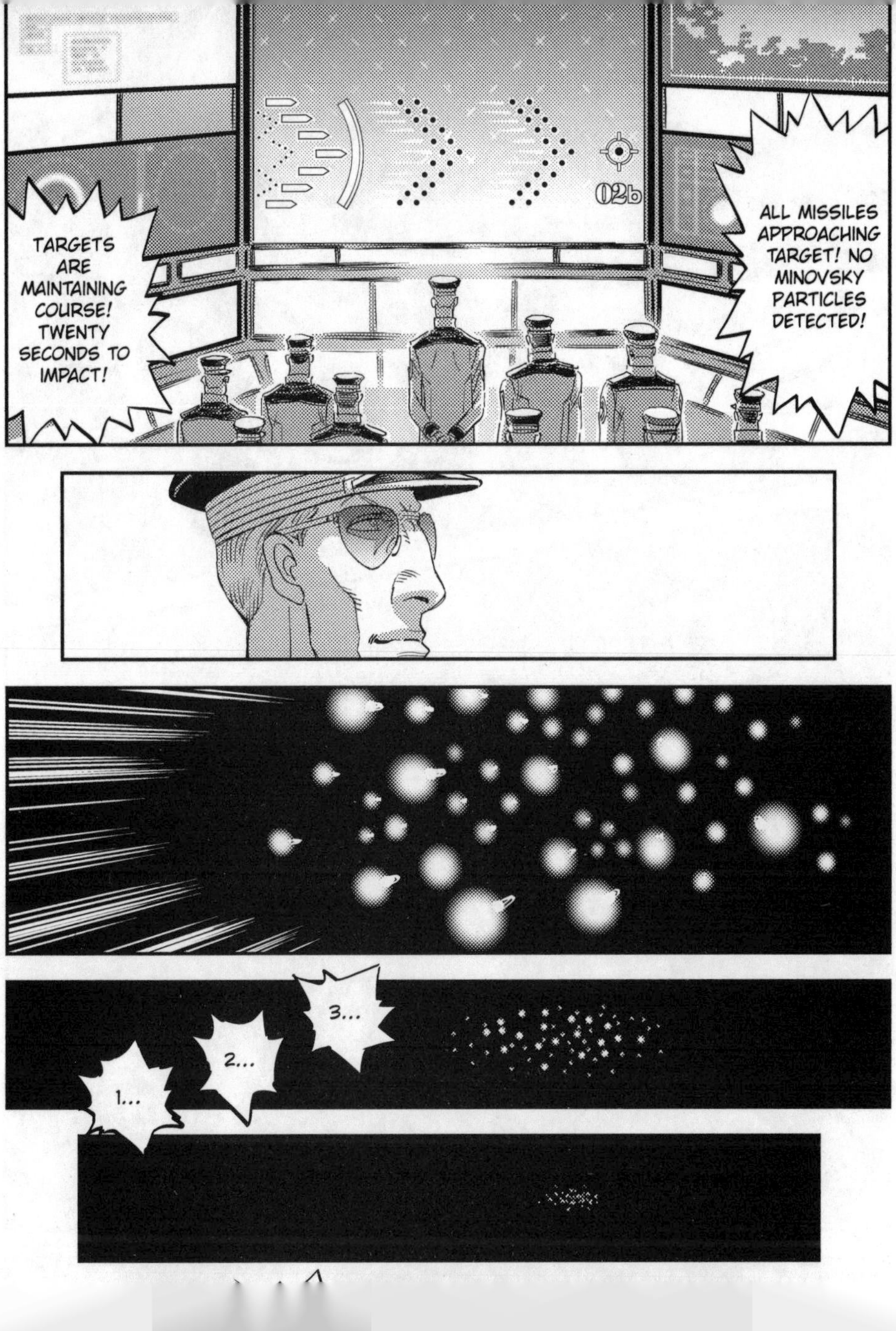
ALL MISSILES APPROACHING TARGET! NO MINOVSKY PARTICLES DETECTED!
TARGETS ARE MAINTAINING COURSE! TWENTY SECONDS TO IMPACT!
3...
2...
1...

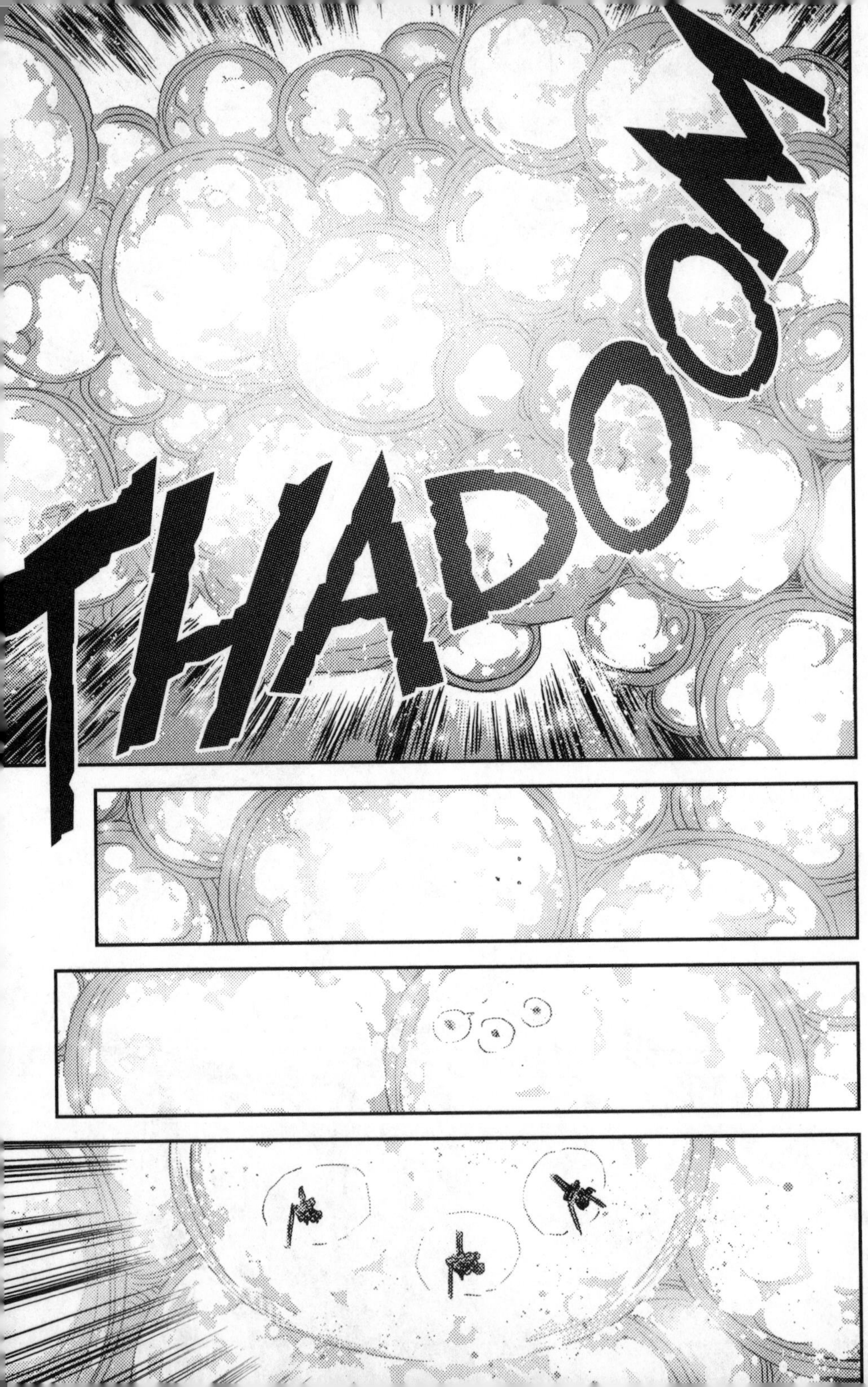
THADOOM

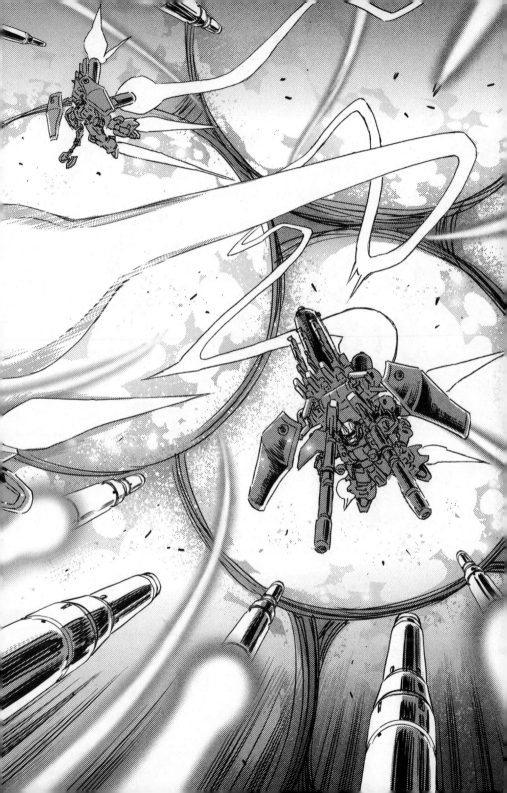

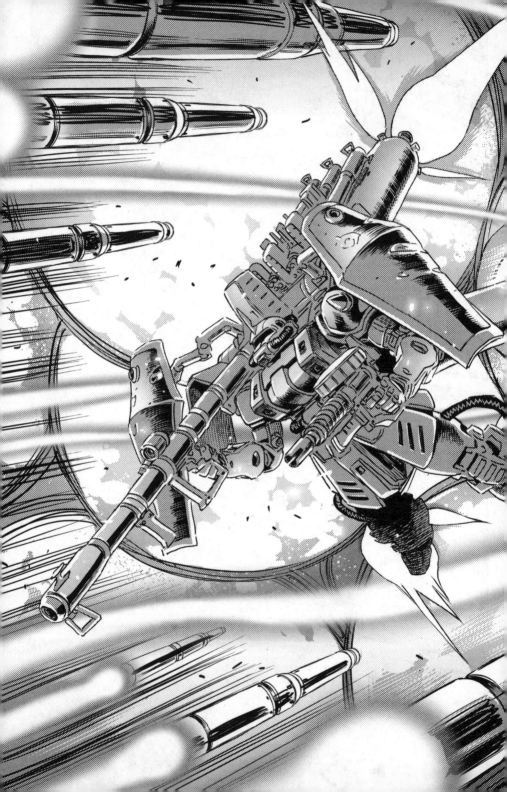

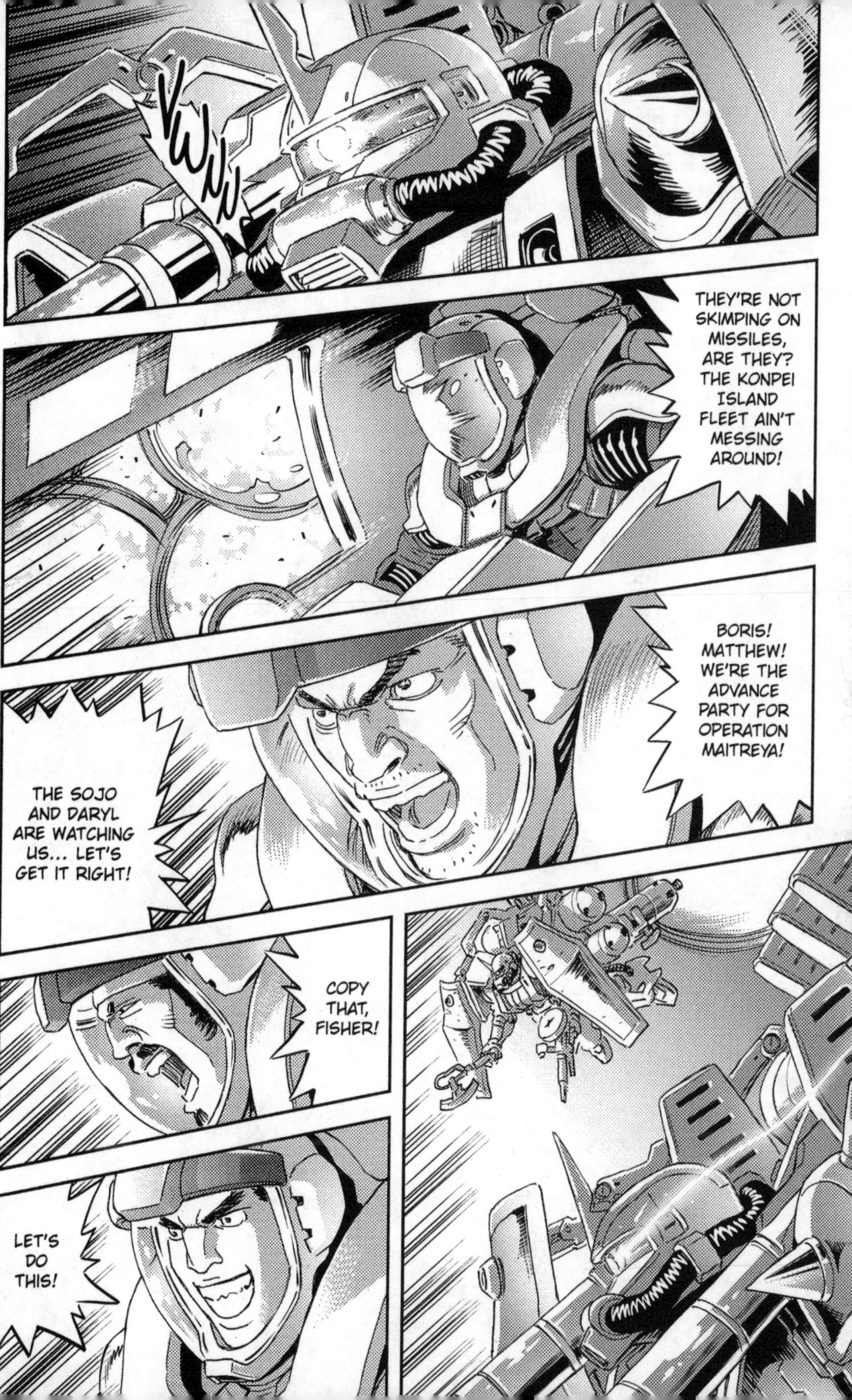
VWNN
THEY'RE NOT SKIMPING ON MISSILES, ARE THEY? THE KONPEI ISLAND FLEET AIN'T MESSING AROUND!
BORIS! MATTHEW! WE'RE THE ADVANCE PARTY FOR OPERATION MAITREYA!
THE SOJO AND DARYL ARE WATCHING US... LET'S GET IT RIGHT!
COPY THAT, FISHER!
LET'S DO THIS!

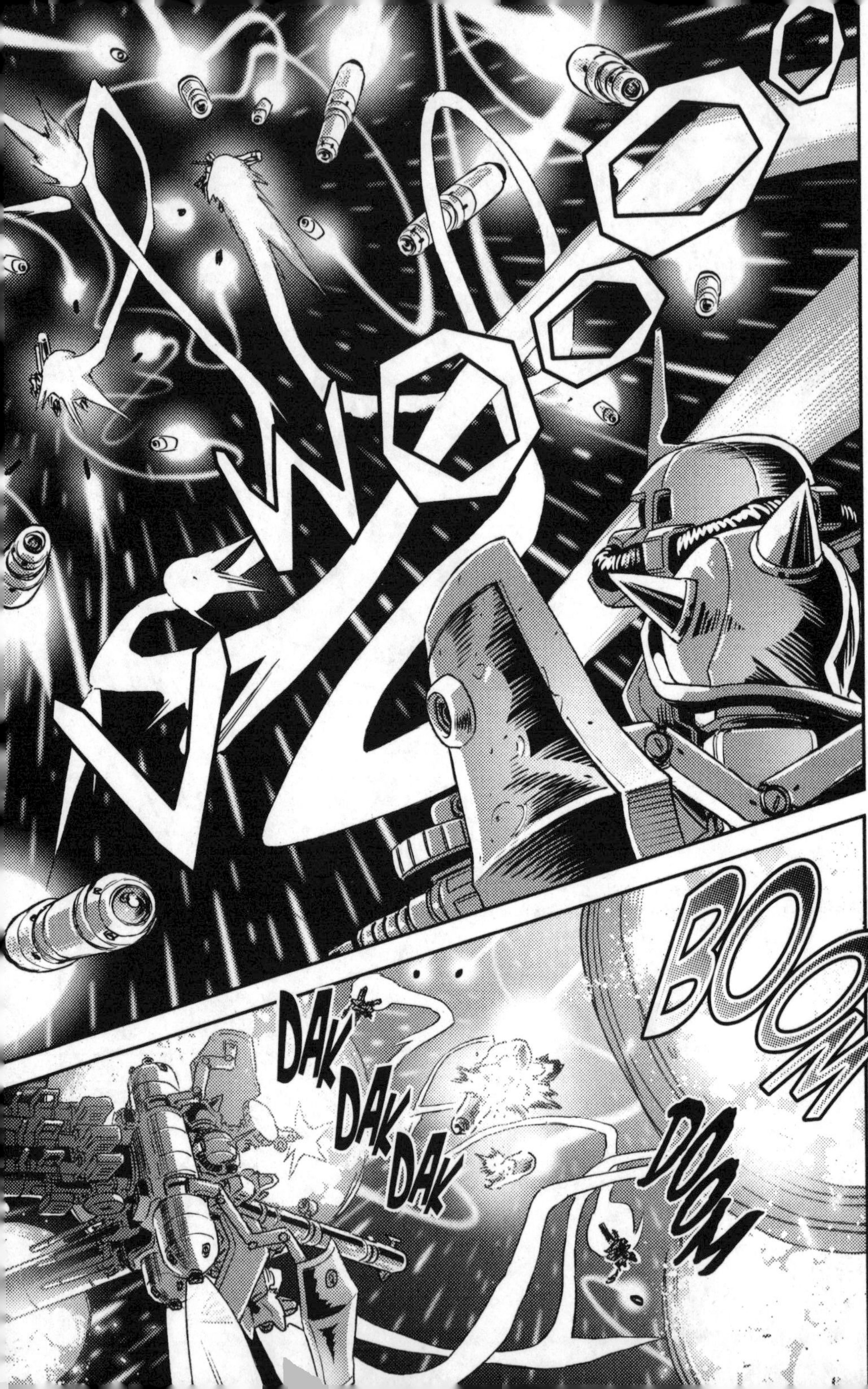
SWOOOO
BOOM
DAK DAK DAK
DOOM

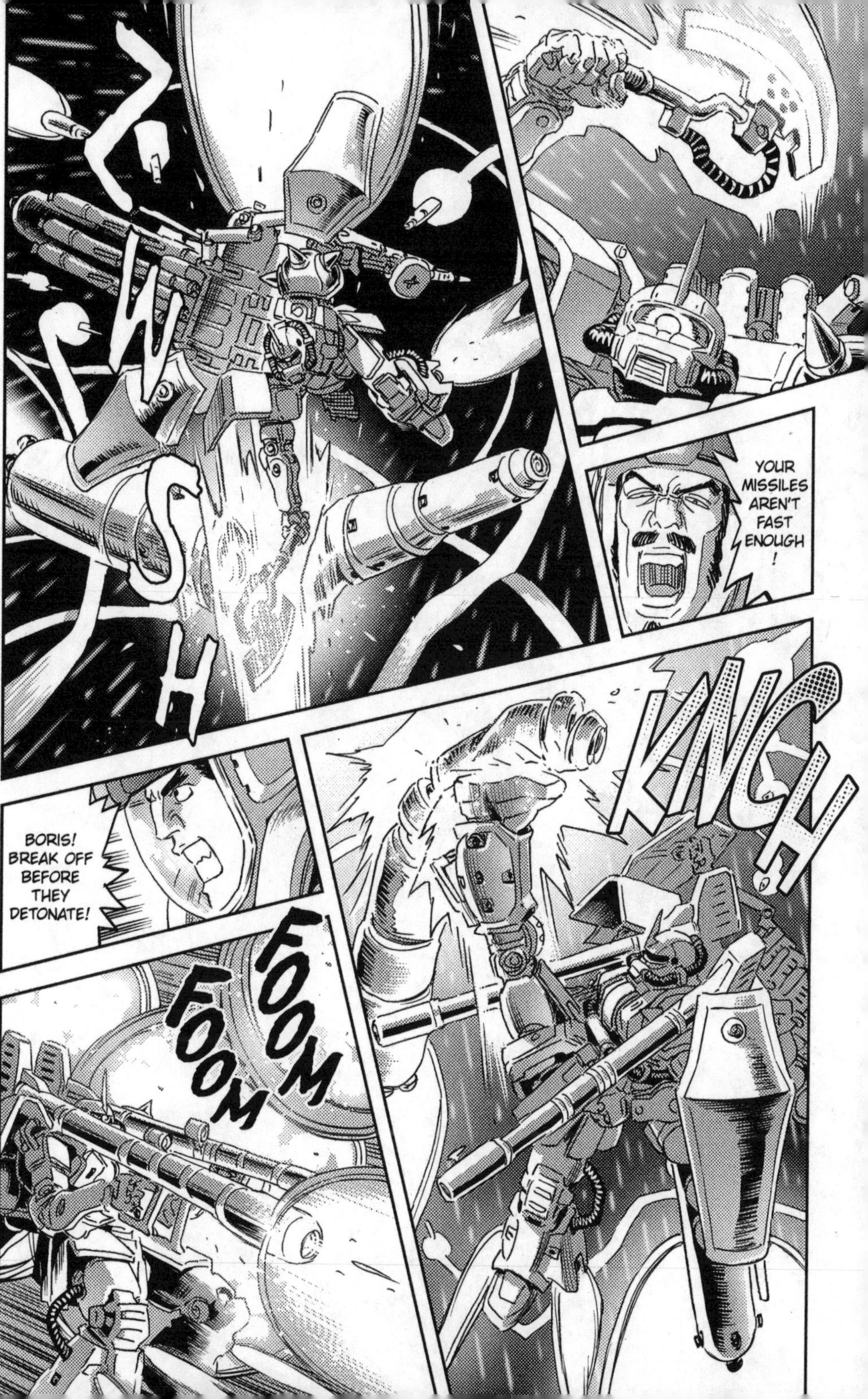
YOUR MISSILES AREN'T FAST ENOUGH!
WSH
KNCH!
BORIS! BREAK OFF BEFORE THEY DETONATE!
FOOM FOOM

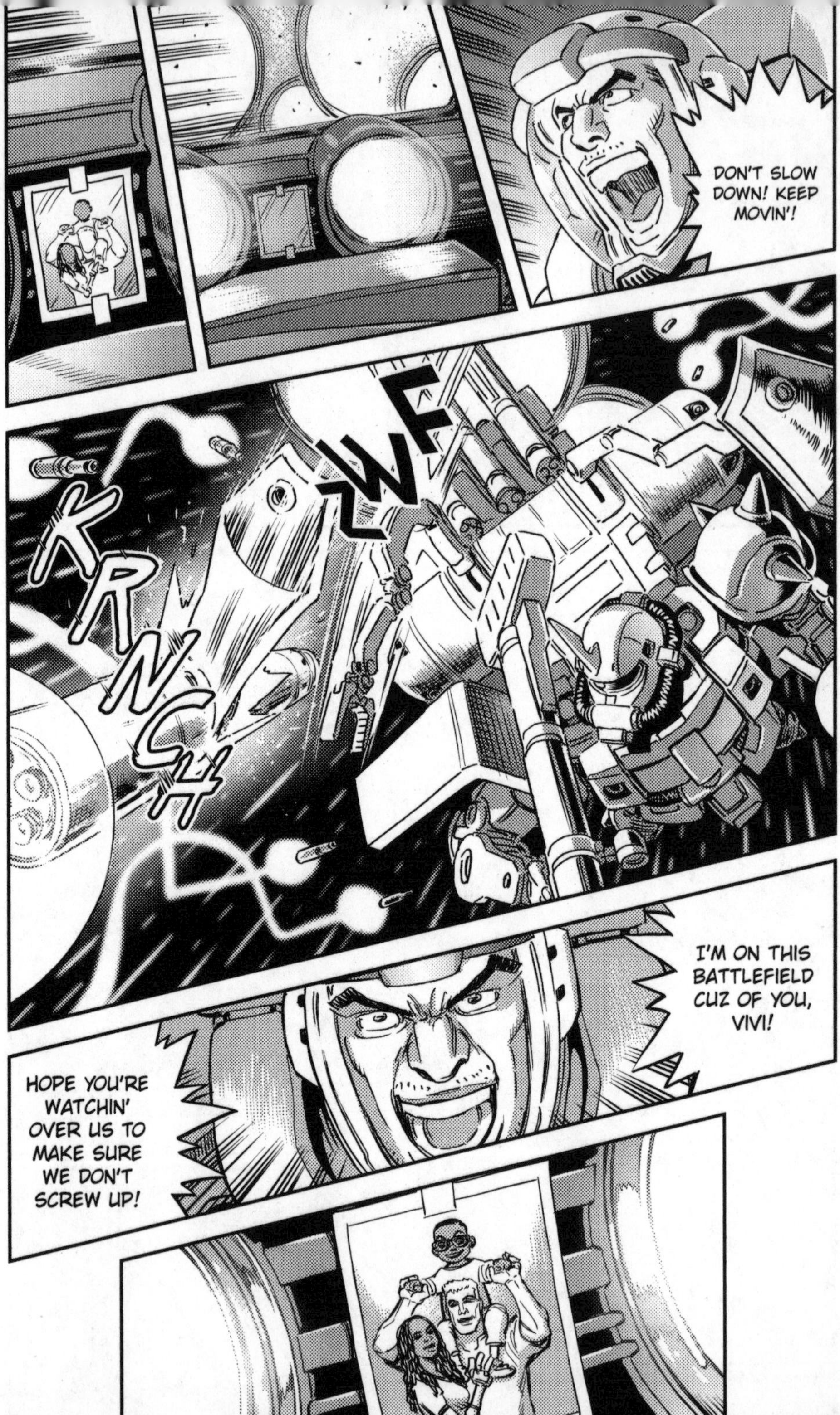
DON'T SLOW DOWN! KEEP MOVIN'!
ZWF
KRNCH
I'M ON THIS BATTLEFIELD CUZ OF YOU, VIVI!
HOPE YOU'RE WATCHIN' OVER US TO MAKE SURE WE DON'T SCREW UP!

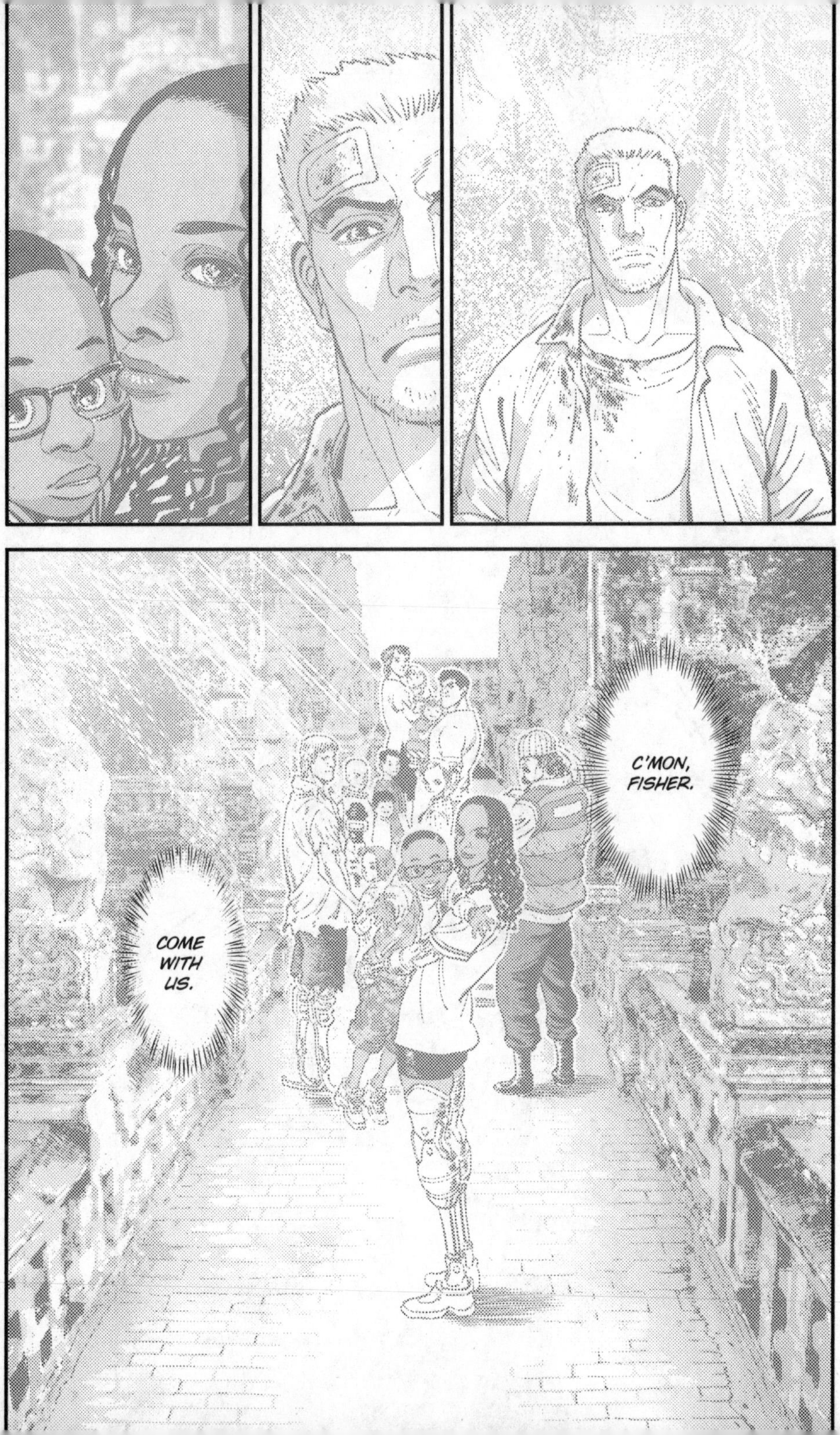
C'MON, FISHER.
COME WITH US.

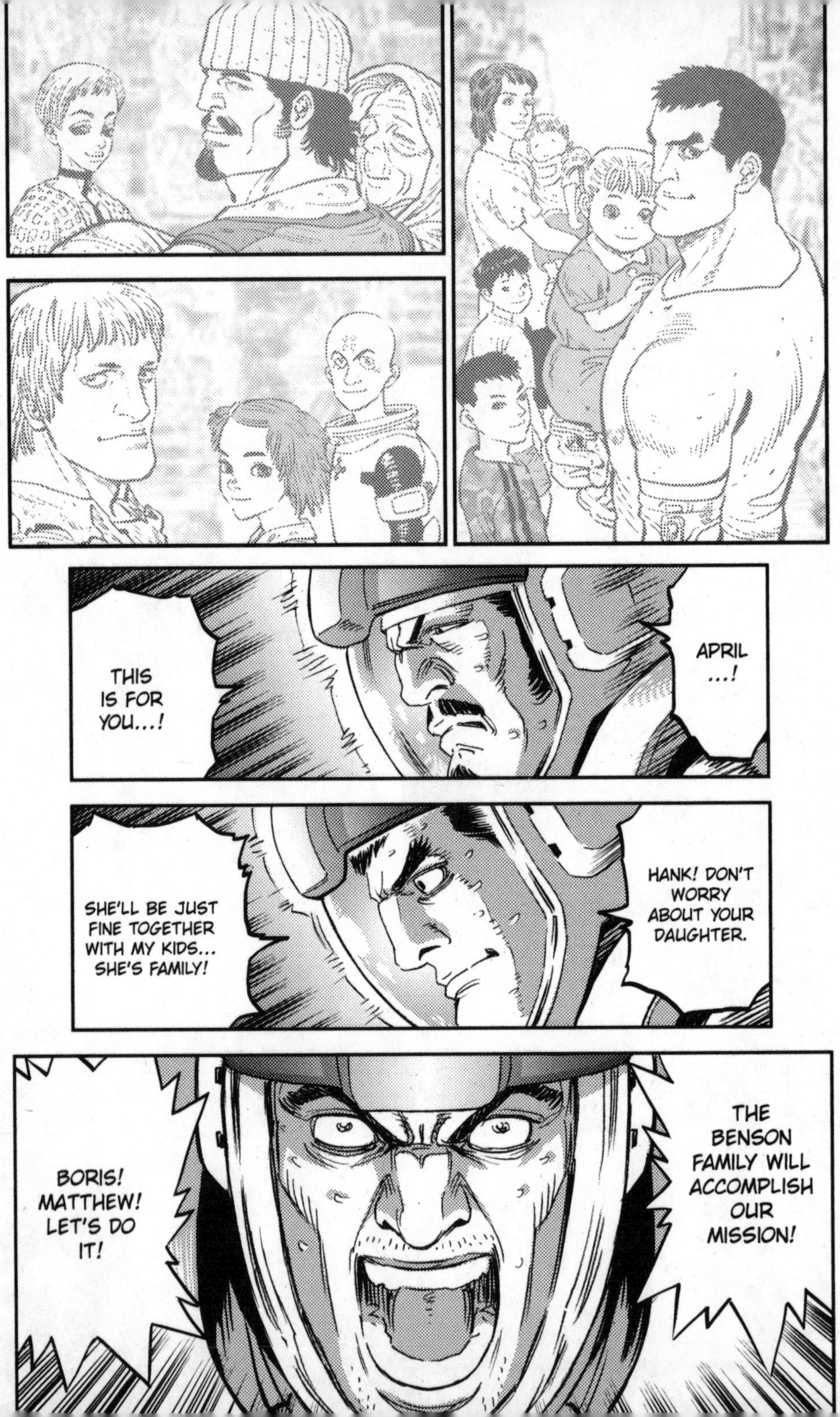
APRIL...!
THIS IS FOR YOU...!
HANK! DON'T WORRY ABOUT YOUR DAUGHTER.
SHE'LL BE JUST FINE TOGETHER WITH MY KIDS... SHE'S FAMILY!
THE BENSON FAMILY WILL ACCOMPLISH OUR MISSION!
BORIS! MATTHEW! LET'S DO IT!

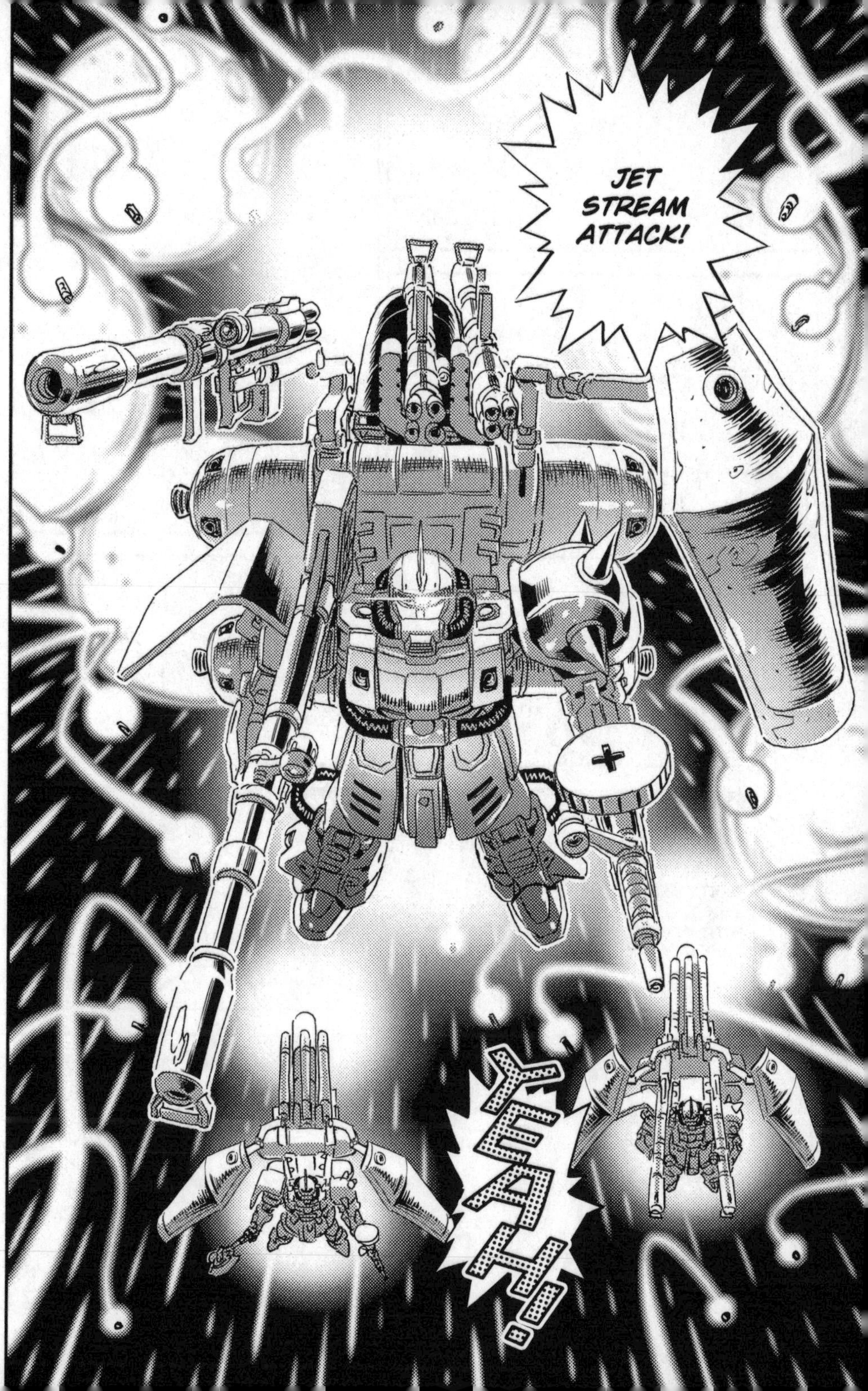
JET STREAM ATTACK!
YEAH!!

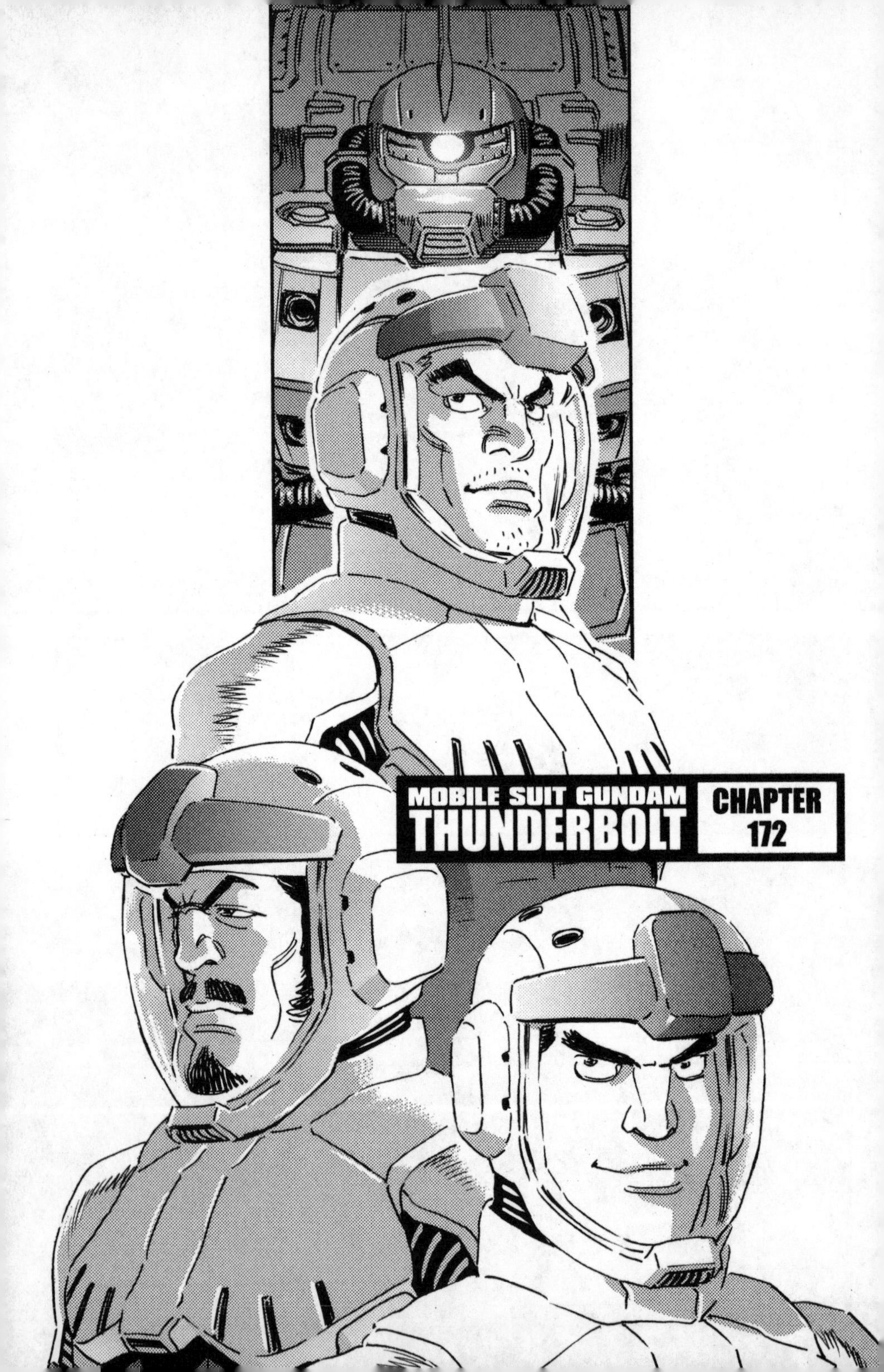
MOBILE SUIT GUNDAM
THUNDERBOLT
CHAPTER
172

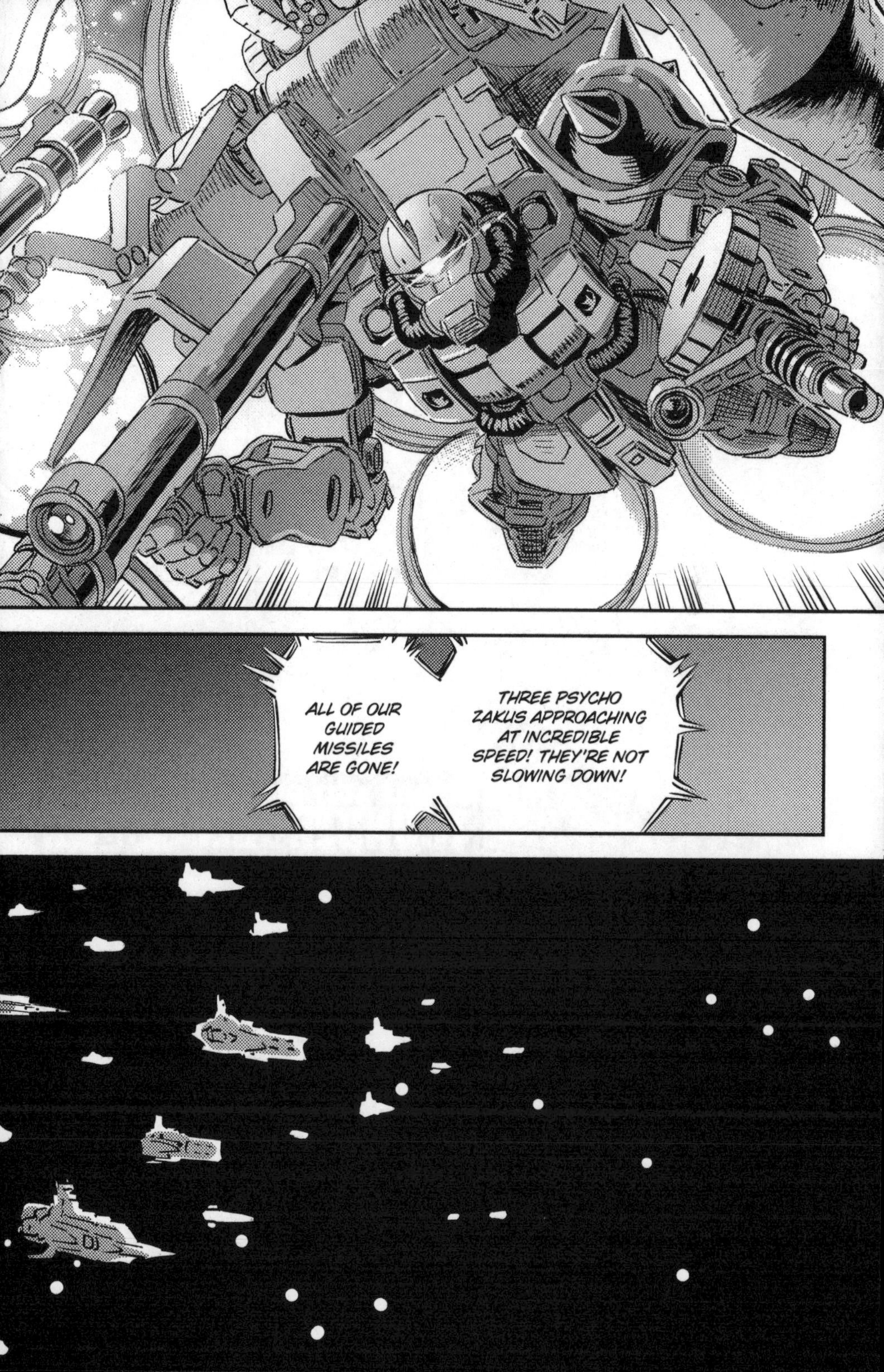
THREE PSYCHO ZAKUS APPROACHING AT INCREDIBLE SPEED! THEY'RE NOT SLOWING DOWN!
ALL OF OUR GUIDED MISSILES ARE GONE!

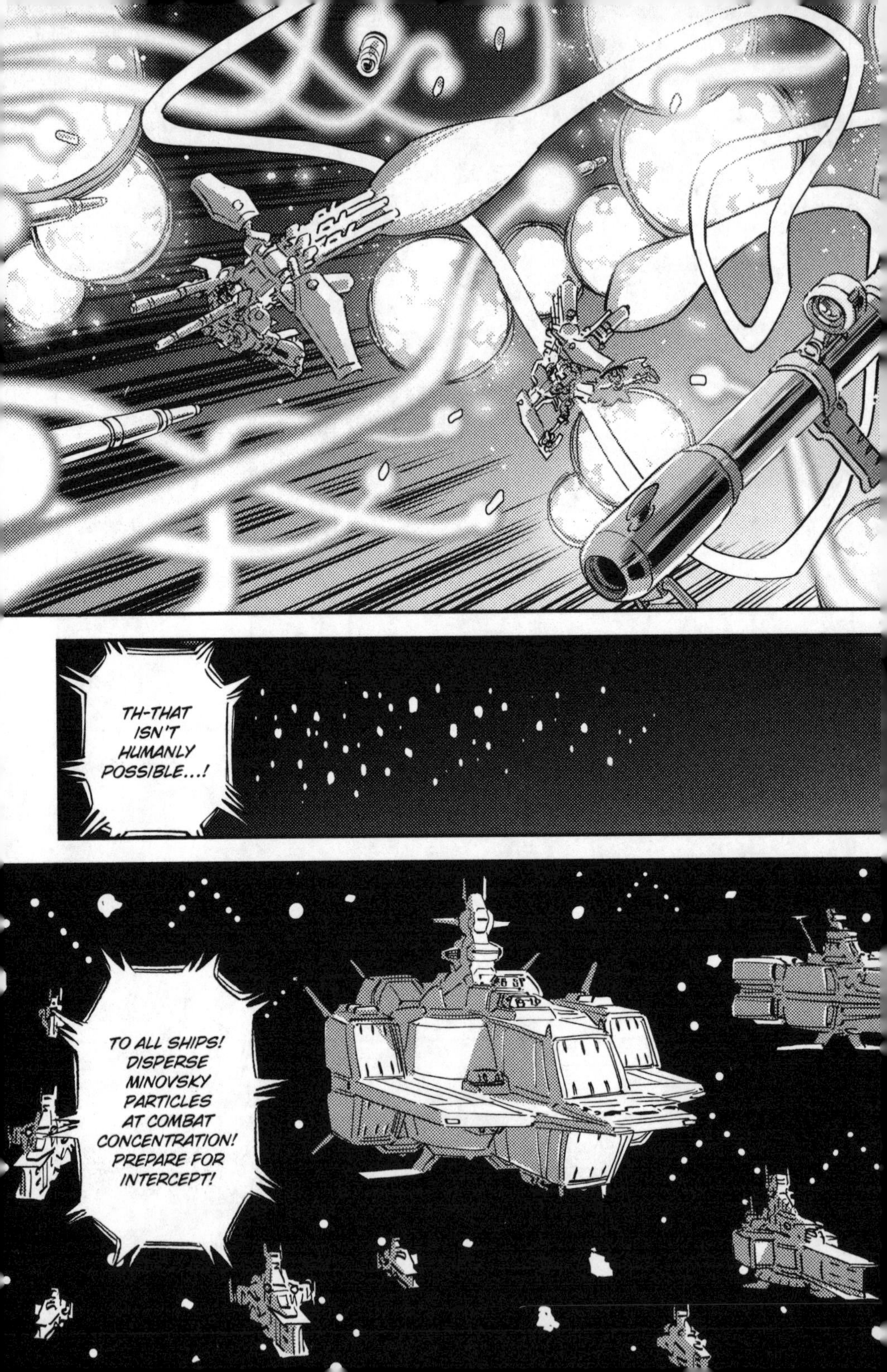
TH-THAT ISN'T HUMANLY POSSIBLE...!
TO ALL SHIPS! DISPERSE MINOVSKY PARTICLES AT COMBAT CONCENTRATION! PREPARE FOR INTERCEPT!

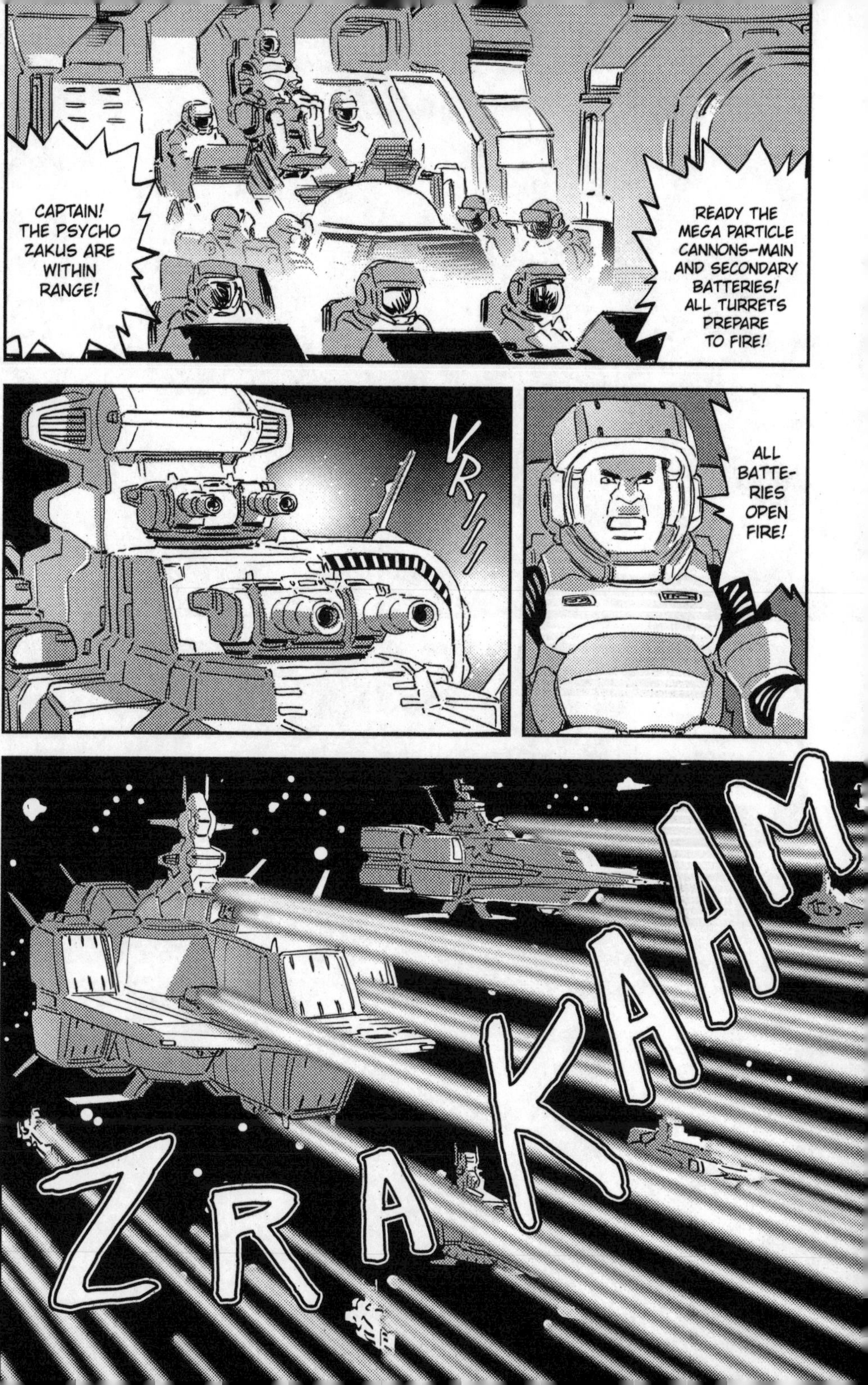
READY THE MEGA PARTICLE CANNONS–MAIN AND SECONDARY BATTERIES! ALL TURRETS PREPARE TO FIRE!
CAPTAIN! THE PSYCHO ZAKUS ARE WITHIN RANGE!
ALL BATTERIES OPEN FIRE!
VRIII
ZRAKAAM

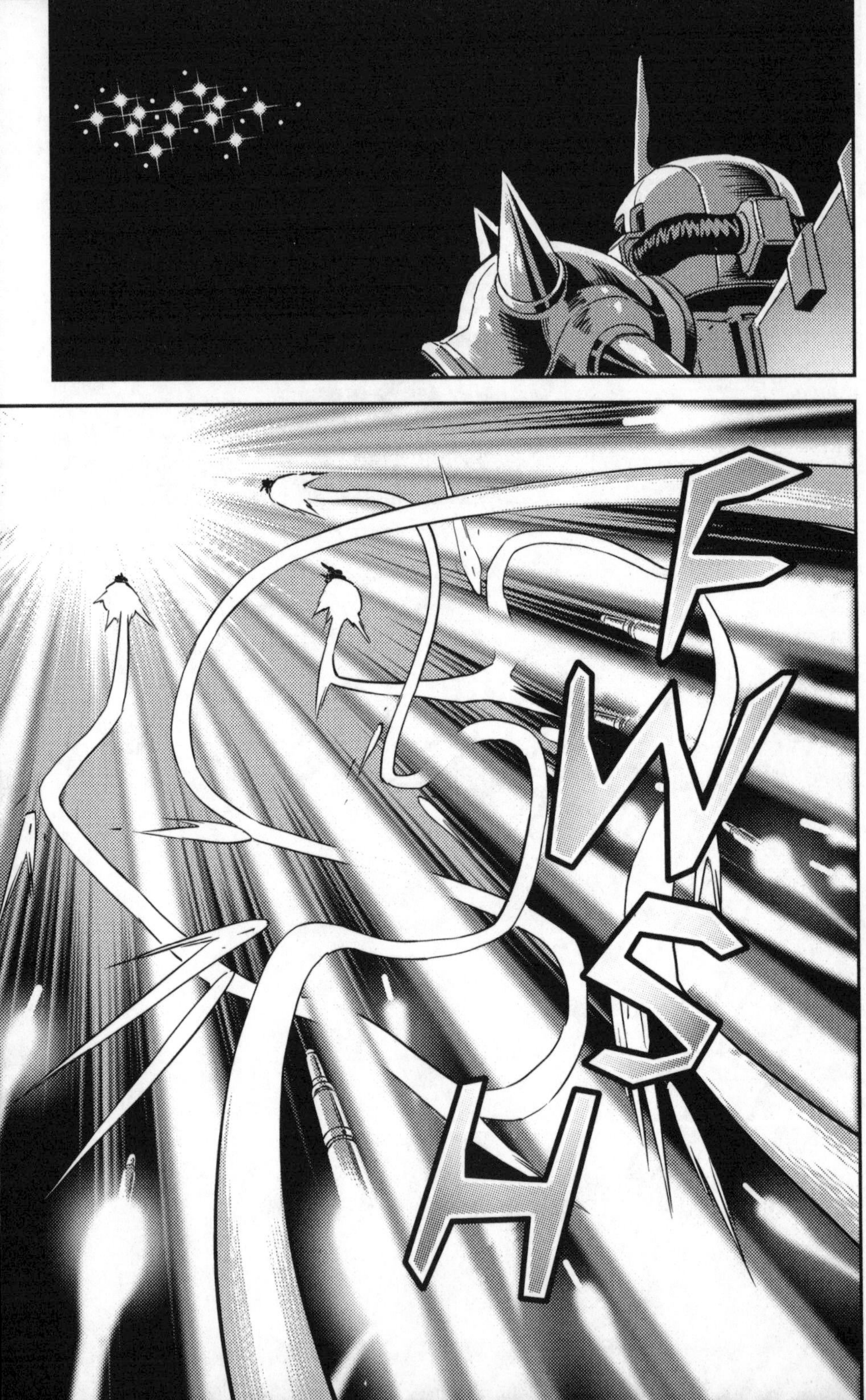
FWSH

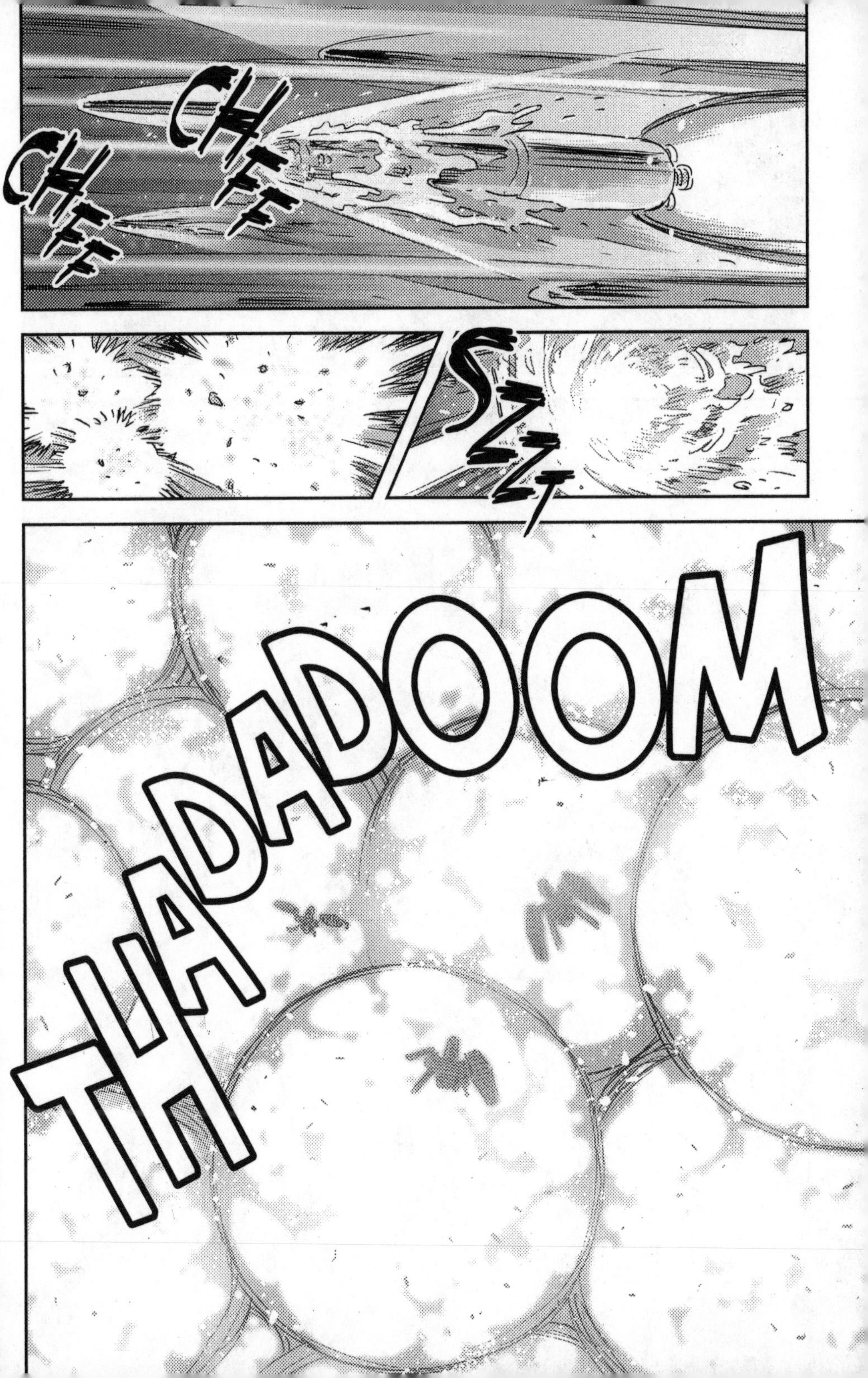
CHFFF
CHFFF
SZZZT
THADADOOM

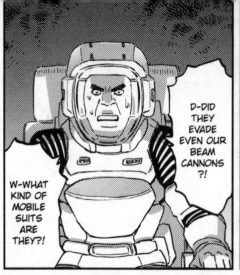

!!
D-DID THEY EVADE EVEN OUR BEAM CANNONS ?!
W-WHAT KIND OF MOBILE SUITS ARE THEY?!
RADAR FUNCTION DECLINING DUE TO THE MINOVSKY PARTICLES!
WE'LL HAVE TO ENGAGE VISUALLY!
ONLINE
MS UNITS ADVANCE! WE **MUST** STOP THEM!

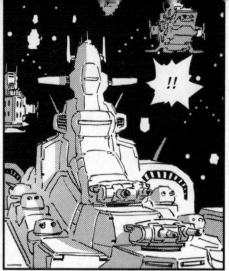

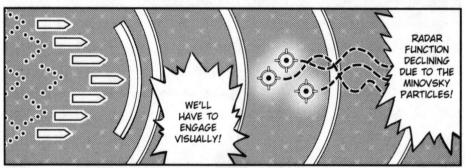

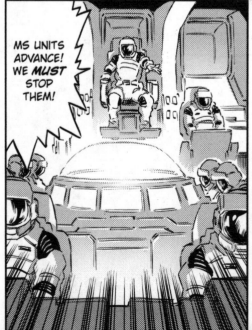

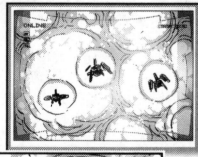

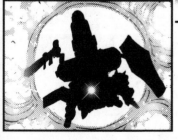

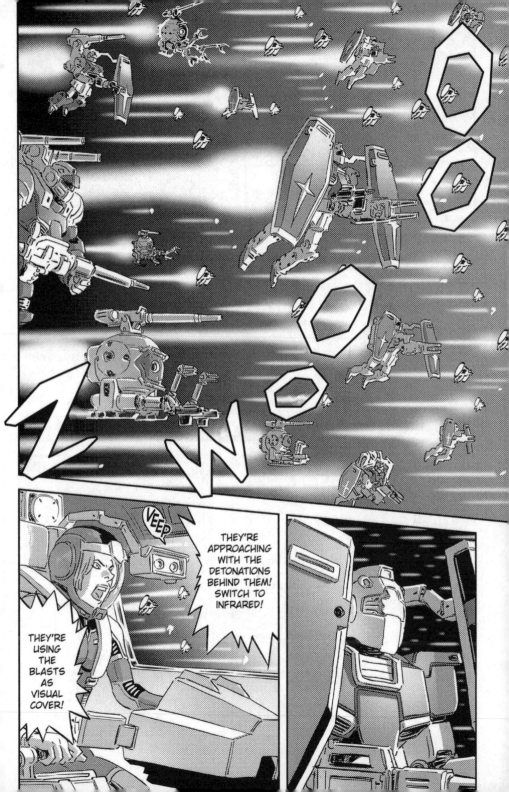

THEY'RE APPROACHING WITH THE DETONATIONS BEHIND THEM! SWITCH TO INFRARED!

THEY'RE USING THE BLASTS AS VISUAL COVER!

VEEP

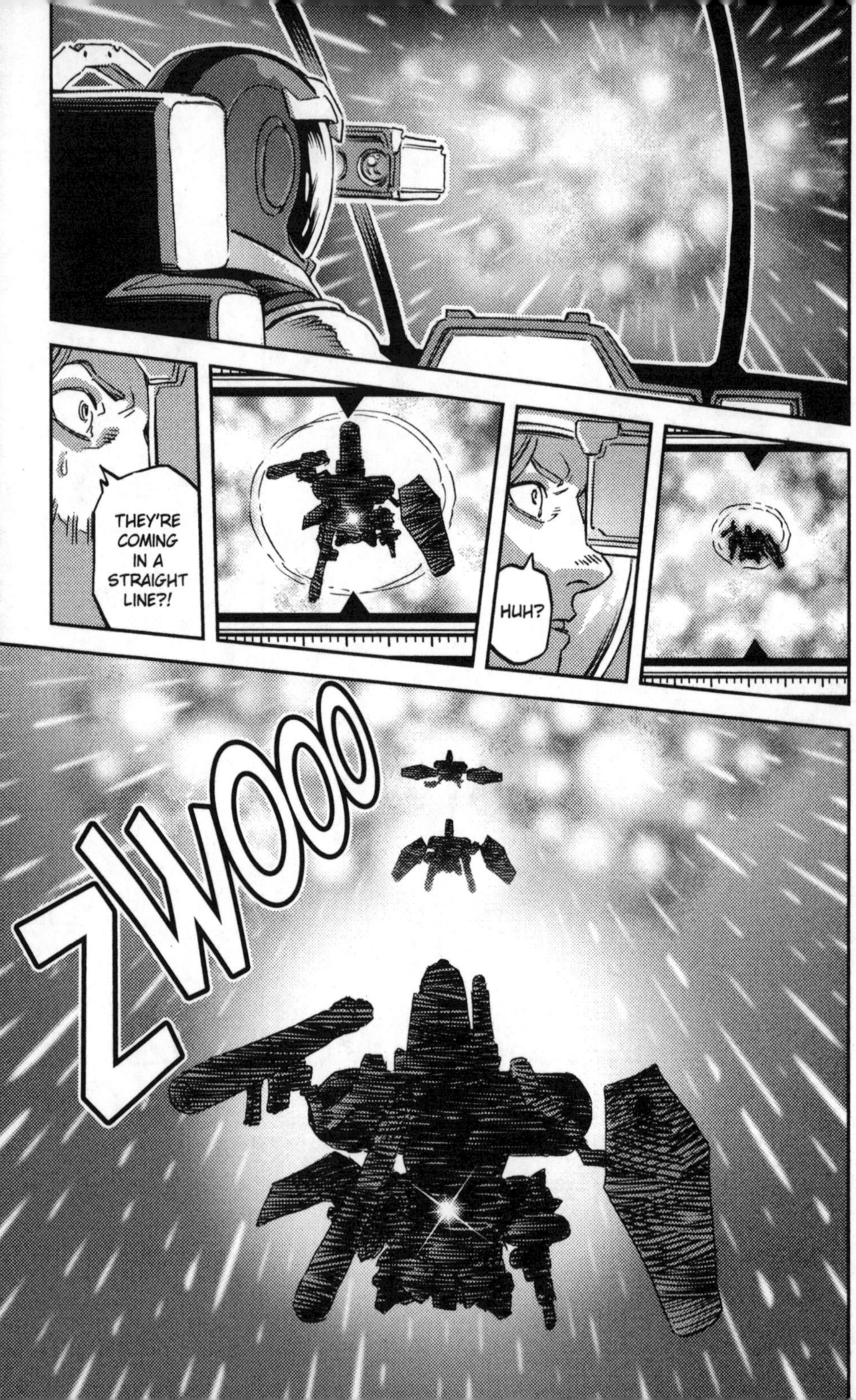
HUH?
THEY'RE COMING IN A STRAIGHT LINE?!
ZWOOO

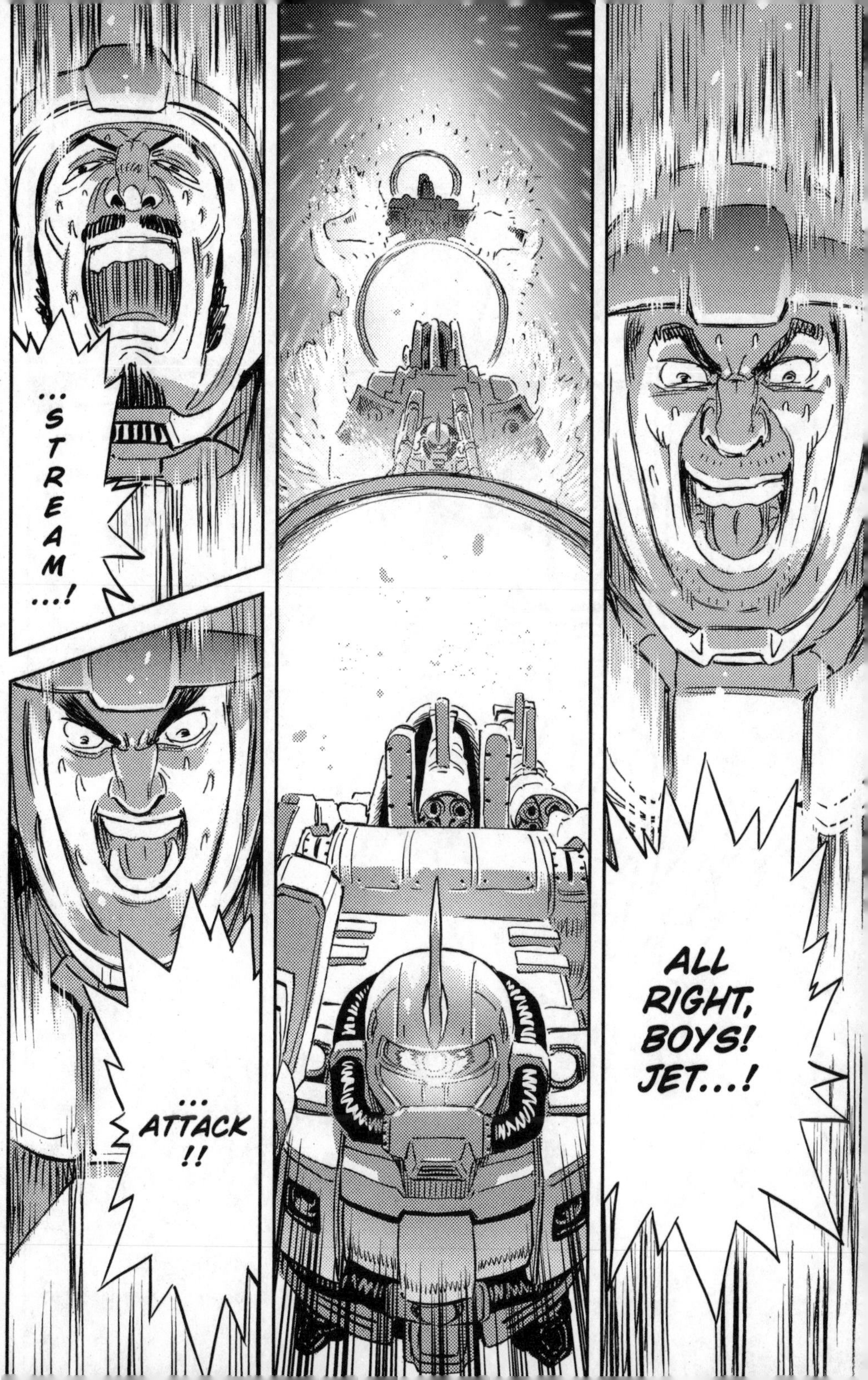
ALL RIGHT, BOYS! JET...!
...STREAM...!
...ATTACK!!

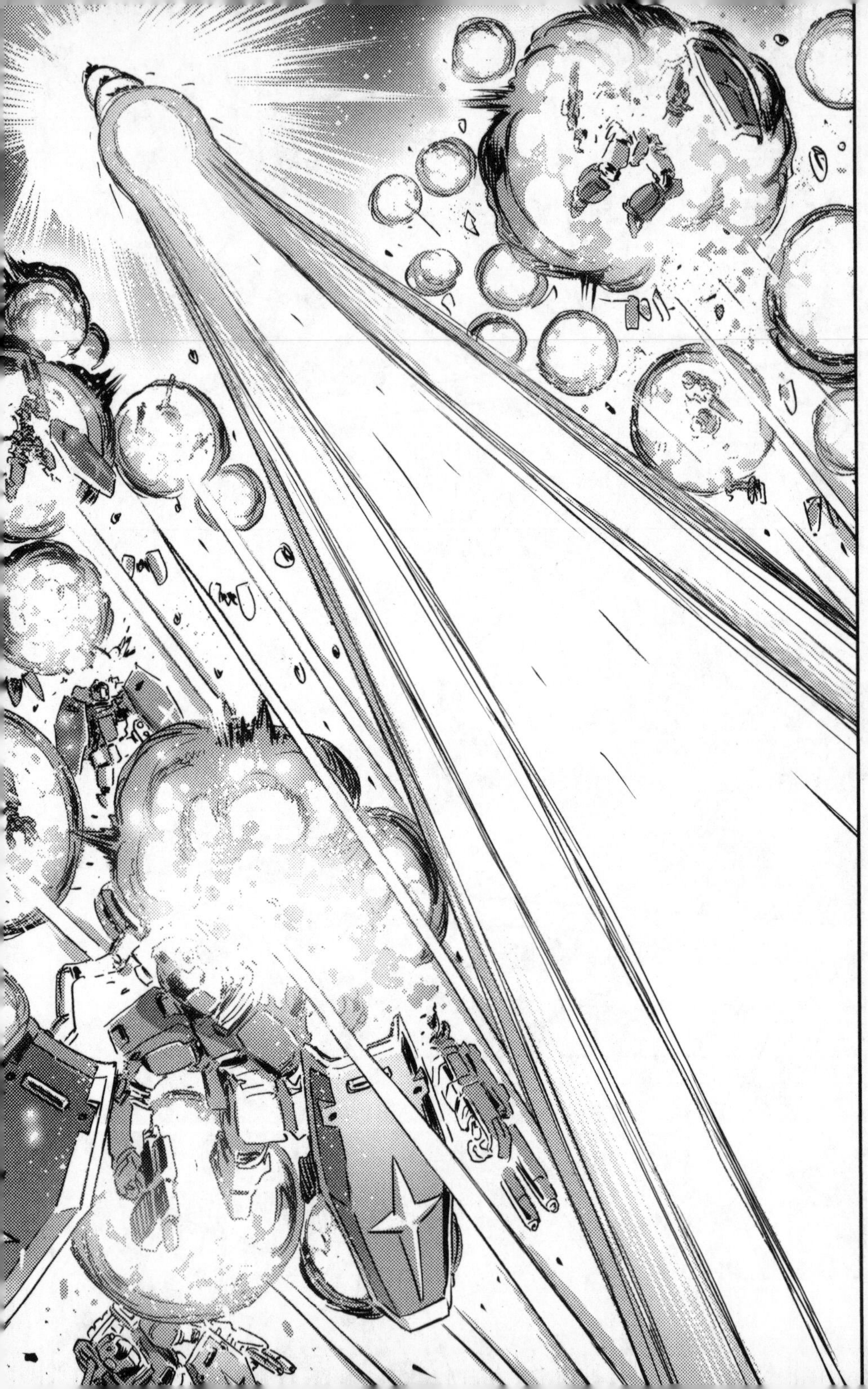

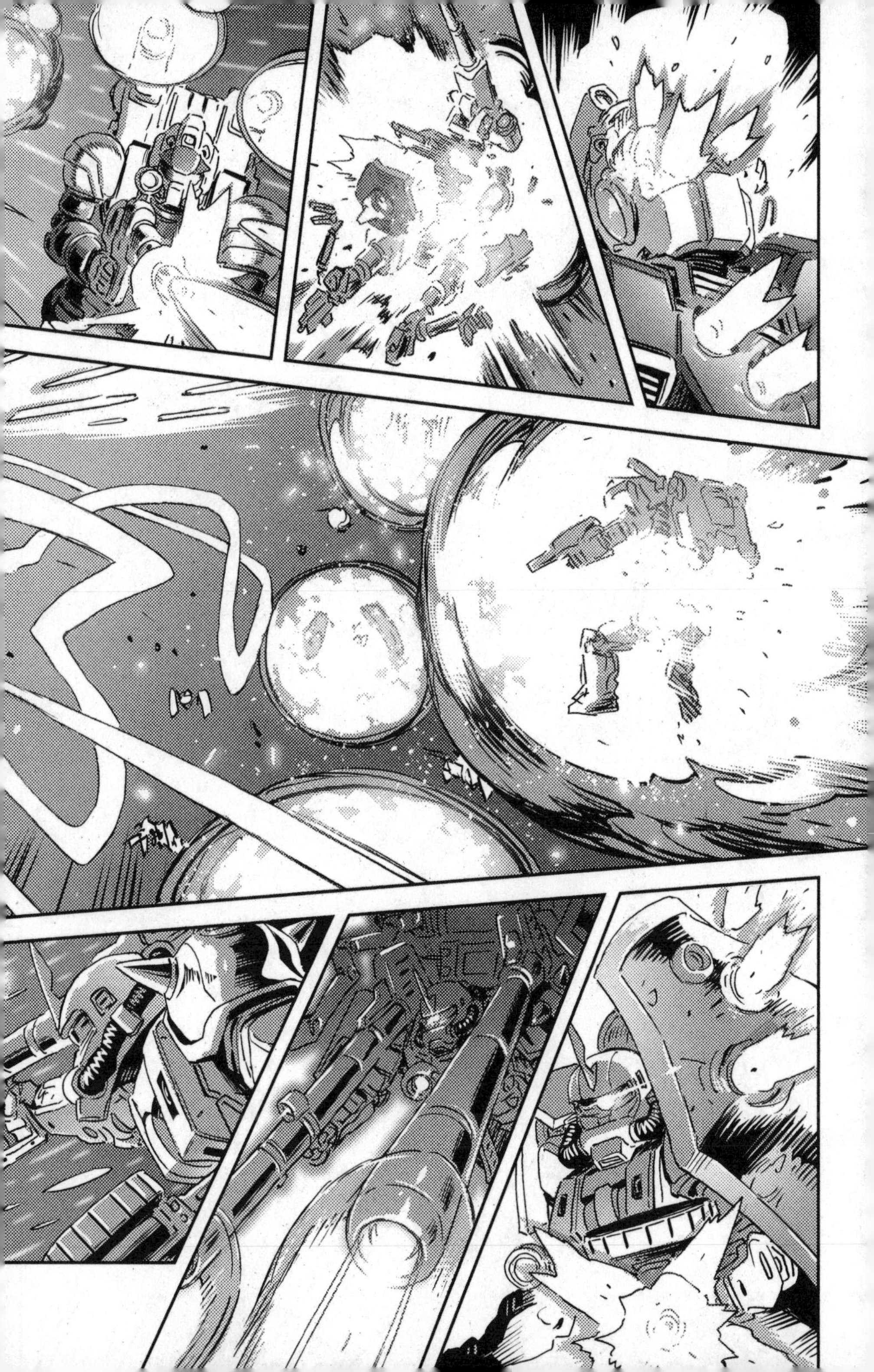

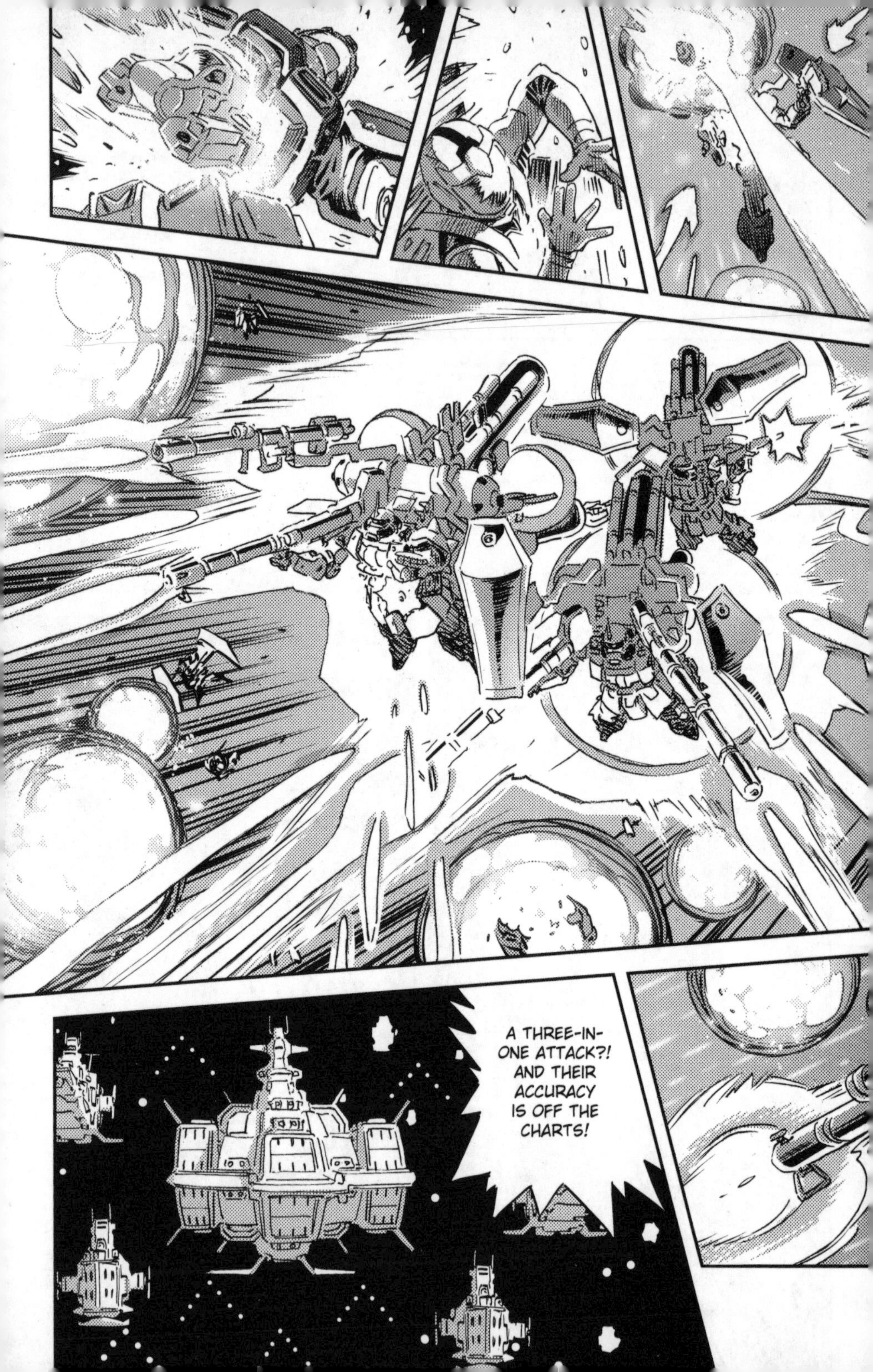
A THREE-IN-ONE ATTACK?! AND THEIR ACCURACY IS OFF THE CHARTS!

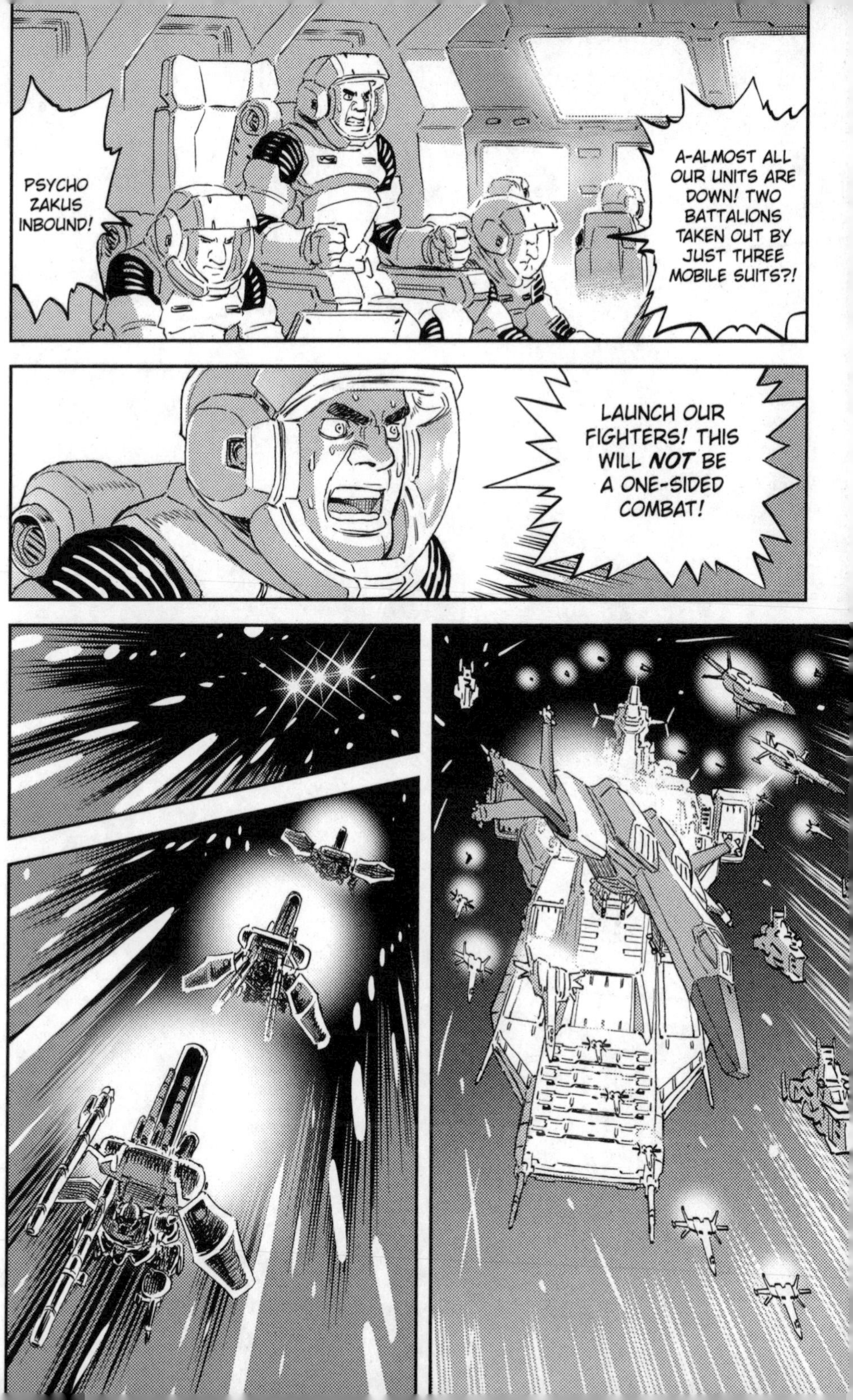
A-ALMOST ALL OUR UNITS ARE DOWN! TWO BATTALIONS TAKEN OUT BY JUST THREE MOBILE SUITS?!
PSYCHO ZAKUS INBOUND!
LAUNCH OUR FIGHTERS! THIS WILL NOT BE A ONE-SIDED COMBAT!

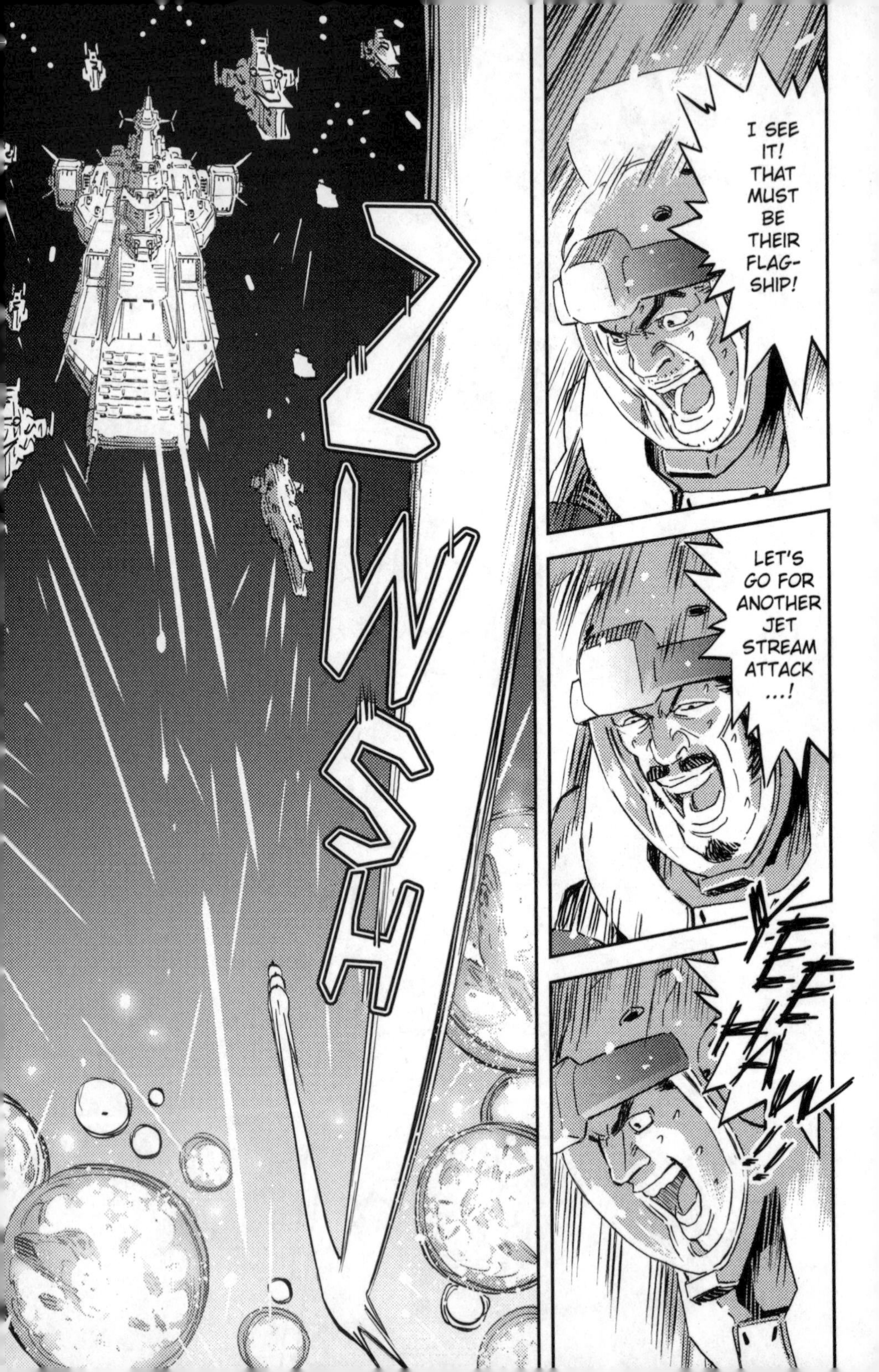
I SEE IT! THAT MUST BE THEIR FLAG-SHIP!
LET'S GO FOR ANOTHER JET STREAM ATTACK ...!
YEEEHAW!!

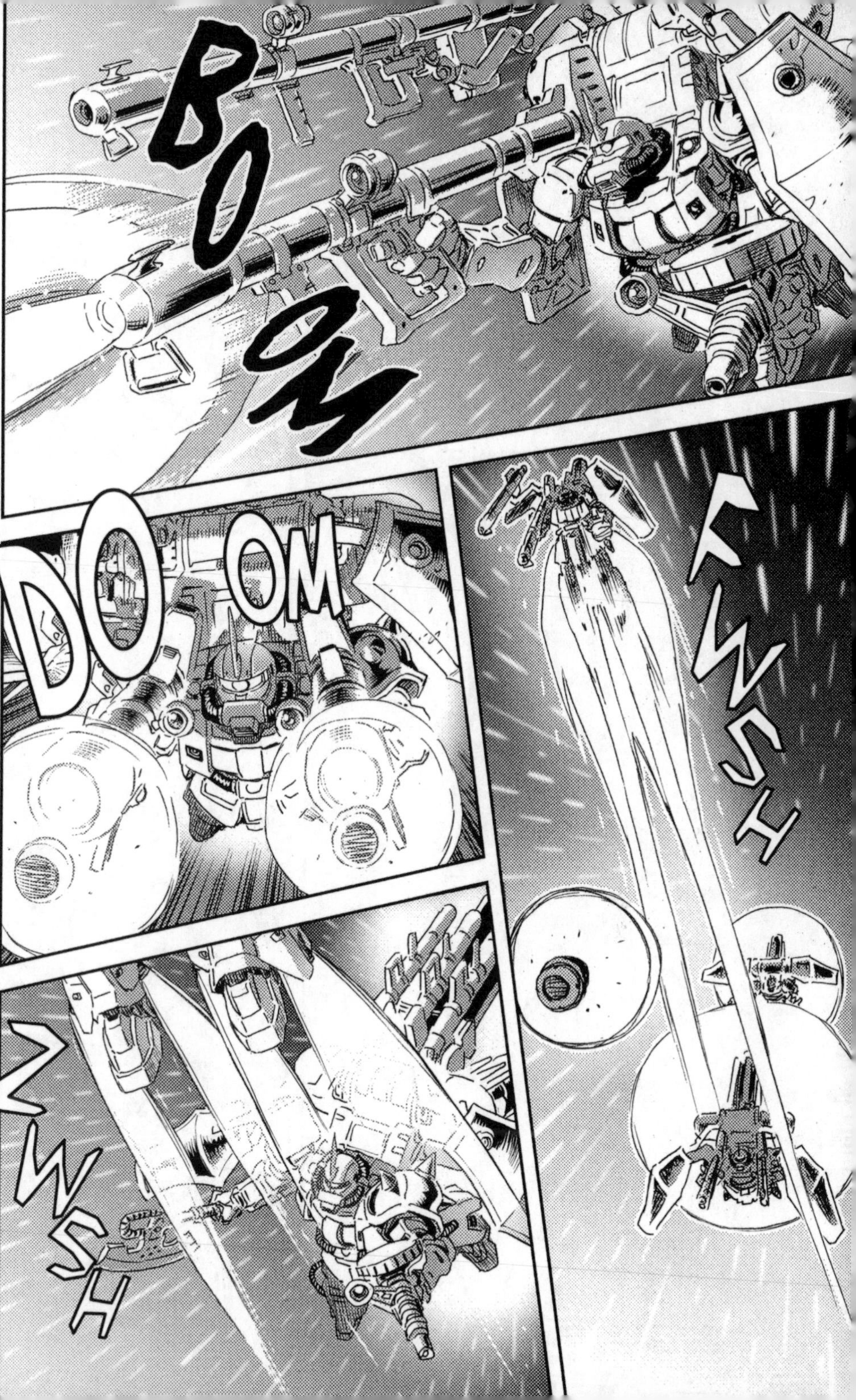
BOOM
KWSH
DOOM
KWSH

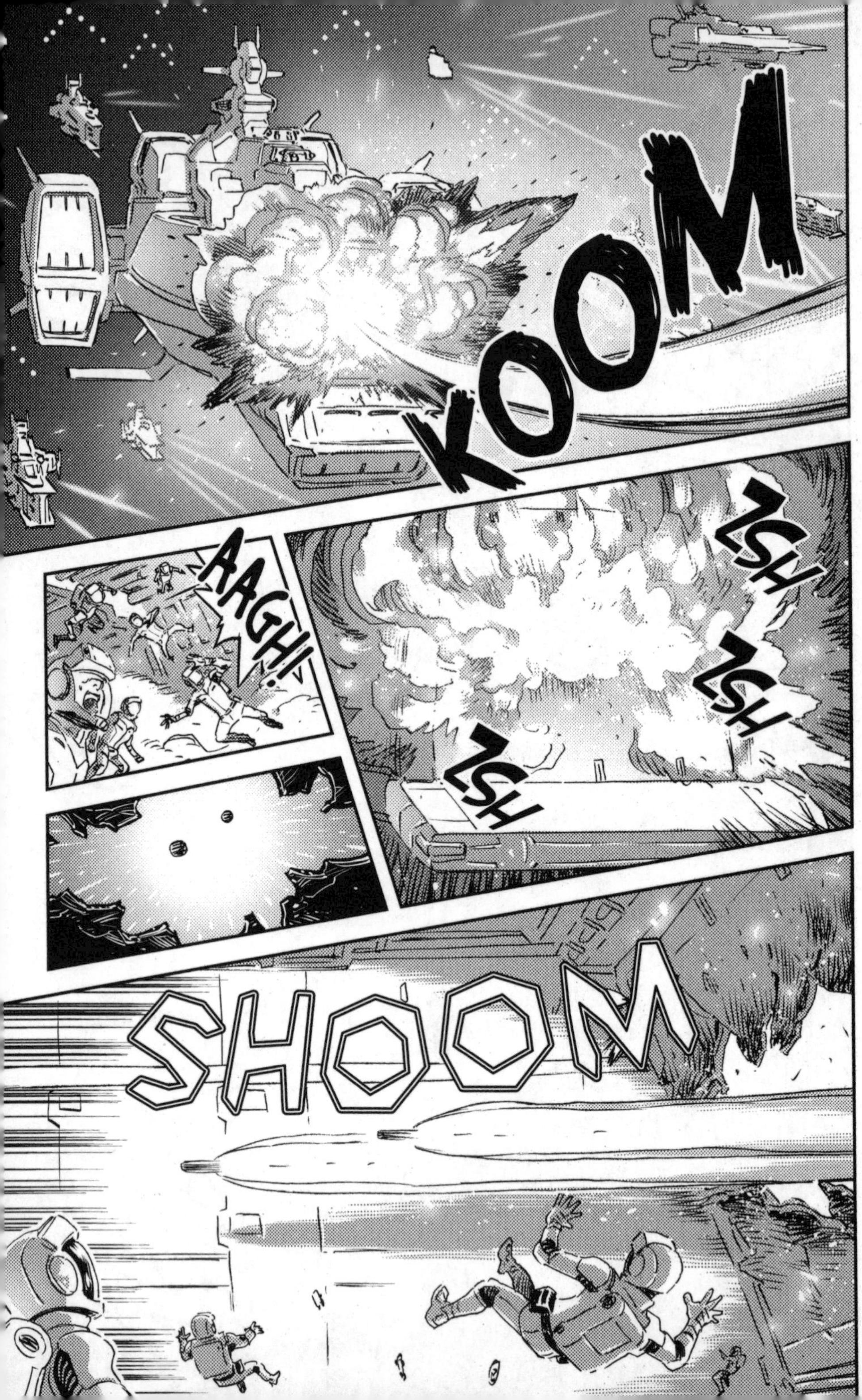
KOOM
ZSH
ZSH
ZSH
AAGH!
SHOOM

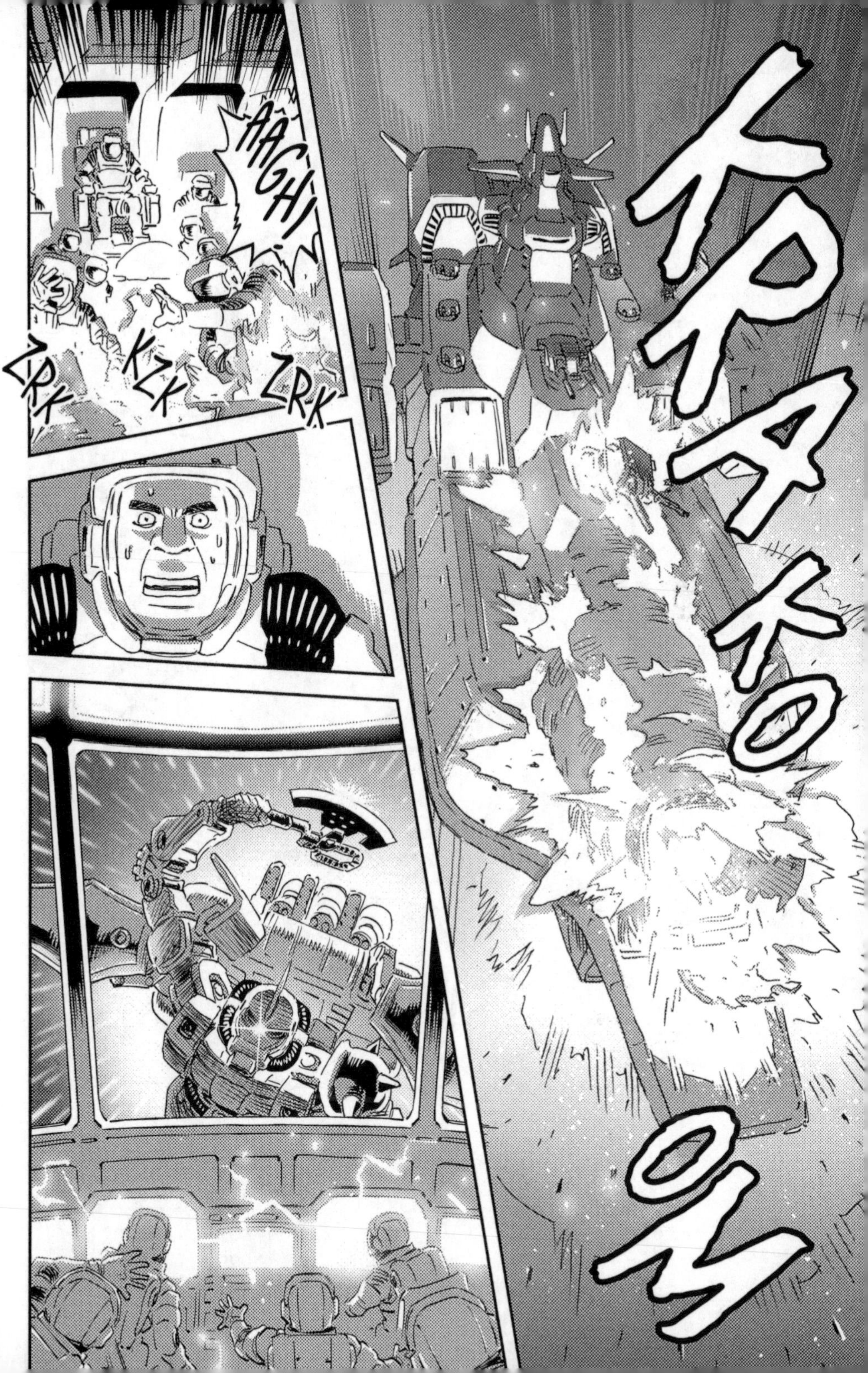
KRAKOOM
AAGH!
ZRK
KZK
ZRK

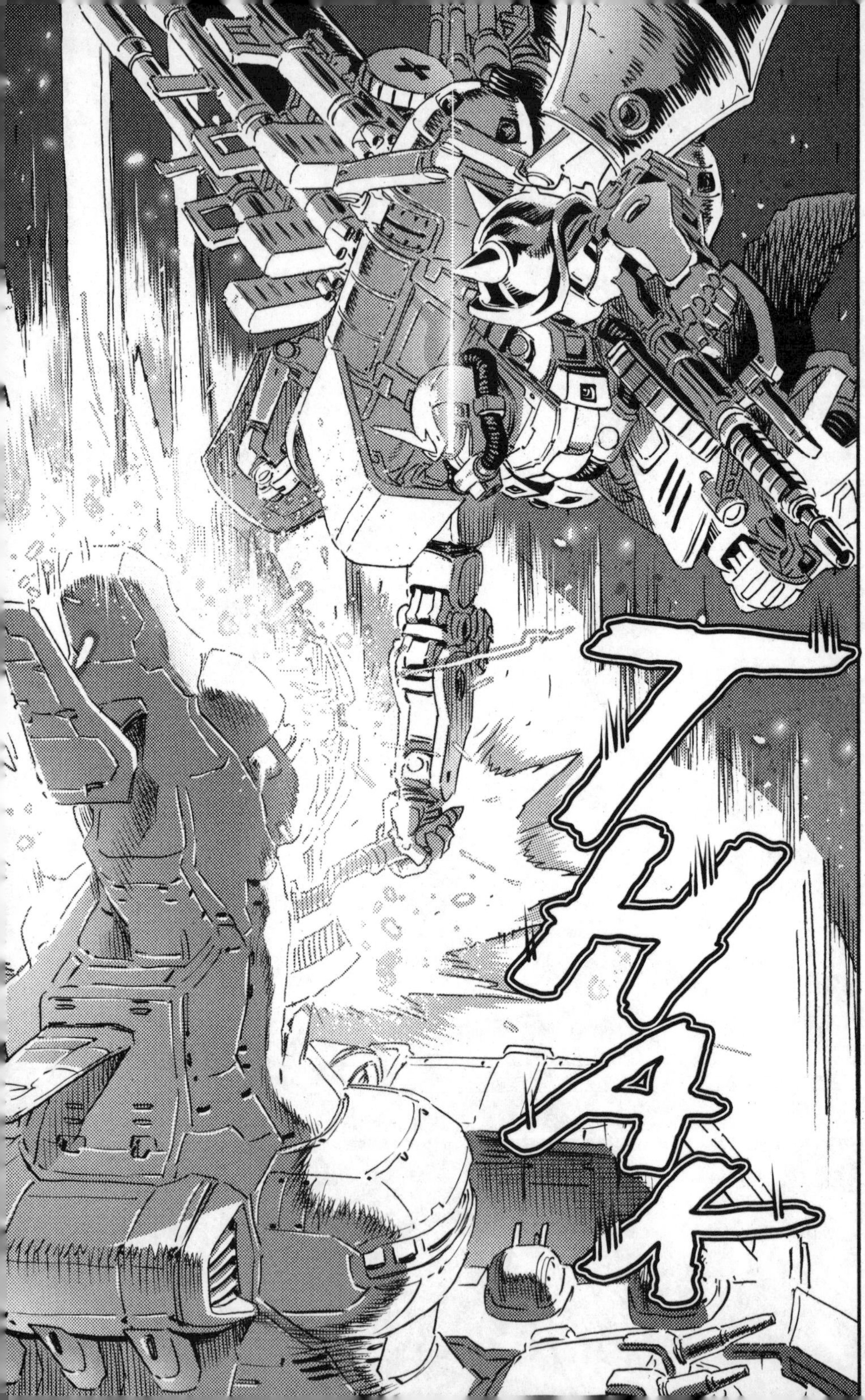

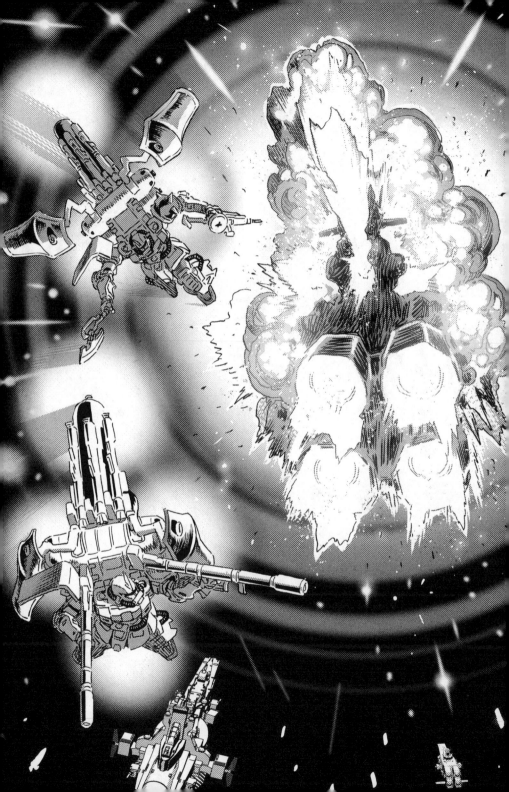

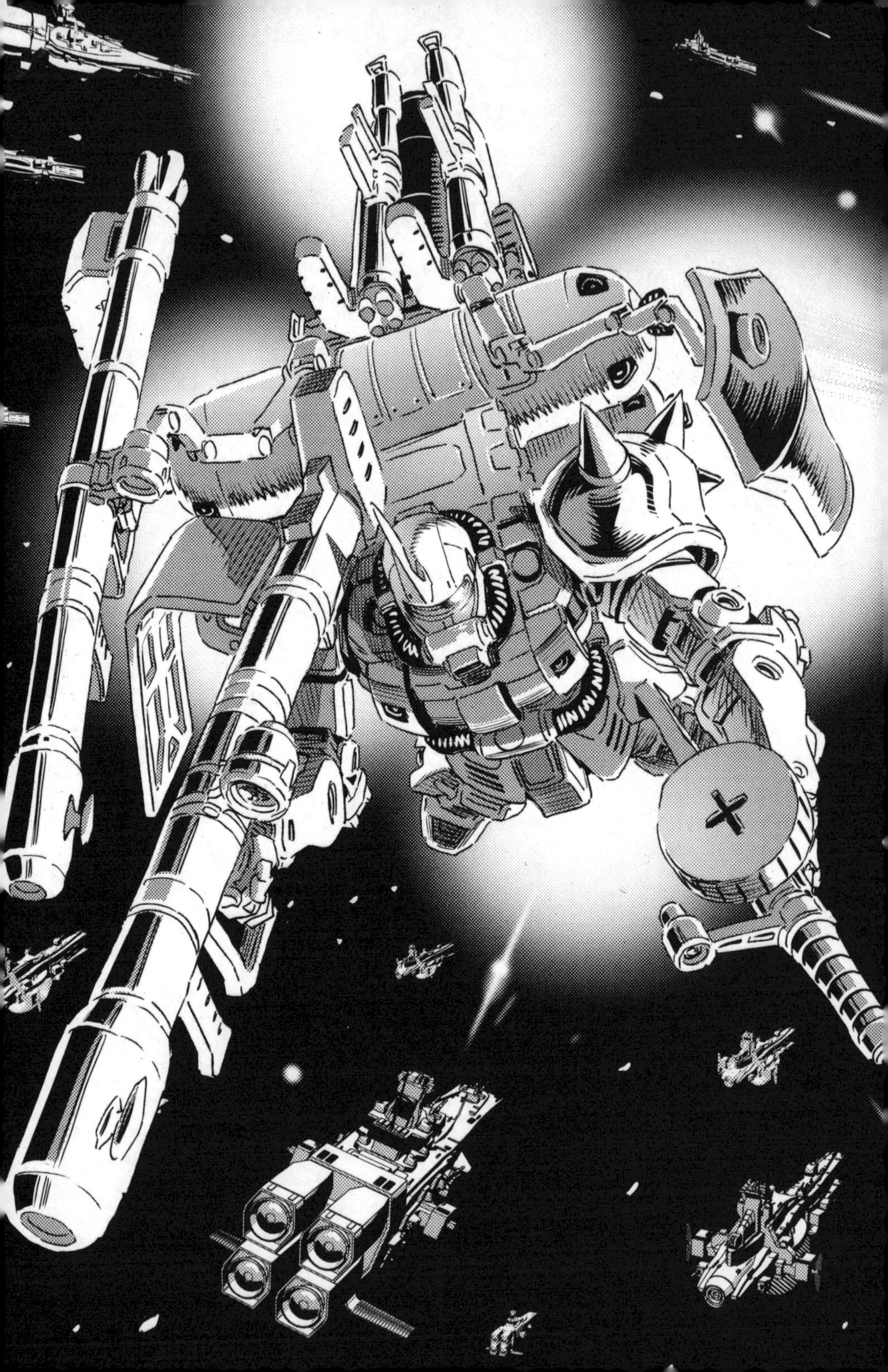

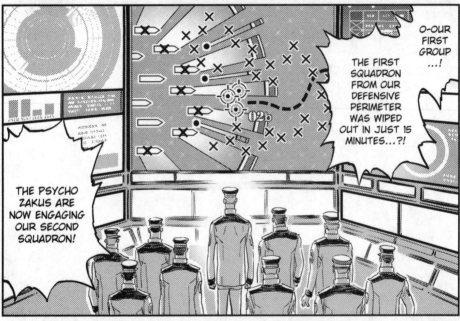

O-OUR FIRST GROUP ...!

THE FIRST SQUADRON FROM OUR DEFENSIVE PERIMETER WAS WIPED OUT IN JUST 15 MINUTES...?!

THE PSYCHO ZAKUS ARE NOW ENGAGING OUR SECOND SQUADRON!

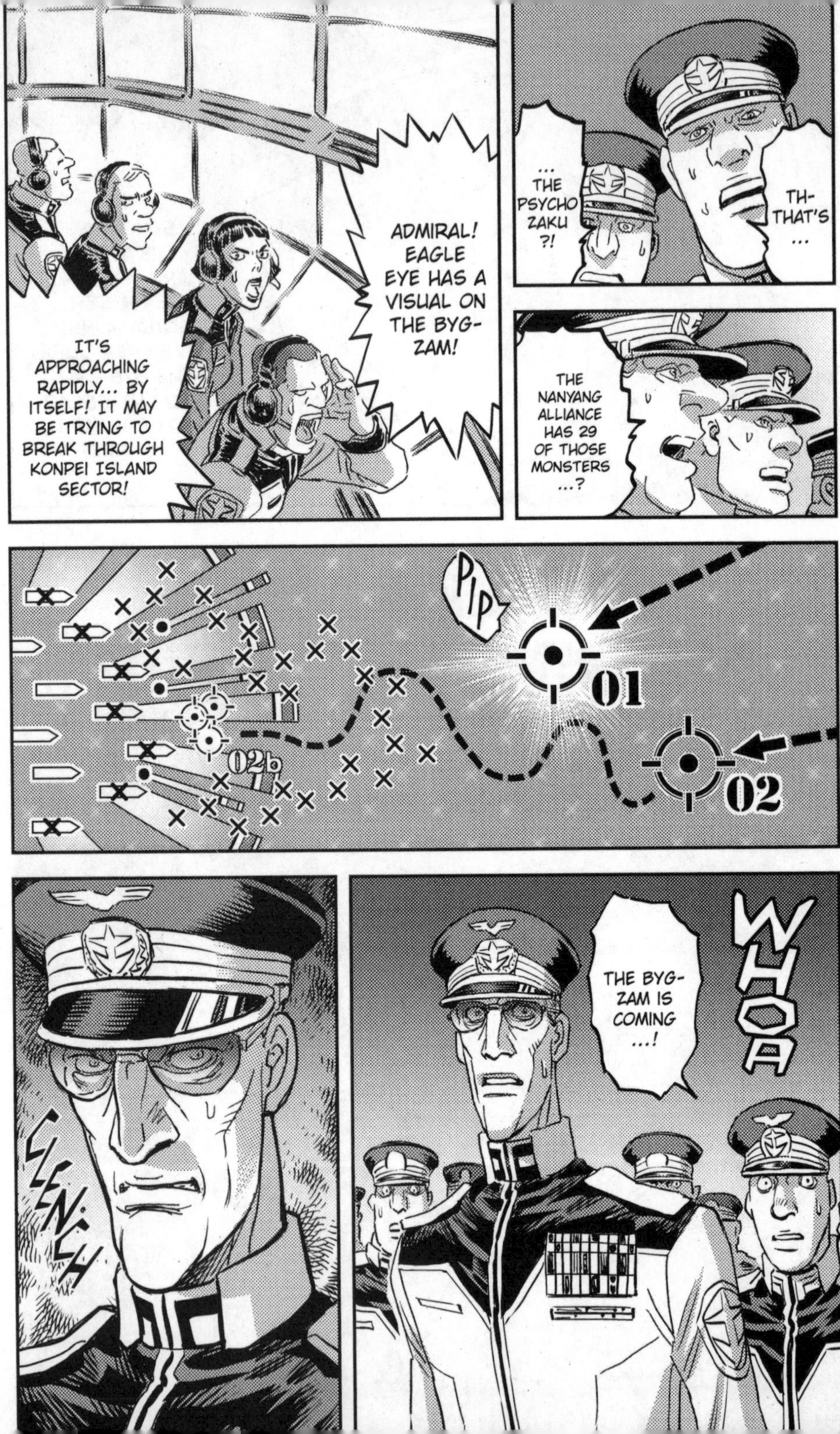
TH-THAT'S...
...THE PSYCHO ZAKU?!
THE NANYANG ALLIANCE HAS 29 OF THOSE MONSTERS...?
ADMIRAL! EAGLE EYE HAS A VISUAL ON THE BYG-ZAM!
IT'S APPROACHING RAPIDLY... BY ITSELF! IT MAY BE TRYING TO BREAK THROUGH KONPEI ISLAND SECTOR!
PIP
01
02
02b
WHOA
THE BYG-ZAM IS COMING...!
CLENCH

SEND OUT THE THIRD AND FOURTH PERIMETER SQUADRONS! HAVE THEM LURE THE BYG-ZAM INTO THE SOLAR RAY'S LINE OF FIRE!

DO NOT LET THEM FLY THROUGH!

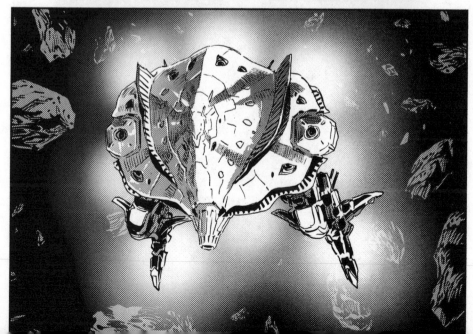

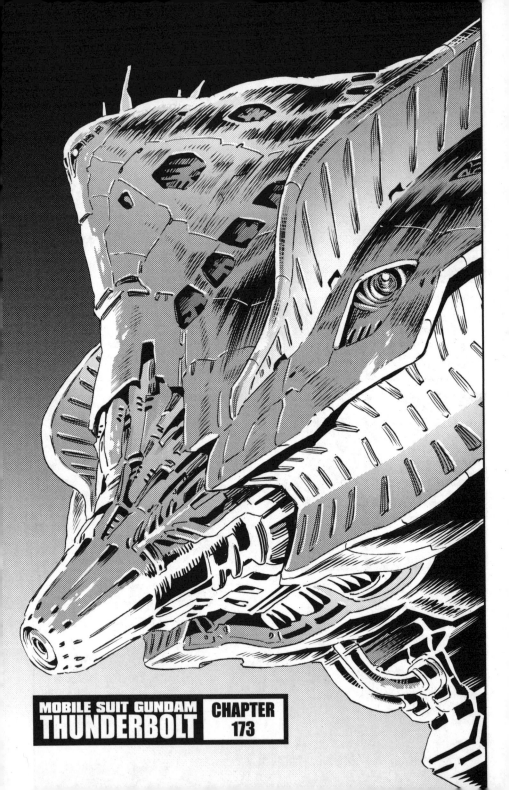

MOBILE SUIT GUNDAM THUNDERBOLT

CHAPTER 173

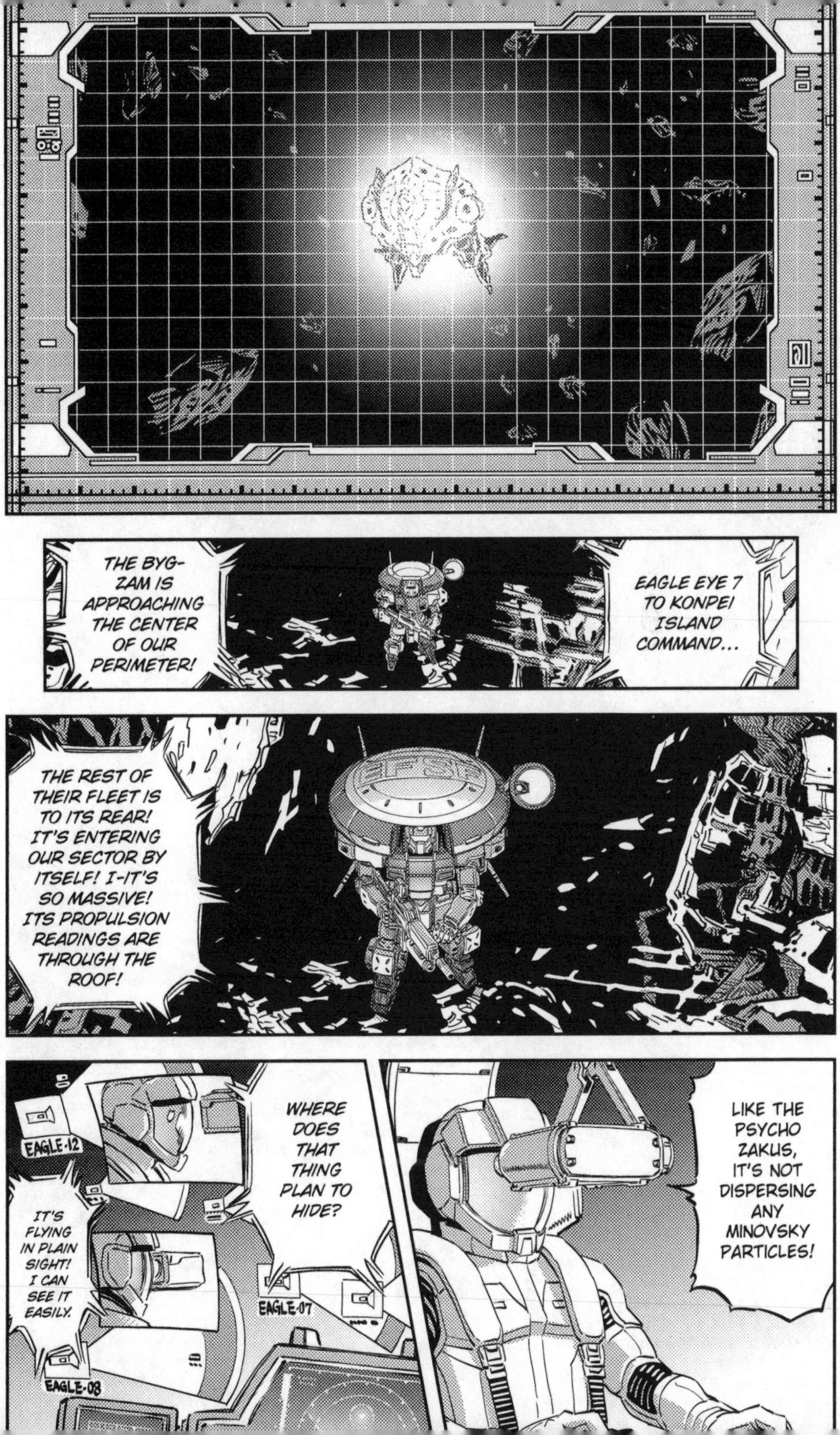
EAGLE EYE 7 TO KONPEI ISLAND COMMAND...
THE BYG-ZAM IS APPROACHING THE CENTER OF OUR PERIMETER!
THE REST OF THEIR FLEET IS TO ITS REAR! IT'S ENTERING OUR SECTOR BY ITSELF! I-IT'S SO MASSIVE! ITS PROPULSION READINGS ARE THROUGH THE ROOF!
LIKE THE PSYCHO ZAKUS, IT'S NOT DISPERSING ANY MINOVSKY PARTICLES!
WHERE DOES THAT THING PLAN TO HIDE?
EAGLE-12
IT'S FLYING IN PLAIN SIGHT! I CAN SEE IT EASILY.
EAGLE-07
EAGLE-08

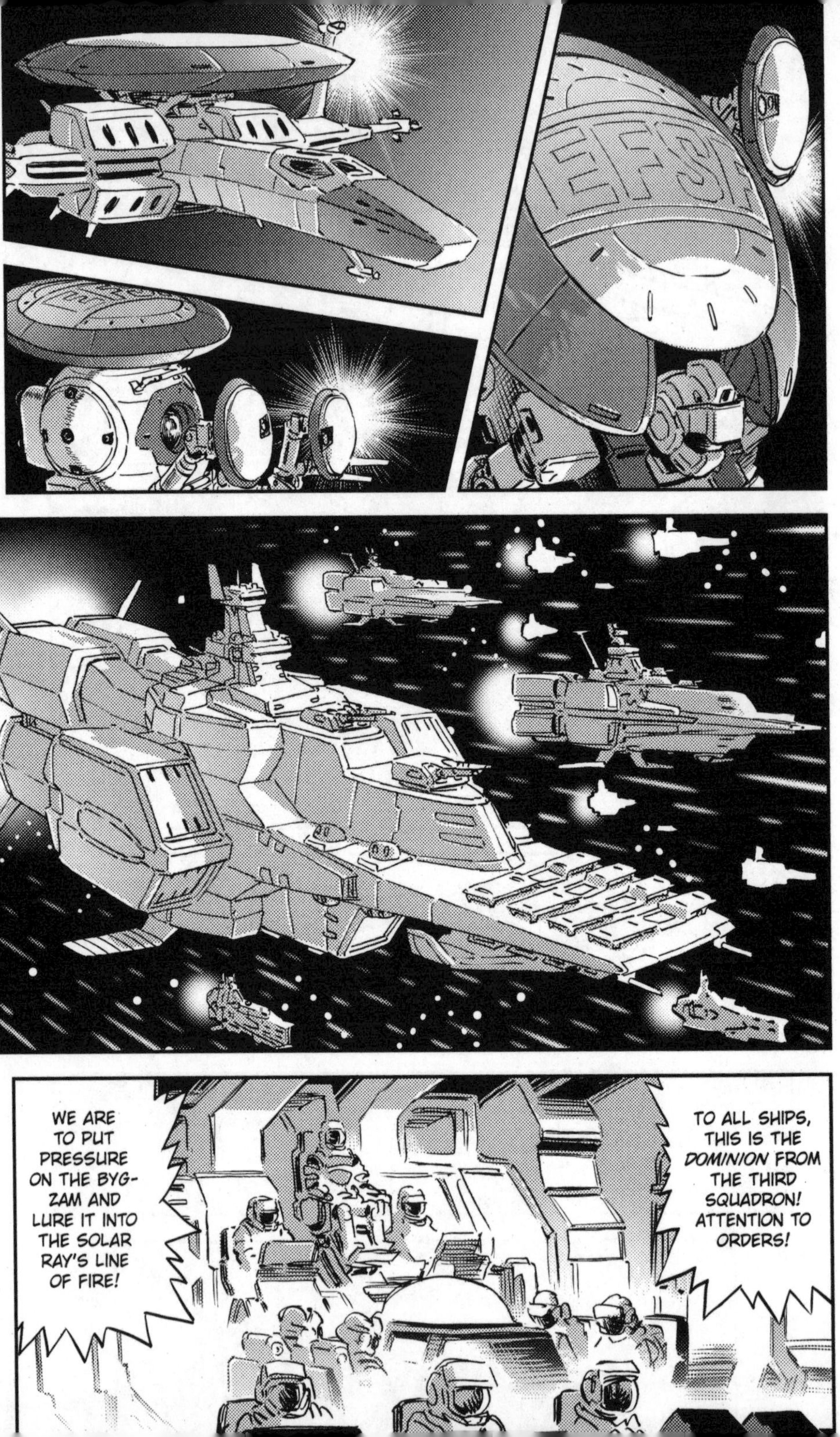
TO ALL SHIPS, THIS IS THE *DOMINION* FROM THE THIRD SQUADRON! ATTENTION TO ORDERS!
WE ARE TO PUT PRESSURE ON THE BYG-ZAM AND LURE IT INTO THE SOLAR RAY'S LINE OF FIRE!

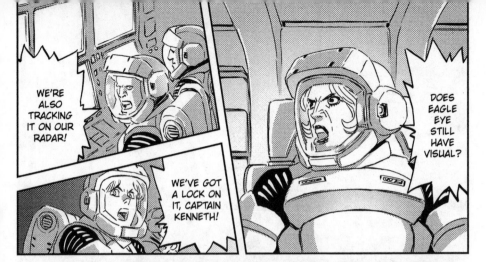

DOES EAGLE EYE STILL HAVE VISUAL?
WE'RE ALSO TRACKING IT ON OUR RADAR!
WE'VE GOT A LOCK ON IT, CAPTAIN KENNETH!
PIP PIP
KONPEITO
01
02b
02
03
AN OVERSIZED MOBILE ARMOR LIKE THAT HAS ALMOST NO MANEUVERABILITY! EXPOSING ITSELF IS JUST MAKING IT A TARGET!
WE'LL DISPERSE MINOVSKY PARTICLES PER STANDARD OPERATING PROCEDURE! PREPARE FOR CONTACT!
01
PIP PIP
01

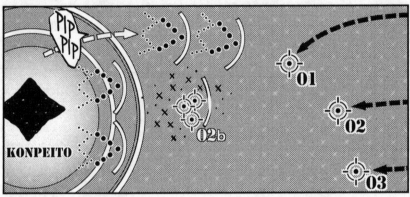

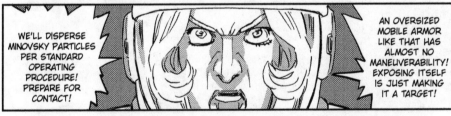

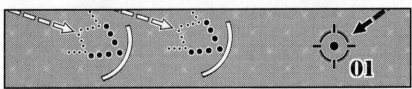

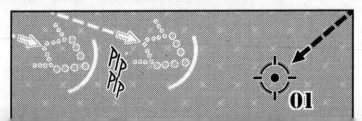

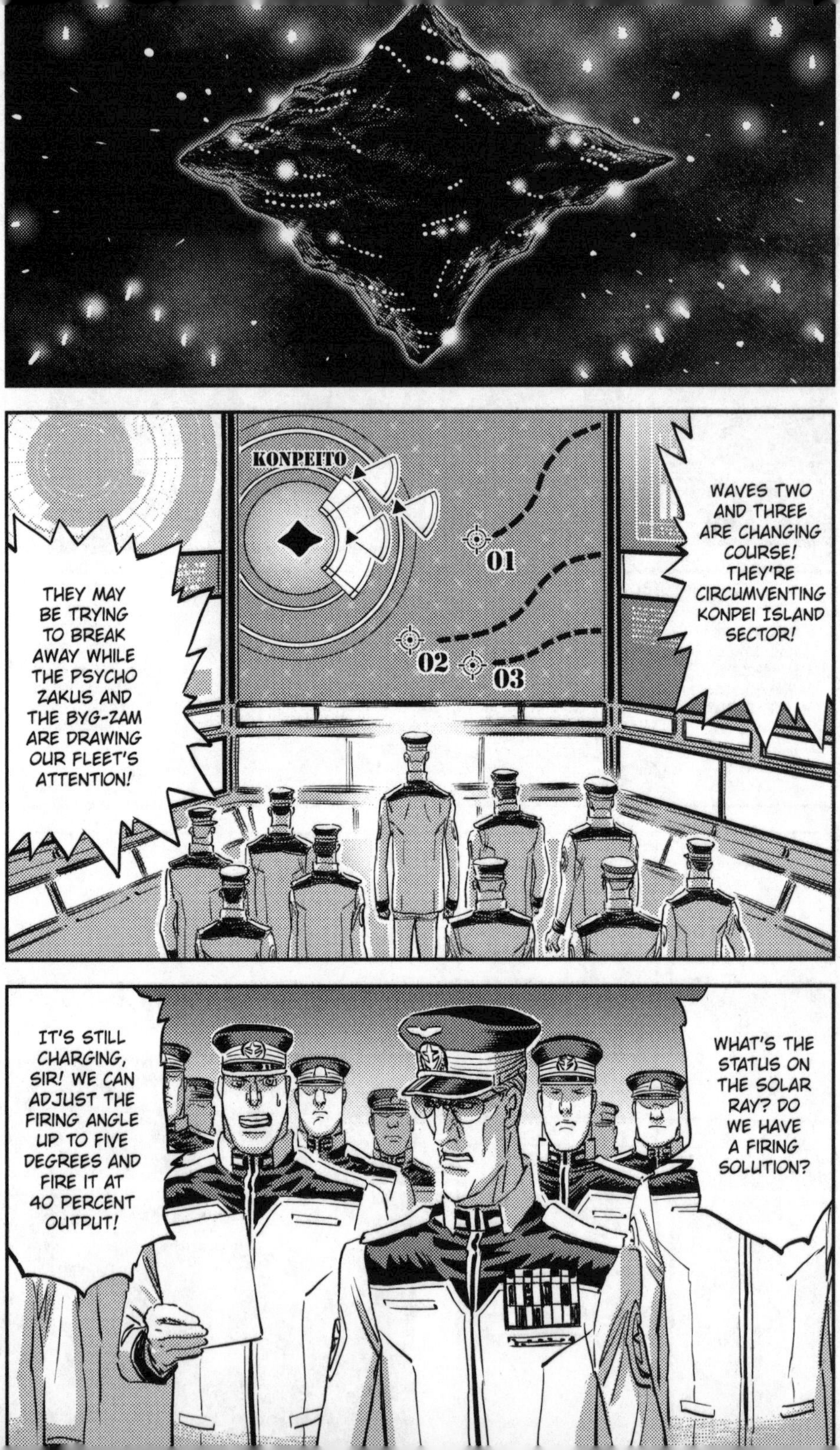
WAVES TWO AND THREE ARE CHANGING COURSE! THEY'RE CIRCUMVENTING KONPEI ISLAND SECTOR!
KONPEITO
01
02
03
THEY MAY BE TRYING TO BREAK AWAY WHILE THE PSYCHO ZAKUS AND THE BYG-ZAM ARE DRAWING OUR FLEET'S ATTENTION!
WHAT'S THE STATUS ON THE SOLAR RAY? DO WE HAVE A FIRING SOLUTION?
IT'S STILL CHARGING, SIR! WE CAN ADJUST THE FIRING ANGLE UP TO FIVE DEGREES AND FIRE IT AT 40 PERCENT OUTPUT!

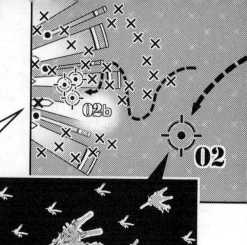

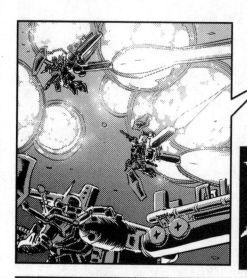

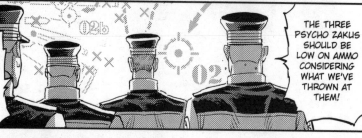

02b
02
THE THREE PSYCHO ZAKUS SHOULD BE LOW ON AMMO CONSIDERING WHAT WE'VE THROWN AT THEM!
02b
02
OUR FLEET HAS TAKEN SIGNIFICANT DAMAGE... BUT IF THE ENEMY REMAINS ON COURSE, THEY'LL ALL BE IN OUR LINE OF FIRE.
02
03
WHERE'S DIRECTOR HUMPHREY'S FLYING SQUADRON?
THEY ENTERED THE SOLAR RAY'S LINE OF FIRE A MOMENT AGO...!
MOON

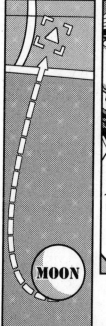

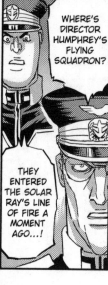

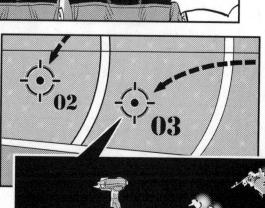

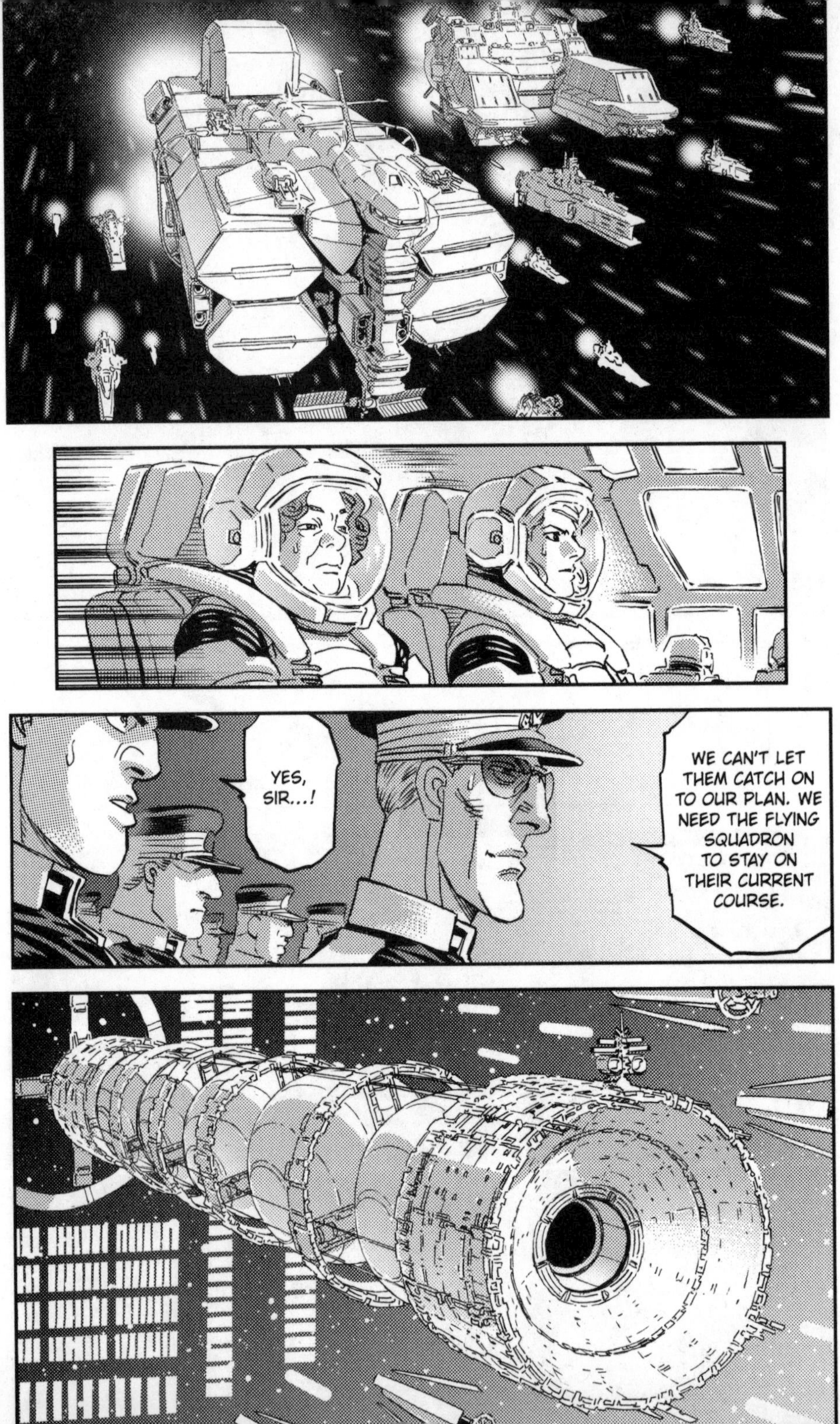
WE CAN'T LET THEM CATCH ON TO OUR PLAN. WE NEED THE FLYING SQUADRON TO STAY ON THEIR CURRENT COURSE.
YES, SIR...!

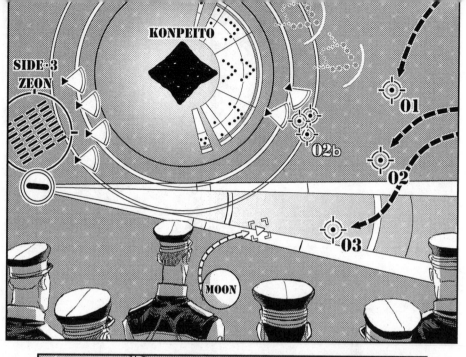

KONPEITO

SIDE-3
ZEON

01

02b

02

03

MOON

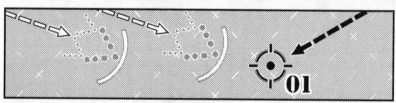

01

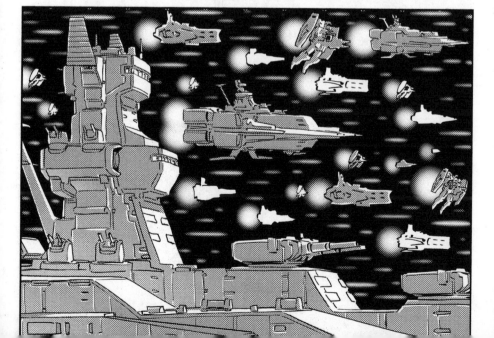

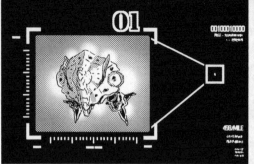

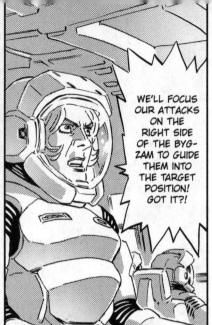

WE'LL FOCUS OUR ATTACKS ON THE RIGHT SIDE OF THE BYG-ZAM TO GUIDE THEM INTO THE TARGET POSITION! GOT IT?!
01
00100010000
STILL NO MINOVSKY PARTICLE DISPERSION DETECTED! WE CAN FIRE OUR GUIDED MISSILES!
WE HAVE A LOCK ON THE TARGET!
01
IGNITE THE SATELLITE MISSILE BOOSTERS! SEND THEM OUT!

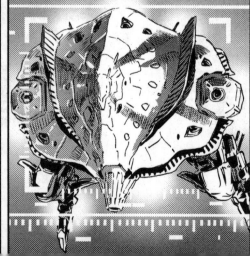

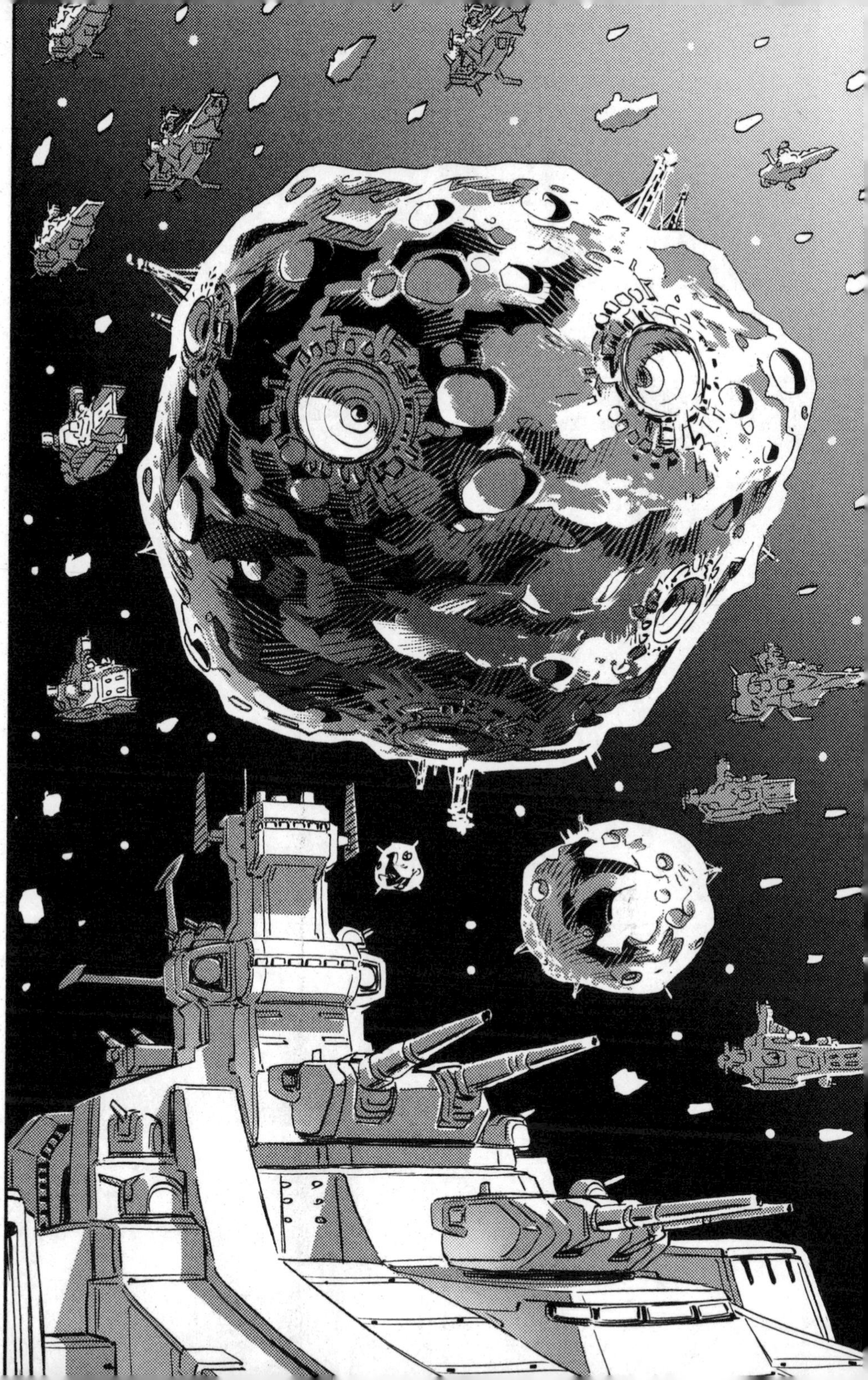

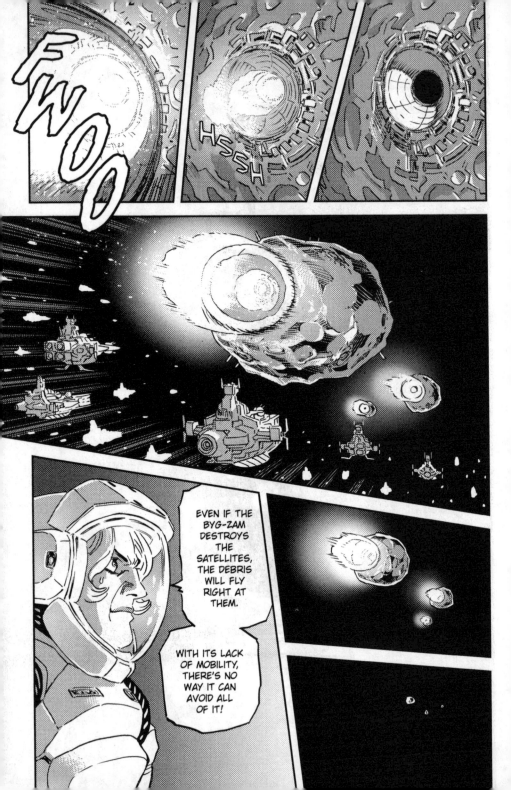

FWOO

HSSH

EVEN IF THE BYG-ZAM DESTROYS THE SATELLITES, THE DEBRIS WILL FLY RIGHT AT THEM.

WITH ITS LACK OF MOBILITY, THERE'S NO WAY IT CAN AVOID ALL OF IT!

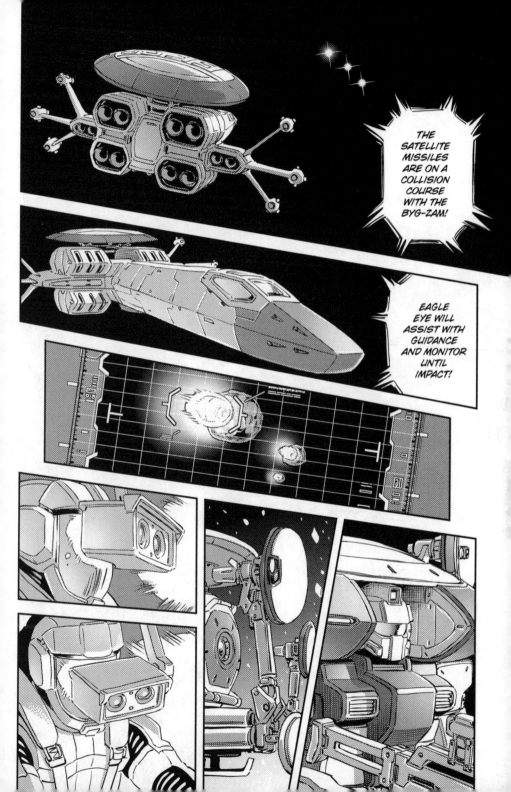

THE SATELLITE MISSILES ARE ON A COLLISION COURSE WITH THE BYG-ZAM!

EAGLE EYE WILL ASSIST WITH GUIDANCE AND MONITOR UNTIL IMPACT!

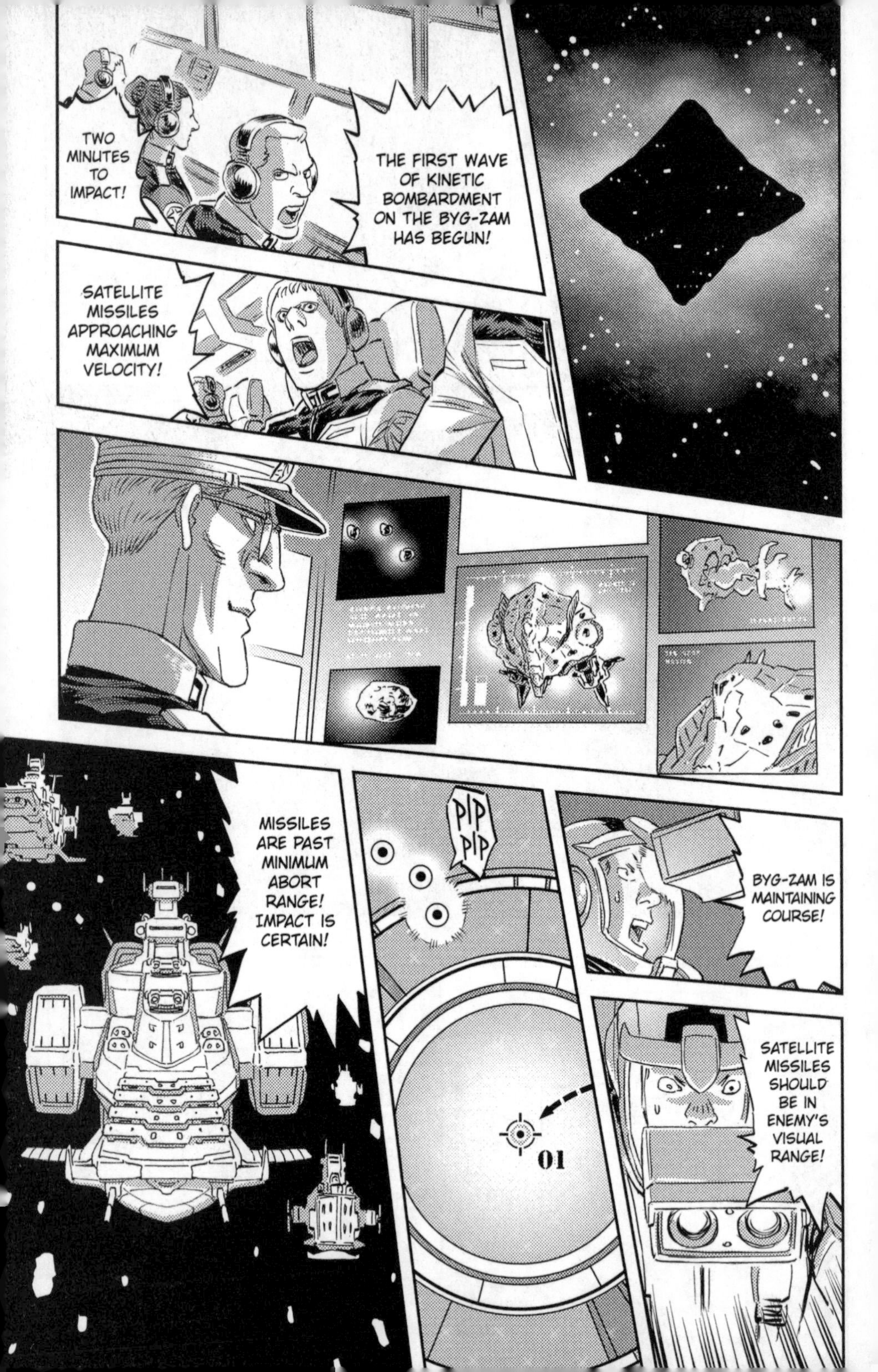
THE FIRST WAVE OF KINETIC BOMBARDMENT ON THE BYG-ZAM HAS BEGUN!
TWO MINUTES TO IMPACT!
SATELLITE MISSILES APPROACHING MAXIMUM VELOCITY!
BYG-ZAM IS MAINTAINING COURSE!
SATELLITE MISSILES SHOULD BE IN ENEMY'S VISUAL RANGE!
PIP PIP
01
MISSILES ARE PAST MINIMUM ABORT RANGE! IMPACT IS CERTAIN!

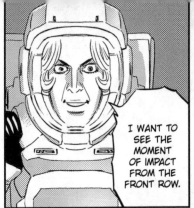

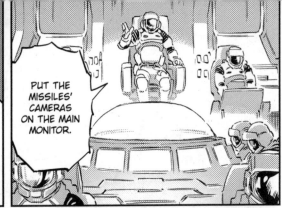

PUT THE MISSILES' CAMERAS ON THE MAIN MONITOR.
I WANT TO SEE THE MOMENT OF IMPACT FROM THE FRONT ROW.
3
2
1
3
2
1
HMM? WHAT?
WHERE'S THE BYG-ZAM?
?

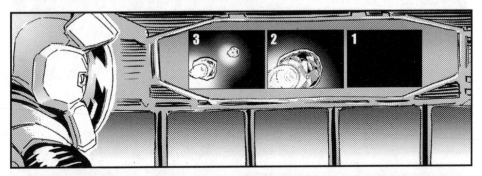

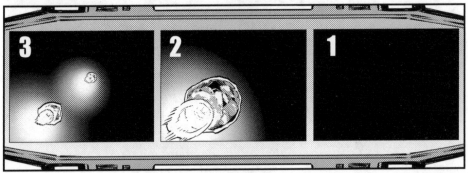

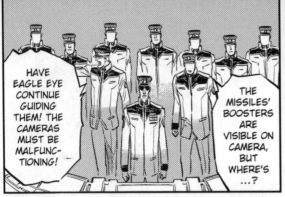

THE MISSILES' BOOSTERS ARE VISIBLE ON CAMERA, BUT WHERE'S ...?
HAVE EAGLE EYE CONTINUE GUIDING THEM! THE CAMERAS MUST BE MALFUNCTIONING!
?
THE BYG-ZAM MUST BE UNAWARE OF OUR ATTACK! NO ANTI-AIR FIRE OR EVASIVE MANEUVERS DETECTED!
01
IMPACT!

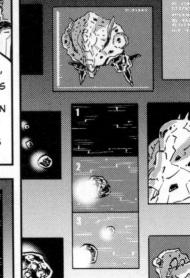

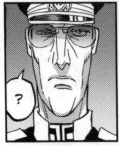

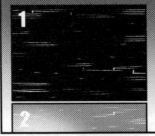

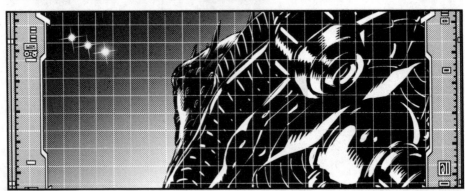

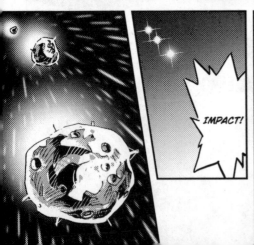

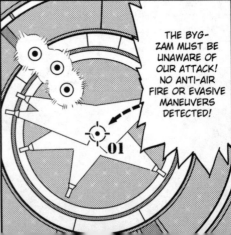

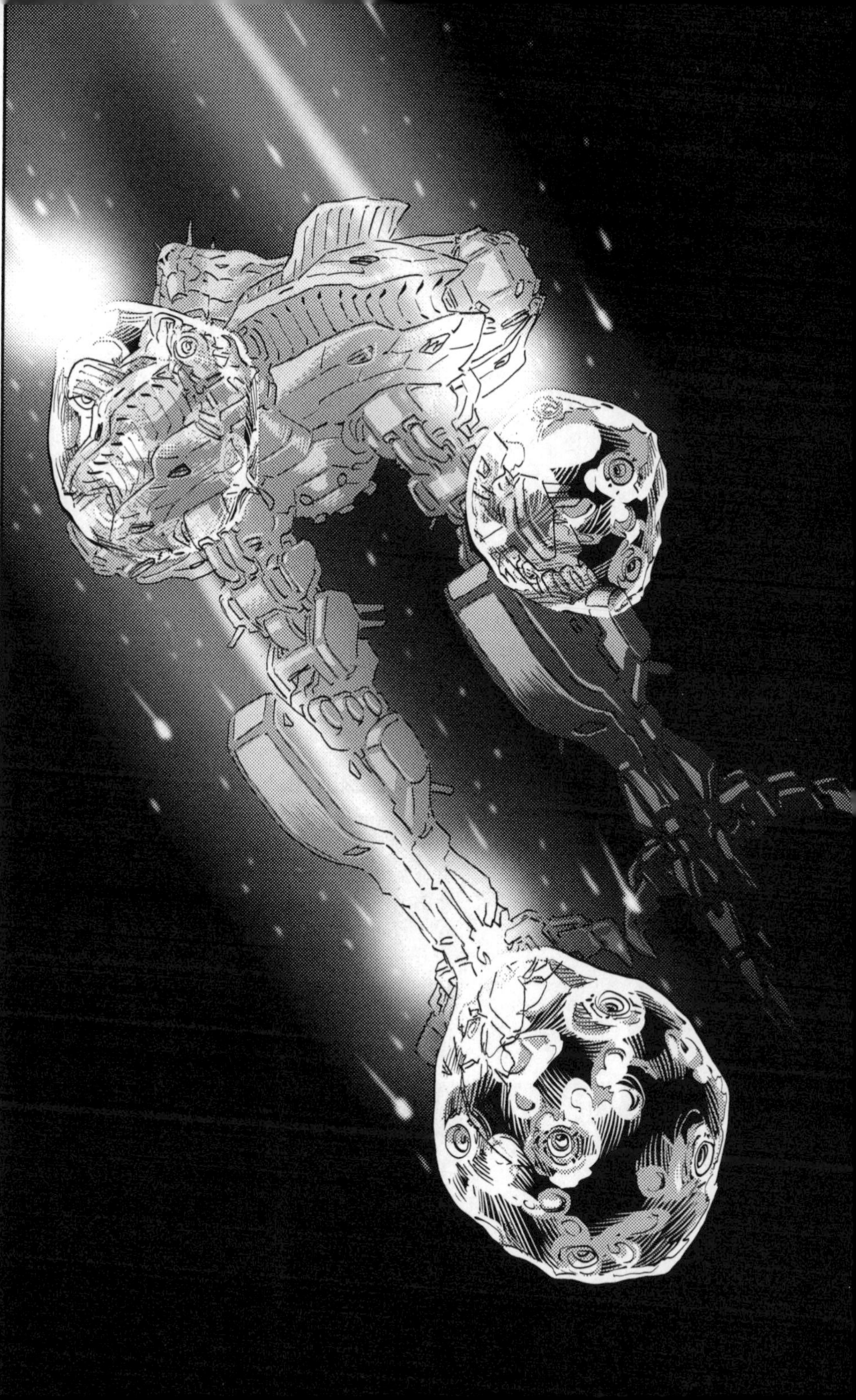

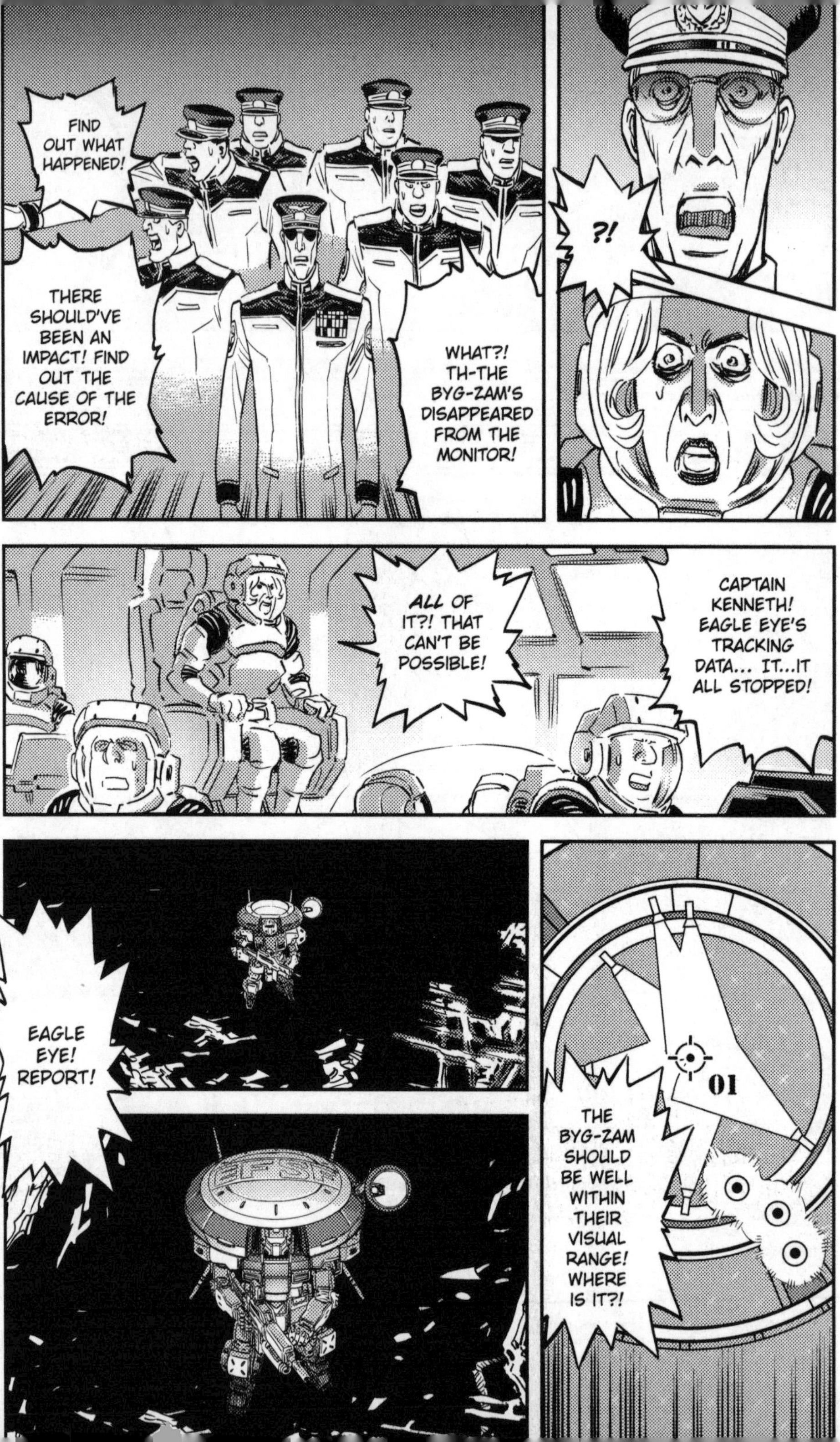
?!
WHAT?! TH-THE BYG-ZAM'S DISAPPEARED FROM THE MONITOR!
FIND OUT WHAT HAPPENED!
THERE SHOULD'VE BEEN AN IMPACT! FIND OUT THE CAUSE OF THE ERROR!
CAPTAIN KENNETH! EAGLE EYE'S TRACKING DATA... IT...IT ALL STOPPED!
ALL OF IT?! THAT CAN'T BE POSSIBLE!
01
THE BYG-ZAM SHOULD BE WELL WITHIN THEIR VISUAL RANGE! WHERE IS IT?!
EAGLE EYE! REPORT!
EFSF

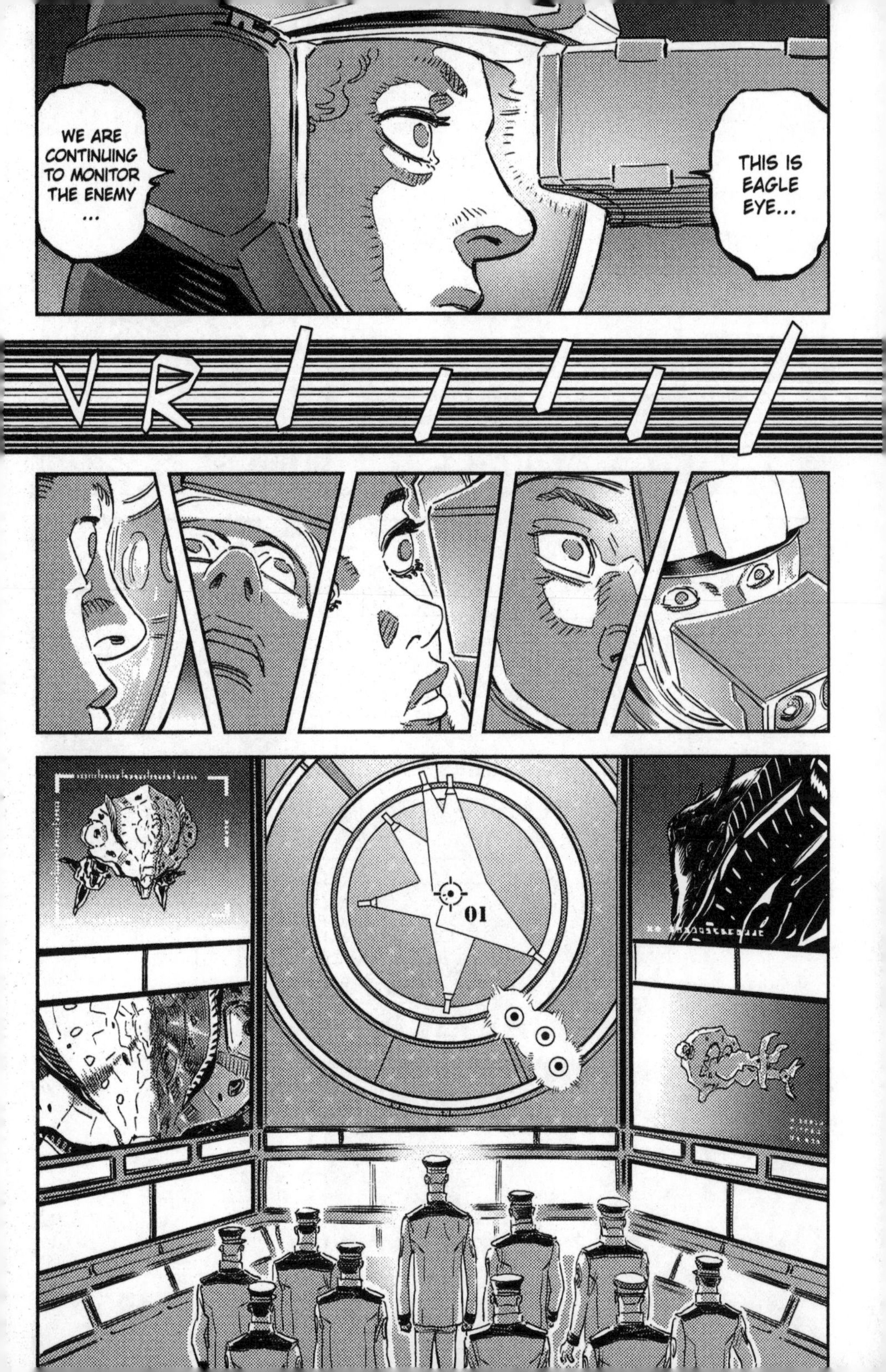
THIS IS EAGLE EYE…
WE ARE CONTINUING TO MONITOR THE ENEMY …
VRIIIIII
01

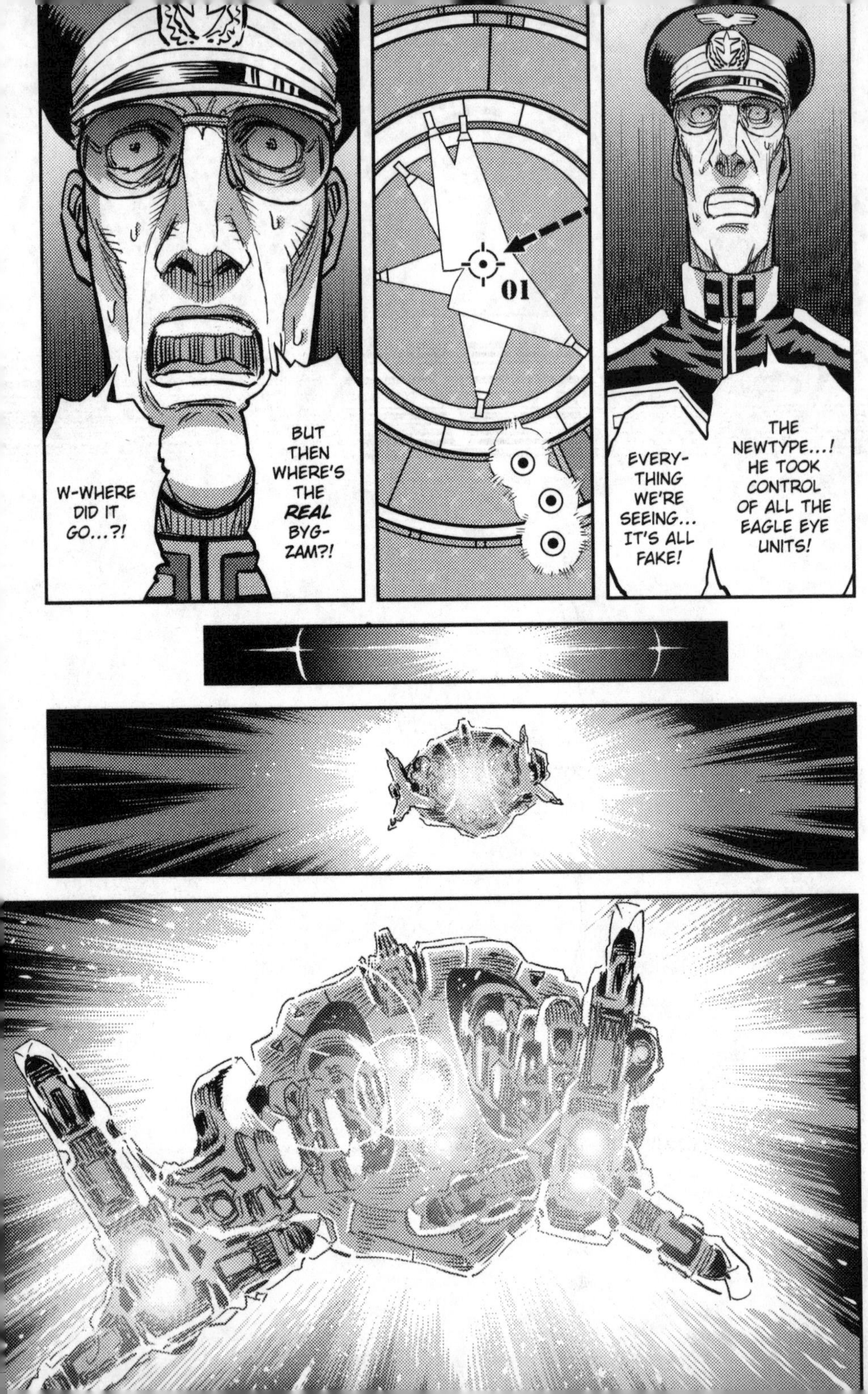
THE NEWTYPE...! HE TOOK CONTROL OF ALL THE EAGLE EYE UNITS!
EVERYTHING WE'RE SEEING... IT'S ALL FAKE!
BUT THEN WHERE'S THE *REAL* BYGZAM?!
W-WHERE DID IT GO...?!

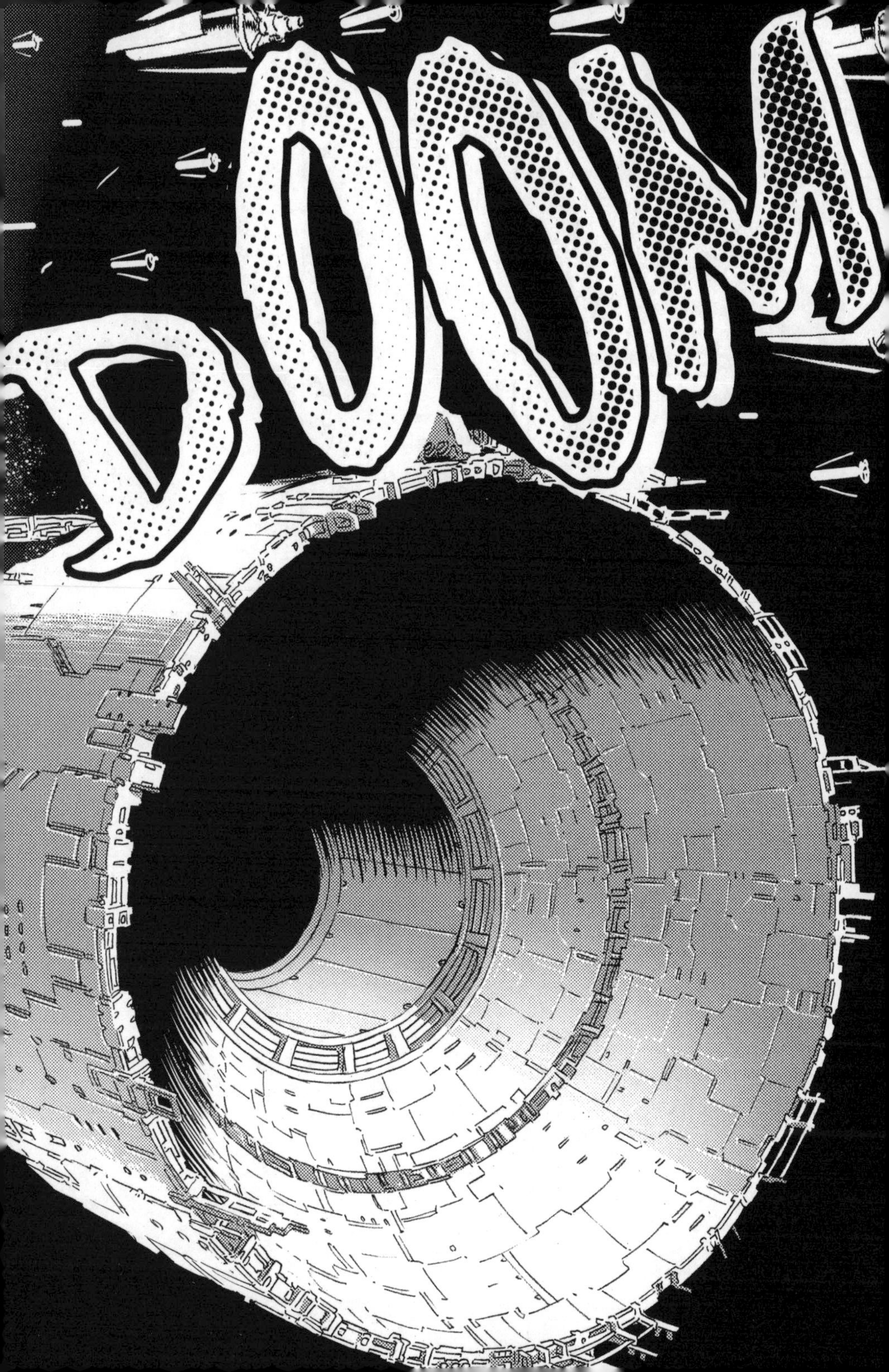
DOOM

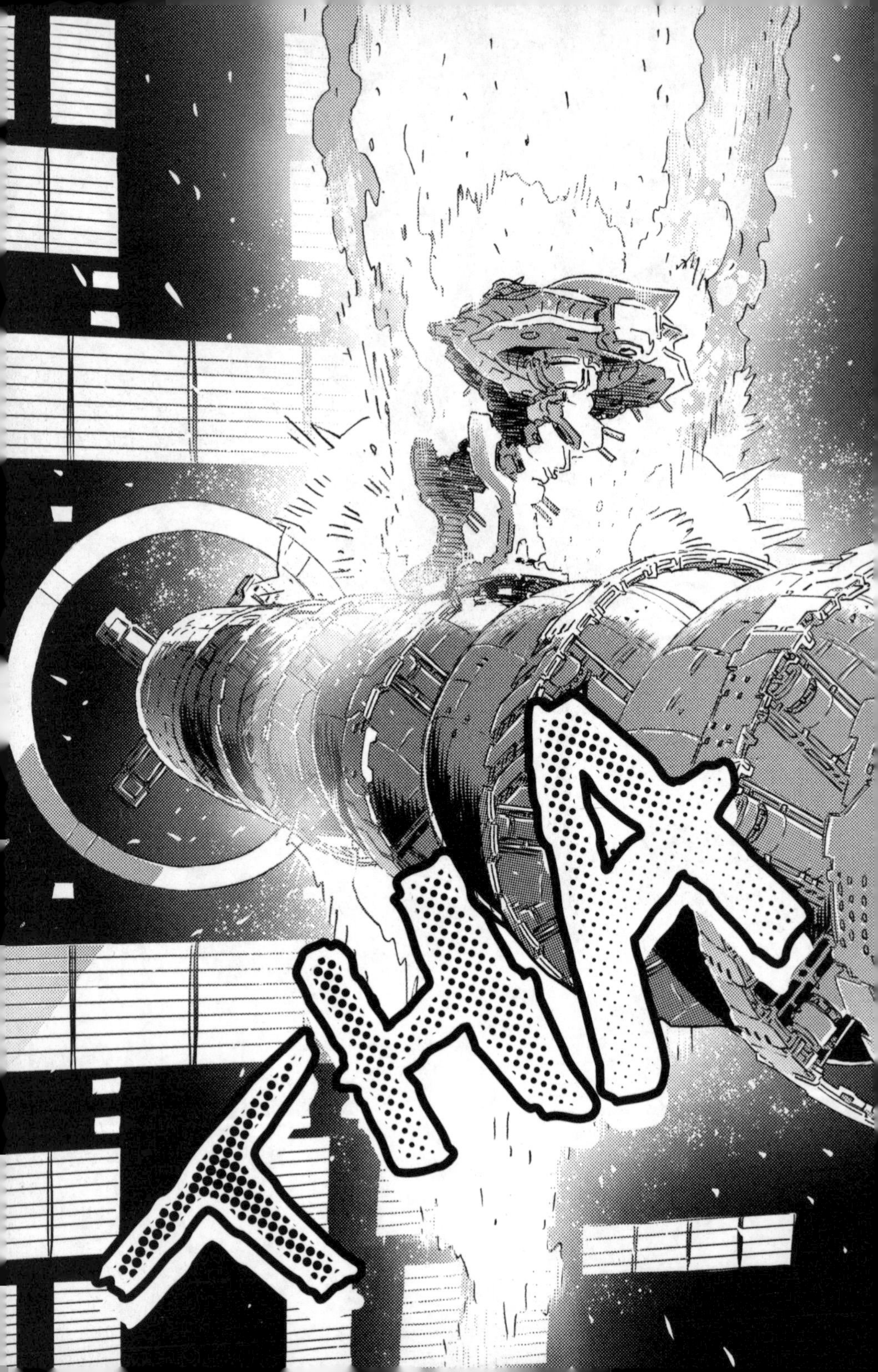

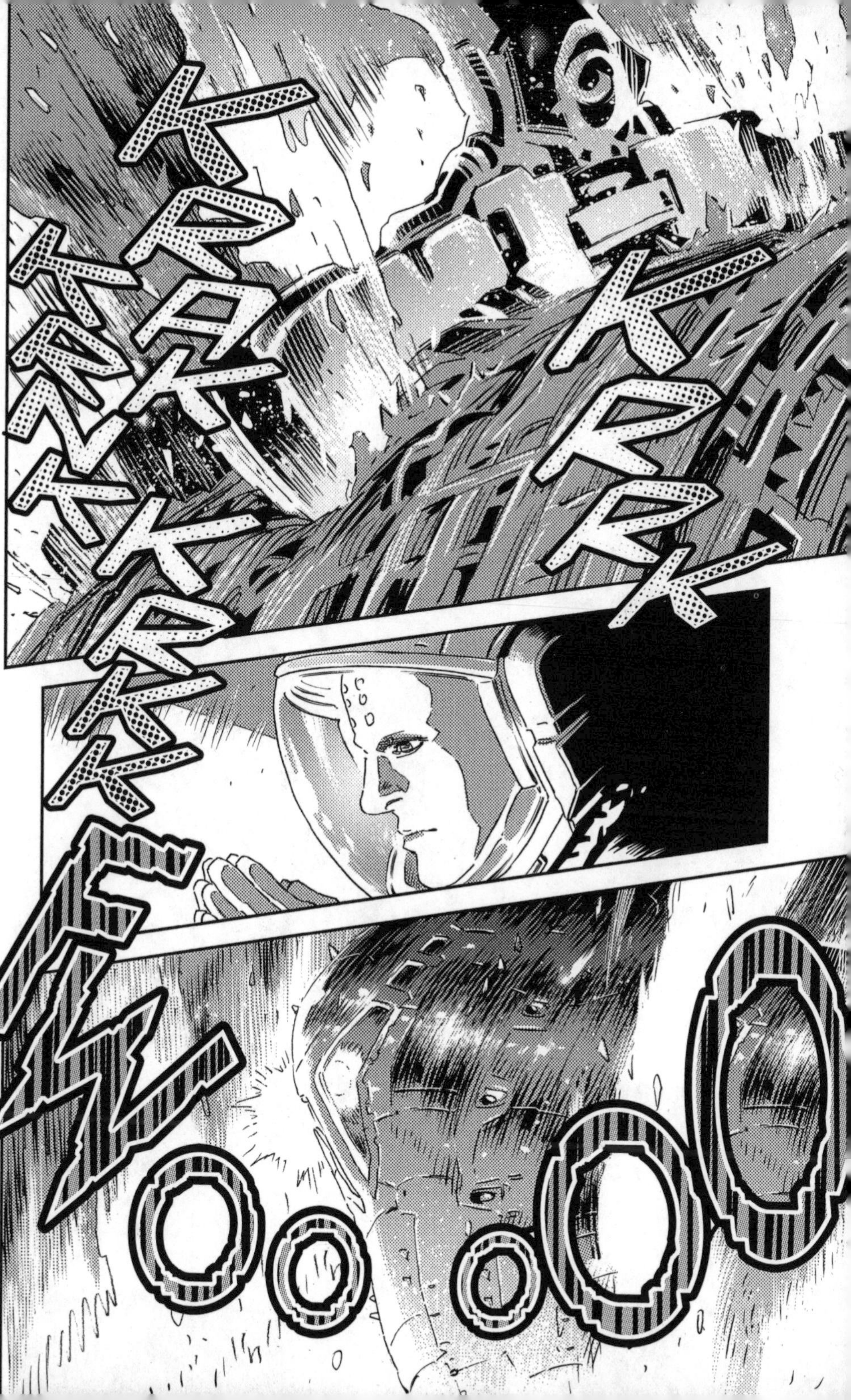
KRRK
KRRKKRRK
KRRKK
FWOO..OOO

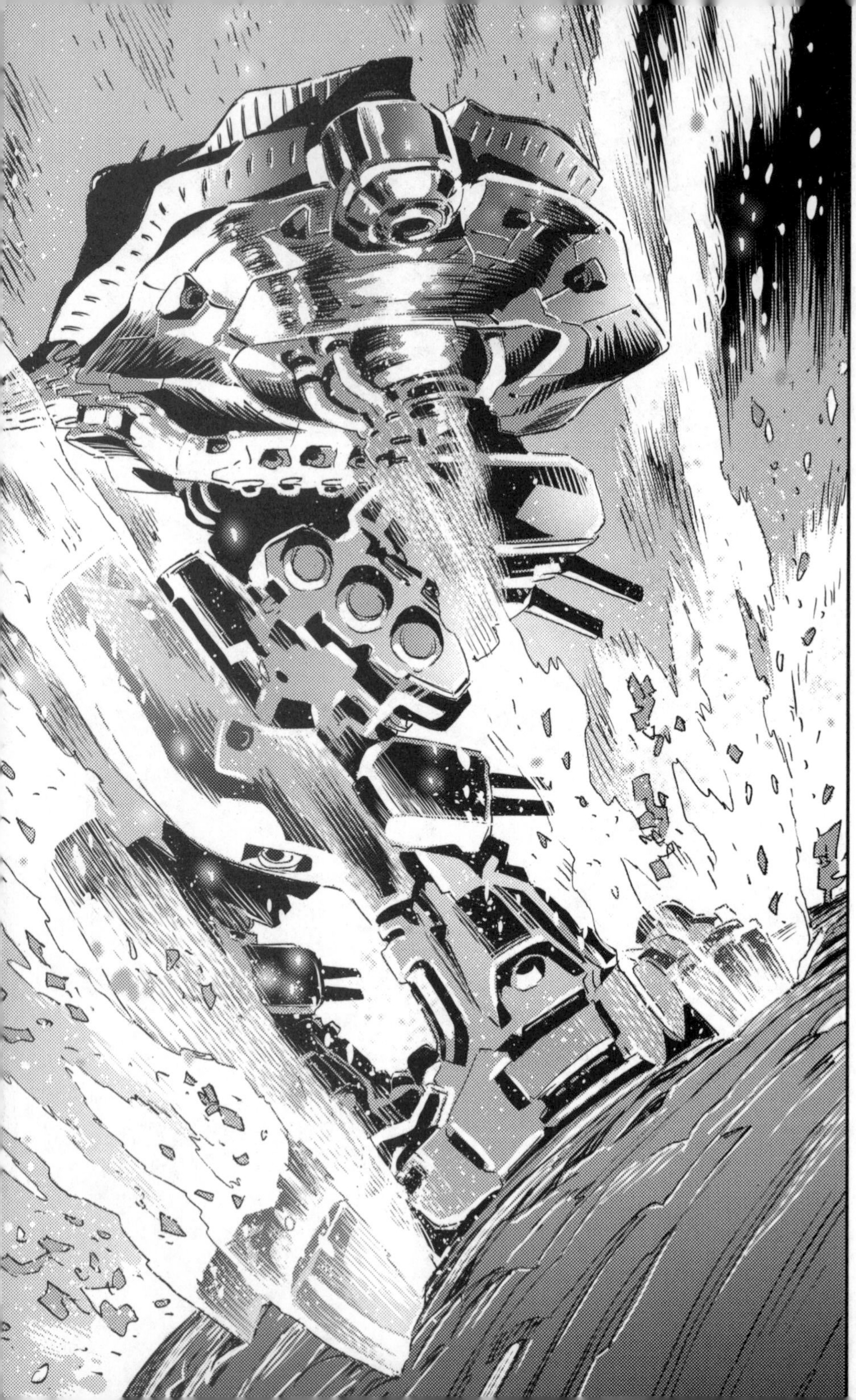

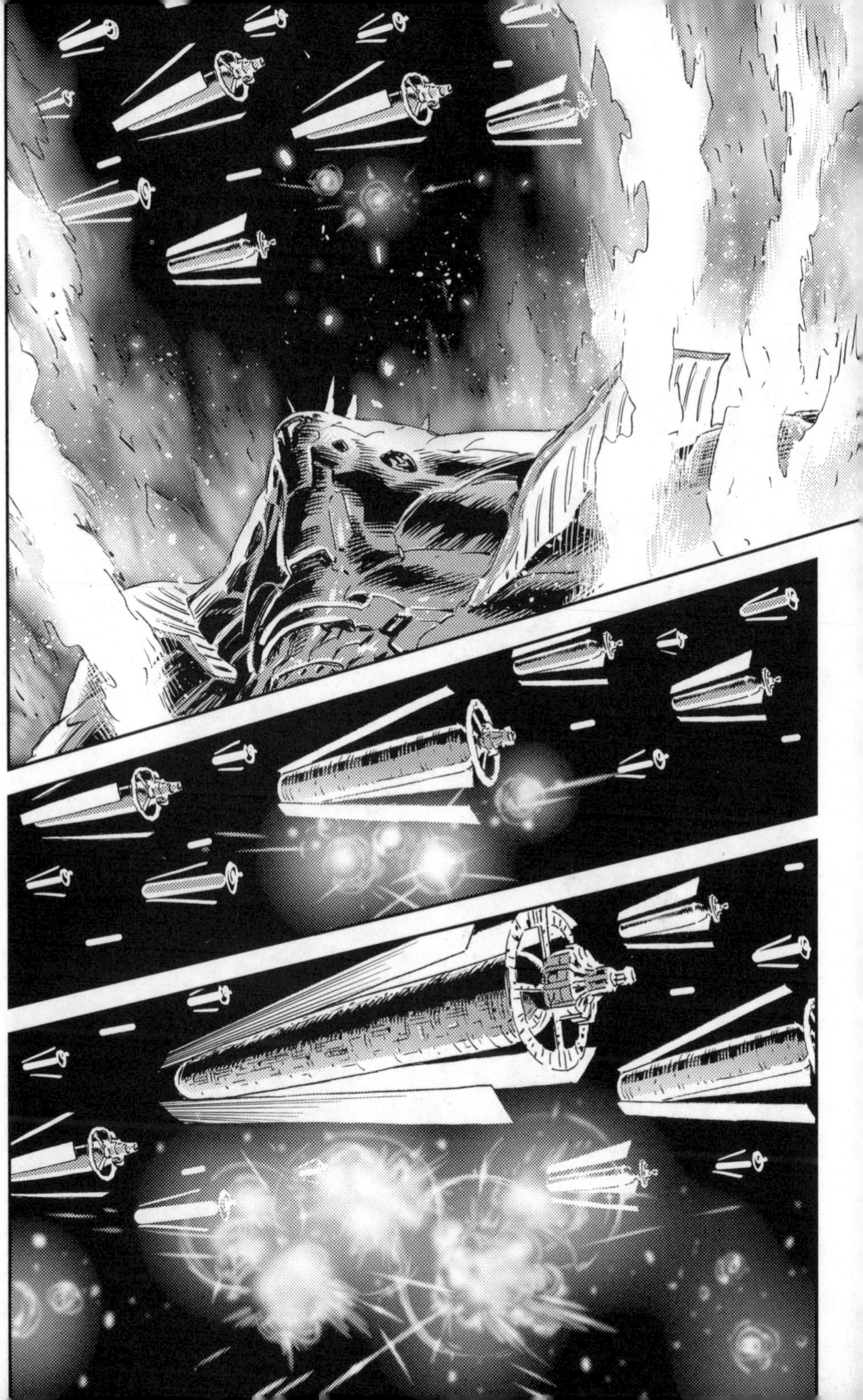

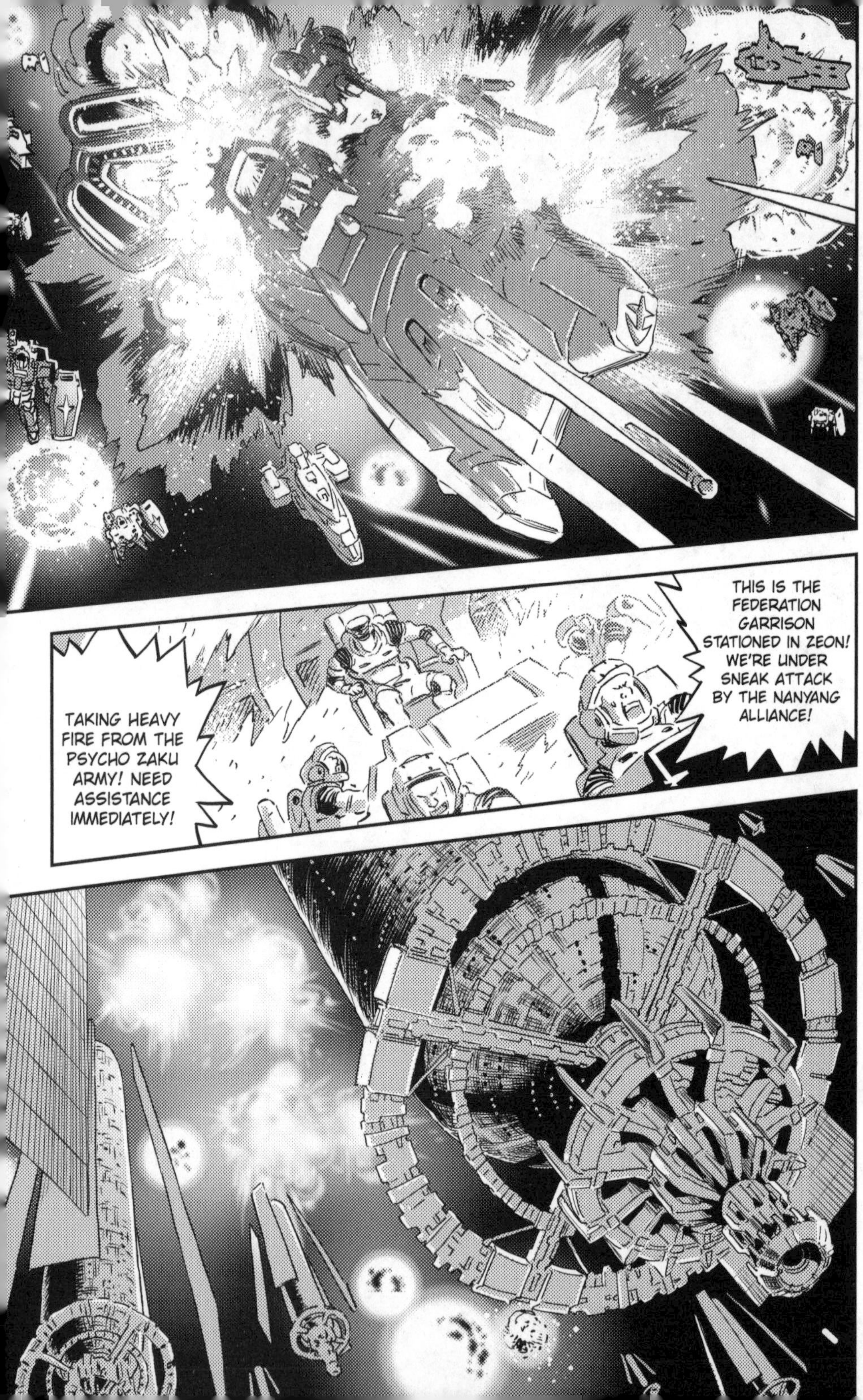
THIS IS THE FEDERATION GARRISON STATIONED IN ZEON! WE'RE UNDER SNEAK ATTACK BY THE NANYANG ALLIANCE!
TAKING HEAVY FIRE FROM THE PSYCHO ZAKU ARMY! NEED ASSISTANCE IMMEDIATELY!

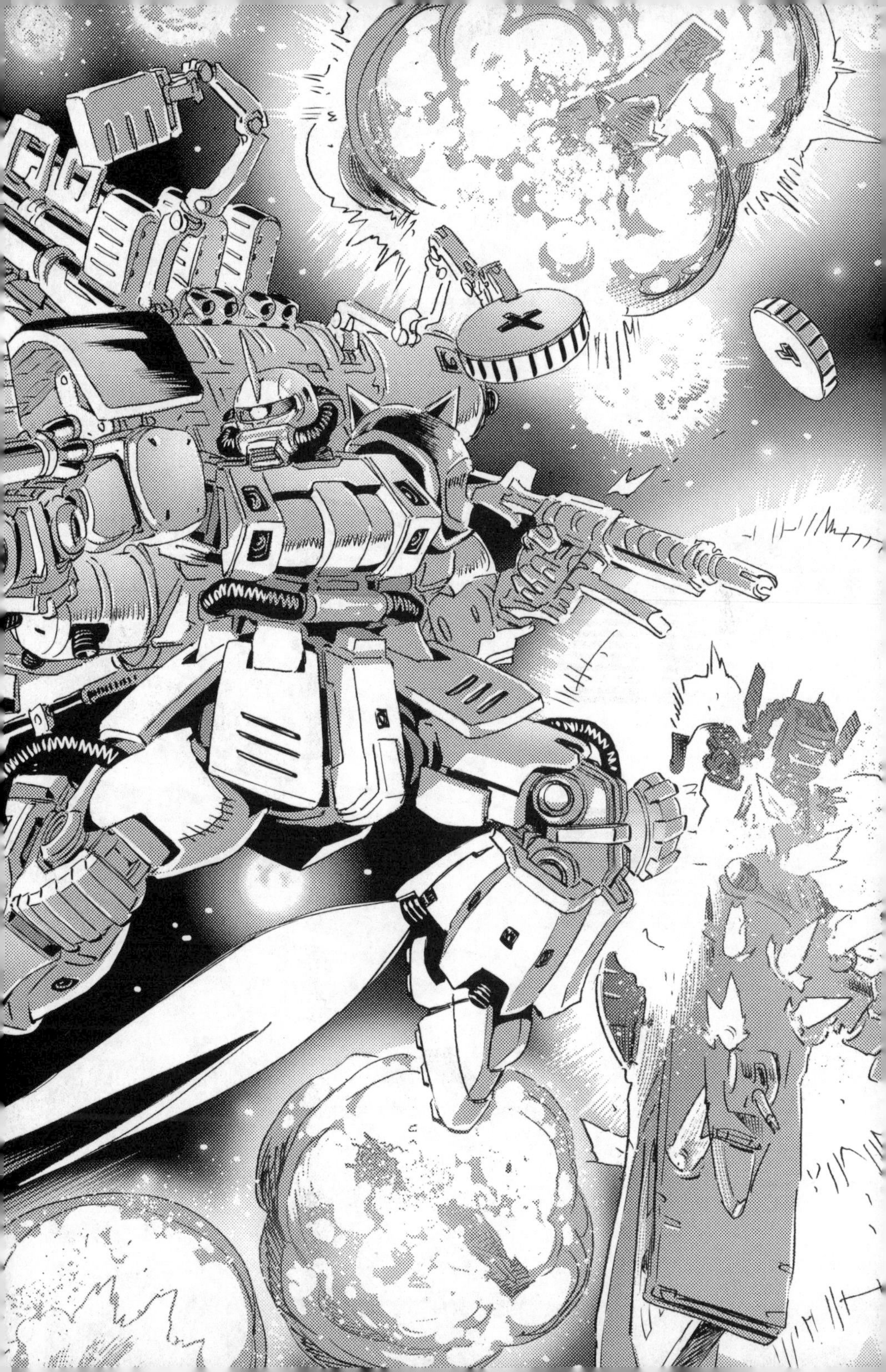

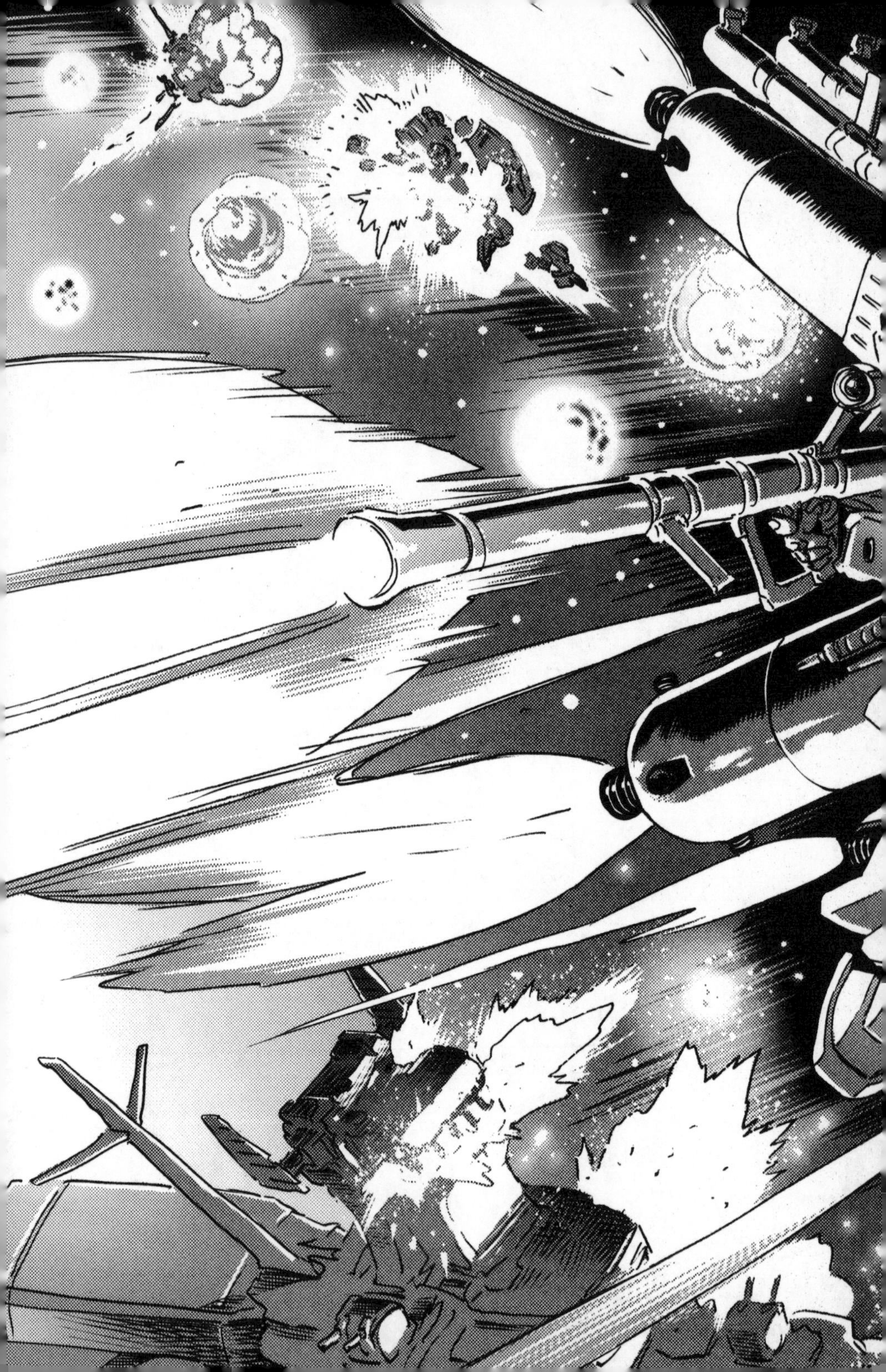

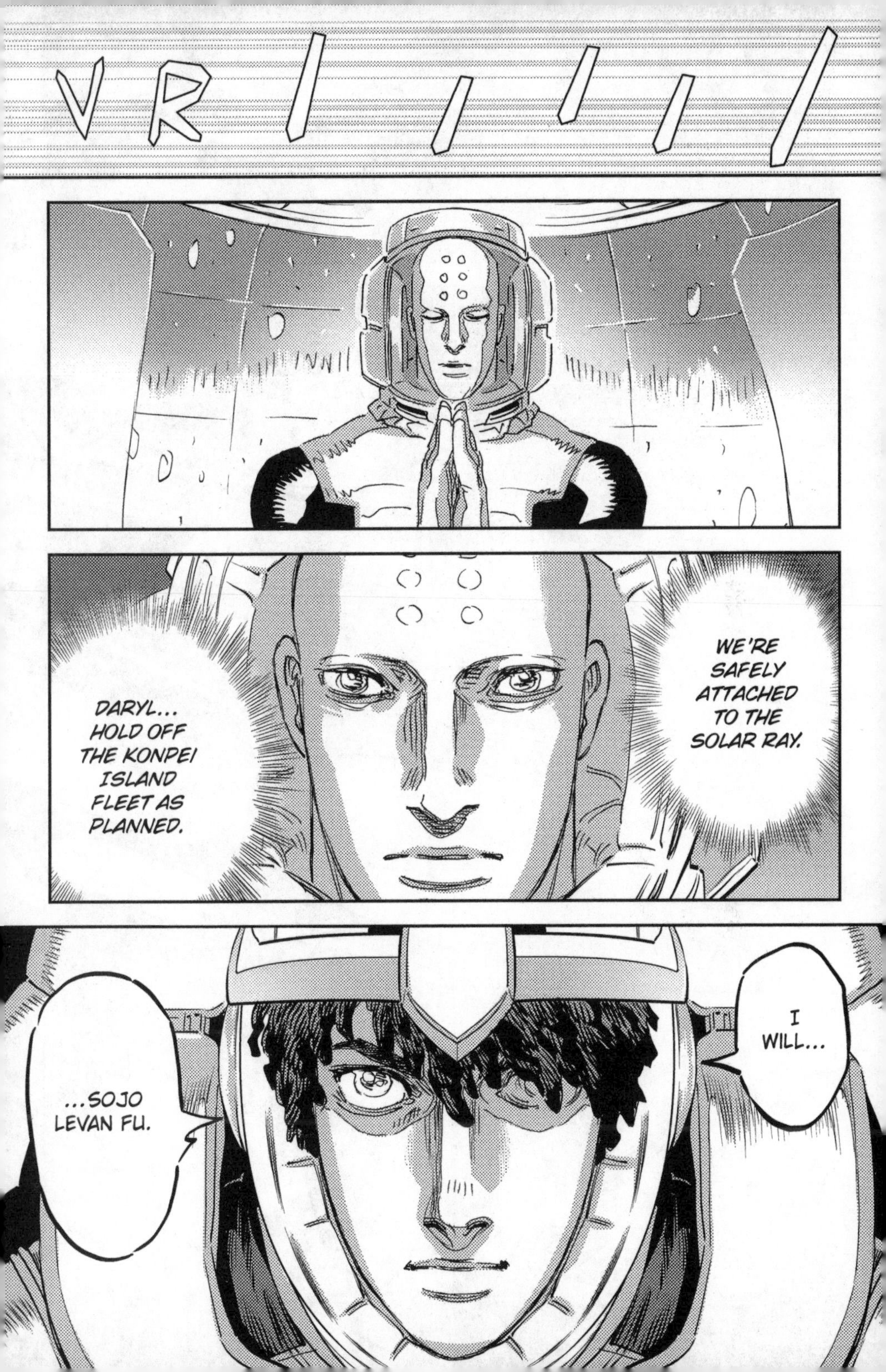
VRIIIII
WE'RE SAFELY ATTACHED TO THE SOLAR RAY.
DARYL... HOLD OFF THE KONPEI ISLAND FLEET AS PLANNED.
I WILL...
...SOJO LEVAN FU.

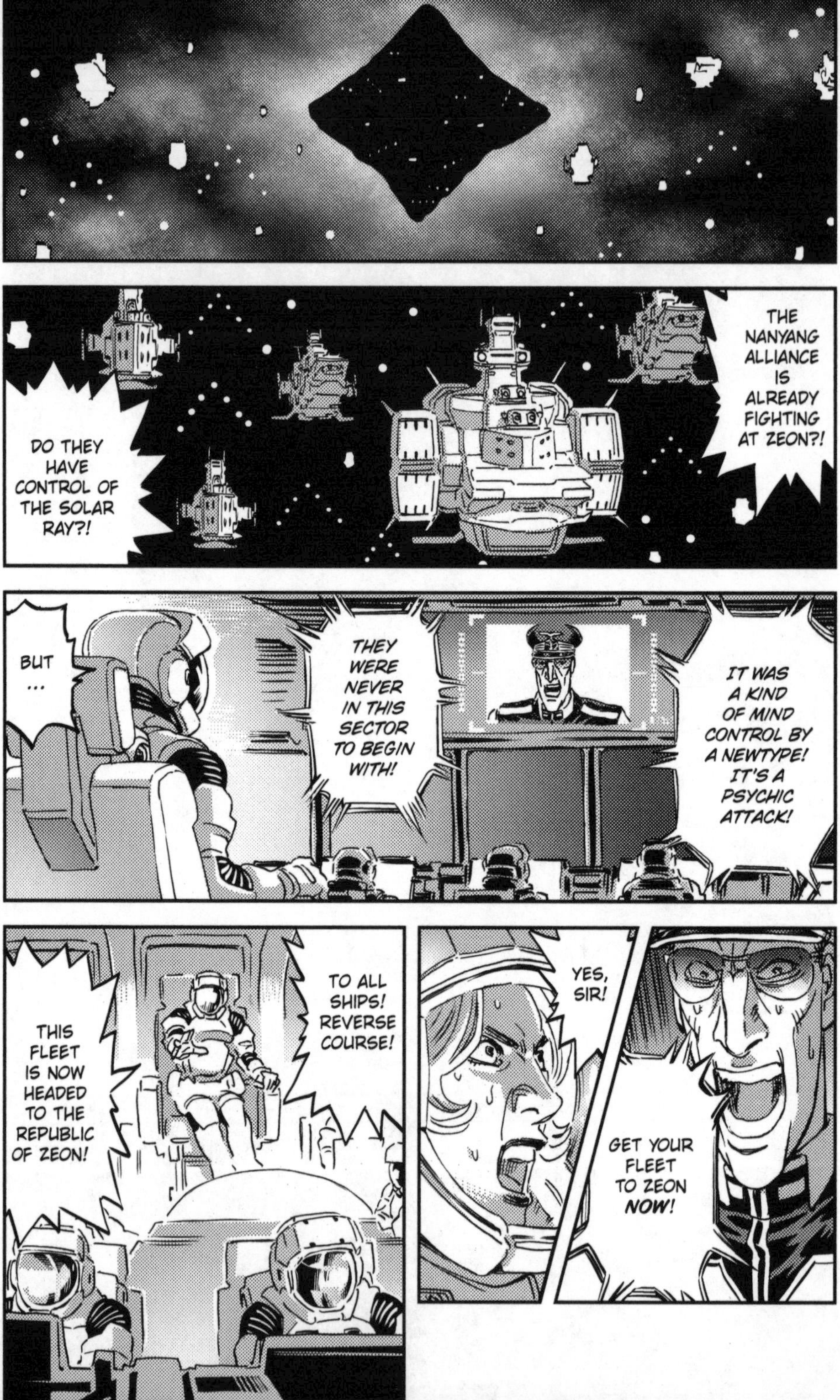
THE NANYANG ALLIANCE IS ALREADY FIGHTING AT ZEON?!
DO THEY HAVE CONTROL OF THE SOLAR RAY?!
IT WAS A KIND OF MIND CONTROL BY A NEWTYPE! IT'S A PSYCHIC ATTACK!
THEY WERE NEVER IN THIS SECTOR TO BEGIN WITH!
BUT ...
GET YOUR FLEET TO ZEON *NOW*!
YES, SIR!
TO ALL SHIPS! REVERSE COURSE!
THIS FLEET IS NOW HEADED TO THE REPUBLIC OF ZEON!

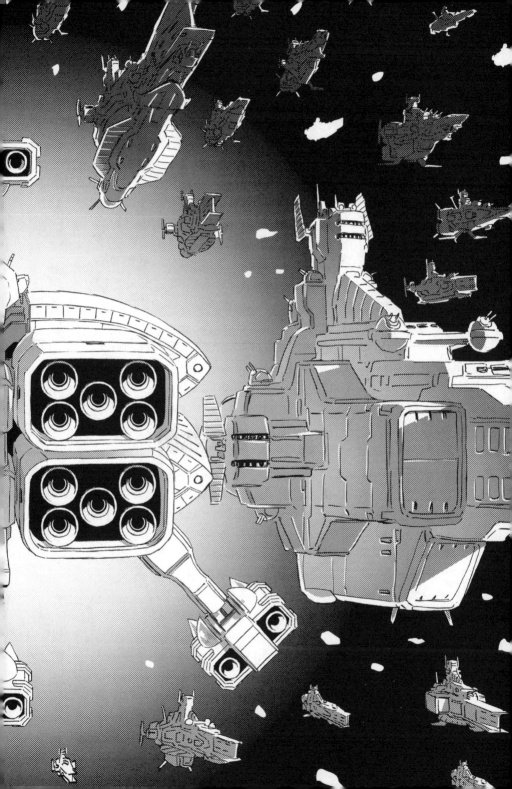

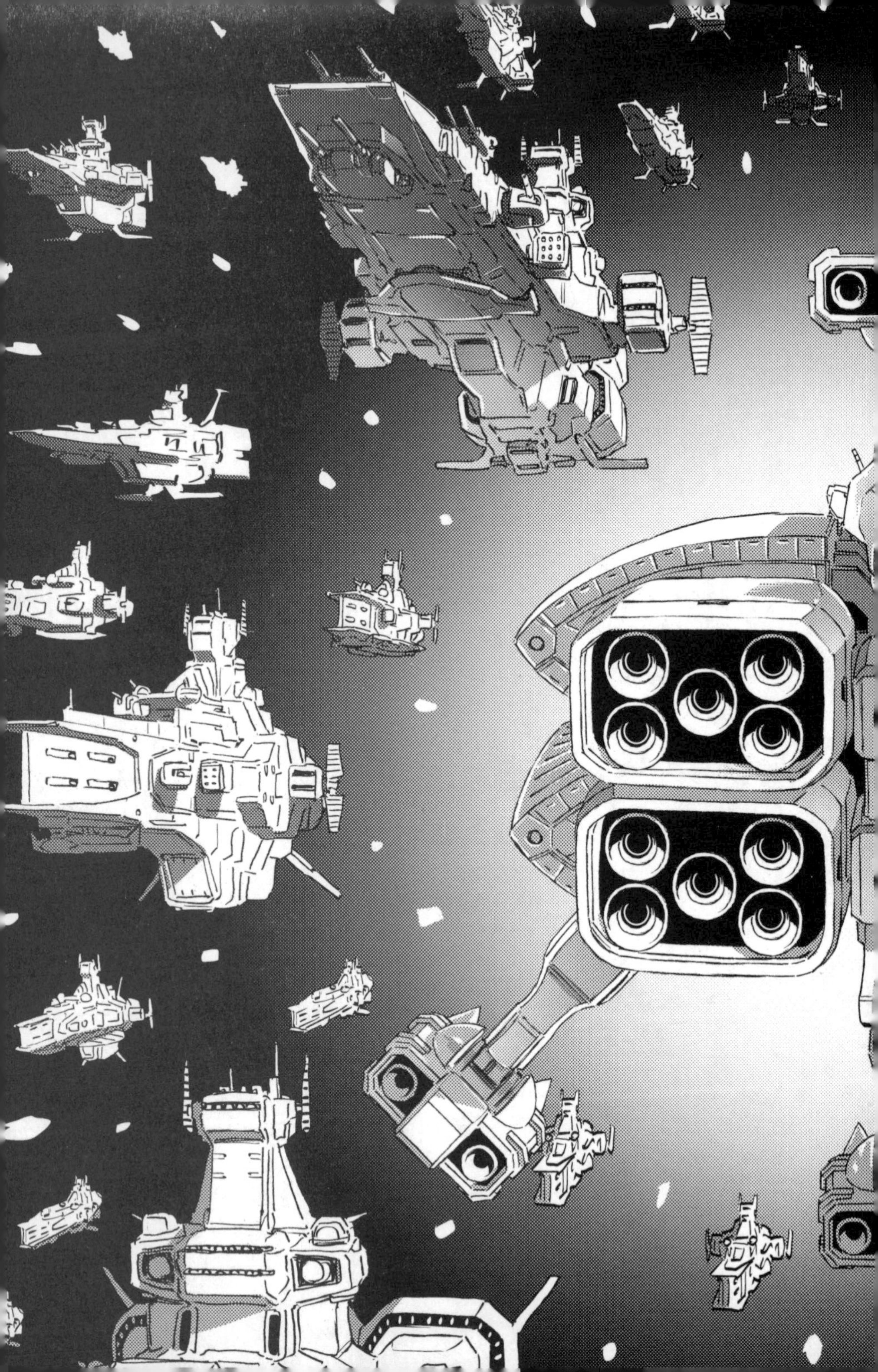

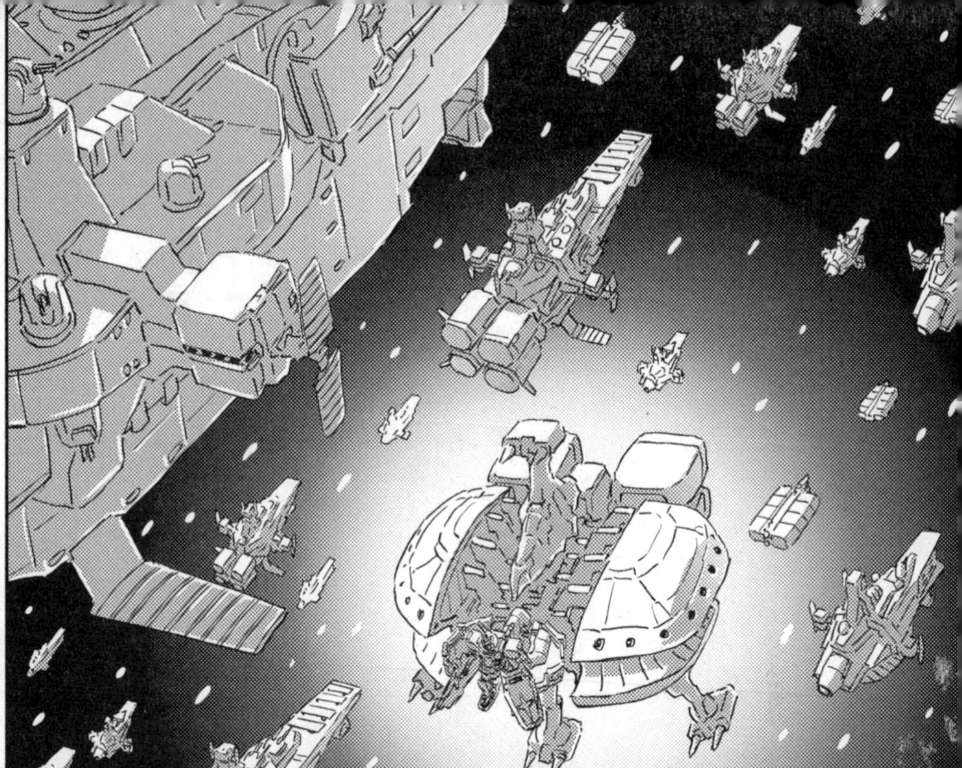

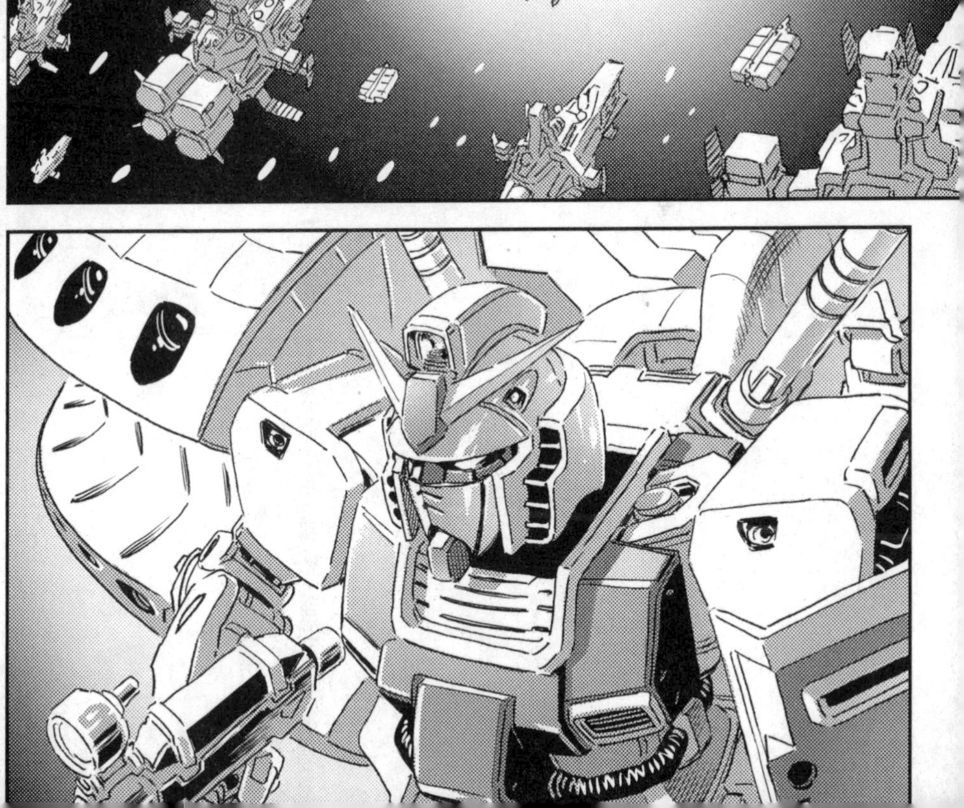

MOBILE SUIT GUNDAM - THUNDERBOLT - VOL. 20 - END

VEEN

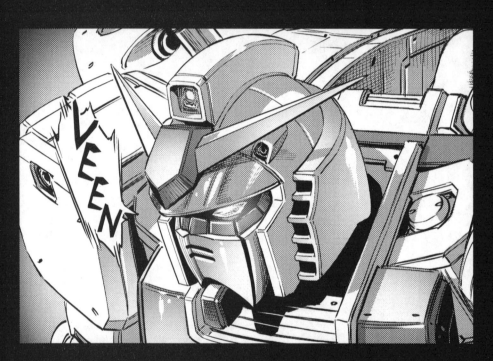

TO BE CONTINUED

STUDIO TOA S.P.A

Executive Director   **Yasuo Ohtagaki**

Special Thanks   **Mizuki Sakura**
umegrafix
Digital Noise Ltd.

MOBILE SUIT GUNDAM
THUNDERBOLT 20

VIZ Signature Edition

STORY AND ART **YASUO OHTAGAKI**
Original Concept by **HAJIME YATATE** and **YOSHIYUKI TOMINO**

Translation **JOE YAMAZAKI**
English Adaptation **STAN!**
Touch-up Art & Lettering **EVAN WALDINGER**
Cover & Design **SHAWN CARRICO**
Editor **MIKE MONTESA**

ORIGINAL COVER DESIGN / Yoshiyuki SEKI for VOLARE inc.

EDITORIAL COOPERATION / Shinsuke HIRAIWA (Digitalpaint.jp)

The stories, characters, and incidents mentioned
in this publication are entirely fictional.

Printed in the U.S.A.

Published by VIZ Media, LLC
P.O. Box 77010
San Francisco, CA 94107

10 9 8 7 6 5 4 3 2 1
First printing, November 2023

viz.com   vizsignature.com

Hey! You're Reading in the Wrong Direction!

This is the **end** of this graphic novel!

To properly enjoy this VIZ graphic novel, please turn it around and begin reading from **right to left.** Unlike English, Japanese is read right to left, so Japanese comics are read in reverse order from the way English comics are typically read.

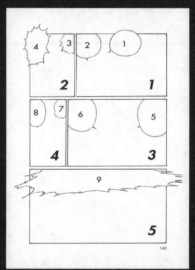

Follow the action this way

This book has been printed in the original Japanese format in order to preserve the orientation of the